MW01201614

Portraits of Conflict

Portraits of Conflict

A PHOTOGRAPHIC HISTORY

OF ALABAMA

IN THE CIVIL WAR

Ben H. Severance

With a Foreword by the General Editors,
Carl Moneyhon and *Bobby Roberts*

Portraits of Conflict Series

The University of Arkansas Press
Fayetteville   2012

Copyright © 2012 by The University of Arkansas Press

All rights reserved
Manufactured in the United States of America

ISBN-10: 1-55728-989-1
ISBN-13: 978-1-55728-989-6

16   15   14   13   12   5   4   3   2   1

Designed by Alice Gail Carter

⊖ The paper used in this publication meets the minimum requirements of the American
National Standard for Permanence of Paper for Printed Library Materials Z39.48-1984.

Library of Congress Cataloging-in-Publication Data

Severance, Ben H., 1966–
    Portraits of conflict : a photographic history of Alabama during the Civil War /
Ben H. Severance ; with a foreword by the general editors, Carl Moneyhon and
Bobby Roberts.
        pages   cm.   — (Portraits of conflict series)
    Includes bibliographical references and index.
    ISBN-13: 978-1-55728-989-6 (cloth : alkaline paper)
    ISBN-10: 1-55728-989-1 (cloth : alkaline paper)
    1. Alabama—History—Civil War, 1861–1865. 2. Alabama—History—Civil War,
1861–1865—Campaigns. 3. United States—History—Civil War, 1861–1865—Campaigns.
4. Alabama—History—Civil War, 1861–1865—Photography. 5. United States—History—
Civil War, 1861–1865—Photography. 6. Alabama—History—Civil War, 1861–1865—Pictorial
works. 7. United States—History—Civil War, 1861–1865—Pictorial works.   I. Title.
    E495.S45   2012
    976.1'05—dc23
                                                2012036555

Dedication

To Tara, Beatrice, and Josie—
the loves of my life

To Bob Bradley—
a superb historian and even better friend

To all of the Alabamians of the Civil War Era—
participants in America's greatest drama

Preface and Acknowledgments

This is the tenth volume in the series of photographic histories of the South during the Civil War. Like the previous volumes, it seeks to give that conflict a human face by presenting the reader an array of still images that preserve the faces of some of the actual participants. Photographs are a valuable primary source, but for the Civil War period—during which they first became widely made—they are often in short supply. Therefore, the images selected for this volume highlight only a narrow sample of the people involved. Nevertheless, the following chapters place these photographs in an historical context that enables the reader to see the war unfold, however unevenly. In telling this story the author has made extensive use of the compiled service records (mercifully digitized by the staff at the Alabama Department of Archives and History) as well as numerous other sources. While this book is hardly an exhaustive study of the war in Alabama or for Alabamians, it does stand as the most thorough overview of the state during that national ordeal.

Over the more than five years that I worked on this project, I took desperate comfort in believing that if this book was ever going to be written, then it was already written, and thus to God goes all of the glory. Nonetheless, I am indebted to a great many people who assisted me along the way. First and foremost, I thank Bob Bradley, a curator at the Alabama Department of Archives and History. From the beginning, Bob guided me through that institution's prodigious collection of photographs (about half of the images presented here come from the state archives). Moreover, he read the entire manuscript, offering insights and suggestions that improved the final product. Finally, he provided the kind of scholarly friendship that makes research a pleasure; I continue to enjoy our many conversations about the Civil War. Other members of the state archives to whom I am indebted include Meredith McLemore, who speedily uploaded hundreds of digital images, and Norwood Kerr, who offered ready assistance whenever I came into the research room.

Another person who deserves many thanks is the late Arthur W. Bergeron, who as a reference historian at the U.S. Army Military History Institute (U.S.A.M.H.I.) smoothed the way for me to acquire many excellent photographs from that repository. In the late 1990s Art actually took on this book assignment, but other obligations interceded. When I resurrected the project in 2005, Art generously gave me everything that he had collected up to that point, including photocopies of relevant articles from the *Confederate Veteran* and a list of possible private donors. I also found of tremendous value his outstanding book *Confederate Mobile* (1991). Sadly, I never got the chance to meet Dr. Bergeron in person. Also of much help from the U.S.A.M.H.I. were Clifton P. Hyatt and Robert M. Mages.

Many other folks at various public institutions deserve praise. I wish to thank Marina Klaric of the W. S. Hoole Special Collections Library at the University of Alabama; Blanton Blankenship of the Fort Morgan Museum; Christine Cramer of the Historic Mobile Preservation Society; Don Veasy of the Birmingham Public Library; Dwayne Cox and Joyce Hicks of the Special Collections Library at Auburn University; Carol Ellis of the University of South Alabama Archives; Kelly M. Kennington of Duke University; Bill Rambo of Confederate Memorial Park; Guy Hubbs of Birmingham Southern College; Rebekah Davis of the Limestone County Archives; Adam Watson of the State Archives of Florida; and from my own institution —Auburn University, Montgomery—Fariba S. Deravi, who handled my Grant-in-Aid account, and Jason Kneip and Samantha McNeilly from the school's special collections, both of whom not only endured my frequent and sudden appearances but also allowed me first dibs on a nearly complete, albeit dilapidated, set of the *Official Records* that had been slated for the trash.

Numerous private citizens also deserve acknowledgment for either donating one or more photographs or for steering me toward useful sources. Among the former, I thank Norman E. Rourke, David Wynn Vaughan, Wayne Wood, Don T. Griffin, John Lloyd and Craig T. Sheldon, John C. Carter, Rayford L. Cannon, Steven R. Butler, Roy H. Bunn, Al Zachry, Wilbur and Illene Thompson, Reita Jones Burress, Barry Lee Collins, Carl S. Smith, J. D. Weeks, and John K. Folmar I. Among the latter, I thank John H. Napier III, Ed Besch, Joe Albree, Ryan Dupree (who oversees an outstanding website on the First Alabama Cavalry, U.S.A.), Donna Collins, and Mary Ann Neeley. Unfortunately, I was not able to integrate every photograph I received into the published book. To those who sent me images that were not used, and to anyone I may have inadvertently left out, I sincerely apologize.

The University of Arkansas Press has earned my eternal gratitude for entrusting this task to me and for patiently awaiting the final product. Specifically, I thank Editor in Chief Larry Malley, who at the outset jokingly asked if I could get it all done in a year (at least I think he was joking); Katy Henriksen, Deena Owens, Brian King, Melissa King, and Kevin Brock for supervising the final stages of publication; and Carl Moneyhon, the coeditor of the series as well as coauthor of four of its volumes. Carl treated my work on the book with salutary neglect; I appreciate that kind of respect. Finally, I would be remiss not to mention Richard McCaslin, author of three volumes in the series. It was he who as part of a casual conversation in Knoxville in 2004 first broached the idea of me taking on this project.

My last word of thanksgiving goes to my family. My parents—RAdm. L. Stanard and Virginia Severance—and my in-laws—John and Jeanette Harmon—provided much love and encouragement, even when they were not entirely sure what it was I was actually creating. And of course, I thank my wife, Tara, and my two daughters, Beatrice and Josephine; those three are the earthly trinity that keeps me going.

Key to photographic and archival collections
ADAH: Alabama Department of Archives and
    History, Montgomery
U.S.A.M.H.I.: The U.S. Army Military History
    Institute, Carlisle Barracks, PA (RG 824S—
    Confederate Alabama)

Contents

Foreword

Portraits of Conflict: A Photographic History of Alabama in the Civil War is the tenth volume in a series that intends to use photographs to tell the story of the individuals and societies engaged in the country's great national conflict. As in previous volumes, the layout involves the use of photographs of individuals accompanied by captions that provide their personal stories. The photographs and individual accounts are then woven into a narrative intended to illuminate the history of a people at war. The series, from its beginning, had a specific purpose—an emphasis upon the individual's experience of war. The first volume made its authors aware that behind the larger stories of war are the thousands of individuals who lived through or died as a result. The series makes no pretense at providing a comprehensive history of the war in each state covered, but we do hope that it brings home the human aspect of this conflict.

With this volume the series turns to the history of Alabama and its people. Alabama presents a special case in that until the war's end, the state saw little fighting inside its boundaries. Nevertheless, over one hundred thousand Alabamians served with Confederate units throughout the South, fighting in most of its great battles. This volume chronicles the lives and experiences of some of these citizen-soldiers. At the same time, it covers life on the home front, where the absence of these men forced major changes in the daily endeavors of those left behind. The book ultimately addresses the conduct of the war when it finally came to Alabama itself in raids by Union forces and the fight for Mobile Bay. The reader will find in *Portraits of Conflict: A Photographic History of Alabama in the Civil War* a large number of previously unpublished photographs, showing the men and women of the state. Its gripping narrative provides one of the few overviews of Civil War Alabama available.

This volume contains the same qualities of photography and story that have attracted readers to the previous volumes in the series. The editors hope that it meets the same approval from readers as well.

CARL MONEYHON AND BOBBY ROBERTS
General Editors

Chapter 1

Photography in Alabama during the Civil War

The Civil War era coincided with the emergence of photography as a profession. As a result, America's Iliad became the first widely photographed military conflict in history. Studio images became especially popular with soldiers on both sides. The volume of such pictures was so great, in fact, that it literally bequeaths for posterity a human face, or rather faces, of the war. Like volunteers everywhere, thousands of Alabamians took the time and spent the money to sit for their share of photographs. The images were, after all, a novel memento of a struggle that all participants seemed to sense was epic in nature.

Civil War photographs reflect a wide range of technological development. One of the earliest processes was the daguerreotype, whereby a cameraman would capture a mirror image of his subject onto a plate of polished silver. Daguerreotypes were expensive to make and by the late 1850s were already outdated. In its place emerged the ambrotype, followed shortly by the tintype. An ambrotype used a wet-plate solution of collodion and silver nitrate to capture a negative image on glass. Once dry, the glass could then be mounted on a dark backing to reveal the positive image. Tintypes involved a similar process, only the image was captured on a thin iron plate rather than glass, which made the final product less fragile. In 1860 yet another technique arose: the *carte de visite* ("visiting card" in French). This was the simplest and least expensive form of photography at the time, entailing the creation of an albumen print (a glass-plate image pressed onto card stock coated in egg white), which could then be used to quickly reproduce multiple copies of the same image. All of these techniques required the subject to remain still for several seconds until the exposure was complete lest the image blur. It is for this reason that, with rare exceptions, no one smiles in Civil War–era pictures and also why there are no action photos of the fighting. Consequently, viewers must use caution if and when they attempt to read character into a given image.

Although the finest studios were in the North, as were the most famous photographers of the period (such as Matthew Brady and Alexander Gardner), the South was hardly delinquent in producing its own high-quality images. The best places to have a picture taken in Alabama were either Montgomery, with at least five studios, or Mobile, with many more, including the reputable Duffee & Sancier studio that specialized in *cartes de visite*. Among the state's other studios were A. B. Avery of Tuskegee and Robinson & Murphy in Huntsville. While soldiers usually wore their actual uniform for a sitting, they also often held any number of studio props, such as muskets or a knife. Therefore, one must be cautious in drawing conclusions about equipment based solely on what is seen in a given photograph. This volume contains nearly 240 images of Alabamians during the Civil War. Selection of these photographs generally conforms to two criteria: one, biographical information sufficient to identify the individual in some depth and, two, a compelling story, such as a battlefield experience, that brings the image alive for a particular time and place. Unfortunately, for a great many photographs the historical record provides little more than the individual's name, rank, and unit (and several others are unidentified altogether). Similarly, many letters and diaries offer compelling stories, but there are no accompanying photographs. Nevertheless, the images presented in the following pages give a face to most facets of Alabama's wartime experience. Moreover, nearly every county in the state is represented. A few caveats are in order, however. The preponderance of subjects are officers. Typically men of means and letters, officers could more easily afford having a picture taken (and having it preserved by descendants) and were more likely to have left behind a written record of their service. Also, most of the wartime images are of soldiers who volunteered early in the conflict. Later enlistees did not display the same martial fervor of their 1861 counterparts and so perhaps were less inclined to have a photographic record of an event in which they only reluctantly participated. Several from this latter group show their subjects posing in civilian attire, which suggests a reason other than obtaining a wartime memento for having the picture made.

Regardless of why a person wanted a photograph of himself or herself, it is fortunate to have any of them at all. Civil War photographs constitute a unique primary source for the period. Happily, hundreds of Alabamians sat for photographers, leaving behind a plethora of images; those that follow in these chapters are but a sample.

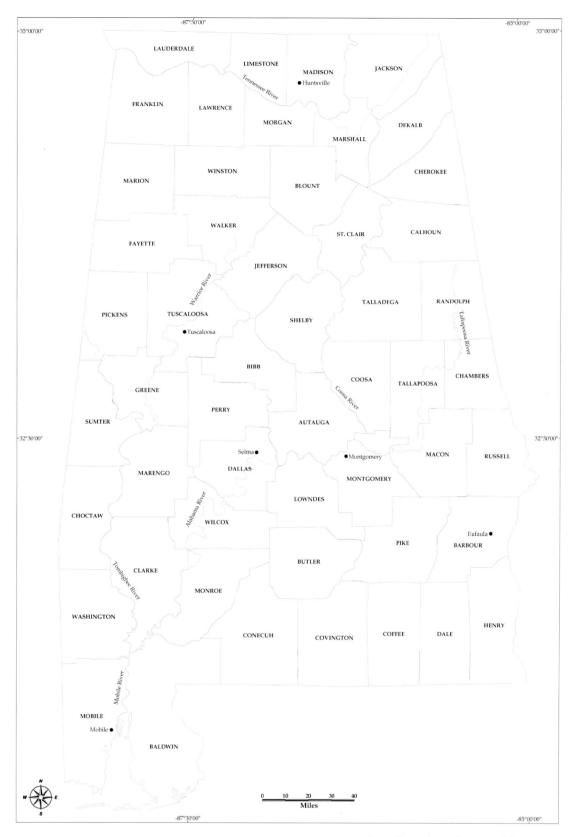

Terance L. Winemiller, Auburn University, Montgomery

3

EDWARD LEGARE MACINTYRE
daguerreotype

A good example of the daguerreotype can be seen in this image. Edward MacIntyre likely posed for this photograph before the war, when he served as a state senator from Pike County, where he also coedited the *Union Advocate,* a Whig newspaper that waffled over the issue of secession. In May 1862 the thirty-one-year-old joined Hilliard's Legion, a brigade-sized unit that was later split into two infantry regiments, the 59th and 60th Alabama. MacIntyre commanded Company G, 59th Alabama, though frequent bouts of illness sidelined him for most of the war. Other than participating in the Kentucky campaign of 1862, he does not appear to have seen any combat. *Photo courtesy of ADAH*

JAMES NICHOLAS
GILMER
ambrotype

James Gilmer was twenty-two years old when he posed for this ambrotype in 1861. A merchant's son from Montgomery, Gilmer first served as a lieutenant in the 3rd Alabama Infantry before accepting a captaincy in Hilliard's Legion in April 1862. When that unit split, he became adjutant of the 60th Alabama Infantry, a position he held for the duration of the conflict. Gilmer saw action at Chickamauga in 1863 and around Richmond during the final months of the war. *Photo courtesy of ADAH*

THomas Peters Lamkin
tintype

The intense patriotism of Alabama's youth is ably captured in this tintype of Thomas Lamkin. The son of a planter from Walker County, Lamkin enlisted in Company F, 16th Alabama Infantry in July 1861; he was only sixteen years old. The specific details of his wartime experience are unknown, but the young man fought as a private in that regiment for the duration, receiving his parole in 1865. *Photo courtesy of ADAH*

6

JOSEPHUS HOLTZCLAW
LAKIN
carte de visite

Few images of Alabama photographers exist, but among them is this *carte de visite* of J. H. Lakin, a specialist in that technique. Lakin operated a studio in Montgomery, where he competed for customers with other local entrepreneurs, including Jerome W. Chambers and F. A. Gerrish. Precise data is not available, but Lakin produced numerous "visiting cards" throughout the war and during the Reconstruction era that followed. *Photo courtesy of ADAH*

JAMES S. HASTINGS
carte de visite
J. H. Lakin, Montgomery

One of Lakin's customers was James Hastings. A twenty-three-year-old druggist from Montgomery at the outset of the war, Hastings served as a private in the 3rd Alabama Infantry. Returning to Montgomery after his term of enlistment, he later accepted command of Company I, 61st Alabama Infantry. Sometime in 1863, while stationed at Pollard in southern Alabama, the young captain lost his right arm in an accident. *Photo courtesy of ADAH*

CHARLES WESLEY FAUST AND
DAVID CLINTON FAUST
ambrotype

The Civil War is sometimes quaintly described as a struggle in which brother fought against brother. In reality, brothers usually fought alongside brothers. Such was the case with Charles and David Faust, siblings from Shelby County. In June 1861 both men enlisted in Company B, 10th Alabama Infantry. Twenty-four years old at the time, Charles left behind a wife and his job as a mechanic in Montevallo. The eighteen-year-old David, who had been working as a small farmer, simply exchanged his plow for a musket. The two participated in plenty of combat together, from the Peninsula Campaign of early 1862 to the Battle of Gettysburg in the summer of 1863. Although David suffered four minor wounds during the course of the war, Charles went unscathed until 5 May 1864, when he was killed in action at the Wilderness. The elder Faust had risen to the rank of sergeant before his demise. The younger brother stayed on, serving as a sharpshooter during the siege of Petersburg. He was paroled at Appomattox in 1865; moved to Jefferson County, where he got married in 1867; and basically resumed his life as a farmer. *Photo courtesy of U.S.A.M.H.I.*

JEFFERSON STRICKLAND AND
MADISON STRICKLAND
copy print

While the Faust brothers experienced the dubious glory of combat, the fate of the Strickland brothers typified the ordeal of most Civil War fatalities—they both died of disease. Jefferson and Madison Strickland were twins from Randolph County. In September 1861 the nineteen-year-old boys joined the Billy Gilmore Greys, a local outfit that was soon designated Company F, 14th Alabama Infantry. At least two other Strickland brothers also served in the company. The twins were proud of their unit and joined the regimen-tal color guard, in which Jefferson attained the rank of corporal and Madison that of sergeant. Sadly, neither experienced the honor of carrying the flags into battle, for in the spring of 1862, while stationed just north of Richmond, Virginia, both boys succumbed to one of the many campground maladies that ravaged Civil War armies during the early months of the conflict. *Photo courtesy of Margaret P. Milford Collection, U.S.A.M.H.I.*

ROBERT THOMPSON COLES
copy print

This photograph of Robert Coles conveys the intensity and determination so often associated with those who volunteered during the first year of the war. An eighteen-year-old student at LaGrange Military Academy when Fort Sumter fell, Coles immediately quit school and joined the Huntsville Guards, a militia unit from his native Madison County. The Guards soon became part of the 4th Alabama Infantry, one of the most renowned regiments the state produced. Serving as an adjutant for most of the war, Coles saw action in every major battle from First Manassas to the surrender of Lee's army in 1865. Miraculously, the youth suffered only one serious wound, during Gaines' Mill in June 1862. Exhilarated by his wartime escapades, Coles kept detailed notes of his regiment's involvement. These became the basis for *From Huntsville to Appomattox,* an outstanding unit history that constitutes an invaluable primary source for the exploits of the 4th Alabama. It is the dedicated patriotism of soldiers such as Coles that continues to dominate the memory of Confederate arms.[1]
Photo courtesy of ADAH

ARMISTEAD L. GALLOWAY
copy print

12

In contrast to the resolute demeanor of Coles is the innocuous image of Armistead Galloway. A twenty-four-year-old married farmer from Tallapoosa County when the war broke out, Galloway waited an entire year before enlisting in Company E, 34th Alabama Infantry. At the risk of photographic overanalysis, Galloway's face depicts the reluctance of so-called "later-enlisters."[2] His apparel is civilian and his expression is arguably apprehensive; he is not even looking at the camera. Galloway's exact motivation is unknown, but most later-enlisters expressed less enthusiasm for the war and perhaps for the Confederacy as well. They served out of a sense of civic duty more so than out of any idealized notion of Southern nationalism. To be sure, such men generally performed well in battle, while many early volunteers crumbled under the rigors of war. In Galloway's case, however, the unwelcome conflict brought only an abrupt and inglorious death, by disease in the autumn of 1862, while his regiment was encamped in Lauderdale, Mississippi.
Photo courtesy of Special Collections & Archives, Auburn University

Chapter 2

The Cradle of the Confederacy

On 11 January 1861, Alabama seceded from the Union and shortly thereafter hosted the newly formed Confederacy's first capital in Montgomery. For Alabamians, secession was the climax to a decades-long power struggle between the North and the South over the political and economic direction of the country. Serious constitutional disagreements over the relationship between federal and state government certainly contributed to the sectional conflict, but the most "vexatious" issue was slavery—the South's "peculiar institution." To more and more Northerners, slavery was not simply immoral but altogether incongruous with the democratic principles of a republic. To more and more Southerners, slavery was a vital component of both their region's agrarian prosperity and its highly structured social order.

Alabama's journey toward secession began in 1848. At the Democratic national convention in Baltimore that year, William L. Yancey of Montgomery presented his Alabama Platform, a radical manifesto that urged the party to make protection of slavery the central feature of its political campaign. The United States had just concluded its successful war with Mexico (1846–48), but that conflict ignited debates over the extension of slavery into the newly acquired territories of California and New Mexico. Northern politicians' bipartisan endorsement of the Wilmot Proviso, a piece of legislation that sought to ban the institution in the Southwest, infuriated the entire Southern delegation in Congress. Though the letter of the proviso died on the floor of the U.S. Senate, its spirit elicited a pronounced antislavery sentiment throughout Northern society. To Yancey, the only antidote for this abolitionist fever was a bold defense of slavery by a national party through states' rights.

While many Southerners sympathized with Yancey's concerns about the South's future in the Union, few at the time displayed the Alabamian's fierce political views. When the convention rejected the Alabama Platform, Yancey stormed out in protest only to discover that he was a minority voice even in his home state. His political rival John Winston persuaded the remaining Alabama delegates to stand with the Democratic majority, while his longtime mentor and states' rights advocate Dixon Hall Lewis tried to comfort him with assurances that party solidarity offered the best guarantee for slavery's perpetuation. Yancey felt betrayed.

Going into the 1850s, Alabama may have been solidly in the Union, but it was a state divided by race, geography, and politics. The racial divide was obvious: by 1860 526,000 whites resided there along with 435,000 blacks, all but some 3,000 of whom were slaves.[1] These slaves typically labored in the cotton fields of the fertile "black belt" running through the central portion of the state or on the plush farms of the Tennessee River valley. Nonslaveholding subsistence farmers—the famed Southern yeomanry—predominated the hill counties in the northern half of the state or resided in the wiregrass region along the border with Florida. Despite these varied demographics, Alabama was generally split between nonslaveholders in the northern half and slaveholders in the southern half. This difference affected state politics throughout the Civil War era.

Like the rest of the nation, Alabama participated in a two-party political system that pitted the Whigs against the Democrats. Generally speaking, the Whig Party, which promoted active government involvement in economic growth, appealed to Alabama's urban middle class and those slaveholders, usually the older, more established planters, who understood that their cash-crop livelihood was tied closely to the national marketplace. The Democratic Party in the state reflected two strains: a Jacksonian tradition of defending common Americans from exploitation by so-called special interests and a Calhounite wing that emphasized state sovereignty. Upstate yeoman embraced the individualism of the former, while a sizeable number of younger slaveholders espoused the latter. This last group comprised ambitious, professional men, such as William Yancey, who coveted the power and status of the planter class, which in turn led them to regard states' rights as an indispensable safeguard to slavery.

Given this diverse political outlook, it appeared unlikely that Alabamians could ever unite around the explosive issue of secession. The state's role in the Compromise of 1850 only reinforced this impression. With tensions running high once again over slavery in the territories, the compromise theoretically offered something for everyone: it admitted California as a free state; it banned the slave trade in Washington, D.C.; it left the matter of slavery in New Mexico Territory to the vagaries of popular sovereignty; and it strengthened the federal fugitive-slave laws. Influential Alabamians of both parties played key roles in enacting these measures. The leading Jacksonian Democrat in the state, Sen. William R. King of Dallas County, supported the compromise as crucial to national harmony (though he actually only voted for the Fugitive Slave Act). King was joined by the eloquent Whig congressman Henry Hilliard of Montgomery County. This political alliance between upstate Democrats and slaveholding Whigs kept Alabama's states' rights Democrats in check. It should be noted, however, that both King and Hilliard understood that Southerners were giving more than they were receiving. "Anything is to be preferred to an ignominious submission to tyranny," Hilliard explained to his Northern colleagues on the floor of the House, warning that if they ever challenged the issue of slavery again, "my mind is made up to stand with the people of that oppressed section of the Union in resistance to your measures and your power."[2] The inherent radicalism of this statement escaped the attention of men like Yancey, who viewed the compromise as a betrayal of Southern principles. In the summer of 1850, Yancey and other states' rights extremists, dubbed "fire-eaters," participated in the Nashville Convention, a stillborn effort to initiate secession throughout the South.

Though compromise and unionism prevailed, the peculiar institution was too entrenched for Alabamians to tolerate further threats to its existence. To slaveholders and yeoman alike, regardless of party affiliation, slavery undergirded the white

South's sense of security and identity. Economically, it was too profitable to abandon. In 1860 approximately 34,000 Alabamians owned slaves (1,700 of whom each owned over fifty), whose total property value capitalized at $200 million. Also in that year the state's plantations produced a record harvest of 990,000 bales of cotton.[3] But slavery represented much more than economic wealth: it reinforced a racial caste system that exalted white supremacy. The paradox of American slavery was that it magnified the importance of liberty to Southern whites. Thus, any attack on black slavery was an attack on white freedom. On this issue there was wide consensus among Alabama citizens.

Indicative of slavery's intrinsic value was the state legislature's passage of a comprehensive slave code in 1852. This code combined a whole series of local statutes and customs into a single state law. It emphasized that slaves were first and foremost property and only secondarily humans with basic rights. But these internal developments paled in comparison to the chain of national events that would polarize the political arena throughout the 1850s and eventually transform the fire-eaters from an impetuous minority into a domineering majority.

The one direct benefit of the compromise for the South was the supposedly stricter Fugitive Slave Act. Several northeastern states, however, refused to comply with its provisions and passed so-called personal-liberty laws that denied the concept of human chattel and offered protection for those involved in the Underground Railroad. As Southerners chafed at this deliberate mockery of federal law, popular polemics over slavery intensified with the 1852 publication of *Uncle Tom's Cabin*. In this best-selling novel, New England–born author Harriet Beecher Stowe condemned the inhumanity of slavery. Southerners denounced what they considered Stowe's naïve misinterpretation of reality. Among the leading critics were two Alabama authors, Caroline Lee Hentz and Augusta Jane Evans. Hentz attempted to counter the influence of *Uncle Tom's Cabin* with

an unabashed proslavery novel, *The Planter's Northern Bride*, published in 1854. Evans was more nuanced in her literary rebuttal. In *Beulah* (1859), the coming-of-age story of a Southern woman, she demonstrates through her discussions of religion, philosophy, and social customs that Southern culture was far too rich and diverse to be viewed exclusively in terms of slavery. Although *Beulah* sold more than 22,000 copies, neither Evans nor Hentz achieved the literary success of their Northern counterpart.

Arguably the most divisive political event of the 1850s was the Kansas-Nebraska Act (1854). Hoping to rally all Americans around a grand economic venture, Democratic senator Stephen Douglas of Illinois proposed construction of a transcontinental railroad. Southern politicians objected, however, because the line was slated to run through Kansas Territory. Given that this land was off limits to slavery due to the Missouri Compromise of 1820, they rightly argued that a railroad would only expedite the settlement and admission of a new free state, which would further weaken the slave states' standing in the U.S. Senate. To placate them, Douglas acceded to a suggestion by Alabama congressman Philip Phillips (Mobile) that the legislation abrogate the Missouri demarcation line with regard to Kansas and leave the fate of slavery in that particular territory to popular sovereignty. So amended, the bill passed—and controversy ensued.

Having gained the right to take their chattel into Kansas, proslavery settlers descended on the territory and soon clashed with Free Soil Northerners for political control. Popular sovereignty quickly deteriorated into the vigilante free-for-all known as "bleeding Kansas." In the spring of 1856, this mini–Civil War erupted as paramilitary forces crossed the Missouri border and attacked Free Soil communities while fanatical abolitionists, such as the notorious John Brown, assassinated slaveholders. In Alabama, proslavery emigration-aid societies sponsored groups of farmers willing to make the trek to Kansas as colonists promoting the Southern way of life. Some went as genuine settlers hoping to acquire a homestead. But others went as filibusters, determined to transform the territory by force into a new slave state. After skirmishing for several months against more-numerous bands of Free Soilers, however, most Alabamians conceded defeat and returned home.

Northern outrage over the Kansas-Nebraska Act and the subsequent violence contributed to the collapse of the Whig Party. Many Northern Whigs, believing that their party had succumbed to a slave-power conspiracy, formed the new Republican Party, an exclusively Northern political organization that made antislavery its central plank. Southerners observed the rise of the Republicans with great alarm. Southern Whigs came to realize that the principle of states' rights in the context of defending slavery was now more important than a party creed; they too quit the ranks. Without a vibrant political replacement, they would lack the institutional means with which to resist the fire-eaters later in the decade.

Since the astonishing rise of the Republican Party made its control over Congress imminent and its eventual capture of the presidency probable, Southerners increasingly looked to the U.S. Supreme Court for protection. Alabamians were especially thankful that one of their own—Justice John A. Campbell, from Mobile—sat on the bench. In 1857 Campbell and his fellow justices rendered a landmark decision on slavery in *Scott v. Sandford*. The case addressed the question of whether residence in a free state or territory bestowed freedom to a slave. In a 7–2 vote the court ruled not only that Congress had no authority to prohibit slavery from the territories but also that blacks had no citizenship rights at all. In voting with the majority, Campbell grounded his arguments on states' rights and stressed the historicity of slavery. Angry Republicans rebuked the court and portrayed the decision as yet another example of a slave-power conspiracy.

Toward the end of the 1850s, many Southerners believed that the Republican Party was on the verge of usurping power for the purpose of implementing an aggressive abolitionist agenda. Stark evidence of this was the propaganda that swirled around John Brown's failed attempt to instigate a slave insurrection during his raid on Harper's Ferry, Virginia, in October 1859. Slave revolts, though rare, were a source of constant worry for white Southerners. To them, Brown became the face of abolitionism, which they further conflated into a psychopathic Republican crusade.

Alabamians felt the gravity of the situation going into the presidential election of 1860. The state assembly reflected this mood. In the event of a Lincoln victory, it ordered the governor to call a special convention empowered to "consider, determine and do whatever in the opinion of said Convention, the rights, interests, and honor of the State of Alabama requires to be done for their protection."[4] The legislature then put the state on a war footing, appropriating $200,000 to finance the militia—the Alabama Volunteer Corps (AVC)—should it be called into service. It also created scholarships for each county to send selected students to the various military academies within the state. Responding to this need, the University of Alabama instituted its Corps of Cadets, among the graduates of this program being future Confederate general J. C. C. Sanders. The people of Alabama matched this martial zeal. On their own initiative, militia companies mustered in several counties, enough to make up two full regiments in the AVC. In other counties States' Rights Democrats raised paramilitary units, often dubbed "Minute Men," or organized into so-called committees on public safety. Such terms were throwbacks to the Spirit of 1776, and their usage was deliberate: liberty or death at the prospect of a ruling Republican Party tyranny.

As Alabama mobilized for conflict, dramatic events unfolded in Charleston, South Carolina, site of the Democratic national convention in April.

Prominent among the delegates was none other than William Yancey. As in 1848, he demanded that the party adopt an unconditional proslavery stance—the Alabama Platform reborn. When Northern delegates unanimously rejected his proposal, Yancey staged another walkout. But this time the entire Deep South delegation marched out with him. The voice in the wilderness had now become the prophet of Southern liberty. Rent into competing factions, Democrats had little chance of defeating the Republicans in November. Undaunted, Southern fire-eaters nominated Kentuckian John C. Breckinridge, who campaigned on the Alabama Platform. Northern Democrats hastily rallied behind Stephen Douglas.

Virtually every white Alabamian loathed the idea of a Republican presidency. Still, there was significant political division among the citizens. States' Rights Democrats endorsed Breckinridge, of course, and enjoyed the support of many disaffected Whigs. Upstate Democrats, however, remained largely devoted to the original party and supported Douglas. Vacillating remnants of the state's Whig Party promoted an odd third candidate—the Tennessean John Bell and his new Constitutional Union Party. Despite the seeming variety of candidates, the differences between each were remarkably slight: in varying ways they all touted Southern rights, a defense of slavery, and a qualified respect for the Union. Under the circumstances, Lincoln's election seemed assured, his absence from most Southern ballots notwithstanding. Nevertheless, Alabamians campaigned with vigor.

The Breckinridge forces proved better organized and more forceful in their campaigning. They portrayed the contest as a choice between "equality in the Union" (as only a Breckinridge presidency could guarantee) "or independence out of it" (which a Lincoln victory would make imperative).[5] Douglas support held strong in the hills as well as Mobile (thanks to the efforts of newspaperman John Forsyth, whose *Mobile Register* was one of the most influential rags in the state). Bell made an impressive showing among conservative slaveholders in the black belt. In the end, however, Breckinridge won the state handily, outpolling his opponents in forty-two of the state's fifty-two counties and garnering 49,000 votes against a combined total of 42,000 for Douglas and Bell. But at the national level, Lincoln's plurality of 39 percent of the popular vote was sufficient for a majority in the Electoral College. For crestfallen Alabamians, this outcome triggered secession.

After waiting for official verification of Lincoln's victory, Gov. Andrew Moore issued the call in early December for a state secession convention. Alabamians elected one hundred delegates, representing every country. Convening on 7 January 1861, the members debated two basic courses: immediate secession by separate state action or secession only in cooperation with other Southern states; one should note that these options reveal that nearly all of the delegates agreed that a Republican presidency was a justifiable rationale to leave the United States. "Present a naked question of resistance to Black Republican rule," said one delegate, "and you will doubtless receive a unanimous vote in favor of it [disunion]."[6] Proponents for immediate secession numbered fifty-four and generally came from the slaveholding regions of the state. Those who urged cooperation numbered forty-six and generally came from the hill counties. Real authority within the convention resided with the Committee of Thirteen, tasked to draft an acceptable ordinance of secession. The fire-eaters on this committee, including William Yancey, barely disguised their intolerance for any hesitation on the matter. Cooperationists argued that secession would enjoy greater legitimacy if multiple states agreed to leave the Union together and only after a final appeal for redress had been made to the federal government. But Yancey and others shrewdly countered that the U.S. Constitution forbade states from forming confederacies while still in the Union; a state had to secede separately under its own sovereignty. Further undermining the cooperationist approach was the fact that South Carolina had already seceded the previous December and that Mississippi and Florida did so during the convention itself.

Even before the delegates had gathered, Governor Moore added impetus to the cause of immediate secession. Consistently moderate for most of his political career, Moore turned into an ardent secessionist after coming to believe that the Republican Party was a foe with which the South could never negotiate favorably. Toward the end of December 1860, he dispatched handpicked commissioners to every slave state. Their mission was twofold: to report on secession proceedings outside of Alabama and to encourage it where the politicians and citizens seemed to waver. The petitions from these officers demonstrate the depth of the crisis and reveal the centrality of slavery to the whole debate. Jabez Curry, commissioner to Maryland, expressed the secessionist mentality as well as any of his colleagues. "Under an abolition Government," Curry warned, "the slave-holding states will be placed under a common ban of proscription . . . to be assaulted, humbled, dwarfed, degraded, and finally crushed out."[7] Rightly believing that secession might entail war, Moore next ordered the state militia to seize all federal arsenals and forts within the state. On 3–5 January Alabama militiamen occupied Forts Morgan and Gaines, both of which guarded the mouth of Mobile Bay, and the federal arsenal at Mount Vernon, with its irresistible stockpile of 20,000 firearms. Though bloodlessly executed, these actions were highly controversial. Given that Alabama was still in the Union, the governor's decision to seize these installations constituted treason. But he speedily reassured authorities in Washington, D.C., that his conduct was nothing more than a preemptive measure intended to avoid hostilities. Fortunately for Moore and for the whole South, lame-duck president James Buchanan accepted this dubious explanation and did nothing to recover the captured property.

On 11 January, after four days of discussion, the Alabama convention voted to secede from the Union. The ordinance read in part, "That the State of Alabama now withdraws, and is hereby withdrawn from the Union . . . and henceforth ceases to be one of the said United States, and is, and of right ought to be a SOVEREIGN and INDEPENDENT STATE."[8] The final tally in the convention hall was 61–39, seven cooperationists having switched their initial stance. Still questioning the prudence of disunion, a few dissenters requested that the ordinance be put before the people for a referendum vote. The secessionist majority, however, quashed this proposal on the grounds that the original vote for delegates, if not the 1860 national election returns themselves, already demonstrated the will of the people. In the end seventy-six delegates signed the official declaration, a figure that suggests that many cooperationists were more concerned with the process than the final outcome.

Most Alabamians did indeed receive the news of secession with jubilation. William M. Brooks, president of the convention, aptly summed up the mood: "Looking back at the many grievous wrongs under which we have so long suffered at the hands of our Northern *brethren,* and reflecting upon the threatened perils from which we have escaped by withdrawing from the Union, I cannot but rejoice at our deliverance."[9] The paramilitary bands that seemed so ubiquitous in 1860 proliferated throughout the state in early 1861, only now they were incorporated into the militia system. Over 150 companies began drilling in colorful new uniforms. Epitomizing the citizens' excitement, these units sported such defiant names as Independent Rifles, Rough and Ready Volunteers, Jefferson Warriors, Jackson Avengers, and LaFayette Guards. Eager to equip the outpouring of volunteers with adequate weaponry, the Moore administration spent $50,000 for additional rifles, many ironically purchased from Northern arms dealers. Taking these developments as their cue, Alabama's delegation in the U.S.

Congress on 21 January 1861 announced its resignation en masse from that body.

On 4 February as per prior arrangements, Alabama hosted a gathering of representatives from the seven states that had seceded thus far. Acting as a provisional congress, the delegates immediately created the Confederate States of America, with Montgomery as the capital. This small city of nearly 9,000 inhabitants now became the bustling center of a new nation, in a matter of weeks becoming home to an additional 7,000 people. In short order the provisional congress drafted a new constitution that explicitly protected slavery and then selected Jefferson Davis of Mississippi as the first president of the Confederacy. Because there was no direct route by rail from Davis's hometown to Montgomery, the president-elect actually entered Alabama via Tennessee and Georgia. The circuitous route, while exposing the South's inadequate rail system, served as a forum to trumpet secession at every stop. On his arrival in Montgomery, the Mississippian received a warm welcome from William Yancey, who famously declared that "the man and the hour have met." On 18 February Davis took the oath of office amid wild celebration punc-tuated by a popular new tune, "Dixie." Before an audience of perhaps 10,000 people, the new president issued his inaugural address. "Doubly justified by the absence of wrong on our part, and by wanton aggression on the part of others," he said at one point, "there can be no cause to doubt that the courage and patriotism of the people of the Confederate States will be found equal to any measures of defense which honor and security may require."[10]

The alacrity with which Alabamians seceded from the Union, raised a sizeable military force, and then helped organize the nascent Confederate States of America is astonishing—and they did it all before Lincoln was even inaugurated. A dozen years of intensifying dissension over slavery and states' rights had culminated in a bold declaration of Southern independence. Alabama had become the "Cradle of the Confederacy." But the euphoria of political self-determination would soon be replaced by the angst of a long military struggle. The militiamen who paraded throughout the state in their fancy uniforms would soon face the test of combat in a modern war.

PHILIP PHILLIPS
daguerreotype
Mathew Brady

On 22 January 1854, Congressman Philip Phillips of Mobile met with Pres. Franklin Pierce at a private conclave in the White House library. Also in attendance were Sen. Stephen Douglas and other leading Democratic politicians. The topic of the meeting was whether the pending Kansas-Nebraska bill would permit the extension of slavery into those two territories. A forty-six-year-old lawyer and Jew originally from South Carolina, Phillips was no extremist, but he did consider slaveholders' equal access to all western lands "a theoretical right" that the federal government could not violate. A Democrat elected in 1852, he served on the House Committee on Territories, from which he sought an opportunity to abrogate the old Missouri Compromise's prohibition on slavery north of latitude 36°30'. When Douglas submitted his bill organizing the Kansas and Nebraska Territories, Phillips's moment to strike had arrived. Whereas the senator preferred cryptic language that left the status of slavery open ended, Southern fire-eaters tried to insert an overt repeal of the Missouri Compromise. At the January meeting with the president, Phillips suggested a provision that semantically satisfied both sides: "That the people of the Territory . . . may legislate upon the subject of slavery in any manner they may think proper . . . and all laws or parts of laws inconsistent with this authority or right shall . . . become inoperative, void and of no force and effect." In essence, Phillips was calling on Congress to "supersede" rather than "repeal" the existing federal restriction, and by doing so he believed that moderate politicians would find it easier to vote in favor of a bill that on its surface seemed less provocative. Regardless of whether such subtlety actually swayed anyone, a revised Kansas-Nebraska bill that closely reflected the Alabamian's terminology soon appeared; it passed in May 1854. "That this measure increased the slavery agitation and hastened the crisis of 1861," Phillips frankly admitted years later, "is very probable."[11]
Photo courtesy of Library of Congress

CAROLINE LEE HENTZ
copy print
Livingston Studio, Montgomery

Like most white Southerners, Caroline Hentz responded to the publication of *Uncle Tom's Cabin* with outrage. To her, the book was nothing more than an obnoxious abolitionist screed written by a woman—Harriet Beecher Stowe of Connecticut—who had no firsthand knowledge of slavery. Conversely, Hentz knew a great deal about both the North and the South. Born in Massachusetts, she grew up a Yankee and developed literary talents of her own. In the 1820s she accompanied her husband to North Carolina, where the two worked as educators. From 1834 to 1848 the couple lived in Alabama, residing in turn at Florence, Tuscaloosa, and Tuskegee, before moving just across the border to Columbus, Georgia. During her fourteen years in Alabama, Hentz fostered close friendships with the state's leading families. Moreover, she came to accept the notion of slavery as a "positive good," where blacks supposedly benefited

from a system that maximized their potential as an inferior race. So when *Uncle Tom's Cabin* came out with its scathing critique of both slavery and slave-holders, Hentz wrote a counter novel in 1854, *The Planter's Northern Bride.* In this work the author emphasizes the paternalistic ideal of plantation life, one where masters were honorable and magnanimous and where slaves were loyal and content. As the title suggests, Hentz insists that if abolitionists would just set aside their sanctimony and observe the world of the slaveholders as she had done for most of her adulthood, then they too would recognize the wisdom and beneficence of race order. Although *The Planter's Northern Bride* did not achieve the far-reaching influence of *Uncle Tom's Cabin,* it did constitute a feminine version of the code duello, with Hentz upholding Southern honor via the pen as opposed to the pistol. *Photo courtesy of ADAH*

JEFFERSON BUFORD
copy print
W. R. Abbott,
Opelika and Auburn

"Who will go to Kansas?" asked Jefferson Buford in November 1855. The question prefaced a call for Alabamians to accompany him on an expedition intended to colonize the newly organized territory with slaveholders. A forty-eight-year-old planter, lawyer, and Indian fighter from Barbour County, Buford believed that Kansas was the crucial battlefield in the South's fight for national honor. He saw it as a "great Thermopylae" against the "free soil hordes" of the North. In other words, Kansas represented his section's last hope for peaceful coexistence in the Union. "If we cannot find some crazy enough to peril even life in the deadly breach," he expounded, "then it is not because individuals have grown more prudent and wise, but because public virtue has decayed and we have thereby already become unequal to the successful defense of our rights."

By April 1856 about 400 men, including some volunteers from neighboring Southern states, responded to Buford's petition. Milling about the streets of Montgomery, they carried banners inscribed "Alabama for Kansas—North of 36°30'"; "Kansas, the Outpost"; and "The Supremacy of the White Race." Many also brandished firearms, though Buford always maintained his mission was one of nonviolence. Buford, elected "General of the force," and his men reached Kansas on May 2. The journey came at great personal expense—the "general" spent approximately $20,000, money largely raised through the sale of many of his own slaves. Once in Kansas the Southerners soon became embroiled in the paramilitary strife running rampant in the territory. They participated in the sacking of Lawrence, a Free Soil bastion, though Buford denounced much of the wanton destruction of private property that he witnessed. Thereafter, he concentrated on acquiring homesteads for his followers. Growing lawlessness in the territory, however, rendered such a pursuit impossible; the men spent more time skirmishing than farming. Desperate for reinforcements, the "general" toured the South over the summer, but his efforts to enlist more emigrants fell mostly on deaf ears. When he returned to Kansas later that autumn, he discovered that most of his original band wanted to go home. The Free Soilers had gained the upper hand; Buford's expedition was a failure.[12]
Photo courtesy of ADAH

JOHN ARCHIBALD CAMPBELL
copy print

To Justice John Campbell, the peculiar institution certainly posed a conundrum, for he believed that it retarded economic development but was always quick to stress that it was the South's problem. So when he wrote his opinion in the Dred Scott case of 1857, Campbell insisted that slavery, as a property-rights issue, was outside the jurisdiction of the federal government, hence untouchable to Northern politicians. At forty-five years of age, Campbell was the junior member of the U.S. Supreme Court, but everyone agreed that he possessed a brilliant legal mind. While still a teenager, he had left his native Georgia in 1830 and opened a law practice in Montgomery. Seven years later he moved to Mobile, where his success in resolving complicated land disputes attracted favorable attention. In 1853 President Pierce appointed him associate justice to the Supreme Court. Despite his cordial association with Southern radicals such as William Yancey, Campbell was no fire-eater. He condemned, for instance, proslavery filibuster adventures then taking place throughout Central America. But when it came to slavery in the territories, the justice was a staunch defender of Southern rights.

In the case *Dred Scott v. Sandford,* Campbell voted with the majority both in denying Scott his freedom and in declaring unconstitutional the Missouri Compromise of 1820. Anticipating charges of regional bias, he averred that his opinion was based solely on the facts in the case while his interpretation of the law reflected an appropriately strict construction. Specifically, Campbell dissected Article IV, Section 3 of the Constitution, granting Congress power over the territories. To him, this provision authorized the federal government to maintain law and order in a territory, but this did not mean it could ban certain settlers (that is, Southerners) from bringing in their chattel property. "A proscription," Campbell explained, "determining property, on the part of the Federal government, by which the stability of its social system may be endangered, is plainly repugnant to the conditions on which the Federal constitution was adopted." Therefore, when it came to slavery in the territories, the justice argued that Congress had to conform to a policy of nonintervention. In a larger, ideological sense, he also exercised vast judicial review with his opinion, asserting in essence that all historical constraints over the extension of slavery, from the Northwest Ordinance through the Missouri Compromise to the Wilmot Proviso, were unconstitutional because they undermined the equality of the Southern states in the Union. Throughout his brief, the principle of federalism, and not some self-serving devotion to slavery, guided his reasoning.[14] *Photo courtesy of Library of Congress*

HENRY DeLAMAR
CLAYTON
from White and
Black under the
Old Regime, *by*
Victoria V. Clayton

In late August 1856, Henry Clayton donned a red-flannel shirt, shouldered a carbine, and led one hundred men into battle against Free Soilers in Kansas. Little did he know that his actions were but prelude to the forthcoming Civil War. A twenty-nine-year-old slaveholder from Barbour County, Clayton shared his friend Jefferson Buford's belief that Kansas was a crucial test of Southern resolve against the growing tide of abolitionism. Earlier in the month Clayton, accompanied by his wife, Victoria, had left his plantation and escorted a party of proslave settlers northwestward. The group was part of a second, smaller wave of Southern emigrants heading to Kansas Territory. They arrived in the wake of John Brown's murderous rampage through the Pottawatomie community; a paramilitary struggle for control was underway.

Leaving their wives behind at the Missouri border, Clayton and his men pitched into the fray, fighting a number of skirmishes before federal authorities imposed an uneasy peace in October. In the immediate aftermath Clayton purchased land and oxen (with money donated by the states of Alabama and Georgia) for each family in his party. "In return for this," his wife noted, "they were to cast their votes for the interest, as we then thought, of our beloved South." Presumably, these men did indeed vote for the Lecompton Constitution of 1857, a fraudulent attempt by the territory's proslave minority to get Kansas admitted to the Union as a slave state. In any event, Clayton himself returned to Alabama and entered politics there as a fire-eater.[13]

WILLIAM LOWNDES YANCEY
copy print

If one man personified Alabama's rebellious spirit, that man was William Yancey. For more than a dozen years, Yancey had called for an independent Southern nation. A lawyer and planter from Montgomery, he espoused strong nationalism in his youth, but after moving from Georgia to Alabama in the 1830s, he evinced a defiant sense of individualism. After dabbling in politics for a few years, he came to realize that great dreams could never be attained through the bureaucracy of a party system, especially one that seemed all too willing to compromise its own principles. Beginning with his Alabama Platform in 1848, a manifesto that utterly repudiated the federal government's authority to regulate slavery in the territories, Yancey emerged in the 1850s as one of the South's most notorious fire-eaters. Although a forceful orator and pamphleteer, the man was no mere demagogue. Rather, he was a shrewd propagandist who skillfully played to his region's sense of honor by launching a compelling attack on the North. As he consistently explained, it was the Yankees who hypocritically demeaned the South as an inferior society somehow in need of change; it was the Yankees who obscenely interjected morality into the slavery debate when in fact their sole interest was the subversion of Southern liberty; and it was the Yankees who blatantly betrayed the heritage of the Founders by conflating the idea of the Union into an unbreakable covenant. Through such steadfast appeals, Yancey candidly reassured Southerners that rebellion was an acceptable course of action. "No national party can save us," he wrote a like-minded friend in a widely circulated letter in 1858. "But if we could do as our fathers did . . . we shall fire the Southern heart—instruct the Southern mind—give courage to each other, and at the proper moment, by one, organized, concerted action, we can precipitate the cotton States into a revolution." The climax of his quest came first at the Democratic Party's Charleston convention in April 1860, when Yancey led the Southern delegates in a dramatic walk-out, then later at the Alabama Secession Convention in January 1861, when he impressed a sense of urgency on the proceedings and thereby stifled any potential hesitation. In the former event he helped destroy the antebellum Democratic Party, in the latter event he expedited his state's withdrawal from the Union.[15]
Photo courtesy of ADAH

LANDON CABELL GARLAND
carte de visite

In July 1860 Landon Garland's half-decade effort to convert the University of Alabama into a military academy came to fruition. A distinguished professor from Virginia, Garland became the school's third president in 1855. His original purpose in introducing what became the Corps of Cadets was to instill discipline and manners into a student body that had grown unruly and disrespectful. As the sectional crisis intensified, however, these martial reforms helped prepare Alabama for war. In fact, it was precisely the impending breakdown between the North and South that prompted the state legislature to finally allocate funds for Garland's project. Within a few months the new military regimen produced a dramatic change. Where the campus once swarmed with young men who were either "rakes or drunkards or problems," now cadets marched in uniform, displaying "punctuality, obedience to authority, and personal neatness." But the students were still exuberant youths. After Alabama seceded from the Union, the fifty-year-old Garland tried to utilize the corps as a training cadre for the rapidly mobilizing Confederate army. Instead, most cadets eventually quit the school to fight. Still, during the first year of the conflict, Garland supervised the drilling of perhaps as many as 12,000 volunteers.[16]
Photo courtesy of W. S. Hoole Special Collections Library, The University of Alabama

FLAG OF THE YOUNG MEN'S SECESSION ASSOCIATION
copy print

Flags symbolize powerful ideologies. A case in point is the flag of the Young Men's Secession Association of Mobile. First unfurled at one of the club's meetings on 18 December 1860, the banner's inscription concisely expresses the prevalent attitude within the state. The pattern is a simple blue column, with the lone star of Alabama in the center, flanked by white columns. Within the star is a magnolia with golden sun rays shining in the background. The upper-left-hand corner exhibits a blue shield with fifteen stars, one for each slave state in the Union. At the December meeting Edmund S. Dargan, a former Alabama congressman and chief justice of the state supreme court, spoke of the sectional crisis and then "pointed to the flag, on the platform, on which were the words, 'The time has come,' and repeated these words three times." The message was clear: no more talk—action.[17]

In 1907 Thomas W. Sims of Mobile donated this flag to the Alabama State Archives. *Photo courtesy of ADAH*

WILLIAM RUSSELL SMITH
copy print

As a self-appointed secretary of the Alabama Secession Convention, William Smith published an invaluable and detailed record of the event. A forty-five-year-old lawyer-politician from Tuscaloosa, Smith opposed immediate secession, partly out of principle but also because he was contrarian by nature. Having grown up an orphan, he had no connection to the state's planter elites. Instead, he pursued the life of a dilettante, periodically writing plays, briefly editing a newspaper, fighting in the militia against the Creek Indians, and engaging in politics first as a Whig, then as a Democrat, and finally as an independent. Dubbed "Little Billy" by his supporters, Smith's personal brand of populism obviously appealed to north Alabama's yeomanry, for he eked out several election victories over more-prominent rivals, and served three terms in the U.S. House (1851–57). During the secession convention, the former congressman firmly denounced the incoming Lincoln administration but urged caution in leaving the Union. Despite the manifest excitement of

the moment, Smith argued that the secessionists' control of the convention was actually out of favor with the real public mood: "I believe that a popular majority of the State is represented here by the minority." Fire-eaters in the chamber bristled at this provocative assertion, but Smith pressed on, comparing their cause to "an apple with gold on its outside, but with ashes on its core." The delegate then asked that he and his colleagues receive "but the ordinary civilities of parliamentary decorum; time to deliberate and examine." The whole speech was "sneeringly" delivered, according to William Yancey, who went on to brand Smith and the rest of the cooperationists "misguided, deluded, and wicked men." Little Billy had successfully goaded Yancey into a verbal misstep, but his efforts to stall the proceedings failed. In the end, though he voted against the ordinance of secession, Smith simultaneously pledged allegiance to Alabama.[18]
Photo courtesy of ADAH

32

JEREMIAH CLEMENS
daguerreotype

As the titular leader of the cooperationists, Jeremiah Clemens was determined to obstruct what he considered a mad rush for secession. A forty-six-year-old politician from Madison County, Clemens was the son of a wealthy Huntsville merchant (and distant relative to Samuel Clemens, the future Mark Twain). His upbringing followed the usual path of the South's upper class: excellent education, law practice, and public service as a state legislator in the 1840s. During the Mexican War, he obtained a regular-army commission but did not see combat. Afterward he won election to the U.S. Senate as a Democrat, but his shifting views on the Compromise of 1850, as well as his private meetings with Whigs, displeased party leaders, who considered the senator an opportunist. Denied a second term, Clemens did indeed briefly align with the Whig Party but spent most of his time writing trite romances and battling alcoholism until his election to the secession convention. There Clemens stated his views with candor. "I am no believer in peaceable secession," he declared, "I know it to be impossible." To Clemens, secession, whether immediate, independent, or gradual, was sure to bring down the military wrath of the North, and he doubted the South's ability to win a full-scale war. When the convention's Committee of Thirteen presented its ordinance of secession, Clemens presented the delegates with the "Minority Report." This document reiterated the cooperationists' demand for a regional convention but also called for a final appeal to the North for political redress over slavery. When Clemens moved that the Minority Report be substituted for the ordinance, secessionists voted him down. He then engaged in a bizarre spate of grandstanding that reminded listeners of his erratic course as a senator. "I shall vote for this Ordinance," he abruptly declared at one point, but at another he admonished, "the act you are about to commit, is, to my apprehension, treason." After rambling on about how he would have voted against secession if his vote really mattered, Clemens closed his speech in dramatic fashion: "it is enough to say that I am a son of Alabama; her destiny is mine; her people are mine; her enemies are mine." He then voted for secession.[19]
Photo courtesy of Library of Congress

SIDNEY CHERRY POSEY
copy print
Campbell and Edens, Florence

One of the most steadfast voices of opposition to secession was that of Sidney Posey. A fifty-eight-year-old lawyer from Lauderdale County who served in the state senate in the 1830s and 1840s, Posey long believed that big political decisions deserved careful deliberation. So, like other cooperationists in 1861, he tried to rein in the surge toward immediate, separate state secession. He particularly disliked the alarmist tactics that invariably came into play. To those delegates who opined that the incoming Lincoln administration planned to destroy the institution of slavery, Posey firmly retorted, "There have been no aggressions on the part of the Federal Government." Moreover, he resented the secessionists' aspersion that the caution of the cooperationists somehow equaled submission to the Republican Party. "We intend to resist," Posey bellowed, "but our resistance is based upon consultation, and in unity of action, with the other slave states." He soon realized, however, that his position was doomed. As the vote on the ordinance neared, Posey tried to persuade the secessionists to at least grant Alabamians the final word via a referendum. "Division at home would be worse than Secession," he warned, only a referendum could properly gauge the people's true feeling. Predictably, secessionists ignored his suggestion. Just as predictably, Posey voted against the ordinance and later refused to sign the official document.[20]
Photo courtesy of ADAH

EDWARD COURTENAY
BULLOCK
copy print

On 3 January 1861 Ed Bullock of Barbour County arrived in Tallahassee, just in time for the opening of the Florida Secession Convention. He carried a commission that authorized him to speak in behalf of Alabama's desire to secede and hopefully join Florida in forming a new nation. A native of South Carolina, the thirty-five-year-old Bullock came to Alabama shortly after graduating from Harvard. He brought with him not only a brilliant legal mind but also an almost fanatical devotion to the political ideology of John C. Calhoun. In addition to practicing law, Bullock ably edited the strident states' rights newspaper *The Spirit of the South.* His enthusiasm, combined with his self-effacing sense of humor, made him a favorite among Alabama's fire-eaters, particularly William Yancey. As a state senator Bullock kept his radical colleagues informed of the latest political developments. In the turbulent months after John Brown's raid, he helped pass both the resolution calling for a secession convention in the wake of Lincoln's election and an appropriation bill for mobilizing the state militia. As commissioner to Florida, Bullock did little more than watch the impetus of secession unfold before his eyes. On 10 January he happily telegraphed Montgomery that Florida had voted to secede by an overwhelming margin: 62–7. Bullock did not know it at the time, but his message when read before Alabama's convention noticeably deflated the cooperationists. He was delighted to learn that Alabama seceded the next day. "The two States, divided by but a single day in their exodus," Bullock exulted, "will soon be closely joined in that new Union of brotherly love, in which a homogeneous people, taking their destiny into their own hands, shall exhibit to the world the noblest phase of Free Government."[21]
Photo courtesy of ADAH

INDEPENDENT BLUES OF SELMA
copy print

On the morning of 11 January 1861, a militia company dubbed the Independent Blues assembled at the wharf on Water Street in Selma, Alabama. There the men posed in full regalia for a photograph while they awaited steamboat transportation to take them down the Alabama River to Mobile. The unit was soon to join a host of other militia companies then gathering to occupy the U.S. military installations around the bay. Organized in the summer of 1859, the Independent Blues exemplified Alabama's early preparation for war. According to one resident of Selma, these volunteers consisted of the "sober, more settled men of the city." They were also among the best dressed. Typical of the state's prewar militia system, volunteer companies wore leftover regular U.S. Army uniforms, often throwbacks to the Mexican War. The dark blue

frock coat and gray pants were standard, but headgear could vary. Most wore shakos, but a few sported kepis and fatigue caps. As they boarded the riverboat *Senator,* the volunteers received word that Alabama had seceded from the Union; much cheering undoubtedly ensued. After spending a couple of months in Mobile, the Blues were designated Company D, 8th Alabama Infantry. True to their volunteer spirit, the men then joined the rest of their new regiment in enlisting for the duration of the war. Before it ended, though, approximately 470 men from the 8th Alabama, including many from the original Independent Blues, had lost their lives. Of course, by then the outfit had long since replaced the snappy uniforms of its halcyon days with the more familiar gray of the Rebel army.[22]
Photo courtesy of ADAH

36

LOUIS ALEXANDER CONOLEY
AND THOMAS P. NORRIS
copy print

For two young men from Dallas County, the call to arms in 1861 was irresistible. Even before their state formally seceded, seventeen-year-old Louis Conoley and his friend Thomas Norris (probably the same age) volunteered to fight with the Independent Blues. Decked out in dark blue frock coats and gray pants, topped off with shako caps, the two teenagers undoubtedly dreamed about winning glory defending their rights as Alabamians and as Southerners. The actual war, however, was not kind to either of them. After serving for a year as part of the Mobile garrison, both youths reenlisted for the duration as privates in Company D, 8th Alabama Infantry. During the Peninsula Campaign in Virginia, the regiment "saw the elephant" at the Battle of Williamsburg on 5 May 1862. Norris suffered a terrible wound during the fighting and fell into enemy hands; he subsequently died in captivity. Before the campaign ended, Conoley transferred to the newly raised 29th Alabama Infantry, a regiment commanded by his father, where he received a commission as second lieutenant. For the next year and a half, the regiment was stationed in southern Alabama, but in early 1864 it joined the Army of Tennessee and participated in the defense of Atlanta. Conoley received a combat wound at Ezra Church in late July. He recovered but in mid-September went on sick furlough with an unspecified illness. Conoley died on 22 November 1864. *Photo courtesy of ADAH*

CLEMENT CLAIBORNE CLAY
daguerreotype
Mathew Brady

Sen. Clement Clay of Madison County was an unabashed Alabama fire-eater, but he tempered his extremism with the gentility of a planter aristocrat. The son of Clement Comer Clay, a powerful politician during the state's early history, the junior Clay benefited from his father's patronage even as he inherited the old man's political enemies. His extensive education—Clay possessed degrees from the Universities of Alabama and Virginia—as well as his marriage to Virginia Tunstall, a high-society debutante, made it difficult for the young planter to connect politically with the yeoman electorate of the Tennessee Valley. In 1850, for instance, he lost a congressional race to the folksy Williamson Cobb, a Jacksonian Democrat whom he considered an insufferable rube. By 1853, however, with the sectional rift widening, Clay's unequivocal stance on states' rights helped him win election to the U.S. Senate; he was thirty-five years old at the time. As a senator he voted for the Kansas-Nebraska Act and supported the Lecompton Constitution, a dubious manifesto that sought to bring Kansas into the Union as a slave state. The concomitant rise of the antislavery Republican Party, however, convinced Clay that the South's ability to defend its peculiar institution was on borrowed time. During a visit home in September 1859, he delivered a speech designed to prepare his state for drastic action. "Property is the basis of the social fabric," Clay declared in reference to slavery, "to protect and preserve it, is the chief end of every government. . . . [W]hen protection ceases, allegiance ceases." Furthermore, he reminded his constituents that Alabama was "one of thirty-three free, sovereign and independent states, composing a confederation, not a consolidation, a union, not a nation." The insinuation—a call for secession—was obvious. John Brown's raid shortly thereafter only added a sense of urgency to this appeal. Though ill for much of the 1860 campaign season, Clay evinced his usual fire-eating spirit following Lincoln's victory: "Since the election of a man to the Presidency pledged to a war of extermination of slavery, the North can offer us no greater insult, or stronger proof of hatred and vengeance." The senator then added, "I am for separating from them immediately and making them a foreign people." Not surprisingly, when Alabama formally seceded in January 1861, Clay resigned his seat accordingly, "to defend her honor, maintain her rights, and share her fate."[23]
Photo courtesy of Library of Congress

BENJAMIN FITZPATRICK
daguerreotype
Mathew Brady

Although he countenanced moderation during the secession crisis, Sen. Benjamin Fitzpatrick seemed resigned to the unfolding revolution in the South. A fifty-eight-year-old politician from Montgomery, Fitzpatrick grew up a common man who started his adult life as a small-town store clerk. Shortly after becoming a lawyer in the 1820s, however, he married into the wealthy Elmore family, which brought him possession of a large plantation with two dozen slaves; by the 1850s he owned over 100 slaves. Fitzpatrick parlayed his economic status into political power, serving twice as governor in the 1840s. In politics he was a solid Jacksonian Democrat promoting fiscal conservatism. Fitzpatrick was dismayed by political developments in the 1850s, considering Southern fire-eaters reckless men but sympathizing with their overall outlook, even when they castigated him for endorsing the idea of popular sovereignty. As for the Republican Party, he could barely contain his disgust. Criticizing its members as "purely sectional candidates" who had destroyed the politics of compromise, the senator denounced "the revolutionary dogmas advanced by that party in utter disregard of the constitutional rights of the Slaveholding States." Declining an invitation to run in 1860 as the vice-presidential candidate on a Democratic ticket with Stephen Douglas, Fitzpatrick watched the election with foreboding. In the aftermath of Lincoln's victory, he approved the course of the cooperationists in the state secession convention, but he almost seemed indifferent to the outcome. "If we cannot live in peace as a nation," he mused, "let us separate and each section provide for itself." Toward the end of January 1861, Fitzpatrick resigned with the rest of the Alabama delegation in Congress. But while colleagues such as Senator Clay delivered impassioned farewell addresses that justified secession, Fitzpatrick merely expressed his loyalty to his home state and then left the capital.[24] *Photo courtesy of Library of Congress*

INAUGURATION OF JEFFERSON DAVIS
copy print

On the morning of 18 February 1861, several thousand people milled about the streets near the Capitol in Montgomery, waiting to watch Jefferson Davis take the oath of office as president of the Confederate States of America. The president-elect had arrived little more than a day earlier and was staying at the Exchange Hotel. Toward noon Davis left his room and took a seat in a six-horse open carriage, resplendent in white ribbons and saffron décor. By this time the now-cheering crowd had grown to an estimated 10,000 people, many coming from well beyond the city, including newspaper correspondents and foreign dignitaries. At Grand Marshal Hugh Watson's signal, the inaugural parade commenced. With Herman Arnold's band blaring "Dixie," the president's military escort—four militia companies from Alabama and one from Georgia—stepped off. Then came Davis, accompanied by Alexander Stephens, the Confederacy's vice presi-dent. Bringing up the rear of the cavalcade was a host of local and regional politicians. On reaching the Capitol, where another band was playing the "Marseillaise," Davis went inside and briefly chatted with various Confederate congressmen. Finally, at 1:00 P.M., Davis took his place on the building's portico, where he delivered a prepared speech, one that reiter-ated the right of revolution and wrapped his new nation in the shroud of the Founding Fathers. He was then sworn in by Howell Cobb, and after kissing a large Bible used for the occasion, the new president basked in the jubilation that followed. Less than a hun-dred yards away, local photographer William Culver captured the moment. "More than any other single event," historian William Rogers Jr. aptly notes, "the inauguration gave focus and a sense of being to the Confederacy."[25] *Photo courtesy of ADAH*

ORIGINAL SCORE OF "DIXIE"
copy print

One of the most popular tunes in the South during the Civil War was "Dixie." Although others claimed authorship, Daniel Emmett of Ohio is the artist who generally gets credit. In 1859 he wrote the lyrics and the music for a minstrel show in New York in which actors in blackface expressed nostalgia for the plantation life of the Deep South. The song's now-famous refrain appealed to the sectional patriotism of virtually all white Southerners: "I wish was in the land of cotton / old times there are not forgotten / Look away, look away, look away, Dixie Land." Prior to the inauguration of Jefferson Davis, Montgomery musician Herman Arnold requested a copy of the sheet music from Emmett, who was then visiting the city. Not having one, or even something to write with, the Ohioan hastily scribbled the music in charcoal on a wall of the Old Montgomery Theater. Arnold then used the notes to compose an original band score, which he first played during the inaugural parade on 18 February 1861. Thereafter, "Dixie" became the unofficial national anthem of the Confederacy. *Photo courtesy of ADAH*

42

GEORGE LITTLE
copy print
Herrick and Dirr,
Vicksburg, Miss.

The sectional conflict was of tangential interest to Dr. George Little of Tuscaloosa, but when Alabama seceded, he performed his patriotic duty and joined the Confederate army. The twenty-three-year-old son of Scottish immigrants, Little was a geology professor at Oakland College in Mississippi when that state declared its independence. For most of the 1850s, he had pursued his education, earning his B.A. from the University of Alabama in 1855 and his Ph.D. from Gottingen University (Germany) in 1859. To the young scientist, the secession debate posed no controversy. "We believed that the original union was a voluntary association of free states," Little candidly admitted years after the war. He did, however, question the timing of the South's revolution: "I thought then, and still

think that the majority of the white people of Alabama were opposed to secession in 1861." Nonetheless, he blamed the Lincoln administration for the carnage that ensued. "When the northern states attempted to force us back into the Union," he explained, "we felt that our liberties were being attacked, and we prepared to defend them with our lives." As for the issue of slavery, Little contended that it "may have had much weight with the men higher up, but it did not enter into the minds of the rank and file. . . . [W]ith us it was purely a question of our right to manage our own affairs without interference from other states." And so, in November 1861 Dr. Little enlisted in Lumsden's Battery.[26] *Photo courtesy of W. S. Hoole Special Collections Library, The University of Alabama*

Alabamians Go to War

In early April 1861, the Confederate government in Montgomery faced a crisis. When South Carolina seceded the previous December, Federal troops under Maj. Robert Anderson concentrated at Fort Sumter, a military installation that controlled the entrance to Charleston Harbor. For several weeks, Confederate diplomats, including John Forsyth of Mobile, had been attempting both to establish peaceful relations with the Union and to negotiate the withdrawal of Anderson's troops. William Seward, President Lincoln's secretary of state, refused to receive Forsyth and his colleagues lest the administration recognize the sovereignty of the Confederacy. Instead, the secretary operated through an intermediary—Alabama's John A. Campbell, who still sat on the U.S. Supreme Court. Based on his conversations with Seward, Campbell assured the Davis administration that an evacuation of Fort Sumter was imminent. As Davis suspected, however, Seward was making promises that were out of step with Lincoln's plans. News on 8 April that the Federals had dispatched a relief expedition to the fort came as a shock to Campbell, but it afforded the Confederates a pretext to take bold action. On 10 April Confederate secretary of war LeRoy P. Walker wired a bellicose order to P. G. T. Beauregard, the Confederate commander in Charleston: "you will at once demand [Sumter's] evacuation, and if this is refused, proceed in such a manner as you may determine, to reduce it."[1] After receiving Anderson's refusal to leave, Beauregard's artillery commenced a bombardment in the morning hours of 12 April. The next day Fort Sumter fell, and Americans, Northerners and Southerners, went to war.

The firing on Fort Sumter is the famous beginning of the Civil War. Yet it all could have easily started months earlier, at a different location, with Alabamians directly initiating the hostilities. When Florida seceded, U.S. troops retained possession of Fort Pickens, which controlled access to Pensacola. Desperate to secure this port as a naval base, Florida authorities called on Alabama for military assistance. With Pickens a mere fifty miles from Mobile, Gov. Andrew Moore rightly concluded that Federal occupation of the fort posed a serious threat to his state's coastline. Before it had even voted on secession,

Alabama's convention approved Moore's request to send a contingent of soldiers to Florida. On 12 January the 2nd Regiment of Alabama Volunteers marched into Pensacola and linked up with units from Florida; some Mississippi troops joined them later. Numbering approximately 515 men, the Alabamians were eager for action, as was their popular commander, Col. Tennent Lomax. At a council of war on 17 January, Lomax and his staff recommended an immediate assault on Fort Pickens, but officers from the other states vetoed the idea as too risky. Had his counterparts been more aggressive, Lomax might have gained eternal notoriety as the man who started the Civil War. Instead, an uneasy truce ensued between Confederate and Federal forces. The impetuous colonel chafed at this inactivity and soon returned with many of his men to Alabama to raise a new regiment and seek martial glory elsewhere.

For the rest of 1861, Fort Pickens remained a military focal point for Alabama volunteers. In February the new Confederate government reorganized many of the state militia companies into a national military authority. Most of the remaining and newly arrived Alabamians at Pensacola merged into the 1st Alabama Infantry, earning the distinction of being the very first regiment of the Confederate army. Other Alabama regiments soon rotated through. Stationed at Fort Barrancas, which stood opposite Fort Pickens at the bay entrance, these men spent the spring and summer improving their position. While the men generally liked their regimental officers, they loathed the stern leadership of Maj. Gen. Braxton Bragg. A doctrinaire West Pointer, Bragg displayed little respect for the citizen-soldier ideal. Military service at Fort Barrancas featured seemingly endless days of drill, including extensive training with artillery for the men of the 1st Alabama, and the tedium of camp life in the sweltering Gulf Coast heat. Rather than the supposed glory of combat, hundreds of Alabamians succumbed to a variety of maladies, such as measles, typhoid fever, or diarrhea.

Adding to the disillusion were the mixed feelings elicited by the capture of Fort Sumter. Alabamians were elated that the war was officially underway but exasperated when plans to seize Fort Pickens were postponed again and again.

Finally, in the autumn of 1861, Confederate forces in Florida saw some action. After Union commandos boarded and destroyed a Rebel privateer at anchor in Pensacola, Bragg devised a counterattack. On the night of 8 October, two companies from the 1st Alabama participated in a raid against Fort Pickens. The ensuing clash amounted to little more than a skirmish, one that never came close to threatening the fort, but it broke the monotony and raised morale. Six weeks later batteries at Fort Barrancas and other positions, all largely manned by the 1st Alabama Infantry, exchanged fire with Fort Pickens and a small squadron of Union warships in an eight-hour contest. By all accounts the Alabamians performed well as artillerists. With Union forces still holding Fort Pickens, however, the Confederate position at Pensacola grew untenable. In the spring of 1862, the Rebels evacuated the city. For the rest of the war, various companies of Alabama cavalry augmented an erratic effort to monitor Union activities along the Gulf Coast.

These desultory operations around Pensacola soon faded into the background. With the secession of the Upper South following Fort Sumter, Virginia and Tennessee emerged as the principal theaters of the war. In May 1861 the Confederate Congress resolved in a close vote to move the national capital to Richmond, Virginia, a decision roundly condemned by most Alabama newspapers. It was painful for Alabamians to witness Montgomery's sudden rise and then fall as the most important city in the fledgling Confederacy.

Alabamians soon swallowed their disappointment and returned to the urgent matter of waging war. Four freshly mustered regiments headed to Virginia to join the growing body of Rebel forces gathering to defend the new capital. The dispositions reflected President Davis's concept of territorial defense: the 3rd Alabama Infantry (under the fiery Tennent Lomax) served with the garrison at Norfolk; the 4th Alabama Infantry linked with units under Brig. Gen. Joseph Johnston in the Shenandoah Valley; the 5th and 6th Alabama Infantry deployed to Beauregard's command at Manassas Junction in northern Virginia. Their arrival was timely, for in mid-July a Union army under Brig. Gen. Irwin McDowell commenced its first major offensive of the war, a direct overland advance by 35,000 men from Washington, D.C., to Richmond, a mere 100 miles to the south.

For several days, Beauregard's division of 20,000 men conducted a series of delaying actions before establishing a ten-mile long defensive line along Bull Run. The 5th and 6th Alabama anchored the Confederates' extreme right wing. On the morning of 21 July, McDowell unleashed an ambitious flank attack against Beauregard's left. Fortunately for the Confederates, General Johnston speedily sent 8,000 reinforcements by rail from the valley to Manassas. At 7:00 A.M. the 4th Alabama Infantry, 750 strong under Col. Egbert J. Jones, disembarked and immediately marched toward the sound of the guns with the rest of its brigade. After a forced march of four miles through oppressive summer heat, the Alabamians formed a line of battle around Matthews Hill just in time to help repel an enemy assault. The brigade commander, Brig. Gen. Bernard Bee, then ordered a counterattack. Still carrying their haversacks, the Alabamians advanced under fire through a cornfield before pressing home an unsuccessful assault of their own. "Our brave men fell in great numbers," remembered Capt. Thomas Goldsby of Company A, "but they died as the brave love to die—with faces to the foe, fighting in the holy cause of liberty."[2] For about an hour, the Alabamians exchanged volleys with the Federals before realizing that neighboring regiments had withdrawn. As the regiment executed a fighting retreat, enemy fire blasted Colonel Jones off his horse. When several more officers went down, the surviving company commanders desperately searched for an escape route. Amid the smoke and din, the Alabamians aligned themselves next to a regiment they assumed was friendly due to its gray uniforms. To their horror, the unidentified unit fired into their ranks. Now thoroughly demoralized, the Alabamians fled toward some high ground around a place called Henry House Hill.

At this new position, the exhausted remnants of the 4th Alabama Infantry reformed and reported to General Bee. At noon, with the Union army resuming its general advance, Bee asked the Alabamians if they still had some fight left in them. The reply was a resounding "to the death!" Bee then uttered his legendary comment about rallying around a brigade of nearby Virginians under Brig. Gen. Thomas Jackson, who were "standing like a stonewall." After helping break the final Union attack of the day, the Alabamians collapsed to the ground while Confederate reserves, including the 5th and 6th Alabama Infantry, pursued the now-routed Federals. At Manassas the men of the 4th Alabama became their state's first genuine war heroes. The gore, however, matched the glory: about forty men were killed and nearly two hundred more wounded.

Many others regiments would replicate the 4th Alabama's example of battlefield courage. Just before Fort Sumter and immediately after, the Davis administration issued a series of measures that mobilized 500,000 Southerners. Alabama responded with alacrity. In December 1861 Governor Moore proudly reported that no fewer than 27,000 Alabamians were serving in the Confederate ranks. Inconsistencies in personnel records prevent absolute precision, but an official estimate in 1864 put Alabama's total volunteer contribution to the Confederacy at 81,000. The state also conscripted over 14,000 more for a final tally approaching at least 96,000 troops.[3] Most of these men served in sixty-three infantry regiments, though Alabama also raised several specialized infantry battalions, fourteen cavalry regiments, and about two dozen artillery batteries. For most of the war, sixteen of the infantry regiments, one battalion, and two batteries (whose total complement eventually amounted to over a fourth of the state's entire manpower contribution) fought on the battlefields in and around Virginia—the eastern theater. The balance, including all of Alabama's cavalry regiments, fought in the various Confederate armies of the western theater—the land in and around Alabama and its neighboring states.

Despite the excitement of the First Battle of Manassas, most Alabamians, along with virtually every other recruit on either side, spent 1861 in training. Civil War combat generally conformed to traditional linear formations, while the standard firearm was the fairly new rifled musket. Unfortunately, the tremendous killing power of the rifle, especially from fortified defensive positions, combined with the offensive nature of open-field linear tactics produced appalling combat casualties.

During the first week of February 1862, the 27th Alabama Infantry sat in the cold, wet confines of Fort Henry, a poorly constructed position along the Tennessee River just south of the Kentucky border. Recruited mostly from the northern part of the state, the 27th Alabama was part of a lengthy line of defense running from the Appalachia Mountains across southern Kentucky to the Mississippi River. On 6 February a flotilla of Union gunboats blasted Fort Henry; the Rebel defenders withdrew to nearby Fort Donelson. These gunboats were the vanguard of Brig. Gen. Ulysses S. Grant's bold thrust against the strategic center of the Confederate perimeter. A week after fleeing Fort Henry, the men of the 27th Alabama found themselves besieged by Grant's army at Fort Donelson. After participating in a failed attempt to break out on 15 February, the Alabamians, along with the rest of the Confederate garrison, surrendered the next day. "Our boys were very much surprised," recalled Pvt. J. P. Cannon, "when they awoke on that memorable Sunday to see the white flag."[4] Under the peculiarities of the prisoner-

exchange system, however, the men of the 27th Alabama would rejoin their comrades later that fall.

The swift capture of Forts Henry and Donelson left Middle and West Tennessee wide open to invasion. Within a matter of weeks, Union forces occupied Nashville and seemed poised to advance in strength into Mississippi and Alabama. Confederate general Albert S. Johnston responded to the crisis with remarkable celerity. Concentrating a sizeable army of 40,000 men at Corinth, Mississippi, Johnston prepared a full-scale counterattack. Among the forces assembled were approximately 6,000 Alabamians distributed among ten infantry regiments, two batteries, and a cavalry unit. A majority of these men served in the division of Brig. Gen. Jones M. Withers of Mobile. All were about to "see the elephant" (a popular expression used to describe one's first combat experience).

On the morning of 6 April, Johnston's army attacked Grant's forces encamped along the Tennessee River; the Battle of Shiloh was underway. Having achieved surprise, the initial Rebel onslaught overwhelmed the Yankees. Withers's Division spearheaded the drive against the enemy left flank. At 8:00 A.M. at a place called Spain Field, four Alabama infantry regiments (the 21st, 22nd, 25th, and 50th) from Gladden's Brigade executed a frontal assault against a hastily formed line of defense. Hampered by swampy terrain, these regiments endured withering enemy fire, and their attack briefly faltered. The Alabamians rallied, however, and with a Rebel yell they carried the Union position. Coming upon a badly wounded bluecoat, Pvt. Liberty Nixon of the 50th Alabama showed his adversary no mercy. "He beged [sic] me to do something for him," Nixon related, but "I asked him why he'd left his home and come here to destroy people who had never harmed him." Ignoring further entreaties for help, Nixon bluntly told the man "to look to a higher power and then left him."[5]

By mid-morning the advance slowed in the face of mounting enemy resistance. Striving to maintain the momentum, Withers advanced his reserve brigade under Brig. Gen. John Jackson, whose command included three more Alabama regiments (the 17th, 18th, and 19th). Toward noon, these fresh units moved aggressively against the defenders' left flank along Locust Grove Creek. For the Alabamians, the fight there was short, intense, and triumphant. Pausing briefly to realign and rest his men, Withers next maneuvered his division against a large concentration of Union forces deployed along a sunken road that arced around a small pond south of Wicker Field; this site became known as the Hornets' Nest. For several hours, the bulk of the entire Confederate army, including sixty cannon, pounded this position. At last the Union line gave way, with Alabamians playing a prominent role in the decisive, final assault. The 18th Alabama received the honor of escorting over 2,000 Union prisoners to the rear.

Unfortunately for the Confederates, these tactical gains had not produced a victory. The Union stand at the Hornets' Nest allowed Grant time to restore cohesion to his battered army and establish a strong defensive line near Pittsburgh Landing, one bolstered by rapidly arriving reinforcements. Even though General Johnston had fallen with a mortal wound, many Confederate officers, including Withers, urged a continuation of the attack. The soldiers, however, were simply too exhausted and disorganized after a full day of combat. Following a chilly, rainy night, punctuated by shelling from Union gunboats, the Confederates failed to withstand Grant's counterattack on 7 April. A near upset thus turned into a terrible defeat. Alabamians accounted for about 15 percent of the 10,700 Confederate losses. Within a few weeks, Union forces secured the Mississippi River down to Memphis (capturing most of the 1st Alabama Infantry at New Madrid in the process), occupied the important rail nexus at Corinth, and conducted forays into northern Alabama.

As the military situation deteriorated in the West,

the Confederacy confronted an equally serious threat in Virginia. In April and May 1862, a formidable Union army approached Richmond from the east in an operation that became known as the Peninsula Campaign. This latest Northern offensive was the brainchild of President Lincoln's new commanding general, Maj. Gen. George B. McClellan. McClellan's strategy was bold in conception but timid in execution. As Federal forces landed and then invested Yorktown, Virginia, only sixty miles from Richmond, a paltry 17,000 Confederates stood between McClellan's army of 100,000 and the Rebel capital; the majority of Confederate forces still held positions in northern Virginia. Fortunately for the Confederacy, McClellan was a cautious man whose pace was meticulously slow. It took the Yankees nearly six weeks to reach the outskirts of Richmond, by which time Gen. Joseph Johnston had assembled an army of 60,000 men. Among this number were a dozen Alabama infantry regiments and two artillery batteries. Several of these units had already sparred with the Union vanguard. For instance, the 8th, 9th, and 10th Alabama Infantry from Wilcox's Brigade had participated in a productive rearguard attack at Williamsburg on 5 May. Though suffering over 150 casualties, the true baptism of fire for these Alabamians, and the rest of the Confederates, came at the end of the month.

On 31 May, with the enemy only five miles outside the capital, Johnston launched a powerful strike against the Union left flank at a crossroads called Seven Pines. But the attack plan proved too complicated for the general's still largely inexperienced officer corps. What followed was a disjointed engagement across rain-soaked, wooded terrain and swollen creek beds that rendered command and control almost impossible. For the five Alabama regiments—the 5th, 6th, 12th, 13th, and 26th—in Maj. Gen. Daniel H. Hill's division, the battle was an especially horrifying ordeal. The first three units, along with a regiment of Mississippians, served in Brig. Gen. Robert Rodes's brigade, the formation assigned to lead the division's attack straight down Williamsburg Road. At 1:00 P.M. an impatient Hill ordered his men to advance without waiting for flank support. Rodes moved forward with vigor and by 3:00 P.M. was heavily engaged on the south side of the road. After literally splashing through a section of forest, his Alabamians had crashed through one line of Yankees, capturing an enemy battery. But a reckless follow-on charge left the brigade isolated and exposed to deadly fire against its front and flanks. For over an hour, it exchanged volleys with surrounding Union regiments, during which time the 6th Alabama was virtually annihilated trying to hold the right flank; that unit lost almost 60 percent of its effective strength. On Rodes's right the 13th and 26th Alabama Regiments (along with some Georgians) in Rains's Brigade skillfully turned the Union left flank around a strong point dubbed Casey's Redoubt, but enemy reinforcements blunted any further success.

Toward sunset, six more Alabama regiments joined the fray as parts of poorly coordinated attacks on the Federal flanks. Their only contribution, though, was to raise the body count. The following morning the 3rd Alabama participated in a perfunctory resumption of the battle. After some inconclusive fighting, the whole affair came to an end. Lt. Edmund Patterson of the 9th Alabama evaluated Seven Pines with sarcasm: "Well, it has been a big battle and both sides, I've no doubt, gained a decided victory, 'so called.'"[6] For a contest that ultimately decided very little, the price in Alabama blood was high. Among the actively engaged regiments, casualties exceeded 1,300 (800 among Alabamians in Rodes's Brigade alone). Given that the Confederate army as a whole lost 6,100 men at Seven Pines, Alabamians accounted for a frightening 21 percent of the total. For the survivors, however, the bloodletting among their ranks was just beginning. Among those wounded was General Johnston. His replacement was Gen.

Robert E. Lee, arguably the most audacious general on either side during the war.

Lee immediately reorganized the forces around Richmond into the Army of Northern Virginia. Included in the ranks of the new command was the 15th Alabama, fresh off its involvement in Stonewall Jackson's remarkable Shenandoah Valley Campaign. Within a month, Lee took the offensive and bludgeoned McClellan's army back down the Peninsula in a series of clashes known collectively as the Seven Days' Battles (25 June–1 July). Much like the Rebel attack at Seven Pines, however, Lee's demanding battle plans invariably degenerated into ferocious piecemeal actions.

Various Alabama units participated in each of these separate engagements, but the best showcase of their overall performance was the pivotal Battle of Gaines' Mill (27 June). After two days of vicious combat, 34,000 men from McClellan's right wing withdrew to Turkey Hill, a piece of high ground due east of the mill. There they entrenched above and behind a creek bed that served as a natural moat. The Union defenses were strong, but the unrelenting Lee ordered a massive assault by 57,000 Confederates. The action developed slowly, but by late afternoon every Rebel soldier was engaged in a general attack. Alabamians participated in the battle at all points: six regiments and two batteries hammered the Union right flank, two regiments charged the center of the line, and six more regiments hit the Union left. The terrain, as well as Yankee firepower, hindered the uphill advance, but Lee's army would not be denied. Toward sundown, Confederate forces penetrated the enemy line at multiple locations and chased the Union defenders off the hill. The most noteworthy breakthrough came in the center, where the 4th Alabama of Col. Evander Law's brigade played a leading role. "Men fell like leaves in an autumn wind," the colonel vividly remembered, "the Federal artillery tore gaps in the ranks at every step." Still, the screaming

Rebels pressed forward and scrambled over the breastworks. "Then we had our 'innings,'" Law continued. "The debt of blood contracted but a few moments before was paid, and with interest."[7] Among the first regiments to reach the summit, the 4th Alabama suffered 132 casualties in this fight, while overall Confederate losses exceeded 8,000 men. Nevertheless, the Army of Northern Virginia inflicted nearly 7,000 casualties and earned an unequivocal victory.

After Gaines' Mill McClellan abandoned his hopes of capturing Richmond and instead concentrated on extricating his army from the Peninsula altogether. On 30 June Lee attempted to trap the retreating Union army around White Oak Swamp. The general envisioned an elaborate pincer maneuver by his entire army, but as it turned out, only the division of Maj. Gen. James Longstreet meaningfully engaged the enemy. Among Longstreet's units was Brig. Gen. Cadmus Wilcox's Alabama brigade, which slammed into a Yankee formation near Frayser's Farm. Attacking at dusk, the Alabamians achieved an impressive tactical success when they overran two six-gun batteries, then staved off a determined counterattack. "Our men do not flee from their prize so bravely and dearly won," Wilcox recalled the twilight melee. "Many of the men received and gave in return bayonet wounds."[8] In all, the brigade sustained an appalling 471 casualties; but once again the bluecoats retreated.

The climax of the Seven Days' occurred at Malvern Hill, where Lee pressed his luck with a foolhardy attack against a virtually impregnable position. The ensuing frontal assault was bloodily repulsed by massed Federal artillery. Of the 5,000 Confederate casualties, Rodes's now all-Alabama brigade suffered a disproportionate share: 425 men, half of whom came from the 3rd Alabama alone. "It was not war, it was murder," General Hill later quipped.[9] Nevertheless, the Army of the Potomac remained passive, and McClellan soon evacuated his men back to Washington, D.C. For the Confederacy, the outcome of the Seven Days' was both miraculous and pyrrhic. Lee's numerically smaller army prevailed but lost over 20,000 men in the process. Nearly 2,500 of the killed and wounded came from Alabama.

As the war moved into its second year, Alabama volunteers could take pride in having acquitted themselves well under fire. William McClellan, a private in the 9th Alabama Infantry and a veteran of Seven Pines, Gaines' Mill, and Frayer's Farm, offered a moving and defiant summary of his state's contribution to this point: "Nobly has Alabamamans [sic] fought in these last desisive Battles for Independence. Many of her brave sons have sealed their devotion to their country by their hearts Blood. Many a Southern fireside has been desolated by the craven messenger of Northern cruelty and oppression."[10] Unfortunately, the war was far from over, and the slaughter at Shiloh and the Seven Days' foreshadowed the tragic pattern of combat for the duration of the conflict. New recruits from all over Alabama soon arrived to replenish the ranks of the fallen, though no regiment would ever reach full strength again. Whether in the Army of Northern Virginia or in the various armies of the western heartland, Alabamians would continue to do their part to drive off the Yankee invader.

LEROY POPE WALKER
carte de visite
E. and H. T. Anthony,
New York

For Leroy Walker, the evening of 12 April 1861 found him in an ebullient mood. Only hours earlier, in his capacity as Confederate secretary of war, he had ordered the attack on Fort Sumter. A forty-four-year-old lawyer and erstwhile state legislator from Madison County, Walker was an ardent States' Rights Democrat. After serving as Alabama's secession commissioner to Tennessee, he joined the cabinet of the Davis administration. Walker and the president were celebrating the commencement of hostilities when a crowd began cheering the two outside Montgomery's Exchange Hotel. Caught up in the moment, Walker addressed the locals with a fiery, impromptu speech. Several Northern newspaper correspondents prickled at an especially bellicose comment the secretary allegedly proclaimed: "In a few months more the flag of the Confederate States [will] wave over the capital at Washington and, if necessary, Faneuil Hall, at Boston." This boastful prophesy did not play well in the North,

which was already afflicted with war fever of its own. Whatever he actually said, Secretary Walker always insisted that his words were either misquoted or taken out of context. It hardly mattered—the sentiment was widely shared throughout the South. Besides, Walker had more urgent matters to attend. Over the summer he strived to convert variegated state militias into a Confederate army, implemented plans to improve coastal defense, and wrestled with the growing bureaucracy of his own department. Despite a genuinely earnest effort, the task of creating a modern, conventional military largely from scratch proved too much for the Alabamian to handle. His relationship with President Davis also soured during these months. In September he resigned and accepted a brigadier generalship, ostensibly to command the garrison at Mobile. When this assignment fell through, Walker became a military judge in April 1862, a position he retained for the duration of the war.[11] *Photo courtesy of ADAH*

First Alabama Infantry
copy print

The many months of digging and training finally paid off for the men of the 1st Alabama Infantry on 22–23 November 1861. On those dates Confederate and Union forces around Pensacola engaged in a grand bombardment. Organized in late March 1861, the 1st Alabama manned the guns at Fort Barrancas outside the Pensacola Navy Yard, where the men eventually developed into "a well-instructed body of artillery." Prior to that, however, the regiment experienced numerous disciplinary problems brought on by the monotony of the hot and sandy camp life, and its men suffered frequent bouts with disease—at least forty members died from measles, typhoid, or malaria. In the autumn of 1861, the regiment saw some real action at last. Companies A and B participated in a failed raid in October on Union-controlled Fort Pickens on Santa Rosa Island. Then at the end of November, the whole regiment fought in the great artillery duel. On the morning of 22 November, Union warships and Federal batteries at Fort Pickens opened fire on Fort Barrancas and the surrounding Confederate defenses. "Ten times more lead and iron were hurled against our positions," recalled Pvt. Edward McMorries of Company C, "but shot and shell made little impression on our batteries of sand bags." Fort Barrancas consisted of earth-covered masonry that made the cannon emplacements nearly invulnerable to anything but a direct hit. Nevertheless, "blood poured

from the noses of men working the guns." After a night-time lull, the enemy fleet resumed its bombardment the next morning. "Frequently several shells would explode almost simultaneously in or above a single battery," McMorries explained, "and the men would take refuge in their 'rat-holes' for protection." The Alabamians claimed to have done some damage to Fort Pickens, but for the most part the entire cannonade was mostly sound and fury; there were very few casualties on either side. After the battle the 1st Alabama received the honor of having "November 22 and 23, 1861" sewn into its regimental banner.[12]

In January 1862 the 1st Alabama deployed to Island No. 10 near New Madrid, Missouri, where it was captured on 7 April. Its men paroled and the unit reorganized, the 1st Alabama helped defend Port Hudson, Louisiana, where it was again captured on 9 July 1863. Paroled a second time, the men joined the Army of Tennessee, in which the regiment was the lone body of Alabamians in Brig. Gen. William A. Quarles's mostly Tennessee brigade. With that unit it fought with distinction throughout the Atlanta Campaign and Hood's invasion of Tennessee. Over the course of the war, some 3,000 Alabamians served in the 1st Alabama, the first regiment in the Confederate army.
Photo courtesy of Florida Photographic Collection, State Library & Archives Florida

JOHN CAMPBELL CHITWOOD,
SAMUEL BROWN, AND
JAMES N. MCDANIEL
copy print

In the early days of the war, many Alabama volunteers approached the conflict as an adventure in which they would play soldier and win glory, or at least have a fun time. So it seemed for three young privates from Lauderdale County. After enlisting in the Florence Guards in the spring of 1861, John Chitwood, Sam Brown, and James McDaniel took a moment to ham in front of the camera. They then set off for Pensacola, where their unit became Company K, 7th Alabama Infantry. Soon the initial frivolity of camp life gave way to rigorous drill in the muggy heat of the Gulf. Like many others, the twenty-year-old Chitwood fell ill and spent the summer in the hospital at Fort Barrancas, where his friend McDaniel worked as an army nurse. Little more is known of the trio other than when their twelve-month terms expired, Chitwood apparently joined the 4th Alabama Cavalry (either Roddy's or Russell's regiment). Brown and McDaniel do not appear on any other Alabama rosters and may well have just gone home. In any event, the goofy innocence of the boys' photograph belies the grim reality of what became the Civil War. *Photo courtesy of ADAH*

54

FLAG OF THE MARION LIGHT INFANTRY
copy print

When the 4th Alabama Infantry went into action at Manassas, Virginia, it sported among its many company standards the colors of the Marion Light Infantry. Consisting of volunteers from Perry County, the Marion Light Infantry became Company G, 4th Alabama shortly before that battle. Toward the end of 1861, the unit's colors briefly served as the regimental flag. The obverse depicts a beautifully rendered cotton plant and cotton bale, both symbols of Alabama's most prosperous economic asset; the reverse exhibits one of the first eleven-star patterns of the Confederate national flag. In the spring of 1862, these colors were officially retired. Capt. Porter King, the company's first commander, kept the flag with his family until his wife presented it to the state in 1904.
Photo courtesy of ADAH

NATHANIEL HENRY RHODES
DAWSON
copy print

As the 4th Alabama Infantry marched into battle at Manassas, Capt. Nat Dawson of Company C brandished his British-made, five-shot Adams revolver. Having boasted that he could kill a man with his prized sidearm at the fantastic range of two hundred yards, the thirty-two-year-old officer was soon to have his chance. A lawyer from Dallas County, Dawson was one of the delegates who stormed out of the Charleston Convention with William Yancey in 1860. After secession he organized the Magnolia Cadets, which later became Company C, and deployed to Virginia. During these months, he became engaged to Elodie Todd, the half-sister of Mary Todd Lincoln and a girl half his age. At Manassas Dawson's martial ardor faded fast. In the cornfields around Matthews Hill, he orchestrated the fire of the fifty men under his command as the 4th Alabama helped blunt a Union drive in that sector. For nearly an hour, "the air resounded with whistling balls and hissing shells," the captain recalled. But with casualties mounting and with Yankee forces turning both flanks, the regiment commenced a difficult retreat. As Dawson climbed over a fence, an enemy cannonball smashed the lower rail, the

impact launching him ten feet into the air. Though dazed by the blast, Dawson suffered only a sprained left ankle, but as he hobbled away, panic spread through the ranks. With bluecoats swarming all around, the captain tried to rally his men. A fresh burst of enemy musketry, however, broke the Alabamians, and when Dawson watched Maj. Charles Scott go down right before his eyes, he fled as well. "The disorder was indescribable," he remembered. After reaching a farmhouse where scores of displaced Rebel soldiers milled about in confusion, Dawson pondered taking charge but instead merely comforted a few wounded men before collapsing under a shady spot, where he lay until the shooting subsided. Rejoining his regiment later that night, the captain learned that his company had lost over twenty men. To his fiancée, who often showered him with romantic praise in her letters, Dawson laconically noted, "it is honor enough to have been in the battle and to have done our duty." He also confessed with some embarrassment that he did not fire his Adams revolver during the battle.[13]
Photo courtesy of ADAH

JOSEPH P. ANGELL
copy print from
Confederate Veteran

While the rest of the 4th Alabama Infantry was retreating from Matthews Hill under heavy fire, Pvt. Joe Angell was rushing to the side of Col. Egbert Jones. Badly wounded and unable to move, the colonel pleaded with the youth to run with the rest, but Angell refused to abandon his fallen leader. The son of English immigrants, Angell grew to manhood in Madison County, where he worked as a mechanic in Huntsville. When war broke out, the twenty-three-year-old joined the Huntsville Guards, which soon merged into the 4th Alabama as Company F. At First Manassas the Alabamian proved his worth as a soldier. Kneeling beside his commanding officer, he realized the man was bleeding to death. After trying in vain to drag the colonel to safety, Angell ran off to get help. As he sprinted through a whirlwind of crisscrossing projectiles, a cannonball caromed off his back, momentarily knocking the lad unconscious. Fortunately, the private's haversack absorbed most of the blow, though its contents were strewn about the ground. After coming to, Angell found a fellow Alabamian and together they retrieved their colonel. Sadly, Jones died a week later. Nevertheless, Angell had more than proved his patriotism by what all of his comrades described as nothing less than "gallant and heroic conduct."[14]

BAILEY GEORGE MCCLELEN
copy print

The Battle of Dranesville, a small town on the Virginia side of the Potomac River, was an inconsequential affair, a minor skirmish in a war renowned for epic battles. For those seeing action for the first time, however, including Pvt. Bailey McClelen of the 10th Alabama Infantry, Dranesville was one of the most thrilling experiences of their lives. A twenty-one-year-old schoolteacher and farmer from Calhoun County, McClelen also owned at least one slave. Believing that Abraham Lincoln had instigated a needless war, the young man enlisted in the Alexandria Rifles in the summer of 1861. This unit soon became Company D, 10th Alabama, which then deployed to northern Virginia, where it was brigaded with regiments from Kentucky, South Carolina, and Virginia, all under the leadership of one of the Confederacy's rising stars, Brig. Gen. J. E. B. "Jeb" Stuart. In the autumn of 1861, after nearly dying from a measles epidemic that ravaged the ranks of the 10th, McClelen endured interminable hours on picket duty, exposed to the chilly winds of the season. The

clash at Dranesville on 20 December came as welcome relief. While conducting a foraging expedition, Stuart's command of 1,200 Rebels encountered a Yankee force of over 3,000 men. The Southerners immediately attacked, with the 10th Alabama in the right wing. According to Stuart, the Alabamians "rushed with a shout in a shower of bullets" and took up a firing position behind a fence, from where "the enemy felt the trueness of their aim at short range." McClelen reveled in his first real combat. "The battle waxed warm and fierce," he recalled, "the missiles of death flew thick and fast and had no respect for persons with whom they came in contact from which carnage was made on both sides." After two hours of sparring, Stuart withdrew his badly bloodied command. While Union casualties were less than 70, the Rebels suffered nearly 200, including 66 in the 10th Alabama. Despite the outcome, McClelen insisted that Dranesville was a draw.[15] *Photo courtesy of Norman E. Rourke*

JAMES HOLT
CLANTON
copy print

Far from Virginia in West Tennessee, on the morning of 4 April 1862, Col. James Clanton of the 1st Alabama Cavalry was scouting Union positions at Shiloh when he came face to face with a Yankee major. The enemy officer demanded the colonel's surrender. What followed was an episode worthy of Homeric legend. According to an anonymous wartime chronicler, Clanton "instantly drew his sword and made at his opponent with his weapon ready for a thrust." The Alabamian chased his now frightened foe through the bushes directly into the lines of several Federal infantry regiments. "But Clanton's blood was up," the chronicler continued, "instead of drawing rein at discovering his perilous situation, he spurred forward into the interval in a more determined pursuit of his enemy." The bluecoats "fired hundreds of shots at short range at the audacious intruder," but amazingly all missed. Clanton somehow managed to maneuver his target away from Union lines and back toward his own regiment, when

the exasperated major submitted at last and became the colonel's prisoner. "Nobody but Clanton could have performed this feat," concluded the writer. "It was madness, and fortune alone saved him."

A thirty-five-year-old lawyer and politico from Montgomery County, the "audacious" Clanton actually discouraged secession in early 1861. (During the election of 1860, he canvassed the state in behalf of John Bell's Constitutional Union Party.) Once the ordinance of secession passed, however, he dedicated himself to the Confederacy. In the autumn of 1861, he raised the 1st Alabama Cavalry, which he led at Shiloh. Setting his incredible encounter aside, Clanton did indeed conduct valuable reconnaissance in the days leading up to the battle. Furthermore, during the action on 6 April, he effectively screened the Rebel army's right flank and later committed his troopers to the fight at the Hornets' Nest. On 7 April he assisted with various rearguard activities.[16] *Photo courtesy of ADAH*

WILLIAM DAVIDSON CHADICK
copy print

Lt. Col. William Chadick assumed command of the 50th Alabama Infantry at a critical juncture during the Battle of Shiloh. After overrunning Yankees at Spain Field and a nearby cotton field, the 50th prepared to engage the main defensive line around the Hornets' Nest when Col. John Coltart went down wounded. For the deeply religious Chadick, a test of faith had arrived. Better known for his knowledge of theology than of warfare, Chadick was a forty-five-year-old Presbyterian minister from Madison County. Serving in 1861 as chaplain in the 4th Alabama Infantry, a unit with which he saw action at First Manassas, Chadick returned to Alabama in March 1862 and helped raise the 50th. The men in his new regiment dubbed him "the fighting parson." During the fighting at midafternoon on 6 April, the Reverend Chadick exercised noteworthy tactical skill. Even though his regiment was badly shot up and had become separated from the rest of the brigade, he ignored advice to retire from the field. Instead, he decided to attack two regiments of approaching bluecoats before they could fortify them-

selves within a peach orchard near the Manse George House, a cluster of buildings that marked the approximate center of the Union lines. Aided by a contingent of dismounted cavalry under Col. Nathan Bedford Forrest, the 50th Alabama charged and carried the enemy position. From there Chadick combined prayer with firepower as his regiment withstood vicious counterattacks. Basically unsupported, his men discharged ten volleys before grudgingly falling back. In the process the Alabamians captured some Yankees, one of whom confessed to Chadick, "you fight d——well." Nonetheless, the regiment had suffered grievous losses: 240 men killed, wounded, and missing out of 440 engaged. The next day the 50th contributed little to the fighting retreat. Most of the men had not unloaded their rifles as they slept exposed on the open ground during the night. The ensuing rainfall wet the powder, thereby clogging the barrels. As for Chadick, he fell ill immediately after the battle, was furloughed home, and never held a field command again.[17]
Photo courtesy of ADAH

JOHN CALHOUN MARRAST
copy print from
Confederate Veteran

Sometime in the early afternoon of 6 April, Lt. Col. John Marrast assumed command of the 22nd Alabama Infantry from Col. Zachariah Deas, who hastily departed to take over the brigade in place of its fallen commander. It was a tense moment during the Battle of Shiloh: the sanguinary clash around the Hornets' Nest was just beginning. A thirty-seven-year-old cotton factor from Mobile, Marrast was the son of French immigrants. While no stranger to combat, having fought at Buena Vista during the Mexican War, he was not in good health at Shiloh. The damp, chilly weather made his rheumatism particularly painful, but Marrast did not shirk his duty. He had already helped drive the enemy from Spain Field that morning, but the Union forces digging in around a nearby cotton field posed a greater challenge. There three artillery batteries effectively checked the Confederate right wing. Ordered to silence these guns, Marrast maneuvered two of his companies through some low-lying woods, from which they launched an assault that disrupted one enemy section. He then speedily brought up the rest of the regiment, the Alabamians occupying several farmhouses from which they exchanged fire with the Northerners for several minutes. Marrast and his men endured concentrated retaliatory fire, but their actions facilitated a successful flank attack farther east that pushed the Yankees back several hundred yards. Having lost almost 300 men in over eight hours of combat, the 22nd Alabama did not participate in the final assault against the Hornets' Nest. Instead, its 140 soldiers still standing went into reserve, later shivering in captured but bullet-riddled Sibley tents during a night of heavy rainfall. For Marrast, Shiloh was the apex of his Confederate service. After conducting an orderly retreat the following day, the commander finally collapsed from physical exhaustion.

JEREMIAH MANASCO
copy print

Among the hundreds of casualties in the 22nd Alabama Infantry at Shiloh was 1st Lt. Jeremiah Manasco of Company A. A physician from Walker County who was around thirty years old, Manasco received a mortal wound at some point during the battle. He lingered for several weeks before finally dying on 1 May. Lt. Col. John Marrast spoke highly of Manasco's bravery at Shiloh and mourned his death. *Photo courtesy of Robert M. Jaffee Collection, U.S.A.M.H.I.*

ROBERT CLEMENT
FARISS
copy print

At midmorning on 6 April, Lt. Col. Robert Fariss advanced with his 17th Alabama Infantry (380 strong) toward Locust Grove Creek as part of an unfolding flank attack against the Union left at Shiloh. Fariss had come to Alabama from Virginia in 1851 to help his brother William manage a plantation in Montgomery County. By 1860 he had become a secessionist Democrat, and with the outbreak of war, he helped raise the 17th in August 1861. Eight months later the thirty-two-year-old Fariss was leading the regiment into its first major engagement. The unit marched on the extreme left of Brig. Gen. John K. Jackson's brigade, the 18th Alabama tying into the regiment's right. After dispersing a line of Yankee skirmishers, Fariss and his men crossed the creek and then executed a series of short charges that helped steadily drive back a brigade of midwesterners. Around 11:30 A.M., how-ever, the 17th Alabama came under heavy fire from a distant cotton field off to the regiment's right. Fariss skillfully re-fused his flank and then exchanged long-range volleys for several minutes. All the while the regimental chaplain, Isaac Tichenor, paced back and forth, shouting scripture and exhorting the men "to stand there, and die, if need be, for their country." Evidently, the Alabamians' aim proved deadly, for "they piled the ground with Yankees slain," according to Tichenor. Next the 17th Alabama, in conjunction with other units, stormed the cotton field and routed the defenders, capturing two flags in the process. Fariss and his men later helped crack the Hornets' Nest, but the fighting around Locust Grove Creek was the high-light of the battle. The day's success, however, was not without a terrible cost: 13 men killed in action and 117 wounded or missing.[18] *Photo courtesy of ADAH*

JOSEPH WHEELER
copy print

formance as colonel of the 19th Alabama Infantry at Shiloh. An 1859 graduate of West Point (ranked nineteenth in his class), the twenty-four-year-old Georgia native assumed command of the regiment in August 1861. While stationed at Pensacola, the young colonel trained his soldiers to a high level of proficiency. Wheeler and his 650 men put that training to the test on the afternoon of 6 April. Part of John K. Jackson's brigade, the 19th Alabama advanced on the brigade's right and participated in the fierce attacks against the Union army's left. As the regiment approached Locust Grove Creek, an impatient Gen. Albert Johnston rode up and ordered the colonel to charge an opposing Illinois regiment. Wheeler complied, but first his men had to negotiate a deep ravine, all the while under fire, before successfully driving off the enemy. Pressing on through woods and over hills, the 19th Alabama struggled to maintain contact with neighboring units. By 3:00 P.M., however, the regiment reached the maelstrom of combat around the Hornets' Nest. After passing through a section of burning trees, Wheeler aligned his men on the northeastern edge of Wicker Field, where they immediately exchanged volleys with the bluecoats at close quarters. In short order the Alabamians lost 20 men killed and 140 wounded, but Wheeler praised their "heroic courage": "they stood their ground with firmness and delivered their fire rapidly, but with cool deliberation and good effect." Suddenly, a white flag appeared among the ranks of one Union regiment, followed quickly by several more. After a full day of grueling fire and maneuver, Wheeler took great satisfaction in rounding up hundreds of prisoners. (For its part, the 19th Alabama lost just under 200 men total that day.) Unfortunately, the feeling of triumph was short lived. After spending a rainy night under arms, Wheeler and his regiment joined the rest of the army in retreating under the pressure of Grant's counterattack on 7 April.[19] *Photo courtesy of Library of Congress*

Though not originally from Alabama, Joseph Wheeler stands as one of the state's most famous adopted sons. Small in stature but combative by nature, he is best known for his role as a Confederate cavalry general. But Wheeler's rise to prominence began with his per-

WILLIAM H. CLARE
copy print from Confederate Veteran

On the morning of 7 April, Capt. William Clare, aide-de-camp to Maj. Gen. William Hardee, frantically raced about conveying his commander's battle orders. Just the previous evening the captain had believed that his side had won a great victory at Shiloh, but he now sensed consternation among the ranks as Grant unleashed a massive counterattack. The twenty-two-year-old son of Irish immigrants, Clare was a commoner from Cherokee County. Nevertheless, he had his eye on a pretty debutante from Nashville—Mary Hadley—and was certain that heroism on the battlefield would win her heart. Accordingly, he joined the 7th Alabama Infantry in May 1861, serving as captain of Company C. When that unit disbanded a year later, Clare joined the corps staff of General Hardee. On the second day of fighting at Shiloh, he found his moment of glory. As the bluecoats' attack got underway, Clare

returned to Hardee's side. At a critical juncture, the general ordered a reserve regiment—the 2nd Texas Infantry—into the fray, but that unit hesitated. "I was surprised at such a doubt entertained of Texas troops," Clare mused. When the regiment finally went forward, it immediately broke under intense enemy fire. Clare galloped among the fleeing Texans "but was unable to rally the regiment or to induce a single man to return to the field." Noticing a group cowering behind some trees, he rode toward them and upbraided the ranking officer with charges of cowardice. "He replied that he didn't care a damn," Clare noted. Before the captain could take further action, a hail of gunfire toppled him from his horse. With two bullets in his side, he faded in and out of consciousness while surgeons extracted the slugs.[20]

JOSEPH MATTHEW ELLISON
copy print

In the Shenandoah Valley of western Virginia, on the chilly morning of 25 May 1862, 1st Lt. Joseph Ellison of the 15th Alabama Infantry had just finished marching seventy miles during the previous four days when he went into his first serious battle at Winchester. That clash marked the midpoint of Maj. Gen. Stonewall Jackson's astonishing springtime blitz through the Valley, one that tied down over 50,000 bluecoats who might otherwise have descended on Richmond. A twenty-six-year-old farmer from Macon County, Ellison served in Company C, 15th Alabama. Attached to Brig. Gen. Isaac Trimble's brigade, Ellison and his comrades fought as part of the Rebel right wing at Winchester, where they attacked the enemy from the south. Advancing at dawn as the brigade reserve, the regiment assumed a support position in a field of wheat, waist high and wet with dew. Though not directly engaged, the Alabamians soon became the main target of a Union battery. "Balls and shells fell & burned all in & around the 15 Ala.," Ellison recalled. "They got the range of our Regt. the first fier [*sic*]." The lieutenant passed on an order for everyone to lie down, then a few minutes later helped herd the still-exposed men into a nearby hollow. About an hour later, the 15th Alabama moved forward to join the pursuit of their now-vanquished foe, during which the lieutenant remembered capturing about a dozen Yankees. Ellison could hardly consider his role in the battle worthy of praise, but he was still proud to be a member of Stonewall Jackson's "foot cavalry."[21]
Photo courtesy of ADAH

66

ROBERT TINGNAL JONES
carte de viste

Bedridden for several days, Col. Robert Jones of the 12th Alabama Infantry was still running a fever as he readied for combat on 31 May. His regiment was going into action for the first time at Seven Pines, and the colonel was determined to lead it. A forty-six-year-old planter from Perry County, Jones brought both military professionalism and managerial skills to his position. In 1837 he graduated thirteen in his class at West Point, later participating in the Seminole Wars. In the 1850s he supervised the construction of the Cahaba & Marion Railroad. After briefly commanding the Confederate garrison at Fort Morgan, Jones accepted the colonelcy of the 12th Alabama in July 1861. He was a strict disciplinarian, whom the men came to respect. At Seven Pines the 12th (400 strong) advanced along Williamsburg Road as part of the right wing of Brig. Gen. Robert Rodes's brigade. A quarter mile from the Yankee lines, the brigade came under sporadic artillery fire. Jones pushed his regiment as rapidly as possible across a grassy bog through knee-deep water, after which his men crashed through dense forest, helping drive off a brigade of Federals. Pressing on through a field of thick brush, the colonel quickly realized that his regiment had moved well ahead of the rest of the brigade. Falling back, the 12th paused long enough for

the 6th Alabama to tie in on its right before resuming its advance into another section of woods. Soon the two regiments encountered a stronger Union position —Casey's Redoubt. For a few minutes, the two sides exchanged volleys, with the Alabamians hugging the ground as they reloaded. Suddenly, Colonel Jones ordered his regiment to charge. Capt. Robert E. Park of Company F recalled the moment: "We moved on to the assault, and under the terrible fire of musketry and artillery which we could not return, because of the abatis in our front, and the difficulty of getting over them, but the brave and devoted men kept moving forward, until at last an open field was reached near the enemy's works." At this point the adversaries engaged in close-quarters fighting. During the melee, the Alabamians captured an enemy gun, but as Jones tried to turn it around for use against the Yankees, a bullet pierced his heart, killing him instantly. Rodes's Brigade held the position but suffered appalling losses. Casualties in the 12th Alabama exceeded 50 percent: 59 dead (including Jones) and 156 wounded. Maj. Gen. Daniel H. Hill, a man not inclined to give praise lightly, lamented the passing of Colonel Jones: "He was one of the very best officers and purest men in the army."[22] *Photo courtesy of ADAH*

REGINALD HEBNER
DAWSON
copy print
W. A. Reed, Mobile

Exhorting his men to keep moving, Lt. Col. Reginald Dawson of the 13th Alabama Infantry galloped about the regiment, dodging tree branches and splashing up mud. He moved with urgency because Union forces around a position known as Casey's Redoubt had checked the advance of Rodes's Brigade; Dawson and his regiment (part of Brig. Gen. Gabriel Rains's brigade) were trying to turn the enemy's left flank. A twenty-four-year-old lawyer from Wilcox County, Dawson joined the 13th Alabama in the summer of 1861, winning election as captain of Company A. Tempering his approach to training with demonstrative compassion, he soon rose to the rank of lieutenant colonel. Seven Pines was Dawson's first engagement and, no surprise given his rather careless exposure on horseback to enemy fire, it was also his last. As the

Alabamians came into line on the south side of Casey's Redoubt, enemy guns shifted their fire accordingly. One incoming round struck Dawson's horse, killing the animal and knocking the lieutenant colonel to the ground. Momentarily stunned and in excruciating pain, Dawson recovered in time to help orchestrate the regiment's fire. Shooting from their knees, the Alabamians poured volley after volley into the enemy flank, their discharges producing a steady, deafening roar for nearly fifteen minutes. Finally, the Yankees fled, the redoubt had fallen, and the Rebel advance continued. For Dawson, however, his injury proved more debilitating than he initially thought; after the battle he received a medical discharge.[23]
Photo courtesy of ADAH

SYDENHAM MOORE
copy print

For a man of his age and professional record, Col. Sydenham Moore of the 11th Alabama Infantry was remarkably giddy at the prospect of leading his regiment into combat at Seven Pines. It was nearing sunset on 31 May, and the 11th had just arrived on the battlefield at the van of Brig. Gen. Cadmus Wilcox's brigade. The brigadier ordered Moore to send three of his companies forward immediately as reinforcements for the Rebel attack still underway along Williamsburg Road. Rather than delegating this task, the colonel insisted on commanding the detachment himself. A forty-five-year-old lawyer and politician from Greene County, Moore was one of his state's more prominent figures. A graduate of the University of Alabama (class of 1836), he had practiced law, held various judicial posts, and in 1846–47 had participated in the Mexican War. In 1857 he won the first of two consecutive terms as a Democrat in the U.S. House. When Alabama seceded, Moore departed Washington, D.C., and helped raise the 11th Alabama. Despite his prior military experience, Seven Pines was the colonel's first real battle. "It will be the greatest perhaps of the war," he wrote

shortly before that engagement, "I hope to acquit myself well." And he did, though not like he expected. Leading his three companies from horseback, Moore charged across a soggy, open field toward what Wilcox described as "a certain point that proved to be very annoying." Specifically, the Alabamians were attacking a nest of entrenched sharpshooters backed by an artillery battery. Moore and his men came under withering fire. In rapid succession the colonel received three wounds: First, he was hit in the lower torso, but his pocket watch absorbed most of the force. Second, after having his horse shot dead from under him, one of Moore's shins splintered under the impact of another projectile. Finally, as he tried to stand, yet another round hit him in the chest and passed through his body, grazing his spine. In all the 11th Alabama suffered sixty-six casualties in less than ten minutes. On his way to the field surgeon, Moore learned that his attack actually dislodged the enemy, a tactical success that helped stabilize the Confederate position in that sector just before sunset.[24] *Photo courtesy of W. S. Hoole Special Collections Library, The University of Alabama*

69

MILTON E. CROXTON
copy print

Though late in the day, the 4th Alabama Infantry trudged hurriedly through mud toward the sound of the guns around Seven Pines. Part of a belated flank attack, the regiment was somewhere in the middle of a divisional formation moving southeast along Nine Mile Road. Among the ranks was 1st Sgt. Milton Croxton of Company F, the Huntsville Guards. A twenty-seven-year-old unmarried druggist from Madison County, Croxton had seen action at Manassas, perhaps as one of the regimental musicians. The way events were transpiring on 31 May, however, it seemed unlikely the newly promoted noncommissioned officer would see any more before darkness brought an end to the fighting. But around 5:00 P.M., as the regiment crossed the tracks near the Fair Oaks train station (a mile north of Seven Pines), the Alabamians came under enemy artillery fire. An entire corps of Union reinforcements was bearing down on the unsuspecting Confederates. For the next hour, Croxton and his comrades participated in a series of confusing firefights, where the combatants mostly floundered around in swampy, wooded terrain, until twilight brought an end to the fighting. Throughout it all, the 4th Alabama suffered a relatively modest eight killed and nineteen wounded. Unfortunately, Sergeant Croxton was one of the dead. *Photo courtesy of Mrs. Earl Holder Collection, U.S.A.M.H.I.*

70

TENNENT LOMAX
carte de viste
Duffee and Sancier, Mobile

With the clangor of battle filling the air on 31 May, Col. Tennent Lomax of the 3rd Alabama Infantry was anxious to see some action. But a series of conflicting orders left him gnashing his teeth while his men aimlessly marked time on the muddy Charles City Road, running south of the battlefield. The colonel need not have worried, for the contest was not over yet. A forty-one-year-old lawyer and planter from Montgomery County, Lomax was born in South Carolina but moved to Alabama as a young man. A veteran of the Mexican War, he became an ardent States' Rights Democrat in the late 1850s. After trying in vain to precipitate a war at Fort Pickens in early 1861, he raised the 3rd Alabama, trained it while stationed at Norfolk, and then participated in the Battle of Seven Pines.

The lone Alabama regiment in Brig. Gen. William Mahone's mostly Virginia brigade, the 3rd finally got into combat on the morning of 1 June. Arriving near the scene of the previous day's carnage, Lomax received orders to advance without delay at the head of the brigade. Inexplicably, Mahone neglected to deploy skir-

mishers and moved his regiments forward in line of column. Before Lomax could ascertain the enemy's dispositions, his command came under heavy fire. Impulsively, the colonel put his men into line of battle and charged into a vast thicket of trees north of Williamsburg Road. Unable to see more than a few dozen yards, Lomax soon lost contact with the right wing of his regiment. Nonetheless, he pushed on with barely half his troops. Upon discovering that he was some two hundred yards beyond the nearest Confederate unit, the colonel at last realized that he was in a perilous situation. Yankee forces rapidly closed in and decimated the outnumbered Alabamians. When Lomax himself went down under a hail of bullets, his men fled. After the survivors reunited with the rest of the regiment, they conducted several unsuccessful attempts to retrieve the dead body of their commander. Although it lasted about an hour, Mahone's attack proved perfunctory and ineffectual. In losing approximately 175 men, including Colonel Lomax, the 3rd Alabama paid dearly for such poor planning. *Photo courtesy of ADAH*

SAMUEL BURR JOHNSTON
copy print

Out of its 530 men engaged at Seven Pines, the 3rd Alabama Infantry suffered about 175 casualties, including 38 killed. Among the slain was Adj. Samuel Johnston, who died near the fallen body of his commander, Colonel Lomax. A lad from Macon County, Johnston graduated from the University of Alabama in 1859 and then devoted himself to the care of his widowed mother and two sisters. Described by a fellow officer as "the impersonation of Virtue, Valor, [and] Truth," Johnston had only recently turned twenty-one when he made the ultimate sacrifice for his new country.[25] *Photo courtesy of W. S. Hoole Special Collections Library, The University of Alabama*

H. W. Grubbs
copy print

Gen. Robert E. Lee opened his Seven Days' offensive with a vigorous assault against an isolated Union corps at Mechanicsville on 26 June 1862. Among the attacking forces was the 5th Alabama Battalion, and among its ranks was Lt. H. W. Grubbs of Company C, the White Plains Rangers. Grubbs was a twenty-six-year-old farmer from Calhoun County, and Mechanicsville would be his first and last battle. The night before the engagement, the young lieutenant joined his fellow officers in telling the soldiers that they "must be brave boys and stand firm, be true to [their] country." The pep talk was as much for him as for the men Grubbs would help lead, for he had no idea what to expect on the morrow. Following several interminable hours of delay, the Alabamians went into action at 4:00 P.M. Part of Brig. Gen. James Archer's brigade, the battalion advanced in the second line of attack. After passing through the little hamlet of Mechanicsville, the battalion stormed a strong Union position along Beaver Dam Creek. Pvt. M. T. Ledbetter, also of Company C, described the moment: "The enemy had felled large trees in their front, and it was with great difficulty that we made our way through this entanglement of tree tops, saplings, vines, and every other conceivable obstruction, under a heavy fire." The Alabamians pushed on in vain before nightfall brought an inconclusive end to the fighting. "Many of the boys were killed in trying to get through," Ledbetter later recalled, with a touch of melancholy. Among the fatalities was Lieutenant Grubbs, one of 1,400 Confederate casualties in Lee's less-than-spectacular debut as an army commander.[26] *Photo courtesy of ADAH*

STEPHEN FOWLER HALE
copy print

Col. Stephen Hale had been in command of the 11th Alabama Infantry for less than a month when he led it into battle at Gaines' Mill on 27 June 1862. The forty-six-year-old had fought at Seven Pines, but the triple-tiered Union defenses his men now faced posed a more daunting challenge. A Kentuckian by birth, in 1837 Hale migrated to Greene County, where he practiced law and served as a state legislator. When Alabama left the Union in 1861, he returned to Kentucky as a secession commissioner and later joined the 11th Alabama as its executive officer. At Gaines' Mill the regiment marched as the right flank of Wilcox's Brigade, which constituted the extreme right of the whole Confederate line of battle. Late in the afternoon Hale received the signal to advance. Immediately, enemy fire raked the Alabamians, who stormed across a creek bed, driving back the first line of Yankee defenders. As the colonel

pushed his men upward toward the second line, he felt the thud of bullets entering his left arm and shoulder. Incredibly, he kept moving, waving his men on with his sword. Moments later, while trying to assist a fallen color bearer, another Yankee bullet lodged itself in Hale's left leg; this time the colonel went down. In a matter of minutes, the 11th Alabama had lost nearly 160 men. While the survivors eventually helped over-run the enemy's third line, Hale was rushed to a nearby field hospital. A fellow officer in the regiment described the gruesome scene: "There were thousands apparently wounded, and of all the groans, cries, curses, and prayers that went from them! Surgeons were busy operating on them, taking off arms and legs." It is unclear whether Hale's limbs were among those amputated.[27] *Photo courtesy of ADAH*

MARSHALL B. HURST
copy print

As chief musician of the 14th Alabama Infantry, Marshall Hurst was accomplished on both the fife and kettle drum, and he likely played one of these instruments as the regiment marched into battle at Gaines' Mill on 27 June 1862. Once the shooting commenced, however, he appears to have shouldered a rifle. A twenty-five-year-old schoolteacher from Chambers County, Hurst originally enlisted in a Georgia regiment, but in December 1861 he received a transfer to the 14th Alabama, half of whose men came from the musician's home county. After "seeing the elephant" at Williamsburg and Seven Pines, he experienced his bloodiest fight at Gaines' Mill. The lone Alabama regiment in Brig. Gen. Roger Pryor's mixed brigade of Floridians, Louisianans, and Virginians, the 14th spent most the late morning and early afternoon demonstrating against the Union left flank. Hurst considered this action frustrating and pointless. "We were suffered to lie in an open field, exposed to the murderous fire of the enemy," he complained, "and were not suffered to fire a gun." Finally, about midafternoon, the regiment moved forward as part of a general attack. The charge

up Turkey Hill had just started when well-aimed enemy volleys forced Pryor's Brigade to seek protection in a nearby ravine. From there Hurst and his comrades shot back until neighboring Confederate brigades came on line and reignited the assault. This time there would be no falling back. Musician Hurst reveled in the excitement: "Our men rushed forward yelling, which, with the rattle of musketry, echoed among the hills for miles around." The 14th Alabama helped overrun one line of defenders, but as the men neared the summit, Yankee grapeshot shredded their ranks. Pausing briefly to reorganize their formation, the Alabamians then made a final lunge. Hurst recalled that some of the men had cast aside their empty rifles and wielded only the bayonet in this final clash. Moments later the hill was taken, and the battle was won. Panting heavily, Hurst barely noticed his flesh wound as he gloried in his army's triumph.

Three days later Hurst saw combat once again at Frayser's Farm, where the regiment's losses raised its tally in the Seven Days' Campaign to 353 casualties.[28]
Photo courtesy of ADAH

JOSEPH DEMARCUS
JOWERS
ambrotype

Pvt. Joe Jowers of the 8th Alabama Infantry did not realize that his regiment was veering off course as it went into battle at Frayser's Farm. But it hardly mattered to him; he was still going to get to shoot at some Yankees. A twenty-eight-year-old farmer from Chambers County, Jowers enlisted in May 1861 into an outfit calling itself the Governor's Guard, which soon became Company B, 8th Alabama. The private had seen plenty of action up to this point in the Peninsula Campaign, but at Frayser's Farm he also literally felt the war when he was wounded by an enemy musket ball. His ordeal in that battle began in the late afternoon, when the 8th Alabama (about 180 strong) advanced eastward as the left flank of Wilcox's Brigade. After crossing a little stream, the regiment entered a field overgrown with high weeds and then came under fire from Union infantry deployed among some pine trees about 400 yards to the left. The regiment wheeled left to return fire, while the rest of the brigade continued forward. After exchanging a few volleys, Jowers and his comrades received orders to drive the enemy from the woods. One officer recollected the ensuing clash: "Advancing steadily under heavy fire, losing men at every step, the regiment gained a point within thirty yards" of the enemy's position. Here the Alabamians unleashed a volley that scattered the defenders. The regiment, however, was badly depleted and without support. When Union reinforcements arrived, the 8th Alabama was compelled to retreat. Private Jowers was one of fifty-seven men wounded in the fight (another sixteen were killed).[29] *Photo Courtesy of ADAH*

WILLIAM J. CANNON
copy print

At Frayser's Farm, the 9th and 10th Alabama Infantry fought as the right wing of Wilcox's Brigade. Advancing with the 9th Regiment was 1st Lt. William Cannon, a twenty-three-year-old farmer from Lauderdale County. As acting commander of Company D, Cannon helped guide his men eastward through a thicket of woods on the south side of Long Bridge Road. Heavy rain the previous night had turned the ground into a mushy bog. Their objective was a six-gun battery less than half a mile distant. One of

Cannon's soldiers nervously observed that the Union gunners were "immediately in front of our regiment, and paid us *very marked* attention." As they approached to within a few hundred yards of the enemy position, the Alabamians came under an intensive barrage of grapeshot. One of these projectiles, "about the size of a hen egg," thwacked Cannon on the side of his head; it was a wound that left Company D without any officers for much of the rest of the battle.[30] *Photo courtesy of U.S.A.M.H.I.*

77

JOHN C. MCKENZIE
copy print

Meanwhile, on the right flank of the 9th Alabama, the 10th Alabama deftly maneuvered through a section of pine trees. Leading Company K of that regiment was Capt. John McKenzie. A thirty-three-year-old farmer from Talladega County, McKenzie evinced remarkable coolness under fire. First, the blue-eyed officer halted his company a mere one hundred yards from the enemy guns in order to deliver a few volleys of aimed fire. Then, he led his men in a final assault. Sometime after this, McKenzie incurred a nasty wound from an exploding shell. Nonetheless, his boys helped capture the battery and fend off a subsequent enemy counterattack. *Photo courtesy of William O. Grimes Collection, U.S.A.M.H.I.*

ROBERT MARTIN SANDS
carte de viste

As he stared up the slope of Malvern Hill on the afternoon of 1 July, Maj. Robert Sands of the 3rd Alabama Infantry flinched as a heavy-caliber shell plowed into the earth about twenty feet from his regiment. Fortunately, the projectile did not explode, but its arrival notified the major that he faced not only the 250 enemy cannon arrayed along the high ground to his front, but he also had to contend with gunboat fire coming in from the nearby James River. A twenty-seven-year-old cotton farmer, Sands hailed from Mobile, where at the outset of the war he had raised the Mobile Cadets, apparently arming his volunteers with rifles seized from the U.S. arsenal at Mount Vernon. Shortly thereafter, the Cadets became Company A, 3rd Alabama.

At Malvern Hill Sands was acting commander of the regiment, which had just been reassigned to Robert Rodes's now all-Alabama brigade. For two hours, the 354 soldiers in the 3rd deployed as a skirmish line, then Sands received the signal to advance with the whole brigade as part of a general assault. On leaving the protection of some woods at the base of the hill, the regiment had to cross at least 700 yards of open ground in order to reach the main Yankee line. Artillery raked the

Alabamians as they rushed upward along the east side of Quaker Road. With 400 yards still to go, Sands instructed his men to hug the earth while he sent forward fifty of his best marksmen to try and pick off the Union gunners. The major's decision backfired: "This was done and brought us to the notice of the battery, which, opening on us with grape, canister, and shell, subjected us to a most terrific fire for some time." Acting brigade commander Col. John Gordon then ordered everyone to charge. With men dropping by the scores, the Alabamians got to within 200 yards of the guns before the hurricane of enemy metal finally broke the assault. Sands's description of his color guard's ordeal vividly testifies to the futility of the overall attack: "There were 6 men shot down while carrying the colors forward, the seventh bringing off the field after the fight a portion of the staff, the colors being literally cut to pieces." After delivering a few ineffectual volleys from a prone position, the 3rd Alabama joined neighboring formations in a hasty retreat. Casualties in the regiment were a staggering 200 killed and wounded, while Major Sands received special mention for his "gallant conduct" during the battle.[31]
Photo courtesy of ADAH

Lee's Alabama Boys

Toward the end of June 1862, three fresh Alabama regiments arrived outside of Richmond. Recruited largely from the northeastern part of the state, the 44th, 47th, and 48th Alabama Infantry added approximately 2,500 badly needed reinforcements to the Army of Northern Virginia. Although disease would soon reduce these regiments to only a few hundred effective soldiers each, their presence raised Alabama's contribution to the Confederate war effort in the East to nineteen units. For the next year, Lee's Alabama boys participated in some of the most famous, albeit horrific, engagements of the entire war.

With his victory over George B. McClellan in the Seven Days' Battles, Robert E. Lee had saved Richmond, but he was determined to stay on the offensive. To the north, a recently organized army of 50,000 men under Maj. Gen. John Pope was threatening another advance on the Confederate capital. Lee meant to expel Pope's command before it received additional forces from McClellan's army. In early August the Rebel general commenced a series of daring movements designed both to con-

fuse and to trap his Union counterpart. Thus began the campaign that culminated in the Second Battle of Manassas. Lee's favorite subordinate, Stonewall Jackson, initiated the operation, moving rapidly north with 30,000 men, including four Alabama infantry units. On 9 August Jackson clashed with enemy forces at Cedar Mountain.

Often overlooked in general histories of the Civil War, Cedar Mountain was a rather fierce contest, one that exhibited the worst and best of the Alabama troops in Jackson's command. Eager to destroy what he assumed was an unsuspecting Union corps, Jackson issued vague orders and rushed his brigades into action. Tactical gains were made by the Rebel right wing, where the 15th Alabama helped secure a good position on the slope of Cedar Mountain. The principal fighting, however, occurred on the Rebel left where Union forces executed an unexpectedly bold attack of their own. Among the regiments protecting Jackson's left flank were the 47th and 48th Alabama (Brig. Gen. William B. Taliaferro's brigade), both untried in combat. Indicative of the soldiers' inexperience was their careless movement under artillery fire as they formed into line of battle. Once in position, they marched into a cornfield with the rest of their brigade and exchanged rifle volleys with nearby Yankees. Fixated on the enemy to their front, the Alabamians were wholly unprepared for the sudden appearance of enemy forces on their flank. The green recruits of the 47th panicked and broke, prompting the now exposed men of the 48th to do likewise. Virginians in the brigade opined that the Alabamians scattered like "turkeys." The timely arrival of a fresh division of Confederates, however, with the 5th Alabama Battalion in the van, averted disaster. The green Alabamians eventually rallied and returned to the battle. By the end of the day, Union troops were in full retreat. Forgetting the indignity of his earlier flight, Pvt. James Crowder of the 47th Alabama recalled matter of factly how he "slep all a monkst the ded yankes that night."[1] But the price for becoming a veteran was high: casualties among the two new regiments amounted to 27 dead and 143 wounded.

After Cedar Mountain, Jackson conducted a wide, northwestward movement through the Blue Ridge Mountains. On 26 August the Confederates emerged behind Pope's main body; pillaged a huge Federal supply depot at Manassas Junction, where the Alabamians joined their Southern brethren in gorging on captured foodstuffs; and then established a strong defensive line behind a forested railroad cut along Stony Ridge. Pope reacted by concentrating his entire force against Jackson's position, fatefully ignoring the remainder of Lee's fast-approaching army. From 28 to 30 August, Jackson's men withstood repeated Union attacks, including several nighttime engagements. The 15th Alabama's experience typified the ferocity of the fighting. Occupying a place near the center of Jackson's line called the "dump," these Southerners bore the brunt of numerous assaults, particularly on 30 August, when they expended virtually every cartridge they had in driving back the Yankee attacks. An Alabama soldier recalled how at one point "the flags of opposing reg-

iments were almost flapping together."[2] Fortunately, Lee arrived with the rest of his army and brought relief in the form of a devastating corps-sized flank attack led by James Longstreet. Six Alabama regiments contributed to this success, particularly the 4th Alabama, which shattered a New York regiment during the advance. Despite suffering over 60 casualties, the 4th Alabama helped rout Pope's army. Overall Rebel losses were 9,000 against 16,000 Yankees.

Its triumph at Second Manassas capped off a summer of stunning victories for the Army of Northern Virginia. Hoping to capitalize on the momentum, Lee received permission from President Davis to launch an offensive onto Union soil. The ensuing Sharpsburg Campaign produced some of the most savage fighting of the war. In keeping with his aggressiveness, Lee divided his army into multiple, fast-moving columns. Stonewall Jackson besieged a Union garrison at Harper's Ferry while other detachments swept through western Maryland en route to Pennsylvania. It was an exhilarating time for the Rebels, but the grim business of combat soon returned. General McClellan, having returned from the Peninsula, monitored Rebel movements with his usual uncertainty. After the serendipitous discovery of a lost copy of Lee's campaign plans, however, the Union commander moved with celerity to destroy in detail the dispersed Confederate forces. Realizing that something was amiss, Lee abruptly ordered his army to concentrate around the small town of Sharpsburg, Maryland, behind Antietam Creek.

To gain time, five Alabama regiments under Robert Rodes participated in a desperate rearguard action around South Mountain. On 14 September some 1,200 Alabamians hastily entrenched themselves at Turner's Gap just as three Union divisions came into sight. The 12th Alabama Infantry barely deployed as skirmishers before the enemy stormed the gap. "It was pitiable to see the gallant but hopeless struggle of those Alabamians against such mighty odds," observed Daniel H. Hill, in overall command at South Mountain.[3] Nevertheless, for perhaps three hours "those Alabamians" repulsed one attack after the next before the weight of the onslaught proved unbearable. Despite the uneven terrain, Rodes withdrew in relative good order and rejoined the main Confederate body at Sharpsburg. The brigade lost over 400 men, but it had accomplished its mission: the Union advance had been delayed.

Two days later Lee and McClellan studied each other across the valley of shallow Antietam Creek, which runs roughly north to south just east of Sharpsburg. Although Lee had managed to gather a sizeable force of 40,000 men, the rank and file were not only tired and hungry but also had their backs to the Potomac River; there was no means of easy escape. But Lee had no intention of retreating. On his left flank, five Alabama regiments (distributed among four brigades) took up forward positions in and around the woods and farms immediately north of the town. The center, facing east, was defended in part by Rodes's battered brigade, whose 750 Alabamians occupied a formidable position along a sunken road. Six more Alabama regiments helped guard the right flank, which extended south along the creek. On the evening of 16 September, McClellan deployed his army of 75,000 Federals with orders to attack at the crack of dawn.

The Battle of Sharpsburg unfolded in distinct phases. Rather than launching a simultaneous attack all along the line, McClellan instructed his corps commanders to advance in seriated waves that started from the northern end of the battlefield and proceeded in turn toward the southern end. Such dispositions allowed Lee to shift units from relatively quiet areas to the most threatened sectors. The result was that the antagonists clashed at numerical parity throughout most of the battle. Among the first Rebel units to see action on the morning of 17 September were the men of the 47th and 48th Alabama. Deployed among the trees of an area known as the West Woods, these men excitedly readied their rifles

as they watched an entire corps of blueclad infantrymen advance through a cornfield. Within moments the battlefront erupted in a crescendo of fire and smoke. After delivering several volleys, acting brigade commander Col. James W. Jackson ordered his men to charge. For the next few minutes, the Alabamians engaged in wild, close-quarters combat before enemy artillery fire and the sheer weight of the attack compelled them to fall back. Nevertheless, at the cost of nearly forty casualties in each regiment, the Alabamians helped slow the initial Yankee attack.

The carnage only increased as the morning progressed. As the wave of Union blue swept onward, fresh Confederate units rushed to the scene. Maj. Gen. John B. Hood, whose division included the 4th Alabama, executed a savage counterattack that temporarily drove the enemy back. After racing across the corpse-strewn cornfield, the Alabamians seized a copse called the East Woods and then added their firepower to the volume of Rebel lead that finally halted the first Union assault. A lack of ammunition, not to mention three dozen casualties, forced the regiment to withdraw just as a second enemy wave came in from the northeast. Against this latest attack stood the 13th Alabama (of Brig. Gen. Alfred H. Colquitt's brigade), whose 330 rifles helped the Confederate defenders shred the oncoming Union ranks. Its marksmanship notwithstanding, this unit was still nearly overwhelmed by the Yankee onslaught. In hastily withdrawing to a better position, the 13th Alabama suffered the ignominy of losing its colors. Finally, after four hours of incessant fighting, the cacophony on the northern part of the battlefield came to a merciful end.

At about 10:00 A.M. the principal fighting shifted to the Rebel center, where the Sunken Road, which served as a perfect trench line, would soon earn the sanguinary nickname "Bloody Lane." Rodes's Alabama brigade held the left flank of the road, the 26th, 12th, 3rd, 5th, and 6th Regiments in line from left to right. For three hours, the Alabamians helped stave off a series of Union assaults, their volleys virtually annihilating a Delaware regiment in one instance. "Heaps upon heaps were there in Death's embrace," recalled Col. Cullen Battle of the 3rd Alabama. "And the adjacent planes were covered with a carpet of red, blue, and gray." He then added, "The men that held that centre could die, but they could not fly."[4] Actually, they did both. The 6th Alabama bore the brunt of most of these attacks, but Col. John B. Gordon's fearless leadership kept the men at their posts. After he was wounded, however, a nearly fatal set of events occurred. As nearby North Carolina regiments finally fell back under increased Union pressure, Rodes ordered the 6th Alabama to re-fuse its flank. Instead, the regiment executed a full retreat. Before the now-exposed 5th Alabama could react, Yankees poured into the gap, and the whole Rebel line gave way. Only the timely arrival of Confederate reinforcements prevented a rout. Among these fresh regiments were the 14th Alabama (of Pryor's Brigade) and the 44th Alabama (of Wright's Brigade), both of which hurled themselves toward the enemy, blunted the breakthrough, and then helped establish a new defensive line about 150 yards behind Bloody Lane.

After the struggle in the center petered out, the battle shifted southward. There four Alabama regiments under Cadmus Wilcox provided support for the Rebel defenders around what became known as Burnside's Bridge. These units and others grudgingly gave ground until still-more desperately needed Confederate reinforcements arrived to halt the last Union attack of the day. In all, the Army of Northern Virginia sustained over 10,000 casualties in what became the bloodiest day of the war (Union forces suffered nearly 13,000 casualties). Alabamians accounted for at least 900 of the overall Confederate losses. Over the next few weeks, Lee's army limped southward and went into winter quarters.

For the first time in months, the rank and file of the Army of Northern Virginia rested. In late November, however, the Rebels prepared for more combat. The refitted Army of the Potomac under its new commander, Maj. Gen. Ambrose Burnside, embarked on another campaign against Richmond. For a brief moment, Burnside stole a march on his adversary and rapidly moved his huge army of 120,000 men down the Rappahannock River to opposite the town of Fredericksburg. There the Union offensive bogged down. Pontoon bridges failed to arrive on time, and Burnside's men sat idle. Lee seized this opportunity and concentrated his army in strength on the high ground west of the town. When Union troops finally began crossing the river on 12 December, they encountered not bewildered Southern civilians, but determined Confederate troops. The ensuing battle (13 December) is best known for Burnside's utterly futile attempt to storm the Confederate entrenchments on Marye's Heights, where the Union army suffered over 8,000 casualties. Five Alabama regiments under General Wilcox anchored Lee's far left flank in that sector, but they saw little action. For the remaining Alabama units holding various positions on the Rebel right to the south of Fredericksburg, the fighting proved sporadic. Throughout the afternoon, the opposing sides sparred aggressively, but the Federals could never quite deliver a coordinated assault. The battle ended in a lopsided Rebel victory. In its immediate aftermath the inuring effect of hard war displayed itself as Confederate soldiers plundered the bodies of the Federal dead and wounded, stripping them of clothing and personal possessions. Pvt. James Hoyt of the 3rd Alabama Infantry shook his head with disapproval: "I felt ashamed of being a southerner from the way our men acted in sight of the Yankee lines."[5]

About the time of the Battle of Fredericksburg, Lee completed a reorganization of the Army of Northern Virginia, a process he had started since taking command. As much as possible, regiments were brigaded together by state in order to improve esprit de corps and to simplify the replacement of personnel. The changes produced three complete Alabama brigades. Cadmus Wilcox continued to command the original Alabama brigade, which now included the 14th Regiment in addition to the 8th, 9th, 10th, and 11th. Rodes's Brigade, now under Col. Edward O'Neal of Madison County, consisted of the 3rd, 5th, 6th, 12th, and 26th Regiments. Finally, Brig. Gen. Evander M. Law commanded the newest Alabama brigade, comprising the 4th, 15th, 44th, 47th, and 48th Regiments. Two other Alabama units, the 13th Regiment and 5th Battalion, served alongside three Tennessee regiments in a hybrid brigade under James J. Archer. Capt. William Robbins of the 4th Alabama proudly assessed Lee's war machine: "No doubt we have a grand army, which has been sifted and sifted until nothing but the very quintessence is left."[6]

The reconfigured Army of Northern Virginia soon clashed again with the Army of the Potomac at the Battle of Chancellorsville (1–6 May 1863). In late April Maj. Gen. Joseph Hooker, the latest Union commander, launched a major offensive, one that caught the Rebels off balance. With a sizeable portion of his army (including Law's Brigade) away on security and foraging duties, Lee opposed the Union advance with a mere 60,000 men against a mammoth army of 130,000. Leaving some 40,000 troops to pin Lee's force at Fredericksburg, Hooker marched over 70,000 men on a wide sweep through the Virginia wilderness ten miles west of the city. The maneuver threatened to either trap the Confederate army or force it to withdraw to Richmond. True to form, Lee rejected both fates and decided to counterattack. Leaving 10,000 men at Marye's Heights, he deployed 50,000 men athwart the enemy's approach. Discovering that the Union right flank was "in the air," Lee further divided his army, sending over 27,000 troops under Lt. Gen. Stonewall Jackson northwest along a forest road on what would lead to the most famous flank attack of the war.

While the whole Rebel army performed well in the ensuing battle, Alabamians played an especially prominent role at several crucial stages. O'Neal's Brigade served as the vanguard of Jackson's force. After marching for several hours, it deployed into line of battle, the regiments aligned perpendicular on the left-hand side of the east–west Orange Turnpike. For two more hours, the Alabamians snoozed while the rest of the Confederate units took up their positions. Then, shortly before 5:30 P.M., Jackson executed his attack. With bugles blaring, the Alabamians lifted a Rebel yell and charged forward. Surprise was almost total; an entire Union corps virtually disintegrated under the Confederate onslaught. As O'Neal's Brigade overran one line of defenders after the next, Capt. Jon Williams of the 5th Alabama exulted, "the bluecoats might as well have tried to stop a cyclone."[7] For the most part, the brigade maintained an unbroken front, but unit cohesion inevitably unraveled the farther the Rebels raced through the forest. By nightfall the enemy rallied, and combat abated as exhausted units on both sides reorganized themselves. For Lee's Alabama boys, the day's success was undeniable. In pushing the Yankees back some two miles, O'Neal's Brigade took over 300 prisoners and captured three pieces of artillery. Casualties were light among the Alabamians.

Despite the triumphant flank attack, the battle was far from over. Though distressed by the loss of Stonewall Jackson, who was mortally wounded during a nighttime reconnaissance, Lee ordered a full-scale attack at dawn against Hooker's now-entrenched army. At the start of the fighting on 3 May, O'Neal's Brigade was held in reserve, but it soon entered the fray, assaulting Union positions around Chancellorsville itself (that is, the Chancellor Home and its support buildings). The density of the forest in that area compelled the Alabamians to fight in loose regimental groups often out of contact with one another. In one particularly desperate engagement, the 5th and 26th Alabama Regiments, with elements of the 6th, briefly broke through the Union lines and silenced an enemy battery before falling back under a heavy counterattack; the 5th Alabama lost its flag in the retreat. Elsewhere, the 3rd Alabama made little headway against a withering hail of artillery fire. Pvt. Nick Weeks of that unit described the audible ferocity of the combat: "the ping of the minnie ball, the splutter of canister, the whistling of grape, the 'where are you, where are you' of screaming shells and the cannon's roar from a hundred mouths went to make up the music for the great opera of death."[8] Eventually, Confederate artillery posted on Hazel Grove, an important piece of elevated terrain that Alabamians in Archer's Brigade helped secure earlier in the morning, compelled Union forces to retreat into the woods north of the Chancellor House. Still, unlike the first day of fighting, casualties among the Alabama regiments mounted sharply on 3 May.

At this point the battle reached a critical juncture. Hemmed in by these relentless Confederate attacks, Hooker ordered his containment force at Fredericksburg to storm the now lightly defended Marye's Heights and hit Lee's army from behind. Until this moment, Wilcox's Brigade (2,000 strong) was guarding a quiet section along the Rappahannock just northwest of the town. When the Union attack overran the heights, Wilcox ignored orders to retreat southward and, on his own initiative, decided to withdraw westward in order to protect Lee's rear at Chancellorsville. The stage was set for one of Alabama's most glorious moments of the war. Wilcox's Alabamians conducted a series of skillful delaying actions that culminated in a ferocious clash around a crossroads near Salem Church. There the brigadier deployed his five regiments astride Orange Plank Road—with two companies from the 9th Alabama occupying forward positions in the red-brick church and a nearby log schoolhouse—just in time to receive a division-sized assault. For several minutes, the massed fire of the Alabama brigade stalled the Union attack, but its sheer weight of numbers nearly swamped the defenders. In wild close-quarters fighting, the Yankees encircled the two buildings and hammered the center of the Rebel line. When the 10th Alabama buckled and gave way, Wilcox hurled the remaining companies from the

9th into the fray. As the Union attack faltered, the whole Alabama brigade charged. Soon both buildings were retaken and the enemy driven from the field. Throughout the contest, other Confederate brigades arrived to shore up Wilcox's flanks, but the Alabamians bore the brunt of the attack. The brigade lost 495 men but helped inflict some 1,500 casualties on the enemy. For the next few days, the opposing sides engaged in sporadic fighting before Hooker withdrew his army back across the Rappahannock. Chancellorsville arguably marks Alabama's greatest contribution to the Confederate war effort in the East. From spearheading Jackson's flank attack, which made a victory possible, to repulsing a dangerous counterattack at Salem Church, which essentially ensured the victory, Alabamians were directly involved at every important stage of the battle.

After Chancellorsville Lee launched a second, more-ambitious invasion of the North. That summer the Army of Northern Virginia reached its peak strength: approximately 75,000 soldiers, most them veterans, including the 6,000 Alabamians in the ranks. Basically a giant raid, the Confederate offensive swept into south-central Pennsylvania in late June 1863. On 1 July a contingent of Confederate infantry engaged Union cavalry troopers near the small town of Gettysburg. Both sides hastily rushed additional troops to the scene; the most famous battle of the war was underway. West of the town, the 5th Alabama Battalion and 13th Alabama Infantry helped open the action with an attack against enemy forces on McPherson Ridge. There the Alabamians grappled in a seesaw contest with the vaunted Iron Brigade of midwesterners. North of the town O'Neal's Brigade (1,800 strong) prepared to join the fray as part of Rodes's division-level attack. Unfortunately, the impetuous Rodes mismanaged his units, particularly his Alabama brigade, ordering it to charge without clear instructions and then abruptly detaching two of its regiments for other tasks. Consequently, O'Neal's three remaining regiments suffered heavy casualties and

86

achieved nothing. Nonetheless, Rebel attacks elsewhere steadily pushed the enemy back through Gettysburg before nightfall ended the fighting. His brigade badly depleted, O'Neal fumed at having had his authority superseded. Conversely, Rodes blamed his brigadier for much of the division's less-than-stellar performance that day.

On the morning of 2 July, the Rebels awoke to find the Army of the Potomac strongly fortified on nearby high ground. Undaunted, Lee decided to resume the battle. He ordered Lt. Gen. James Longstreet, whose corps was still arriving on the field, to execute a sweeping flank attack against the Union left just south of Cemetery Ridge. After some lengthy preparation, Longstreet commenced his assault at 4:00 P.M. On the extreme right was Law's Brigade of 1,700 Alabamians, all of whom had spent the previous ten hours marching more than twenty miles through stifling summer heat. With no time to spare, most of the men went into action with empty canteens. Fierce fighting soon erupted throughout the sector, with the 44th and 48th Alabama Regiments engaging the enemy in a boulder-strewn area aptly called Devil's Den. The large rock formations hindered visibility, forcing officers to direct their units by sound rather than sight; thus, the opponents often found themselves in sudden, point-blank combat. Still, after repeated assaults the Alabamians overran an enemy battery and helped secure the area after an hour of intense fighting.

Rather than commit the rest of his regiments to this particular fight, Law belatedly realized that Little Round Top, a hill a bit farther south that commanded a view of the entire battlefield, was the key terrain. Accordingly, he directed the rest of his brigade toward this position, even as local Union commanders rushed in defenders. The 4th Alabama hammered the enemy center in vain, sustaining 25-percent losses before falling back. Pulled from Devil's Den, the exhausted 44th and 48th Alabama linked with two Texas regiments for an all-out assault against the right flank on Little Round Top.

Clambering uphill through trees and over rocks, the Alabamians nearly broke a Michigan regiment before additional Union forces arrived to prevent a breakthrough. All the while the 47th and 15th Alabama strived to seize the other side of the hill. As best they could, the men of the 47th attempted to charge, but fatigue brought on by thirst took as great a toll as Yankee musketry; caught in a crossfire, the regiment's attack failed. The 15th's attempt came closer to success. With Col. William Oates exhorting his men, the Alabama boys engaged in what later became a legendary duel with the 20th Maine under Col. Joshua Chamberlain. After several desperate minutes, the Alabamians finally gave way when the bluecoats launched a bayonet attack. Despite the defeat, Oates praised his men: "Greater heroes never shouldered muskets than those Alabamians."[9]

As the fighting around Little Round Top transpired, Wilcox's Brigade participated in a sizeable supporting operation a mile to the north, one designed to threaten the Union position on Cemetery Ridge. Maintaining remarkably good alignment, the five Alabama regiments steadily moved over fence rails and around farm buildings, all the while exchanging a brisk fire with retreating bluecoats. When Union rearguard batteries slowed the advance, Wilcox ordered a general charge that "swept like a hurricane over cannon and caissons."[10] With the help of nearby brigades, the Alabamians badly bludgeoned the defending Union division. At that moment Wilcox determined that instead of simply supporting Longstreet, his brigade seemed on the verge of ripping a serious gap in the Union lines. The Yankees apparently agreed and frantically hurled reinforcements against the Alabamians. In one instance, the 10th and 11th Alabama Regiments virtually annihilated a Minnesota regiment that hastily arrived to seal the breach. Fading light and a lack of reserves, however, prevented Wilcox from exploiting the day's success; his brigade soon withdrew to its starting point.

The climax of the Battle of Gettysburg came on 3 July with Lee's controversial decision to launch a full-scale frontal assault against the center of the Union line along Cemetery Ridge. Though most of the Confederate soldiers involved came from either Virginia or North Carolina, two Alabama units played a prominent part. The 5th Alabama Battalion and the 13th Alabama Infantry Regiment constituted the very center of the Rebel battle line, around which all other units were to align themselves. The ensuing attack has entered Civil War lore as Pickett's Charge, the futile "high tide of the Confederacy." Trudging nearly a mile over exposed ground, the Rebels suffered appalling losses from concentrated artillery and rifle fire. Like many of their Southern compatriots, however, the Alabamians persevered and actually penetrated the Union lines. For a few minutes, the opposing forces wrestled in furious hand-to-hand combat before sheer numbers overwhelmed the Alabamians, many of whom were captured along with both units' flags. Not far away, Wilcox's Brigade conducted another supporting attack, but coming under intense artillery fire as well as enfilading musketry from a Vermont regiment, it retreated well short of the positions it had nearly seized the previous day. In the days that followed, the surviving Alabamians joined the rest of Lee's army in a general retreat back to Virginia. Total casualties among Alabama units at Gettysburg were frightful: about 200 men lost from Archer's Brigade, 525 from Law's Brigade, 700 from O'Neal's Brigade, and 780 from Wilcox's Brigade—some 2,200 in all.

Lee's Alabama boys had performed well in more than a year of grueling conventional warfare. But attrition had taken its toll. In future contests the Alabama brigades would never display quite the same fearlessness that characterized their performance in battle during 1862 and 1863.

JAMES WASHINGTON JACKSON
ambrotype

Despite the shell bursts overhead, Lt. Col. James Jackson of the 47th Alabama Infantry kept his 300 men calm as he hurried them into line of battle just north of Cedar Mountain. It was late afternoon on 9 August, and the regiment was going into its first fight; everyone was both excited and apprehensive. A military novice, Jackson was about to receive a humiliating lesson in tactics. A thirty-year-old physician from Tallapoosa County, he first served as a captain in the short-lived 7th Alabama Infantry before becoming lieutenant colonel of the 47th at its organization in May 1862. Now, at Cedar Mountain, he was acting commander and responsible for the extreme left flank of Taliaferro's Brigade, which constituted part of the Confederate left wing. Initially, all went well for the lieutenant colonel and his men. The Alabamians advanced in good order across a stretch of farmland to within a few hundred yards of the Yankee lines. For about twenty minutes,

Jackson orchestrated some effective volley fire, then disaster struck. "We found ourselves attacked from a very unlooked-for quarter," Jackson remembered. "The enemy, having flanked us, had come around to our rear, and were pouring heavy volleys on us at the distance of 40 paces." Having neglected his security, Jackson attempted to save the situation by re-fusing his left flank. Unfortunately, the companies assigned to this task gave way and fled; soon the entire regiment was running in confusion off the battlefield. Once safely out of danger, though, Jackson managed to rally most of his survivors and lead them back in time to participate in the closing stages of the battle. At 9:00 P.M. the fighting ended, and the Alabamians happily bivouacked on the ground that had earlier witnessed their rout. Satisfied that honor had been redeemed, Jackson counted his losses: 12 men killed and 85 wounded.[11]
Photo courtesy of ADAH

EDWARD HENRY VANCE
DAVENPORT
copy print

Toward dusk on 29 August, the 4th Alabama Infantry hustled across a broken landscape just north of Warrenton Turnpike. The Alabamians were part of a large reconnaissance in force dispatched by James Longstreet both to determine enemy strength around Groveton—due east—and to establish contact with Stonewall Jackson's embattled forces to the northeast. One of the men in the 4th was Pvt. Edward Davenport of Company H. A twenty-three-year-old mechanic from Lauderdale County, Davenport was a veteran of the Peninsula Campaign. Unfortunately, the imminent clash around Groveton, part of the larger Second Battle of Manassas, would be the private's last experi-

ence on earth. Advancing as the left flank of Law's Brigade, the 4th reached the outskirts of Groveton at 6:00 P.M. Seeing a Yankee battery unlimber to their front, the Alabamians attacked. Davenport and his comrades fired and reloaded over and over as they moved rapidly forward. After helping drive off the enemy gunners, the regiment consolidated with the rest of the brigade astride the turnpike, where the Alabamians beat off an infantry probe during the night. Somewhere and at some point in all that darkness, Davenport went down with a fatal wound. He was one of nineteen men killed in the regiment in the course of the battle. *Photo courtesy of ADAH*

DAVID BARNUM
copy print

As he fired down at Federal infantrymen darting among the rocks and trees covering the slopes of South Mountain, Maryland, Pvt. Davy Barnum of the 5th Alabama Infantry had no idea that he was about to be captured. The nineteen-year-old son of a slaveholder from Greene County, Barnum resigned from the U.S. Naval Academy and in the summer of 1861 joined the Greensboro Guards; this outfit soon became Company I, 5th Alabama. A physically small boy, he possessed a seemingly fearless personality. In camp Barnum once challenged a soldier to a knife fight, and after receiving a bullet wound at Seven Pines, he stoically carried the slug in his side for months before the pain became too great to bear. On the afternoon of 14 September, the private was part of a large-scale delaying action at Turner's Gap. The 5th Alabama (of Rodes's Brigade) helped defend the left flank of the Confederate position. From Barnum's perspective, however, Company I might as well have been all alone. The brigade's dispositions were thin to begin with, and the rugged, forested terrain made visual contact with neighboring units virtually impossible. Nevertheless, he and his comrades fought with determination. As Union forces approached to within a couple of hundred yards, the Alabamians began sniping away from behind a patch of boulders. When the Yankees began shooting back, Barnum's company commander noted that "the balls would hit those rocks and it sounded like heavy hail." At first Company I checked the Union advance, but enemy forces eventually turned both flanks and trapped the Greensboro Guards, along with two other companies. While a few Alabamians managed to escape, Private Barnum was one of thirty-two men taken captive.

His ordeal as a prisoner actually had its perky moments. For instance, at a holding area in Frederick, Maryland, the Yankees provided Barnum and his mates a smorgasbord of coffee, sugar, hardtack, and pork. The private's incarceration also proved short lived; within a few months after his capture, he was exchanged.[12] *Photo courtesy of Richard K. Tibbals Collections, U.S.A.M.H.I.*

OWEN KENAN
MCLEMORE
copy print

As exhausted Confederate forces withdrew out of Turner's Gap and trudged through the streets of Boonsboro, Maryland, Lt. Col. Owen McLemore rushed the 4th Alabama Infantry forward to renew the delaying action that was still buying precious time for General Lee to concentrate his army at Sharpsburg. A twenty-three-year-old professional soldier from Chambers County, McLemore was serving as a lieutenant in the 8th U.S. Infantry when Alabama seceded. He resigned his commission and helped raise the 14th Alabama Infantry, holding the rank of major. Due to attrition among officers in the 4th Alabama after First Manassas, McLemore accepted the lieutenant colonelcy of that regiment in the spring of 1862. Though a West Pointer (class of 1856), he respected his men as citizen-soldiers, and they responded in kind. Having fought with valor during the Peninsula Campaign and at Second Manassas, the officer was no stranger to combat crises. On the evening of 14 September, he understood that the enemy had to be kept at bay until sundown. Part of Law's Brigade, McLemore's men moved toward the gap with bayonets fixed, while their lieutenant colonel held his sword high and shouted, "Never will they get over this!" The 4th Alabama held firm behind a road embankment, but McLemore went down under a Yankee volley; he was standing on a fence to get a better view when a bullet ripped through his right shoulder. As his regiment withdrew during the night, it left behind McLemore's sword. The lieutenant colonel's wound proved mortal, and he died quietly on 30 September in a private residence in Winchester, Virginia. Maj. Gen. John Bell Hood grieved the loss, describing McLemore as "a most efficient, gallant, and valuable officer."[13] *Photo courtesy of ADAH*

Isaac Ball Feagin
copy print
G. V. Buck,
Washington, D.C.

At dawn on 17 September, Capt. Isaac Feagin of the 15th Alabama Infantry roused his men from their fitful slumber on the fields around the Mumma Farm. The captain and his men had occupied their position for only a few hours and now braced for the opening Federal attack at Sharpsburg. A twenty-eight-year-old merchant from Barbour County, where he also served as deputy sheriff, Feagin helped raise the Midway Southern Guards, which became Company B, 15th Alabama, with himself as captain. He had participated in all of the regiment's major engagements, but at Sharpsburg Feagin was the acting commander of 300 very tired veterans. As a division of bluecoats crashed through the East Woods north of the Mumma Farm, the 15th deployed into line of battle as the right flank of Trimble's Brigade. Feagin and his men soon found themselves embroiled in a vicious standup fight, one that rapidly exhausted the regiment's supply of ammunition. This disconcerting news, combined with his mounting casualties—eighty-four killed and wounded before the fighting was over—compelled Feagin to withdraw with the rest of the brigade to a rally point on the outskirts of town. Once there, the captain coordinated efforts to resupply his men. While looking through a cartridge box discarded behind a haystack, Feagin was taken aback by the unexpected arrival of Daniel H. Hill. The general berated the captain for wasting time seeking bullets when he could just as well fight with the bayonet—or even rocks; Feagin simply stared back in silent disbelief. The 15th Alabama saw little combat for the rest of the battle.[14]
Photo courtesy of ADAH

JULIUS A. KIMBROUGH
ambrotype

Since 10:00 A.M., Capt. Julius Kimbrough of the 6th Alabama Infantry had been orchestrating the volley fire of Company I along the Sunken Road just outside Sharpsburg. Part of Rodes's Brigade, the regiment anchored the right, with Company I deployed near the extreme end where the Alabamians tied into a brigade of Tarheels. The captain and his men were therefore a vital link holding together the center of the Rebel line in that sector. A thirty-three-year-old slaveholder from Choctaw County, Kimbrough had enlisted in the 6th Alabama in May 1861. He appears to have served alongside several brothers and cousins. When the regiment reorganized in early 1862, Kimbrough won election as captain of Company I. The new company commander fought unscathed through the entire Peninsula Campaign. Unfortunately, at Sharpsburg Kimbrough suffered a mortal wound. Before his final moment, however, the captain ostensibly led his men with valor. He and his comrades helped repulse three Yankee assaults until around 1:00 P.M., when a fatal miscommunication undermined the linear cohesion of the Alabama line. General Rodes tried to coordinate a sortie, but the officers in the 6th never heard the order over the clamor of battle, staying put while other units charged without support. Whether such an attack would have accomplished anything became moot when the neighboring brigade of North Carolinians gave way, exposing the 6th Alabama to enfilade fire. Captain Kimbrough likely prepared for the regiment to re-fuse its flank, but Lt. Col. James Lightfoot abruptly called for a general retreat. In the panic that followed, swarming bluecoats blasted the right wing of the 6th, inflicting in a frightful instant most of the 156 casualties suffered by the regiment that day. The remaining Alabamians managed to fall back and rally, but they did so without Julius Kimbrough, one among the dead who gave the "Bloody Lane" its terrible name.
Photo courtesy of David Wynn Vaughan

George Croghan Whatley
copy print
Russell Studios, Atlanta

The fighting around Sharpsburg was well underway as Capt. George Whatley of the 10th Alabama Infantry hastily guided his regiment across the Potomac River at Shepherdstown, Maryland. The only thing the captain knew about the struggle was that his army's center along the Sunken Road was buckling under a massive Union assault. A lanky forty-one-year-old lawyer and politico from Calhoun County, Whatley was a diehard Confederate. Representing his county at the secession convention in January 1861, he unhesitatingly voted for independence, afterward recruiting Company G (the Pope Walker Guards) for the newly organized 10th Alabama. He proved his zeal for the cause at Gaines' Mill, where he was wounded leading his men in that battle's climactic charge. At Sharpsburg Whatley took on greater responsibility: he was the regiment's acting commander. Following the sound of the guns, the cap- tain arrived in time to help shore up the Rebel right flank. Other units had stanched the primary enemy breakthrough, but there was still plenty of fighting left to be done. The 10th quickly deployed and commenced volley fire into the nearest Yankee formation. An Alabama private in the regiment recalled a scene of hectic violence: "I passed several Confederates who had fallen before getting close enough to the enemy to do an execution. I passed one whose head had been severed from his body by a shell just in front of me." Whatley and his men helped stop any further advance by Yankee infantry, but the Alabamians then came under merciless Union artillery fire. At this point, whether by musket ball or cannon shot, Captain Whatley went down, one of 10 men killed in the regiment that day; another 53 were wounded.[15]
Photo courtesy of ADAH

JOHN PELHAM
copy print
Gilbert Studios, Philadelphia

In a war filled with heroic moments, the artillery exploits of Maj. John Pelham certainly rank among the most remarkable. A twenty-four-year-old daredevil and heartthrob from Calhoun County, Pelham was a cadet at West Point when the war broke out. Known for his athleticism and horsemanship, the young man also proved a natural cannoneer. Quitting the academy, Pelham joined the Confederate service, and at First Manassas he garnered attention for his skillful handling of a section in Imboden's Battery. After that he commanded a battery of his own in Jeb Stuart's cavalry. In all of the Army of Northern Virginia's major battles during its first year, Pelham always seemed to place his guns at the right place and time, delivering barrages with uncanny accuracy. His record earned him accolades and promotion to major, yet it was his performance at Fredericksburg that brought him eternal fame. In the days leading up to the battle, Pelham harassed enemy traffic on the Rappahannock River, puncturing the hull of a Union gunboat in one instance. On the morning of the battle itself (13 December), Pelham's Battery anchored the Confederate right flank at Hamilton's Crossing. Due to a thick fog, General Stuart dispatched the major and a section of horse artillery to reconnoiter. When Pelham reached the road leading into Fredericksburg, the fog cleared and the youth beheld an impressive array of bluecoats—40,000 of them—formed into three lines of battle along the near bank of the river. The Yankees were just starting to advance when the major unlimbered his guns among a copse of cedars. Pelham exulted at the prospect of enfi-

lading the lines of the entire Federal army and ordered his crews to fire. Nine hundred yards away, pandemonium erupted as their shots plowed into the tightly packed Union ranks. Enemy gunners soon retaliated, as first three, then five, and finally six Union batteries bombarded Pelham's position. Unfazed, the young officer coolly rode between his guns, displacing them as necessary, yet maintaining steady fire. Eventually, the Yankees disabled one cannon, but the other— a Napoleon smoothbore—continued to blast away. The crew of this piece consisted of French immigrants from Mobile, who reportedly sang the "Marseillaise" throughout the exchange. On the ridge overlooking the scene, most of the Rebel army watched the duel and cheered, including General Lee, who exclaimed, "It is glorious to see such courage in one so young." After nearly an hour, Stonewall Jackson ordered Pelham to fall back lest the Confederacy's newest hero be killed. The major duly complied, salvaging his disabled gun and taking great satisfaction in having singlehandedly disrupted the attack plans of his foe. For the rest of the day, Pelham directed additional artillery fire that helped repulse the ensuing Union assault that he had so admirably delayed. Thereafter, Lee referred to his now-favorite artillery officer as "the Gallant" Pelham. A few months after Fredericksburg, on 17 March 1863, Major Pelham participated in a skirmish at Kelly's Ford. During the fight, a shell fragment penetrated his skull. The young man died as a result, but a legend was born.[16]
Photo courtesy of ADAH

Watkins Phelan
copy print
L. D. Benton,
Waterbury, Conn.

As he nibbled some cornbread, Capt. Watkins Phelan of the 3rd Alabama Infantry could just see the Orange Turnpike off to his right through the trees and brush of a forested snarl known as the Wilderness. In command of the regiment's left wing, the young officer understood that that road was the principal landmark that would guide Stonewall Jackson's corps-sized attack straight into the right rear of the Union army at Chancellorsville. The twenty-six-year-old son of one of Alabama's most prominent jurists, Phelan had participated in every major engagement since Seven Pines, where he was wounded. Prior to Fredericksburg he received promotion to captain of Company F (the Metropolitan Guards). At Chancellorsville the 3rd Alabama anchored the right flank of O'Neal's Brigade. Shortly before 6:00 P.M., the whole Confederate line went into action. For the next hour, Phelan and his fellow Alabamians exulted in what became their greatest success of the entire war. After thrashing several hundred yards through thick woods, the regiment burst into a clearing and embarked on a glorious charge through poorly organized enemy resistance. Throughout the assault, Phelan helped maintain impressive linear discipline as the men fired and loaded while on the run. The regimental commander vividly described the scene: "Leaping over the [Union] breastworks, we swept onward and over a line of intrenchments, routing the enemy, capturing one cannon and two caissons, and, through a hot fire of shell, grape, canister, and musketry, moved forward to a second and stronger line of intrenchments, which were speedily occupied, the enemy retiring in disorder after a few rounds." Phelan and his men had helped destroy the entire right flank of the Army of the Potomac. Slightly wounded in the fighting, the young captain earned praise for his gallant conduct. The next morning Phelan and the 3rd Alabama participated in further assaults, but nothing compared to the triumph of the previous day.[17] *Photo courtesy of ADAH*

98

WILLIAM BRYAN HUTTON
copy print from Confederate
Veteran

Shortly before dawn on 3 May, the men of the 5th Alabama Infantry Battalion received orders to form the skirmish line for Archer's Brigade. The tactical objective was the high ground around Hazel Grove, a position that would give Confederate batteries an excellent field of fire on Union forces entrenched to the north around Chancellorsville. Commanding Company A that morning was 2nd Lt. William Hutton of Sumter County. A graduate of the University of Virginia (class of 1861), the twenty-two-year-old Hutton was well on his way toward becoming a professor of ancient languages when the call to duty reached him while studying abroad in Germany. Well liked by his soldiers, with whom he frequently discussed the political views of John C. Calhoun, Hutton was a strict yet congenial drillmaster who never flinched in combat. At sunrise the lieutenant and his company ascended Hazel Grove just as the enemy was inexplic-

ably evacuating the heights. Rushing his men forward, Hutton scattered the remaining Federals and helped the brigade capture four pieces of artillery and one hundred enemy troops. As Rebel gunners arrived and set up, Archer's Brigade resumed its advance toward a crossroads due west of Chancellorsville. The 5th Battalion once again served as skirmishers, this time with Hutton commanding in place of the injured Captain A. N. Porter. A few hundred yards from a thick patch of woods infested with Union infantrymen, the Alabamians came under heavy fire. Hutton collapsed with a bullet in his chest. As comrades carried him to the rear, another bullet struck the lieutenant in his arm. The battalion fell back to Hazel Grove after suffering thirty-three casualties. Rebel reinforcements eventually drove the Yankees back, but Hutton never learned of the day's success; he died that evening of his wounds. Alabama had lost a brilliant young scholar.

CECIL CARTER
on the right, with Willis E. Hall
copy print

As he stepped over the prone bodies of a brigade of Virginians, Pvt. Cecil Carter of the 3rd Alabama Infantry empathized with those men's refusal to advance. Up ahead, Federal artillery around the Chancellor House was blasting anything that moved. Regardless, Carter and his fellow Alabamians pressed forward. A twenty-one-year-old student from Mobile, Carter was attending the University of Alabama when Fort Sumter fell. Two weeks later he and his friend Willis Hall joined the Mobile Cadets, which soon became Company A, 3rd Alabama. (Hall later transferred to a North Carolina regiment.) In the campaigns that followed, Carter seemed to attract bullets. Wounded at Seven Pines, the youth had barely recovered when he was wounded again at Malvern Hill. His next wound would nearly prove fatal. Advancing along the Orange Turnpike on the morning of 3 May, the 3rd Alabama (of O'Neal's Brigade) was part of a division-sized reinforcing attack. As Carter neared the main line of Union batteries, incoming canister balls ripped his regiment apart. A fellow private graphically described the carnage: "I saw the arm and shoulder fly from the man just in front exposing his throbbing heart. Another's foot flew up and kicked him the face as a shell struck his leg. Another disemboweled crawled along on his fours, his entrails trailing behind, and still another held up his tongue with his hand, a piece of shell having carried away his lower jaw." Private Carter and a handful of other Alabamians found relative cover in a thicket, where they briefly exchanged point-blank volleys with opposing bluecoats. Rising on command to resume the charge, Carter immediately crumpled with a shot to the chest. A comrade propped him against a tree and tried to give aid, but the private was gushing blood. Absently poking a finger into his wound, Carter babbled a few nonsensical sentences before leaning back and fading into unconsciousness. He was one of the more than one hundred men in the regiment wounded that day.[18] *Photo courtesy of W. S. Hoole Special Collections Library, The University of Alabama*

100

JOHN PURIFOY
copy print
Jerome W. Chambers,
Montgomery

The gunners of the Jeff Davis Artillery had not partici- pated in Stonewall Jackson's famous flank attack on 2 May, but they fired nearly all of their rounds the fol- lowing morning. Commanding one of the battery's four guns was Cpl. John Purifoy, a twenty-one-year- old law student from Wilcox County. The war inter- rupted his education at East Tennessee University in Knoxville, but since joining the artillery, Purifoy had seen plenty of action, going back to the Peninsula Campaign. Chancellorsville, however, proved the youth's most unforgettable experience. At dawn the battery deployed behind the 3rd Alabama Infantry in preparation for a renewal of the attack. Located on the northern edge of the Orange Turnpike, the gunners enjoyed a relatively clear field of fire down the road. At 8:00 A.M. the infantrymen advanced; Purifoy and his comrades followed. With some difficulty the gunners

maneuvered their pieces through the exhausted ranks of Confederate regiments that had attacked in vain earlier that morning. Finally, as the 3rd Alabama initi- ated its assault, the Jeff Davis Artillery unlimbered and laid suppressive fire on a large body of Union guns posted on the not-too-distant Fairview Heights. As Purifoy lined up one of his shots, he noticed an enemy cannonball bearing down upon his section. The corpo- ral coolly calculated that the trajectory was off, so he stood to his gun. The projectile whizzed past the right side of his head, grazed another gunner, and then landed harmlessly behind the battery. Almost immedi- ately Purifoy gave the command to fire in return. By 10:00 A.M. the Jeff Davis Artillery had expended over 300 rounds, firepower that helped drive their Yankee rivals off Fairview.[19] *Photo courtesy of ADAH*

101

Henry Black Wood
ambrotype

Resting among the trees due west of Chancellorsville, Pvt. Henry Wood of the 12th Alabama Infantry could hear the cacophony of battle raging less than a mile away. He knew it was only a matter of time before he and the other fifty men in Company B would be ordered to join the fight. A thirty-three-year-old overseer from Coosa County, Wood was also the proud father of a toddler named Willy, a child he had not seen since his enlistment in the summer of 1861. As his many letters home reveal, frequent thoughts of his son and wife, Sarah Jane, sustained his morale. On the morning of 3 May, however, the imminent clash of arms harshly pushed aside these dreamy images. Part of O'Neal's Brigade, Wood and the 12th Alabama (300 strong) occupied the center of the formation, whose immediate task was to maintain the momentum of the ongoing Rebel assaults against Union forces entrenched around Chancellorsville. Unfortunately, as the Alabamians marched through the dense forest, unit cohesion unraveled. Somehow the two regiments to the left of the 12th fell behind and drifted over to the brigade's right.

Though not realizing it at the time, Private Wood and his comrades were now responsible for protecting the entire Rebel army's left flank. Pressing on, the regiment occupied some abandoned breastworks and commenced firing on enemy units to its front, specifically a nearby battery of Union guns. Just then the Alabamians discovered a large body of bluecoats tramping through the woods to their left. The regiment re-fused its flank in time to repulse a strong enemy assault before launching one of its own. Private Wood recalled the ensuing, desperate clash: "It was an awful time, the heaviest shelling and graping that I ever saw. For any one to pass threw the woods where we went it would loock impossible for men to go threw there without being tourn up with grape shot or shell. The timber is literly torn down. I went threw safe but I thought several times that I had gawn up the spout." The Alabamians held but suffered eighty-two casualties. Company B was especially hard hit, losing twenty men, including its commander, Capt. Henry Cox, whom Wood greatly admired.[20] *Photo courtesy of Wayne Wood*

ENOCH M. VAN DIVER
copy print
May's Studio,
Columbus, Miss.

After weathering a hail of shot and shell for nearly an hour, Capt. Enoch van Diver of the 26th Alabama Infantry could see his unit's tactical objective—the Chancellor House, just north of Orange Plank Road. A thirty-one-year-old resident of Fayette County, Van Diver joined the regiment in October 1861 as a lieutenant. Immediately after the Seven Days' Battles, he gained promotion to captain of Company A (the Dixie Boys). Now, on the morning of 3 May 1863, Van Diver was part of a desperate fight to dislodge the Yankees from their principal stronghold around Chancellorsville. The 26th Alabama originally advanced as part of the left wing of O'Neal's Brigade, but in the chaos of combat and the disorienting nature of the dense forest, the regiment ended up on the brigade's right by the time it reached the Chancellor House. Union batteries and musketry had greatly thinned the brigade's ranks—of its five infantry regiments, only the 26th and 5th Alabama were able to press home an effective assault. Exploiting some confusion among the Yankees, who evidently were readjusting their formations, the Alabamians successfully carried the enemy position sometime after 9:00 A.M. Van Diver and his company helped capture five pieces of artillery and cheered wildly as the regimental colors were planted near the now-gutted home. But the triumph proved short lived, for a Union counterattack hit the Alabamians' left flank and drove them off, with the loss of both regimental flags. Captain Van Diver and other officers in the 26th rallied their men, pitched back into the fray, and managed to recapture their standard (though that of the 5th Alabama remained in enemy hands). Although the regiment suffered over one hundred casualties, including Van Diver, who went down with a shattered ankle, the outcome of the contest was a gratifying moment for all involved. The Union army retreated; the Rebels held the field.
Photo courtesy of ADAH

FLAG OF THE
5TH ALABAMA
INFANTRY
copy print

During the Civil War, battle flags were sacred to the soldiers who fought under them. And so for the men of the 5th Alabama Infantry, the capture of their colors at Chancellorsville was devastating, a loss made all the more exasperating because the Confederates won the battle. Raised at the outset of the war, the 5th comprised Alabamians from the west-central part of the state. Beginning with First Manassas, the regiment saw action in every major engagement in the East. By the spring of 1863, the 5th Alabama marched under a banner sporting a blue St. Andrew's Cross, woven with thirteen stars, on a red background. This pattern was prevalent among all of the regiments in the Army of Northern Virginia—and has since become the endur-

ing symbol of the Confederacy itself. At Chancellorsville the 5th Alabama was part of Stonewall Jackson's storied flank attack on 2 May and the next day was among the few formations to penetrate the inner line of Union entrenchments around the Chancellor House. At this stage of the battle, the 5th Alabama found itself engulfed by a Yankee counterattack. The regiment managed to fight its way out of trouble, but in the process it lost its standard to the 111th Pennsylvania Infantry. The 5th eventually received a replacement flag, and the unit went on to further military heroics, but nothing could ever quite atone for the disgrace of losing the regimental colors on the battlefield. *Photo courtesy of ADAH*

SALEM CHURCH
(postwar image)
copy print

A red-brick edifice built in 1844, Salem Church served the Baptist community of Fredericksburg. On the afternoon of 3 May 1863 (a Sunday), it became the main landmark in a desperate clash during the Battle of Chancellorsville. After falling back before a much larger Union force, Cadmus Wilcox decided to make a final stand with his Alabama brigade on the gently upward-sloping ground just west of the church, which sat at an intersection on Orange Plank Road. The general placed a company from the 9th Alabama Infantry inside the church to act as sharpshooters. The men fortified their position inside by using furniture, stored in the building by local civilians who had evacuated their homes, to reinforce the doors and windows. Around 5:00 P.M. the Alabamians opened fire on the rapidly advancing Yankees. Within minutes hundreds of blue-coats swarmed about the churchyard, striving to hack their way into the sanctuary. One Alabamian reportedly shot at the intruders from the pulpit; another lamented that the fighting had turned the "House of God into a charnel house." Although Union soldiers overpowered another company from the 9th holed up in a nearby log schoolhouse, the Alabamians fighting on the holy ground of Salem Church staved off their assailants. Soon a Confederate counterattack drove away the Yankees and relieved the hard-pressed men inside the church. In 1881, veterans of the engagement around Salem Church revisited the scene. Exterior and interior damage from cannon fire and musketry were still visible. Happily, this later encounter was one of peace.[21] *Photo courtesy of Duke University Rare Book, Manuscript, and Special Collections Library*

YOUNG LEA ROYSTON
daguerreotype

At six feet, seven inches in height, Col. Young Royston of the 8th Alabama Infantry was an officer whom soldiers obeyed. With as many as 1,000 bluecoats bearing down on his position at Salem Church, the colonel ordered his men to stand fast. It was 3 May and this particular Union advance threatened the rear of Lee's army around Chancellorsville. A forty-three-year-old lawyer from Perry County, Royston raised Company A for the 8th Alabama in June 1861, after which he rapidly rose to regimental command. Badly wounded during the Seven Days' Battles, Royston had only recently returned to duty at Chancellorsville, but he showed no signs of hesitation. At Salem Church the colonel deployed his men as the extreme right of Wilcox's Brigade, which held a line perpendicular to Orange Plank Road. Having participated in delaying actions all afternoon, Royston did not have time to entrench his regiment. A slight elevation in ground and a smattering of new-growth trees constituted the only natural cover. Shortly after 5:00 P.M. a massive Union assault struck the brigade's whole line. Charging toward the 8th was a regiment of Pennsylvanians. Royston waited until they were within eighty yards before giving the command to fire. The Alabamians' volley decimated the Keystone ranks, but the enemy returned fire with deadly effect of its own. Among the dozens of Alabamians who fell was Royston himself, several bullets having ripped through his left arm, leaving it dangling at the elbow. Rushed to a field hospital, the colonel likely received medical attention from his brother, Dr. R. T. Royston, the regimental surgeon. Colonel Royston survived and apparently was spared an amputation, but his wound left him permanently crippled. *Photo courtesy of ADAH*

HILARY ABNER HERBERT
copy print

For Lt. Col. Hilary Herbert of the 8th Alabama Infantry, Salem Church was the ultimate test of his combat leadership. While directing fire against Yankee forces to his front, command of the regiment devolved to him when Col. Y. L. Royston went down with a terrible wound. Moments later the 10th Alabama Infantry, on Herbert's left, gave way under a furious assault by a New York regiment. At every point waves of bluecoats seemed poised to engulf the lieutenant colonel and his men. A twenty-nine-year-old lawyer from Butler County, Herbert was born in South Carolina but in 1847 moved to Alabama, where he spent his teenage years on the family's new plantation. After attending school first at the University of Alabama and then the University of Virginia, he practiced law in Greenville. During the secession crisis, Herbert raised a company of state militia that later merged into the 8th Alabama. Wounded and captured at Seven Pines, he was exchanged in time to fight at Sharpsburg, where he was again wounded. These

ostensible heroics aside, it was at Salem Church where the battle-hardened Herbert displayed true tactical brilliance. With Union forces surging on front and flank, the lieutenant colonel ordered seven of his companies to hold the center and right at all costs while he personally led the remaining three companies on his left in a deftly executed backward wheel. This difficult maneuver enabled the Rebels to fire down the whole line of charging New Yorkers. The ensuing volley virtually destroyed the enemy regiment, the Alabamians shooting down over 200 bluecoats. Having broken the Union attack, the men of the 8th participated in a general pursuit of their now-fleeing adversary. "Forward we rush through the woods, and into the fields," Herbert jubilantly recalled, "driving the enemy's line[s] over one another, and as they mingle pell mell in the open field, high above the Confederate yell are heard the voices of officers and men shouting, 'take good aim, boys! Hold your muskets level, and you'll get a Yank!'"[22] *Photo courtesy of ADAH*

ELIHU HAULBY GRIFFIN
ambrotype

They were supposedly looking for shoes, or so thought Pvt. Elihu Griffin and the rest of his comrades in the 5th Alabama Battalion as they neared the western outskirts of Gettysburg, Pennsylvania. Instead, what they found on the morning of 1 July was a strong contingent of Union cavalry armed with breech-loading carbines. Griffin was a twenty-five-year-old overseer from Calhoun County. In August 1861 he and his brother Gabriel joined the Calhoun Sharpshooters, an outfit that soon became Company B, 5th Alabama Infantry Battalion. Beginning with the Peninsula Campaign, Elihu participated in all of the Army of Northern Virginia's major operations without harm, but at Gettysburg his luck ran out. At 8:00 A.M. the battalion formed as the skirmish line for Archer's Brigade, which held the right flank of Maj. Gen. Henry Heth's unfolding divisional attack. The Alabamians' task was to help carry the Union position along McPherson Ridge. Against increasing carbine fire, Griffin trotted toward Willoughby Run, a shallow creek that ran perpendicular to the Confederate line of advance. After thrashing through some thick undergrowth, according to an official report, "the brigade rushed across with a cheer, and met the enemy just beyond." At fifty yards the Alabamians began exchanging volleys with their dismounted adversaries. Griffin went down with a serious wound. Not long after, the just-arrived Iron Brigade of midwesterners launched a powerful counterattack that drove the Rebels back. The bluecoats took seventy-five prisoners, including Griffin and his brother. For the young farmer, his role in the engagement was over, but he enjoyed the dubious distinction of being one of the first casualties in what would become the war's bloodiest battle.[23] *Photo courtesy of Don T. Griffin*

JAMES ERVIN TOMLIN
copy print

Sgt. James Tomlin of the 26th Alabama Infantry had only just rejoined his mates in Company K (the Looxapalila Guards) when the whole regiment went into battle at Gettysburg. Less than two months before, Tomlin had been captured at Chancellorsville and then exchanged shortly thereafter. Much to his imminent chagrin, this twenty-seven-year-old farmer from Fayette County was about to be captured again. Around noon on 1 July, the 26th advanced as the center of O'Neal's Brigade as part of a general attack against Union forces northwest of Gettysburg. The ensuing clash was a disaster for the Alabamians. After only fifteen minutes of ineffectual fire and maneuver, the regiment succumbed to a blistering enemy fusillade that routed the 6th Alabama, to the left of the 26th Alabama, and exposed Tomlin and his comrades to a Yankee flank attack. The sergeant was shot in the groin and left behind as his regiment fell back in confusion. A prisoner once again, this noncommissioned officer would no doubt have taken great offense at his regimental commander's summary of the action: "The loss of the regiment was heavy," reported Lt. Col. John Goodgame. "Some 40 were taken by the enemy, but it is my opinion that every man could have escaped being captured had they done their duty."[24] *Photo courtesy of Eddie Womack Collection, U.S.A.M.H.I.*

ADOLPH PROSKAUER
copy print

Known as the "best dressed man in the regiment," Maj. Adolph Proskauer of the 12th Alabama Infantry was about to get his uniform ruffled as he helped deploy his men into line of battle northwest of Gettysburg. A twenty-five-year-old Jewish immigrant from Breslau, Germany, Proskauer came to Alabama in 1854 and settled in Mobile, where he earned a living as a bookkeeper. In May 1861 he enlisted in the Independent Rifles, a unit made up primarily of fellow Jews and Germans, which became Company C, 12th Alabama. Proskauer rose quickly through the ranks, in part because of his charming rapport with the men (particularly his peculiar fondness for fried mushrooms), but mostly because of his combat abilities. His wounds at Sharpsburg and Chancellorsville attested to his courage, while his brilliant performance on a tactics examination in early 1863 displayed his military intellect. Going into Gettysburg, Proskauer was a proven leader. Around noon on 1 July, the 12th Alabama marched as the right-flank regiment in O'Neal's Brigade. The overall attack was ill conceived; enemy forces to the regiment's front were strongly posted behind a stone wall abutting Mummasburg Road, leading into the town. Moments after advancing, the Alabamians came under fire and for the next fifteen minutes engaged in a furious standup fight. Having detailed his horse to speed wounded men to the rear, Proskauer strode the line directing volleys. In the words of one officer in the regiment, "Our gallant Jew Major smoked his cigars calmly and coolly in the thickest of the fight." Suddenly, the brigade's left gave way under a Union flank attack that compelled the 12th Alabama to beat a hasty retreat. Proskauer helped rally the men and get them back into the fight later in the day.[25]

After resting on 2 July, the 12th Alabama would go into action again on 3 July as part of a full-scale assault on Culp's Hill. O'Neal's Brigade failed to make any headway then and for three hours would remain pinned along the slopes. Either here or earlier in the battle, Proskauer received a flesh wound to his cheek. Regardless, the "Jew Major" would continue to encourage the men of his regiment throughout their three-day ordeal. *Photo courtesy of ADAH*

LAWRENCE HOUSTON
SCRUGGS
copy print
Anderson and Webb,
Huntsville

Perspiring heavily, Lt. Col. Lawrence Scruggs of the 4th Alabama Infantry quickly put his regiment into line of battle just east of Emmitsburg Road on the afternoon of 2 July. Although he and his men had just finished marching two dozen miles, their next movement would be under fire from Union defenders gathering on and around Little Round Top. A cotton factor from Madison County, the twenty-seven-year-old Scruggs had fought in every engagement with the 4th Alabama since First Manassas. As captain of Company I, he proved his valor with wounds received at Malvern Hill and at Sharpsburg. As the acting regimental commander at Gettysburg, Scruggs enjoyed the unwavering trust of the 340 men in the ranks. It was nearly 4:00 P.M. when he led the 4th into action, guiding them straight toward the base of Little Round Top. Crossing a plowed field on the Slyder Farm, the Alabamians came under long-range artillery fire and sporadic rifle shots from a Yankee skirmish line along Plum Run. Scrambling over this natural obstacle, Scruggs urged his screaming men forward. "We arrived at a stone fence, behind which the enemy's first line of infantry was posted," he remembered, "which position we soon succeeded in carrying with the bayonet." Halting briefly to realign his companies, Scruggs resumed the advance "up the mountain under a galling fire." Suddenly, a day's worth of physical exertion caught up to Scruggs; he collapsed, joining scores of other men prostrated by the heat. While he recovered in the rear, command passed to Maj. Thomas Coleman, who conducted a series of vain attacks farther up the slope. That evening Scruggs resumed command, distributed fresh supplies, and fortified his position. He also counted the cost of failure at Little Round Top: eighty-seven men killed, wounded, and missing.[26]
Photo courtesy of ADAH

112

"Slaughter Pen"
stereograph
Alexander Gardner

A rocky patch of ground lying in the Plum Run gorge between Devil's Den and Little Round Top, the Slaughter Pen was the scene of a fierce clash between the 44th Alabama and the 4th Maine. Late on the after-noon of 2 July, Evander Law dispatched the 44th, under Col. William Perry, to eliminate a Union battery lobbing shells from Devil's Den. As the Alabamians entered the gorge, Yankee infantrymen hiding in support of the guns rose and fired at short range. Within seconds two dozen Alabamians lay dead and another sixty sustained wounds—fully a quarter of the entire regiment. The survivors hunkered behind boulders and shot back as best they could. Refusing to stay pinned, Colonel Perry

shouted above the din a command to charge. "The men sprang forward over the rocks," he proudly recalled, "swept the position, and took possession of the heights, capturing 40 or 50 prisoners around the battery and among the cliffs." Soon the 48th Alabama and other friendly forces arrived to consolidate Confederate con-trol over Devil's Den, repelling several enemy counter-attacks in the process. In the days after the battle, wartime photographer Alexander Gardner captured this gruesome image of the Slaughter Pen, one that included two Rebel corpses, in all likelihood the remains of two soldiers from the 44th Alabama.[27]
Photo courtesy of Library of Congress

113

WILLIAM CALVIN OATES
copy print

After wasting time chasing a team of U.S. sharpshoot-ers through the trees and then arguing with a brigade staff officer over tactical options, Col. William Oates of the 15th Alabama Infantry finally executed his part of Law's assault on Little Round Top. As the extreme right of the Army of Northern Virginia, the colonel and his men would soon be fighting against the extreme left of the Army of the Potomac. A twenty-nine-year-old lawyer from Henry County, Oates was a powerfully built man with the mien of natural leadership. After raising Company G, 15th Alabama, his combat ability gained him steady promotion to regimental command. Late on the afternoon of 2 July, he led more than 400 men into the fully raging battle at Gettysburg. The steep, wooded slopes of Little Round Top, combined with thickening gun smoke, made it difficult for the colonel to orchestrate the actions of more than a few dozen men at a time. Nevertheless, Oates pushed his weary soldiers forward. Moments later at least two blue regiments opened fire from behind stone breast-works. Oates recalled that his boys "advanced about half way to the enemy's position, but the fire was so

destructive that my line wavered like a man trying to walk against a strong wind, and then slowly, doggedly, gave back a little."

Determined to prevail, the colonel rallied his men, who charged and retreated as many as five times, driv-ing back Yankee follow-on sorties in each instance. At one point, in an effort to spur the men on his left wing, Oates leaped onto a boulder and rapidly emptied his revolver at the Federal lines. That having failed to moti-vate, he then dashed to his right wing and led several companies in a final, futile lunge toward the summit. The Alabamians soon engaged their adversary in chaotic hand-to-hand combat. "My dead and wounded were then nearly as great in number as those still on duty," Oates noted years later. "They literally covered the ground." As he tried to disseminate an order to retreat, the bluecoats launched a full-scale counterattack that shattered the remnants of his regiment: "we ran like a herd of cattle." In all the 15th Alabama suffered over 160 casualties. Among them was the colonel's beloved younger brother, John, who died from his wounds while in captivity.[28] *Photo courtesy of ADAH*

FRANK HENRY MUNDY
copy print from
Confederate Veteran

For several hours, 1st Lt. Frank Mundy of the 11th Alabama Infantry loitered with the rest of the regiment in an open field under a hot sun waiting for orders to commence their portion of a massive echelon attack against the Union left flank at Gettysburg. A twenty-six-year-old store clerk from Greene County, Mundy was a well-educated Englishman who immigrated to Alabama in 1855. He was a gregarious individual who excelled at sports and saw the war as an adventure. Among the first to enlist in what became Company B, Mundy had participated in every major engagement since the Peninsula Campaign. At 6:30 P.M. on 2 July, he and the 11th advanced as the center of Wilcox's Brigade. The Alabamians were soon exchanging fire with two regiments of bluecoats deployed behind plank fences along Emmitsburg Road. The lieutenant

and his comrades never slowed their pace as they struck the right flank of a New Hampshire regiment, rolled up the enemy formation, and basically shattered the Union position in that sector. As they pursued their adversary up Cemetery Ridge, the Alabamians encountered much-stiffer opposition. Mundy's company commander, George Clark, vividly related the scene: "The air was thick with missiles of every character, the roar of the artillery practically drowning the shrill hiss of the Minnies." Although the men of the 11th Alabama inflicted many casualties, General Wilcox ordered the whole brigade to fall back under the mounting pressure of Union reinforcements. Unfortunately, Mundy did not retreat quickly enough and found himself a captive as the sun went down.[29]

JOHN CHAPMAN
GOODGAME
copy print

As he stared up the wooded slopes of Culp's Hill in the early morning hours of 3 July 1863, Lt. Col. John Goodgame of the 26th Alabama Infantry did not relish the idea of storming the strong Union forces posted there. The Battle of Gettysburg, however, was entering its third day, and duty called. A twenty-seven-year-old schoolteacher from Coosa County, Goodgame was actually a member of the 12th Alabama Infantry, having risen from orderly sergeant to executive officer in just over a year. But after Chancellorsville, where the 26th lost a great many officers, including its commander (John Garvin, wounded in action), Goodgame assumed temporary command during the Gettysburg Campaign. His unfamiliarity with the men may have contributed to the regiment's uneven performance on the first day of the battle, when the 26th Alabama suffered over forty casualties as part of a poorly executed brigade attack just outside of town. There was little time to lament that day's mistakes, though, for after resting on 2 July, Goodgame and his men went into action again at Culp's Hill. The overall plan was for the Confederates in that area to draw enemy reserves away from Cemetery Ridge in preparation for Lee's grand attack against the Union

center later in the day. Advancing as part of O'Neal's Brigade—the Alabama regiments in line from left to right: 6th, 12th, 26th, and 3rd—Goodgame and his men hit the Union position at 8:00 A.M. The assigned target was a log fort situated on a spur on the northern side of the hill; it proved impossible to reach. "The brigade moved forward in fine style," Col. Edward O'Neal recounted, "under a terrific fire of grape and small-arms, and gained a hill near the enemy's works." From that point, however, the Alabamians hugged the ground, "exposed to a murderous fire," pinned and useless for the next three hours. Shortly before noon, the brigade managed to extricate itself, with O'Neal recasting the failure as a tactical triumph: "Officers and men fought bravely, and held their ground until ordered to fall back." In his own report Lieutenant Colonel Goodgame was more forthright: "Engaged the enemy at an early hour, but were unable to dislodge him from his fortified position." He then listed the regiment's losses for the entire battle at seven killed, fifty-eight wounded, and sixty-five missing (mostly captured), about two-thirds of that tally coming around Culp's Hill.[30] *Photo courtesy ADAH*

BIRKETT DAVENPORT FRY
from The Photographic
History of the Civil War,
by Francis T. Miller

Col. B. D. Fry of the 13th Alabama Infantry had seen more combat in his forty-one years than just about anyone else in the Army of Northern Virginia. A cotton manufacturer from Tallapoosa County, Fry had fought under Winfield Scott during the Mexican War, had filibustered with William Walker in Nicaragua, and had suffered gunshot wounds at Seven Pines, Sharpsburg, and Chancellorsville. Yet as he gazed across a sunny Pennsylvania landscape toward the fortified Union lines along Cemetery Ridge, the colonel sensed that his most exciting exploit lay just across the fields. Only two days before he had assumed command of Archer's Brigade amid hot fighting. Now, on 3 July, he was to lead his old regiment, the 5th Alabama Battalion, and two regiments of Tennesseans as the vanguard of Lee's grand frontal attack at Gettysburg. "It was then understood that my command should be considered the centre," Fry recalled, "and that in the assault both divisions should allign themselves by it." After briefly reminiscing about Chapultepec with Maj. Gen. George Pickett, for whom the great charge would

be named, Fry ordered his men to lie down during the preparatory cannonade. At 3:00 P.M. the colonel gave the signal to move out: "The men sprang up with cheerful alacrity, and the long line advanced." Immediately Union batteries opened on Fry's brigade; the colonel received a shell fragment in his right shoulder. Despite mounting casualties, the Rebel infantrymen pressed onward. "Strong as was the position of the enemy," Fry noted, "it seemed that such determination could not fail." Mere yards from the Yankee breastworks, the colonel went down with a bullet to his thigh. He waved off assistance and instead urged his men to carry the ridge. Lying prostrate in a cloud of smoke, Fry soon heard the disheartening jubilation of the Union defenders: the assault had failed, and the colonel became a prisoner. As he rested in a field hospital, Fry noticed a Yankee soldier with a nasty shoulder wound. The man explained that the color bearer of the 13th Alabama had impaled him with the lance head of the flag shaft. Fry inwardly chuckled at his foe's misfortune.[31]

117

Chapter 5

Defending the Heart of Dixie

In the early summer of 1862, the military situation in the western Confederacy was bleak. One Union army of nearly 70,000 under Maj. Gen. Ulysses S. Grant was preparing to advance deeper into Mississippi—its goal, Vicksburg and with it control over the mighty river. Another Union army of more than 30,000 under Maj. Gen. Don Carlos Buell was already marching through northern Alabama toward Chattanooga, possession of which would open Georgia to invasion. For Alabama Confederates, the outcome of these two operations was of particular concern, for failure to halt them risked exposing their native state—the "Heart of Dixie"—to invasion and conquest. In 1862 and 1863 the geography of war in the West formed a destructive arc around Alabama; titanic battles occurred in northern Mississippi, Middle Tennessee (and beyond into Kentucky), and northern Georgia. The Alabamians who participated in these campaigns won fewer laurels than their counterparts in the Army of Northern Virginia, yet their perseverance in combat helped temporarily spare their homeland the depredations of hard war.

Confronting the dual Yankee invasion was an array of small Confederate armies and detachments spread over a wide front from East Tennessee to central Mississippi. Alabamians composed a significant portion of this manpower: at least two dozen regiments of infantry, nine batteries of artillery, and three regiments of cavalry. By this time they had also gained a nickname—"Yellowhammers"—after the common flicker that would become the state bird in 1927. The principal fighting force in the area was the Army of Mississippi under Gen. Braxton Bragg. Though disliked by soldiers for his rigid sense of discipline and by officers for his irascible personality, Bragg was an able strategist who understood the principle of offense. Beginning in June, he dramatically turned the military tide by implementing one of the most ambitious Confederate operations of the entire war. Leaving a sizeable contingent to contain Grant, Bragg concentrated the bulk of his forces, in all about 40,000 men (including 5,000 Alabamians), in the eastern half of Tennessee, where his army crossed in two columns into Kentucky in mid-September. These unexpected movements forced

Buell to cancel his ponderous drive on Chattanooga and pursue the Rebels north.

Bragg's promising invasion, however, soon bogged down as the commander brooded over what to do, especially after Kentuckians refused to rally around the Confederate banner. After several weeks of cautious maneuvering in central Kentucky, the opposing forces clashed in the bizarre Battle of Perryville. Incorrectly concluding that a Union army approaching from the west was a feint, Bragg kept his main body, including most of his Alabama regiments, farther north at Frankfort, the state's capital. Thus, a mere 16,000 Confederates faced an imposing adversary of 55,000 Federals. Nevertheless, it was the Rebels who, on the afternoon of 8 October, initiated the main action at Perryville. While the 1st and 3rd Alabama Cavalry distracted Union forces due west of the town, three infantry divisions attacked from the northern outskirts, slashing into the Union left wing. Advancing as part of the Rebel left, the 33rd and 45th Alabama Infantry Regiments were heading into their first major military engagement. Fighting in a brigade commanded by Brig. Gen. S. A. M. Wood, the 33rd Alabama helped storm a key Union position at Dixville Crossroads. Determined to hold the junction, these Yellowhammers gamely stood their ground until sunset, delivering numerous volleys into nearby Union lines before finally falling back under the weight of enemy counterattacks. Out of 380 men engaged, the regiment sustained 170 casualties. Just to the south, the 45th Alabama (of Col. Samuel Powell's brigade) participated in a fierce supporting attack. One observer noted that the Alabamians went into battle "yelling like fiends broke loose from pandemonium."[1] Caught in Yankee crossfire, the 45th withdrew with the rest of its brigade under cover of darkness. Happily for the Confederates, many Union formations sat idle during the contest; an acoustic shadow left them unaware that combat was raging only a few miles away. But Perryville was hardly the decisive battle Bragg desired, instead marking an anticlimax to the whole invasion. Logistically unable to stay in Kentucky, the Rebel army retreated back to Middle Tennessee.

While Bragg's invasion of Kentucky unfolded, those Alabama regiments assigned to protect northern Mississippi participated in the often-forgotten battles of Iuka and Corinth. The Confederate commanders in the area—Maj. Gens. Earl Van Dorn and Sterling Price—sought to destroy Grant's occupation forces, now depleted after sending reinforcements to Buell's army. Grant was no idler, however, and ordered two of his detachments to converge on Price's 15,000-man force at Iuka, one to go in from the west and the other from the south. On 19 September Price preempted the trap with a sortie against the southern column of 17,000 Federals. In the wild melee that followed, the 37th Alabama Infantry received its baptism of fire. Held in reserve at the outset, the regiment participated in a late-afternoon attack against the Union right flank. Toward dusk, the Yellowhammers fixed bayonets, charged into a regiment of Missourians, and clashed in hand-to-hand combat before retiring from the field; both regiments sustained seventy-five casualties each. Iuka was a tactical defeat, but during the night, Price's army slipped away and linked with Van Dorn's command.

At the end of September, Van Dorn and Price moved their combined forces to Corinth, possession of which would undermine Union control over the region. The town was well fortified and the opposing forces about equal in strength at roughly 20,000 men apiece, but the Rebels attacked nonetheless. On 3 October they overran the outer defenses to the north of the town, though the combat was fierce. The performance of the 35th and 49th Alabama Infantry Regiments during an assault on the Union left flank epitomized the war's oscillations between cowardice and courage. Part of Brig. Gen. Albert Rust's brigade, both were veteran units, but charging over uneven terrain against an entrenched enemy proved too much for the men of the 49th; decimated by canister from sixty yards, these Alabamians broke and fled the battlefield. The 35th, however, though similarly rent, rallied and successfully carried the Union position, capturing two guns. The division commander, Maj. Gen. Mansfield Lovell, paid the regiment a high compliment: "Well, boys, you did that handsomely."[2]

On 4 October the Confederate army launched a full-scale assault against the inner defenses at Corinth. The outstanding Yellowhammer unit on this day was the 42nd Alabama Infantry, 700 strong. Part of a general attack against the Union left flank, it marched alongside regiments from Arkansas, Mississippi, and Texas. Their objective was the formidable Battery Robinette, whose three guns commanded a vast stretch of open ground over which the Alabamians had to advance. Despite intense artillery fire, the 42nd Alabama briefly seized the strong point, though losing over half its strength in the process. But other Rebel attacks failed all along the line; the Federals had won.

The Battles of Perryville and Corinth proved inconclusive for the Confederacy. Grant remained strongly entrenched in northern Mississippi, while Buell's old command, now under Maj. Gen. William Rosecrans, posted itself in Nashville. Still, Confederate forces had bought their nation precious time. For Alabamians in particular, the recent offensive operations also had the salutary effect of liberating the northern part of their state from Union occupation. Moreover, the autumnal campaigns, combined with Shiloh earlier in the year, had transformed most Alabama regiments in the West into veteran outfits. And in defending the Heart of Dixie, combat experience soon became the Confederacy's most valuable asset. While encamped in Middle Tennessee, Bragg reorganized his extant force of 36,000 into the Army of Tennessee. Alabama's contribution consisted of thirteen infantry regiments, five artillery batteries, and four cavalry units. Nine of the infantry regiments and two batteries served in the division of Maj. Gen. Jones Withers of Mobile.

Toward the end of December 1862, the new Army of Tennessee went into action at the Battle of Murfreesboro. Ordered to drive the Rebels out of Tennessee, Rosecrans sallied out of Nashville with an army of 42,000 bluecoats. Shortly after Christmas Day, the opposing forces deployed astride Stones River northwest of Murfreesboro (thirty miles east of Nashville). Intent on seizing the initiative, Bragg shifted most of his army to the western side of the river and ordered an attack against the Union right flank at dawn on 31 December. Leading the first wave was Withers's Division, posted in the center of the Confederate battle line where it would constitute the pivot upon which the Rebel left wing would swing in behind the Union position. Bursting through the frigid, early morning mist, the graybacks caught many Federal units by surprise. An Alabama brigade under Col. John Q. Loomis rapidly gained ground, his regiments advancing in line of battle, from left to right: the 50th, 39th, 25th, 19th, and 22nd—in all about 2,000 soldiers. Screaming the now familiar Rebel yell, the Alabamians sloshed over a muddy cornfield, driving the Union defenders back about 300 yards. As the brigade entered a forested area, however, regimental cohesion unraveled just as enemy resistance stiffened. The 50th Alabama, for example, pushed beyond the support of friendly formations and soon found itself fighting alone. Pounded by a Union counterattack, the regiment fell back after losing 200 men out of 600 engaged. The brigade as a whole suffered 670 casualties; the Yellowhammers had been soundly repulsed. Although Confederate units elsewhere tore through panicked Union formations, it had been Loomis's bad luck to run into Federal veterans led by the fiery Brig. Gen. Philip Sheridan. As a brigade of Tennesseans passed through to resume the attack, a dejected Alabamian warned them, "You'll find it the hottest place that you ever struck."[3]

Attacking alongside Loomis's right flank was Col. A. M. Manigault's brigade containing three Alabama regiments (the 24th, 28th, and 34th) along with two from South Carolina. Copses of cedar trees delayed the advance of these units so that their attack on Sheridan's line went in largely after Loomis's had already played out. Nevertheless, the Yellowhammers in this sector mounted three charges, the last one, ably supported by Capt. John Waters's Alabama battery, finally helping dislodge the Union defenders. Exhausted and almost out of ammunition, only a few Alabama units were involved in the later fighting that day. Instead, many of the enlisted men prowled abandoned parts of the battlefield, scooping up better-quality rifles or looting the bodies of the enemy dead. At the distant front, the now fully rallied Union army withstood late-afternoon Rebel attacks; the day ended in stalemate.

After a one-day lull, Bragg renewed the battle with an impetuous assault against the Union left flank on the other side of Stones River. All of the general's subordinates discouraged such an attack, for the Federals there held fortified high ground backed by nearly sixty cannon. The result was a disaster. Among the unfortunate participants were the men of the 41st Alabama Infantry in Brig. Gen. R. W. Hanson's brigade. Under relentless shelling, the Alabamians were ripped apart along with the rest of the attacking force. An Alabama battery under Capt. Henry Semple tried in vain to suppress the Yankee artillery but lost twenty gunners and fourteen horses without inflicting any serious damage. In two days of combat, the rival armies each lost a third of their combat strength, but Murfreesboro was a Confederate defeat. The Army of Tennessee withdrew to south-central Tennessee and went into winter quarters. Pvt. Thomas Warrick of the 34th Alabama aptly summed up the downcast spirits among the rank and file: "I can inform you that I have seen the Monkey Show at last and I dont Waunt to see it no more," he wrote his wife soon after the battle. "Men was shot Evey poshinton that you mit Call for. . . . Som had there hedes shot off and som ther armes and leges. Som was Shot too in the midel. I can tell you that I am tirde of Ware."[4]

After Murfreesboro the cynosure of war in the West moved squarely over Vicksburg. In the spring of 1862, Grant executed his most skillful offensive of the war: a swift, indirect approach toward the city that left the Confederate high command confused at every turn. Opposing this incursion was a Rebel army of 40,000 men under Lt. Gen. John Pemberton. Eleven regiments of Alabama infantry served in this force, but the five in Brig. Gen. Edward Tracy's brigade—1,500 men in all—saw the most action. Their efforts to defend the "Gibraltar of the Confederacy," however, proved an exercise in gallant futility.

At the end of April, Grant began transporting his field army of 40,000 across the Mississippi River forty miles south of Vicksburg. In a belated effort to contest the crossing, Pemberton sent a contingent of 6,000 men, including Tracy's Brigade, to block Federal access to the nearby town of Port Gibson. After an all-night march, the Alabamians deployed against the enemy left wing and then dozed in line of battle along one of only two serviceable roads in the area. The immediate terrain was heavily wooded and cut by numerous ravines. At dawn on 1 May, the brigade roused for action, its regiments facing southwest and aligned, from right to left: 20th, 30th, 31st, and the 23rd Alabama. (Tracy later reluctantly dispatched the 23rd Alabama to help reinforce the Confederate left astride the other road but soon restored his line with the arrival of his last regiment, the 46th Alabama.) The Yankees, confident that sheer numbers would bowl their foe over, lunged against Tracy's position with a frontal assault. Topography and Alabama tenacity, however, stymied the initial charge. While striving to launch a counterattack, Tracy received a fatal wound. Col. Isham Garrott assumed command and, with the help of a battery of Virginians, fended off repeated attacks until sunset. During the night, the Alabamians slipped back to Vicksburg. Port Gibson was a nasty scrap that cost the Alabama brigade 272 casualties with little to show for the sacrifice.

Over the next fortnight, Grant's bluecoats moved quickly into central Mississippi, where they sacked Jackson, the state capital, before turning sharply westward back toward Vicksburg. On 16 May Grant's vanguard of 29,000 men smashed into Pemberton's hastily established defensive line along Baker's Creek, twenty miles outside the city. Tracy's Alabama brigade, now commanded by Brig. Gen. Stephen D. Lee, anchored the Rebel left flank at Champion Hill. Lee braced for an enemy approach from the east until scouts from the 20th Alabama warned him of a massive Union column coming in rapidly from the north. With noticeable urgency, Lee realigned his infantry along a forested ridgeline just as the Yankees came into sight. The regiments now faced north, their front extending a mile, from left to right: the 23rd, 30th, 46th, 31st, and 20th Alabama. After repulsing the first wave of attackers, the 23rd Alabama carried out a foolhardy sortie against a well-placed enemy battery; heavy cross-fire sent the Yellowhammers scampering back up the ridge. Nonetheless, Lee's men held their ground until the Yankee onslaught routed a brigade of Georgians tied into the Alabamians' right flank. After falling back 600 yards, Lee established a new line, from which his men participated in a mid-afternoon general counterattack. Here the brigade's luck ran out as the five regiments lost cohesion and direction in their pell-mell rush through the woods. The Alabamians were soon engulfed in a tide of charging Yankee formations. The 46th was cut off entirely, and many of the men forced to surrender; the rest of the brigade narrowly avoided a similar fate. Even as the whole Rebel army retreated, Lee found an opportunity to praise his soldiers. "Boys, there are not enough of you," he declared. "If there were, we would redeem the day yet."[5] The Alabama brigade lost 263 men at Champion Hill.

No sooner had Pemberton's demoralized forces withdrawn into the ostensible safety of Vicksburg's fortifications than Grant's victorious army stormed the city on 19 and 22 May. Lee's brigade bore the brunt of the second attack. Occupying the Railroad Redoubt, a strong position southeast of the city, the Alabamians endured a heavy artillery barrage, then barely withstood the subsequent assault. For the next six weeks, they stolidly held their section of an eight-mile defensive perimeter until Pemberton formally ended the siege by surrendering both the army and the city on 4 July. Five days later a smaller Confederate garrison at Port Hudson, Louisiana, farther south along the river, also surrendered. Within days of these inglorious defeats, the surviving Alabamians began a long trudge home as parolees. Most eventually returned to fight another day.

The twin disasters at Gettysburg and Vicksburg in early July 1863 prompted Josiah Gorgas of Tuscaloosa to opine in his diary, "the Confederacy totters to its destruction."[6] Adding to the misery was the capture of Chattanooga in early September. After reorganizing his Army of the Cumberland in the wake of Murfreesboro, General Rosecrans conducted a skillful campaign of maneuver throughout the summer that ousted Bragg's Army of Tennessee from the state altogether. As the Union army proceeded to advance into northern Georgia, however, the Rebels lashed back on 18–20 September at the Battle of Chickamauga. Frustrated by a season of retreat, the Army of Tennessee was eager for a fight, and with the arrival of Longstreet's I Corps from the Army of Northern Virginia, the Confederates actually outnumbered their adversary during the battle,: 66,000 to 58,000. Among the reinforcements was Law's Brigade (temporarily under Col. James Sheffield), with its five regiments of seasoned infantrymen. Bragg's force, therefore, contained a sizeable contingent of Alabamians: twenty-three infantry regiments, six infantry battalions, eight batteries, and four cavalry units.

Chickamauga was the bloodiest engagement of the war in the western theater. Probes and skirmishes on 18 September gave way to an all-out slugfest the following afternoon. The armies faced each other in roughly parallel lines running northeast to southwest. Bragg concentrated his attacks that day against the Yankee left flank (the northern end of the line). Due to the densely wooded countryside, the fighting occurred mostly as fierce, chaotic clashes between isolated formations. Thrashing through the trees southwest of some farmland called Brock Field, three Alabama regiments (the 18th, 36th, and 38th) under Brig. Gen. Henry Clayton soon found themselves pinned down by withering fire from eight enemy regiments. Clayton managed to extricate his men and later rejoin the battle, but the brigade's losses exceeded 600 for the day. Colonel Sheffield's command fared little better. Rushing into action shortly after Clayton, these regiments crashed blindly into the Union lines along LaFayette Road. "We got scattered as we always do in the charge," griped Capt. Joab Goodson of the 44th Alabama.[7] A savage Federal counterattack blindsided the Alabamians, driving them back several hundred yards. Reinforced later by other units, the two Alabama brigades helped push the enemy across the road but advanced no farther.

Nightfall brought no relief as several commanders continued to press their attacks. The 16th, 33rd, and 45th Alabama Regiments in Wood's Brigade suffered grievously from this rash decision. Stumbling across Winfrey Field, these units came under coruscating bursts of rifle fire from the tree line opposite. Despite the ensuing chaos, which included some instances of friendly fire, the Alabamians managed to capture the field and bivouac on the far side, though at a cost of 200 men.

The next day brought more relentless pummeling against the Union left flank. About 11:00 A.M., however, the Confederate left wing under Longstreet achieved a genuine, and sudden, breakthrough farther south against the Union right. His corps charged just as a Union division departed the line to strengthen beleaguered defenders at the northern end of the battlefield. Into this gap streamed thousands of howling Rebels. Advancing on Longstreet's right, Sheffield's brigade routed an enemy regiment

that had just left its breastworks but then stalled against desperate Union rearguard actions. The Confederates' greatest success came on their far-left flank, where eight fresh Alabama regiments under Brig. Gens. Zach Deas and Arthur Manigault waded into unhinged Union formations. Deas's Brigade (in line, from left to right: 22nd, 50th, 39th, and 19th Alabama, with the 25th in reserve) bounded 600 yards, overwhelming a hapless Illinois regiment in the process. A hasty Union counterattack failed to stop the brigade's progress. Instead, Deas again plowed into his opponent and pushed his brigade on several hundred more yards. The Yankees "scattered to the four winds," an ecstatic Lt. James Frazer of the 50th Alabama recalled, "it was the quickest and prettiest fight I ever saw."[8] On Deas's left, Manigault's three Alabama regiments, plus two from South Carolina, made similarly impressive gains. At a place known as the Widow Glenn House, the Alabamians turned the flank of a brigade of midwestern regiments, shot down a full battery of gunners, and bagged hundreds of prisoners. The sudden appearance of Union reinforcements armed with repeating rifles, however, hindered any further advance. But the damage was done; Yellowhammers had helped shatter the entire right flank of the Union army.

By early afternoon, with half of Rosecrans's army fleeing to Chattanooga, the Army of Tennessee was on the verge of a fantastic victory. Remaining Union forces under the redoubtable Maj. Gen. George Thomas, however, waged a dogged rearguard action along an eminence called Snodgrass Hill. Bragg hurled his whole army against this well-fortified position, but every assault failed. For their part, Deas and Manigault came up from the south and tried to get in behind the hill at Horseshoe Ridge, but Union reinforcements arrived just in time. With swollen tongues, black lips, and hoarse lungs, the Alabamians' assault lacked cohesion and vigor. The climax of the battle came at 4:00 P.M., when Longstreet ordered his final reserves, a brigade comprised mostly of Alabama volunteers under Brig. Gen.

Archibald Gracie, to crack the Union line. The nearly 1,900 soldiers (including a regiment of Tennesseans) in Gracie's Brigade were well trained and just about the only fresh troops anywhere on the battlefield, but they were not combat tested. Nevertheless, they stormed Snodgrass Hill with élan. Passing through a blizzard of musketry and canister, the Alabama formations reached the crest, where they grappled with the enemy for ninety minutes before attrition and lack of ammunition compelled them to retreat; the brigade lost 700 men. During the night, Thomas conducted an orderly withdrawal. Still, Chickamauga was a victory for the Confederacy. "Never did men more fully perform their whole duty," Pvt. W. H. Cunningham of the 19th Alabama exulted in its aftermath. "The day's work was one continual charge of the bayonet—that terrible weapon which invariably wins when properly manned and used in the right cause."[9] This glowing assessment belies the grim reality of the battle's casualty list: 18,000 Rebels lost to 16,000 Federals.

Toward the end of September, the Army of Tennessee besieged their vanquished foe in Chattanooga. Confederate forces occupied all of the high ground, specifically Tunnel Hill to the northeast, the six-mile long Missionary Ridge due east, and Lookout Mountain, which towered 1,100 feet over the city from the southwest. From these vantage points, the Rebels denied Rosecrans the Tennessee River as a supply line. The Union army in and around Chattanooga appeared doomed, but never were looks more deceiving. The Confederate chain of command suffered from longstanding internecine rivalries that both undermined morale among the soldiers and fostered careless leadership in the battles to come. Conversely, Federal generalship proved bold and resourceful. Within a month, Grant arrived with substantial reinforcements and initiated a series of actions that lifted the siege. Throughout, Alabama soldiers witnessed firsthand each phase of the campaign. On the night of 27 October, a Union strike force crossed the Tennessee and surprised the

4th and 15th Alabama Infantry Regiments at Brown's Ferry, just downriver from Chattanooga. The following night Law's Brigade participated in a bungled counterattack in the Wauhatchie Valley. Union forces had reopened the city's lifeline and gained a foothold at the base of Lookout Mountain.

For the next few weeks, Grant steadily improved his position around the city, his combat strength growing to 56,000 men, while Bragg either remained passive or unwisely dispatched badly needed units on far-flung operations that reduced his numbers to 46,000 troops. (In mid-November, for instance, he sent Longstreet's corps, including two brigades of Alabamians, on a boondoggle to capture Knoxville.) Toward the end of November, Grant confidently attacked Bragg's inert army with a double envelopment against the flanks at Lookout Mountain and Tunnel Hill. As a diversionary prelude to these turning movements, two Union divisions moved against a Confederate outpost on Orchard Knob, a small hill between Missionary Ridge and the outskirts of the city. Defending this position was the 24th Alabama Infantry on the right and 28th Alabama Infantry on the left. On the afternoon of 23 November, the men in these regiments watched nervously as nearly 5,000 bluecoats methodically advanced toward them. The 24th Alabama delivered a few harassing volleys, then beat a retreat back to the ridge, but Maj. Lavelle Butler of the 28th Alabama foolishly ordered his men to hold their ground. Assailed from front and flank, these Alabamians soon fled in disorder, the regiment losing its flag and almost 200 of its men.

On 24 November Union forces commenced their assault up the slope of Lookout Mountain. Despite the terrain advantages, Confederate resistance was hampered by an intermittent fog that ensconced enemy movements. Among the defenders were two brigades containing eight Alabama regiments that had surrendered at Vicksburg and only recently been reconstituted. Serving as the main picket line, the 37th Alabama was nearly overwhelmed by fast-moving Yankee columns. Reforming at the northern summit of the mountain, the regiment joined the 40th Alabama and two Mississippi units in a hectic clash around the Craven House. The wet ground posed as great a challenge as the swirling gunfire. "I stepped on a slippery rock," Lt. Samuel Sprott of the 40th Alabama remembered, "and went sliding down the mountain like a shot out of a shovel."[10] (Sprott survived and returned to the fight.) Just before 2:00 P.M. the 20th Alabama arrived to deliver a timely flank attack, which helped stabilize the line until nightfall. But the Confederate hold on the mountain was now untenable; Bragg abandoned it and withdrew his men to Missionary Ridge.

The climax at Chattanooga came on 25 November. When his attack against the Confederate right at Tunnel Hill bogged down, Grant sought to break the deadlock with a massive demonstration against Missionary Ridge. Among the defenders dispersed along the crest of the ridge were four Alabama infantry regiments protecting the left, eight more dug in at the center, and eleven posted on the right to bolster the line during the fight around Tunnel Hill. Bragg's defenses should have been impregnable; its 400-foot elevation offered natural defenses and the Rebels had had weeks to fortify themselves. But a host of preparatory missteps made the Confederate line shockingly vulnerable to a frontal attack. The most egregious was an engineering blunder that resulted in many units digging in not on the military crest of the ridge, which would maximize their field of fire, but on the physical crest, which limited their view of the terrain directly to their front.

At midafternoon, when the Yankees hit the first line of trenches at the base, chaos swept the Rebel ranks. In Deas's Brigade, for instance, some Alabamians scurried up to the summit while others held their ground only to get swamped by waves of bluecoats. Riding the impetus of this initial success, the attacking Federals decided impromptu to storm the whole ridgeline. Unable to lay down effective fire, the Confederate center disintegrated as over 20,000 screaming Yankees penetrated the summit entrenchments at multiple points. Alabamians in Manigault's Brigade managed a patchwork holding action near the center, but when neighboring brigades gave way, they too retreated, having suffered about 370 casualties (including some South Carolinians). On the extreme left flank, Union forces literally overran the Alabama brigade of Col. James Holtzclaw (18th, 32nd/58th, 36th, and 38th Regiments), which lost nearly 700 men as prisoners. Among the captured was an exasperated Lt. Col. John Inzer of the 32nd/58th Alabama, who lamented, "I never worked so hard in my life as I did at this time to rally my command."[11] But his efforts, like those of countless other officers, were for naught; the Union army had achieved one of its most astonishing victories of the war.

On 27 November Confederate forces conducted a strong rearguard action at Ringgold Gap in northern Georgia. There the 16th, 33rd, and 45th Alabama Infantry Regiments in Brig. Gen. Mark Lowery's brigade helped maul pursuing Yankees and thereby allow the Army of Tennessee time to reorganize after the debacle at Missionary Ridge. Success at Ringgold, however, brought small comfort to the Alabamians involved. To them it seemed only a matter of time before the bloodletting that had ravaged newly hallowed fields in Mississippi, Tennessee, and Georgia spilled over into their native state. But as the military campaigns of 1864 would demonstrate, defending the Heart of Dixie was worth continued sacrifice to those sons of Alabama still devoted to the cause of independence.

JAMES THOMAS
SEARCY
ambrotype

Union artillery rounds were already peppering the ground around them when Pvt. James Searcy and his fellow gunners in Lumsden's Battery hurriedly unlimbered their four 12-pounder Napoleons. It was early afternoon on 8 October 1862—the Battle of Perryville was underway. A graduate of the University of Alabama (class of 1859), the twenty-two-year-old Searcy hailed from Tuscaloosa, as did just about everyone else in the battery. The private dreamed of becoming a doctor one day, but at the moment he thought only of working his gun as efficiently as possible. Searcy's cannon occupied a portion of a hill near the Widow Bottom House. From there the battery covered much of the left flank of the Rebel right wing. For two hours, Lumsden's Battery traded shots with enemy guns over a distance of about a half mile. Searcy recalled the duel with metaphorical understatement: "the music of twelve Yankee guns and their whistling shells is not the most pleasant I have heard." The Alabamians lost one gun and suffered two wounded, but they knocked out as many as four Yankee pieces. When the main Confederate attack went in, Searcy and his mates shifted their fire to the enemy infantry. By 4:00 P.M. Lumsden's Battery had expended over 200 rounds and greatly contributed to their side's tactical gains. "It was awfully exciting while going on," Searcy reflected as the fighting petered out, "but the after sight of the battlefield is horrible." Nevertheless, he joined his comrades in pilfering some fine blue overcoats left behind when their foes retreated.[12] *Photo courtesy of W. S. Hoole Special Collections Library, The University of Alabama*

RICHARD ORRICK PICKETT
copy print

Among the Alabama infantry regiments that fought at Corinth, the 42nd understandably garners the most attention with its forlorn assault on Battery Robinette. The 35th Alabama, however, earned its share of glory as well. One of the officers in the regiment was Capt. Richard Pickett of Company H. A state politician from Lawrence County, the forty-eight-year-old Pickett would have rather served in some government capacity, as he had done throughout the 1850s. The call to duty, however, compelled the erstwhile Whig legislator to resign his post as inspector general and accept a commission in the 35th Alabama. At Corinth on the morning of 3 October, Pickett and his men were a small part of Rust's Brigade, which attacked the Union left wing. The Alabamians deployed in the center (with Company A on the right of the line) between an

Arkansas regiment on their left and a Kentucky regiment on their right. The tactical objective was a Union battery posted behind a railroad cut. Dense forest protected the Yellowhammers for most of the advance, but as they emerged from the trees a mere sixty yards from the enemy lines, canister ripped through the ranks. At the order to fix bayonets and charge, Pickett and his company rushed into the storm of lead. The regiment buckled under the enemy barrage, but officers such as Pickett helped rally the men and keep them moving. Following the Arkansans, who had found a way around the railroad cut, the Alabamians helped silence a section of Yankee guns. Pickett and his men saw little fighting for the rest of the battle, but they participated in plenty of action during the subsequent Confederate retreat. *Photo courtesy of ADAH*

BATTERY ROBINETTE
(Alabamians and Texans killed in action)
copy print

The climax of the Battle of Corinth came with the 42nd Alabama Infantry's ill-fated assault on Battery Robinette, a bastion mounting three 30-pounder Parrott guns manned by soldiers from the 1st U.S. Infantry. Organized in May 1862, the 42nd drew its men primarily from the recently disbanded 2nd Alabama Infantry. Part of Brig. Gen. John C. Moore's brigade, which included regiments from Arkansas, Mississippi, and Texas, the regiment went into action at Corinth with approximately 700 men under Col. John W. Portis of Clarke County. On 3 October, the first day of battle, the Alabamians helped drive the defenders back to the outskirts of Corinth itself. Late the following morning, Portis led his regiment directly against Battery Robinette. Marching on the brigade's right, the 42nd Alabama ensconced much of its movement within nearby woods, but the final hundred yards were across open ground. The Yellowhammers charged and, despite canister blasts that killed or maimed some forty men, including Colonel Portis,

they stormed the parapets. With Capt. George Foster now in command, the Alabamians clambered over abatis, all the while dodging grenades, until they reached the embrasures, where they poured volleys of fire through the openings. After scattering the artillerymen, Foster and his men rushed inside and planted the regimental colors. Though soon reinforced by the 2nd Texas Infantry, the 42nd proved too tired and disorganized to resist an ensuing Union counterattack. "Boys, you had better get away from here," shouted Captain Foster, but his men were quickly overwhelmed. In the frenzy of the close-quarters fighting, the Yankees shot down dozens of Rebels as they tried to surrender. Among the slain was Captain Foster, who suffered a swift, albeit gruesome death: "The top of his head seemed to cave in," recalled an officer in the regiment, "and the blood spouted straight up several feet." In all the 42nd Alabama lost 370 men, many of the dead intermingled with the bodies of their brethren from Texas.[13] *Photo courtesy of ADAH*

129

JONES MITCHELL WITHERS
carte de viste
Duffee and Sancier, Mobile

As dawn approached on 31 December 1862, Jones Withers anxiously awaited the moment to advance his division against the Union center at Murfreesboro. The situation was strikingly reminiscent of the Battle of Shiloh, where Withers ably led his troops in a devastating early morning surprise attack. This time, however, the general understood that his task was not simply to charge, but to serve as the hinge for a massive turning movement designed to sweep around the enemy right and drive them into the icy waters of Stones River. A forty-eight-year-old politico from Mobile, Withers was one of the most prominent Alabamians then serving in the Confederate army. He graduated from West Point in 1835 (forty-fourth in his class), fought in the Creek War of 1836, volunteered for service in the Mexican War (though his regiment never saw action), became a lawyer and businessman in the early 1850s, and in 1856 won the first of five consecutive elections for mayor of Mobile. At the outset of the Civil War, he commanded the 3rd Alabama Infantry but soon thereafter received rapid promotion to major general.

At Murfreesboro Withers's Division totaled almost 7,800 men divided among four brigades. A plurality of his soldiers came from Alabama, the Yellowhammers making up nine of the division's twenty-one infantry regiments and two of the four batteries. At 7:00 A.M., with gunfire already crackling to his left, Withers sent forth his brigades in seriated waves, beginning with

Colonel Loomis's five Alabama regiments on the left and ending with Brig. Gen. James Chalmers's five Mississippi regiments on the right, which bordered the western bank of the river. Within minutes all of these units were engaged in a ferocious seesaw struggle. For the next four hours, Withers directed the action as best he could, but for the most part, the slugfest boiled down to a test of willpower. When the Union line finally gave way, Withers's Division was unfit for further combat that day: over 300 of its men lay dead, some 2,100 more were wounded, and another 100 were missing—2,500 casualties in all. Still, the general had nothing but praise for his men: "In temporary repulses and the most trying positions, the total absence of everything like panic, and the cool self-possession and alacrity with which they rallied, reformed, and moved forward against the enemy, was as truly remarkable as it was most honorable."

On 2 January 1863, the division probed and skirmished along the Union position at Round Forest, but after a failed attack by divisions on the other side of the river, Withers joined a chorus of generals who urged Braxton Bragg to withdraw his badly damaged army. Defeat did not tarnish the admirable performance of Withers at Murfreesboro. Bragg singled out the general from Mobile for his "valor, skill, and ability."[14] *Photo courtesy of ADAH*

MARCUS E. WESTBROOK
copy print

As he advanced toward the Yankee campgrounds west of Murfreesboro, Sgt. Marcus Westbrook probably calmed his comrades' nerves with jokes and words of encouragement. Ever since their baptism of fire at Shiloh, the boys in Company I, 19th Alabama Infantry, looked to their sergeant for combat fortitude. Evidently, the twenty-one-year-old Westbrook combined youthful courage with preternatural maturity. In August 1861 he had left the family farm and enlisted in Company I (the Cherokee Rangers). Though recognized for his natural soldiering abilities, he consistently refused promotion, preferring to serve as a private. Prior to every battle, however, he acceded to his officers' request to become an acting sergeant.

At Murfreesboro on 31 December, Westbrook and the 19th Alabama marched as part of the right wing of Loomis's Brigade. After racing across a muddy field and chasing panicked Yankees toward a wooded ridge,

the brigade splintered; the 19th drifted to the right, where it joined the 22nd Alabama Infantry in an unsupported attack against Union forces in a particularly thick section of forest. Hacking its way forward, the regiment further separated from the 22nd. Alone and disoriented, the men then came under fire from multiple directions. The Alabamians fought back, however, exchanging volleys for half an hour before extricating themselves from the untenable position. All the while Westbrook calmly fired his rifle despite receiving a flesh wound. A fellow sergeant in the regiment described the carnage: "i saw more dead men in one field than i Saw in the hole Shilow battle." In all the 19th Alabama suffered 154 casualties out of about 400 men engaged. A few days later Westbrook reverted back to the rank of private of his own volition.[15]
Photo courtesy of Jack E. Westbrook Collection, U.S.A.M.H.I.

Julius Caesar
Bonaparte Mitchell
copy print

Julius Mitchell had been colonel of the 34th Alabama Infantry for almost ten months when he led it into its baptism of fire at Murfreesboro. A forty-four-year-old planter from Montgomery County, Mitchell was an energetic organizer for the Confederate army, raising nine companies for the 13th Alabama Infantry, eight for the 45th Alabama Infantry, as well as the ten he now commanded. Moreover, Mitchell had the first and middle names of two of history's greatest warriors— did he have their fighting spirit? Part of Manigault's Brigade, Mitchell's regiment was assigned the front rank of an echelon attack. Around 8:00 A.M. on the morning of 31 December, the colonel slowly maneuvered the 34th Alabama westward through a section of woods as the roar of combat grew ever closer from units already engaged off to the left. On reaching the tree line, Mitchell's boys made contact with a sizeable enemy skirmish line, which they easily dispersed. From there, however, they entered a small cotton field and immediately came under heavy fire, particularly from two Union batteries posted on high ground across the field to the northwest. Mitchell pushed his men forward and briefly engaged several Illinois regiments in a furious standup fight. The whirlwind of shot and shell, however, was too much to withstand; the regiment fell back. The colonel rallied his men and led them forward once again, but once again they fell back. The regiment also participated in a third brigade attack, one that finally dislodged the Yankee defenders, but two hours of fighting had left the Alabamians too exhausted for further action. Nevertheless, Julius Caesar Bonaparte had lived up to the reputations of his namesakes.[16] *Photo courtesy of U.S.A.M.H.I.*

WILLIAM JEFFERSON
BICKERSTAFF
copy print

The 34th Alabama Infantry suffered eighty-eight casualties at Murfreesboro. Among them was Capt. William Bickerstaff of Company I, mortally wounded during the regiment's first charge. The forty-three-year-old Bickerstaff was well liked by his men. He personally raised Company I in April 1862, recruiting friends and neighbors from among the yeomanry of Russell County. One of the company's lieutenants was Bickerstaff's eighteen-year-old son, James. The men had all participated in Bragg's invasion of Kentucky but had seen little action; Murfreesboro was their first major engagement. Early on the morning of 31 December, Bickerstaff aligned Company I on the regiment's right wing (the 34th was spearheading an echelon attack by Manigault's Brigade). He then led his men across a cotton field into the maw of enemy rifle and artillery fire. The whole unit buckled under the whirlwind of projectiles. At some point a piece of lead pierced Bickerstaff's side. The captain staggered a few steps, dropped his sword, and collapsed. As the 34th Alabama fell back, young James recovered his father's sword and led the company for the rest of the battle. Unfortunately, Captain Bickerstaff did not survive his wound. After lingering for several weeks, he died on 14 February 1863. *Photo courtesy of ADAH*

134

John Henry Turpin
copy print
Tresslar Studio, Montgomery

As Capt. John Turpin of the 28th Alabama Infantry stepped out from some woods and onto a smoke-filled cotton field on the last day of 1862, he undoubtedly felt a certain amount of trepidation. Like many of the Alabamians in Manigault's Brigade, Murfreesboro was Turpin's first big fight. A druggist from the Canebrake region of Greene County, he came to Alabama from Virginia in 1856. As the sectional crisis intensified, he switched his political affiliation from Whig to Democrat. After war broke out, in March 1862 Turpin organized, at personal expense, the Confederate Sentinels, an infantry unit that became Company B, 28th Alabama. He and all of his men enlisted for the duration of the war. Now, on 31 December, just three days after his twenty-fifth birthday, Turpin was leading his Sentinels into battle.

The 28th Alabama was the second line of Manigault's echelon assault; Company B anchored the regiment's left flank. Fifty yards to his front on the cotton field, Turpin watched as soldiers of the 34th Alabama furiously exchanged near-point-blank volleys with the enemy. The men of the 28th hurried to come alongside their hard-pressed comrades, then heard the order to charge. In the melee that ensued, a Yankee soldier shot Turpin through his left shoulder. Moments later Company B fell back in confusion, leaving their commander behind. The 28th Alabama, which sustained 116 casualties that day, would rally and eventually help drive back the bluecoats, but by then the captain was writhing in agony on the floor of a Union field hospital, where surgeons amputated his arm.
Photo courtesy of ADAH

FLAG OF WATERS'S BATTERY
copy print

Artillery played an invaluable combat role on virtually every Civil War battlefield. Exemplifying such service was Waters's Battery, organized in October 1861 by Capt. David D. Waters of Mobile. Initially stationed around the Bay City, in April 1862 the unit was assigned to Manigault's Brigade in the Army of Tennessee. Seeing action in every major engagement from Perryville to Chattanooga, the four-gun battery's performance at Murfreesboro stands out. On the morning of 31 December, it helped the brigade overcome an especially difficult enemy position. When Manigault's first assault failed, Captain Waters repositioned his guns to within 500 yards of the Yankees and raked their lines. "I think I must have done them some damage," he reported, "as I saw my shell burst and shot strike among them." Consequently, a second Rebel charge achieved greater success, though it would take a third attack, one supported by close-range canister fire from Waters's Battery, to finally dislodge the defenders. In this contest the cannoneers suffered six casualties and lost four horses. In the aftermath the battery received its own banner, a white St. George's Cross on a dark blue background—the so-called "Polk and Bragg" pattern also shared by the 22nd and 24th Alabama Infantry Regiments. Proudly sewn into the right side of the flag is the name of its greatest battle.[17]

Waters's Battery did not survive the war. At Chattanooga on 25 November 1863, it lost three guns and half its manpower during the Confederate flight. Disbanded as a result, the survivors transferred into other units. Captain Waters, however, retained personal possession of his battery's flag. His descendants presented the flag to the Alabama State Archives in 1959. *Photo courtesy of ADAH*

FREDERICK OSCAR
ALEXANDER SHERROD
copy print

For 1st Lt. Fred Sherrod of the 16th Alabama Infantry, the Battle of Murfreesboro was a painful and frustrating experience. The twenty-year-old son of a slaveholder from Lawrence County, Sherrod had been in the Confederate service since early 1861 but had not seen any significant action. All of that changed on the morning of 31 December, for the lieutenant was acting commander of Company B—the Lawrence Guards—and his regiment was part of the massive left hook that sought to smash the Union right wing. Part of Wood's Brigade, the 16th deployed on the right flank. After advancing approximately 100 yards, the whole regiment came under fire from Union forces posted among cedar trees and boulders. Sherrod orchestrated his company's fire for about thirty minutes when General Wood "gave the order to 'charge,' and the men,

with a yell, made a charge in gallant style, dislodging the enemy from their strong position and killing scores of them as they fled." It was probably at this point that Sherrod went down with a severe wound. Company command passed to 2nd Lt. Chesley Davis, who won accolades for his participation in a later charge that nearly captured an enemy battery. On that day the 16th Alabama suffered 166 casualties. Col. William Wood, commanding the regiment, singled out by name most of his company officers for various heroics. Unfortunately, Lieutenant Sherrod's name was not among them; having been incapacitated during the first hour of combat, he missed out on the ostensibly more noteworthy events of the day-long struggle.[18]
Photo courtesy of Mrs. Lloyd E. Nelson Collection, U.S.A.M.H.I.

137

HENRY MAURY
copy print

Around 2:00 P.M. on 31 December, Lt. Col. Henry "Harry" Maury led the 32nd Alabama Infantry across a ford over Stones River. Maury and his men were the odd-regiment out in Brig. Gen. Daniel Adams's brigade of Louisianans. Nevertheless, the Alabamians moved with a sense of urgency; they were to participate in the ongoing assaults against the Yankee's last, albeit formidable, line of defense—the Round Forest. A Virginian by birth, the thirty-five-year-old Maury spent most of his life in Mobile, where he practiced law, engaged in politics, and sailed the Gulf waters. Combative by nature, he gained notoriety both as a duelist and as a filibuster, skippering a schooner for the infamous William Walker. With the outbreak of war, Maury first commanded the 2nd Alabama Infantry (which was subsequently disbanded) and then accepted the lieutenant colonelcy of the 32nd. Captured at Lavergne, Tennessee, in early 1862, he was exchanged in time to command the regiment at Murfreesboro.

After crossing the river, the 32nd Alabama deployed on the brigade's left flank. The men then advanced northwest past the detritus of previous Rebel charges, including the charred ruins of the Cowan House. The scattered fence rails of that farmhouse interfered with the alignment of his companies, but Maury pushed his men forward. Three hundred yards from the Round Forest, with enemy artillery now raining down, the lieutenant colonel wheeled his regiment to the right and brought it in line with the rest of the brigade. "At this point we commenced firing," he recalled, "but finding that it was not efficient on account of the excellent cover of the enemy, I ordered the regiment to cease firing and charge." Union canister tore through the Alabamians. When the regimental color bearer went down, Maury himself recovered the flag and brandished it before also falling with a Minié ball in his side. After suffering 126 casualties in nearly an hour of combat, the 32nd Alabama retreated. That bitter afternoon constituted Maury's most intense moment of the war, yet, he took pride that ten of his soldiers were listed on the army's Roll of Honor for their heroism in the battle.[19] *Photo courtesy of ADAH*

138

DAVID WARDLAW RAMSEY
carte de viste

As the long roll drummed out its tocsin on the night of 14 March 1863, Capt. David Ramsey of the 1st Alabama Infantry readied his men for action. Union admiral David Farragut was attempting to run a squadron of gunboats up the Mississippi River past the Confederate citadel at Port Hudson, Louisiana. Ramsey, who commanded Battery No. 5—one 10-inch mortar and two heavy smoothbores—was eager to thwart his adversary's intentions. A twenty-three-year-old medical student from Wilcox County, Ramsey joined the 1st Alabama in February 1861 and rose to captain of Company B the following year. He saw action during the bombardment of Fort Pickens in November 1861 and was captured at Island No. 10 in March 1862. Exchanged that September, Ramsey arrived at Port Hudson, where the 1st Alabama was part of a large garrison that was striving to keep the Mississippi open to the Confederacy. Battery No. 5 guarded a bluff on the east side of the river about one mile south of the port city. Against any threat coming upriver, Ramsey and his men would constitute one of the last lines of resistance. Around 11:00 P.M. the Yankee ships made their bid, steaming rapidly along the western bank. Immediately Rebel guns opened fire. By the time Ramsey's battery chimed in, the Union fleet was in disarray. The Alabamians helped pound the 27-gun USS *Richmond,* which weaved an erratic course before finally hobbling back downriver. Ramsey next concentrated his guns on the USS *Mississippi,* a 24-gun frigate that was already reeling from damaging hits. To the captain's frustration, though, the vessel ran aground at a point where he could not depress his guns. Decisively, Ramsey ordered his crews to grab their muskets and rake the decks of the stricken ship with small-arms fire. While other grayback batteries shelled the *Mississippi,* Ramsey and his men reveled in its imminent destruction. "The prettiest sight I ever saw," Pvt. Marcus Sanford declared, "was the red hot balls screaming through the air at night seeking to locate her." Sensing their fate, the Yankee sailors fired their vessel and abandoned ship. Early the following morning, the still burning *Mississippi* broke free, drifted downriver, and exploded. For three hours, Ramsey had stoutly defended his section of the river. Because of his efforts, and scores like it, the Union operation was a complete failure.[20]
Photo courtesy of David Wynn Vaughan

139

SAMUEL CAMP KELLY
copy print

The morning of 1 May 1863 brought pandemonium to Capt. Samuel Kelly of the 30th Alabama Infantry. Strong Yankee columns were bearing down on the Confederate position at Port Gibson, Mississippi, and he was among the 2,000 Alabamians in Tracy's Brigade tasked with stopping the enemy's progress. A thirty-eight-year-old planter from Calhoun County, Kelly descended from proud Irish stock. He joined the 30th Alabama in March 1862 and soon gained the captaincy of Company E. Assigned to the garrison around Vicksburg in January 1863, the regiment performed various mundane duties until Union forces crossed the Mississippi River below the city. Tracy's Brigade rushed south to contest the enemy landing.

After an exhausting two-day forced march, the brigade reached the woodlands around Port Gibson on the night of 30 April. There the Alabamians bivouacked in line of battle. At dawn Captain Kelly roused his company—twenty-four men in all—and moved them into a better defensive position around a nearby cluster of cabins, home to several dozen slaves. "The poor things were scared," Kelly said of the occu-pants, "running and hollering from the time we got there." The captain ordered them to clear out. At 7:00 A.M. the battle opened, and two Union regiments soon pitched into the 30th Alabama. Kelly remembered a lit-eral shower of bullets: "It seemed at times as if they came as thick as drops of rain." Nevertheless, he kept his men calm and directed their fire toward a group of bluecoats attempting to advance out of gorge. "Every evidence goes to show that we killed lots of them," Kelly remarked. At 8:00 A.M. the brigade commander, Edward Tracy, rode up to encourage the 30th, but he drew the attention of Yankee sharpshooters. "Gen. Tracy fell within five feet of me," Kelly recalled. "He was shot through with a minie ball." As he helped carry the fatally wounded general to the rear, the whole Rebel position gave way. A series of rearguard actions ensued, but by nightfall all Confederate forces were in full retreat. Despite the defeat and the loss of eighty men from the regiment, Captain Kelly remained upbeat. "My men all acted bravely," he beamed after-ward. "We are not half whipped even if we did fall back twenty miles."[21] *Photograph courtesy of ADAH*

James Fleming
Waddell
copy print
Jerome W. Chambers,
Montgomery

As the Confederate left wing around Champion Hill collapsed on the afternoon of 16 May, Capt. James Waddell ordered his gunners to stand fast in the face of onrushing Yankees. A lawyer from Russell County, the thirty-seven-year-old Waddell was a veteran of the Mexican War and an early volunteer for the Confederate military. After serving as a company commander in the 6th Alabama Infantry, he helped organize an eight-gun battery in February 1862 made up of fellow soldiers from that regiment. At Champion Hill his command was not only down to six field pieces but also was overextended as a result of hasty changes in the dispositions of Pemberton's forces. Posted to cover an important crossroads, Waddell's Battery guarded the hinge of a line where the left wing faced north and the right wing faced east. For much of the day, the gunners harassed enemy forces approaching from the east. Shortly after 2:00 P.M., however, the Rebel left gave way under tremendous pressure. Supporting infantry regiments fell back, exposing Waddell's sections to charging bluecoats. The Alabamians feverishly loaded their guns and delivered point-blank salvos: "Double-shotted, they were fired until in many instances the swarms of the enemy were in among them. Officers and men stood by them to the very latest moment that they could be served." For a few agonizing minutes, Waddell feared that he had lost his entire battery, not to mention most of the horses and two dozen of his men, killed, wounded, or captured. Fortunately, a timely Rebel counterattack enabled the captain to recover four of his guns, which he briefly turned on the Yankees before extricating them to safety.[23]
Photo courtesy of ADAH

ALBERT THEODORE GOODLOE
copy print

The 35th Alabama Infantry fired some of the first and last shots of the Battle of Baker's Creek, Mississippi. One of the officers in this regiment was 1st Lt. Albert Goodloe of Company D (the Mollie Walton Guards). A resident of Nashville, Goodloe relocated his wife and children to Franklin County, Alabama, when Union forces invaded Middle Tennessee in February 1862. Leaving his family in the care of relatives, Goodloe enlisted in the newly raised 35th Alabama. "I did not feel that I had cast my lot among strangers," he later reminisced, "for the spirit of devotion to our Southland bound us together as comrades in a holy cause." His comrades reciprocated the good will, electing Goodloe to a lieutenancy in September. He saw plenty of action at Corinth and plenty more at Baker's Creek. At 7:00 A.M. Goodloe and the rest of the regiment deployed as the skirmish line for Brig. Gen. Abram Buford's brigade. Within minutes they made contact with elements of the Union army along Raymond Road, about three miles south of Champion Hill. After a brisk exchange of fire, the Alabamians fell back to the main body, but the enemy did little more than probe; the main action was unfolding to the north.

As the day wore on, the brigade responded to frantic pleas for reinforcements by marching toward the fight raging around Champion Hill. En route, a Confederate general commandeered the 35th and ordered its men to protect a nearby Missouri battery. The Alabamians complied and took up a good position among some trees just in time to repel an enemy assault. "We disputed his way as best we could with an insufficient force," Goodloe later recalled. In actuality the Alabamians provided cover fire for the artillerymen for almost an hour, from 3:00 to 4:00 P.M., until Rebel resistance in general played out in the face of a growing Yankee onslaught. As demoralized graybacks from other regiments fled through his regiment's ranks, Lieutenant Goodloe and other line officers tried in vain to stop their flight. In desperation the Alabamians even leveled their bayonets to induce the panic-stricken men to rally, though all for naught. To its credit the regiment maintained discipline throughout and conducted a fighting retreat that helped buy time for the Confederate army to reorganize. For Goodloe, this admirable rearguard action brought small comfort, for his close friend and fellow lieutenant, George Hubbard, went down with a fatal shot to the head. The retreat lasted well into the night, but rather than fall back toward Vickburg, Buford's Brigade withdrew to the south. Thus, Goodloe and the 35th Alabama avoided the siege and the eventual capitulation.[22] *Photo courtesy of Charles A. Stuck Collection, U.S.A.M.H.I.*

WILLIAM JAMES SAMFORD
copy print

As he watched several thousand fast-moving midwestern soldiers approach his position along Champion Hill, 1st Lt. William Samford of the 46th Alabama Infantry may well have yearned for his carefree college days of just the previous year. The eighteen-year-old son of a prominent Methodist preacher from Chambers County who also enjoyed connections by marriage to the aristocratic Dowdell family, Samford could have avoided military service. In the spring of 1862, however, he emulated the patriotism of his older brother and enlisted. While big brother Thomas went into the 37th Alabama, William joined the 46th, in which he quickly became the regiment's sergeant major. Prior to the Vicksburg Campaign, Samford received a promotion to first lieutenant in Company G, a unit with whom he "saw the elephant" at Port Gibson.

At Champion Hill the 46th Alabama (approximately 300 strong) occupied the very center of Stephen Lee's brigade. About 2:00 P.M. Samford and his men helped repel a full-scale attack against the left half of the brigade's line, but a later assault on the right flank forced the Alabamians to retreat. After falling back 600 yards, General Lee ordered the brigade to participate in a general counterattack. The 46th Alabama in particular "made a most gallant charge," one that exploited a gap in the Union lines. Unfortunately, these Yellowhammers pressed their attack beyond the support of friendly units and soon found themselves trapped in a ravine, caught in crossfire by foes holding the high ground. A few companies managed to hack their way out, but Lieutenant Samford and over 100 of his comrades surrendered.[24] *Photo courtesy of Special Collections & Archives, Auburn University*

FRANKLIN KING BECK
copy print

The road from Baker's Creek to Vicksburg, whether in retreat or in pursuit, entailed crossing the Big Black River. On 17 May Confederate forces attempted a holding action in front of the two bridges over that stream. Col. Franklin Beck of the 23rd Alabama Infantry (in Lee's Brigade) defended one of them from a strong position on the western banks. A planter and lawyer from Wilcox County, the forty-nine-year-old Beck possessed an enviable pedigree: his father, John Beck, was one of the state's earliest political leaders, and his uncle, William R. King, had been the state's most distinguished U.S. senator. A politician himself, Beck endorsed the fire-eating agenda of many Southern Democrats prior to the war, and in 1861 he represented his home county in the secession convention, where he voted in favor of Alabama's declaration of independence. In the autumn of 1861, Beck won election to command the 23rd Alabama. Known for his temerity in battle, the colonel earned his greatest laurel at the Big Black, where his regiment guarded a railroad bridge. When Yankees forces bowled over the Confederate rear guard east of the river, Beck provided effective covering fire until all friendly forces were safely across and the bridge set ablaze. Lee's Brigade then also withdrew, except for the 23rd, which inexplicably never received the order. Steadfastly adhering to his original instructions, Beck and his regiment remained at their post alone for the next twelve hours, disrupting Union efforts to throw pontoons across the river. Finally, at midnight, with ammunition running low, Beck slipped away and entered the fortifications around Vicksburg. His men were greeted with cheers for their remarkable feat at arms. *Photo courtesy of ADAH*

145

RICHARD HENRY BELLAMY
copy print

Since placing his 6-pounder along the Vicksburg fortifications, 1st Lt. Richard Bellamy had spent the first few days of the siege shelling Union targets of opportunity. On 22 May, however, he was on the receiving end, in what became one of the most intense bombardments of the war. A thirty-three-year-old lawyer from Russell County, Bellamy had been a section leader under Capt. James Waddell since the battery's formation in early 1862. He performed well at Port Gibson and helped salvage his one remaining field piece during the chaos at Champion Hill. Now at Vicksburg, he was responsible for augmenting the defenses around a bastion known as the Railroad Redoubt. At midmorning on 22 May, scores of Union guns commenced a heavy cannonade against selected points in preparation for a general assault. When the barrage fell upon his section, Bellamy may have tried to shoot back or may have simply hunkered behind the earthworks and prayed. Regardless, an incoming round hit the lieutenant's ammunition cache, setting off a huge explosion. The blast stunned the whole crew and wounded four, including Bellamy. When the Yankees stormed the redoubt an hour later, Bellamy's gun was silent, leaving just one other operable fieldpiece in the immediate vicinity. Fortunately, Alabama regiments from Lee's Brigade beat back the assault, but the practical loss of Bellamy's section made for a difficult fight. Lieutenant Bellamy later recovered and resumed his post along the Vicksburg line. *Photo courtesy of ADAH*

JOHN BASS SMITH
copy print

Despite the shot and shell whizzing around him, Lt. Col. "Jack" Smith of the 30th Alabama Infantry still managed to catch disconcerting glimpses of Union formations lining up a few hundred yards to his front. When enemy artillery knocked out one of the gun emplacements inside the Railroad Redoubt to his immediate left, the officer knew that his men would be hard pressed to resist the imminent assault. Smith was a forty-year-old slaveholder from Jefferson County, where he and his wife, Sara, raised six children. When the 30th Alabama formed in April 1862, he won election as captain of Company K. In short order he earned promotion to major and, just prior to the Vicksburg Campaign, was again promoted to lieutenant colonel. On 22 May Smith was the regiment's de facto commander, Col. Charles Shelley being sick at the time. Although the 30th Alabama technically defended the southern end of the redoubt, several companies from the regiment actually occupied the strongpoint, where they reinforced the understrength

46th Alabama. Smith also enjoyed the support of the 31st Alabama, which tied in to his unit's right flank. Not long after the Union artillery barrage subsided, waves of bluecoats charged, with the redoubt their main objective. As per brigade orders, Smith made sure that his men did not shoot until the enemy came into optimal killing range, then the whole Yellow-hammer line opened fire. Volley after volley of concentrated musketry shattered the attack; hundreds of Yankees lay dead or wounded on the field, while the survivors hastily fell back. One group, however, successfully breached the redoubt and scattered the defenders. Desperate to retake this vital position, Lieutenant Colonel Smith unwisely mounted his horse, perhaps either to rally his men or to muster reinforcements. In any event, Union sharpshooters quickly shot him down. An improvised commando unit of Alabamians and Texans eventually recaptured the redoubt, but Smith was lying in a Vicksburg hospital when he heard the news. *Photo courtesy of ADAH*

147

MICHAEL B. LOCKE
copy print

The siege of Port Hudson is overshadowed by the Vicksburg Campaign, but this small post in eastern Louisiana was actually the last Confederate stronghold on the Mississippi River to fall. Among the garrison of 7,000 was Lt. Col. Michael Locke, acting commander of the 1st Alabama Infantry. The twenty-five-year-old Locke, a resident of Pike County, had already been captured once, at Island No. 10 in March 1862. He did not relish the possibility of surrendering a second time at Port Hudson. In mid-May 1863, however, a Union army of approximately 30,000 men under Maj. Gen. Nathaniel Banks invested the Rebel citadel. For the rest of the month, Locke was actively engaged in trying to defeat the siege. On 17 May he led three companies on a raid across the river intended both to disrupt Union communications and to secure several hundred head of cattle. Unfortunately, this force clashed unsuccessfully with a troop of Yankee horsemen that made off with the herd. On 23 May Locke deployed six of his companies to the northern outskirts of Port Hudson, where they helped thwart an enemy reconnaissance in force. Two days later he repelled a Union probe against his lines, a stretch of entrenchments dubbed the "bull pen." Then on 27 May the lieutenant colonel coordinated efforts to resist an all-out Union assault; he had

just assumed command of a regiment of Arkansas infantrymen and a contingent of Mississippians in addition to his own Alabamians. After enduring an early morning bombardment by enemy gunboats and land batteries, this combined force repelled with relative ease what turned out to be a poorly executed attack. Buoyed by this success, the lieutenant colonel led a twilight sortie with four Alabama companies against enemy forces in some thick woods nearby. After several minutes of severe fighting, the Alabamians withdrew to their trenches, having accomplished little for their audacity. For his part, Locke received a deep, grazing wound to the neck, but after "bandaging it with his pocket handkerchief[, he] stood bravely to his post." The following morning, under a flag of truce, he supervised a Confederate detail that removed and buried the many corpses strewn about the battlefield. Casualties within the 1st Alabama were high after more than a week of protracted combat: thirty-two killed, forty-four wounded. When the Port Hudson garrison formally surrendered on 9 July, Locke may have expected a speedy exchange, but the victorious General Banks decided to parole only the enlisted men. The lieutenant colonel spent the rest of the war in a prison camp.[25] *Photo courtesy of ADAH*

148

AQUILA D. HUTTON
copy print from
Confederate Veteran

For Pvt. Aquila Hutton of the 36th Alabama Infantry, even a bloodbath such as Chickamauga had its light-hearted moments. A nineteen-year-old son of a Sumter County physician, Hutton enlisted into Company A—the Sumter Warriors—in March 1862. After serving a year as part of the garrison around Mobile, his regiment joined the Army of Tennessee in the spring of 1863. About that time Aquila learned that his older brother, William, had been killed at Chancellorsville. On the afternoon of 19 September 1863, Private Hutton marched on the extreme right flank of his regiment, which in turn held the right flank of Clayton's Brigade. Company A tramped westward through some fairly thick forest when the Alabamians came under enemy fire. Hutton and his comrades dropped to the ground and exchanged vol-leys until they had nearly expended all of their ammunition. After falling back to replenish their ordnance, the 36th Alabama participated in an assault on a contingent of Indianans defending the Brotherton Farmhouse. It was at this point that the battle turned into something of a game, for the line officers exhorted their men to capture the colors of the rapidly retreating Hoosiers. Company A concentrated on a section of gunners fleeing across a nearby cornfield. A bemused Col. Lewis Woodruff commented that his men "desired rather to obtain the flag than capture the battery." The Alabamians chased their foe for half a mile before finally returning empty handed. Unfortunately, Hutton received an incapacitating wound during the pursuit, becoming one of over one hundred casualties in the regiment that day.[26]

EDWARD CRENSHAW
copy print

Capt. Edward Crenshaw of the 58th Alabama Infantry was eager for combat on the afternoon of 19 September. Although he had been in the army since the autumn of 1861, the twenty-one-year-old had yet to participate in a full-blown battle. That all changed at Chickamauga. A law student from Butler County, Crenshaw was attending the University of Virginia when the war broke out. He enlisted as soon as he returned home, but his initial military experience was anything but glorious. In the spring and summer of 1862, Crenshaw languished in a hospital, where he nearly died from typhoid fever. After recovering, he accepted a commission in the 58th Alabama and, in the summer of 1863, assumed command of Company B. When the regiment went into action at Chickamauga, Company B deployed on the extreme left flank. In fact, Crenshaw's men anchored the entire left flank of Brig. Gen. William B. Bate's brigade. With the battle well underway, the 288 soldiers in the 58th headed to the front as part of a concerted effort to drive the blue-coats away from Brotherton Field. The regiment had advanced several hundred yards through thickening clouds of smoke when Col. Bushrod Jones barked the command to charge. "With loud and enthusiastic

cheers," the Alabamians waded into the Union ranks and routed their foe. Crenshaw recalled the scene with aplomb: "Passed a Chinese Sorghum patch while double-quicking . . . charged the enemy with two stalks apiece—one in mouth and one in hand (nearly starved)." The young captain and two other company commanders pushed their men so hard and fast that they broke contact with the rest of the regiment. Their impetuosity, however, contributed to the capture of an unprotected Union battery whose gunners fled, leaving behind three field pieces.

The following day, the 58th Alabama supported a general attack against a formidable Union position just west of LaFayette Road. One hundred yards from the enemy lines, Colonel Jones strived to orchestrate an assault, but a "terrific storm of Minie balls made dreadful havoc in the ranks." Jones withdrew to safety, his regiment having lost 95 men to no avail (149 for the entire battle). Among that day's casualties was Captain Crenshaw, who received multiple, deep lacerations to his face. Colonel Jones praised his fallen captain's brav-ery, but Crenshaw's days with the 58th Alabama were over.[27] *Photo Courtesy of ADAH*

REUBEN VAUGHN KIDD
copy print

Above the clangor of battle along LaFayette Road, the stentorian voice of Capt. Reuben Kidd of the 4th Alabama Infantry could be heard with clarity by every man in the regiment. The Alabamians were heading into the thick of battle at Chickamauga on the afternoon of 19 September, and the captain's crisp commands helped calm apprehensive nerves. A twenty-three-year-old merchant from Dallas County, Kidd enlisted into the 4th Alabama in April 1861, immediately winning election to captain of Company A. He believed in the cause, but his motivation reflected a more familial patriotism. "The love of country that will lead a man to suffer martyrdom, that will uphold him amid startling scenes on the ensanguined field," Kidd once wrote, "is nought compared to the love of mother, home and sisters." A veteran of some of the 4th Alabama's most grueling combat, including both

battles at Manassas, Sharpsburg, and Gettysburg, Kidd seemed unaffected by the chaotic conditions in the sprawling woodlands of northern Georgia. A little after 3:00 P.M., Law's Brigade advanced westward across the road near the Brotherton House, with the 4th Alabama aligned on the right. "Forward, men, forward!" Kidd reportedly bellowed, "On to victory!" Suddenly, heavy enemy musketry erupted from front and flank. A bullet pierced Kidd's heart, killing him instantly. His company fought a few minutes longer before falling back with the rest of the brigade. Kidd's body lay in the underbrush until nightfall, when the captain's personal servant, a slave named Joe, dragged it to the rear and buried the young officer under an oak tree. Someone also fetched the dead man's sword, which was returned to the family.[28] *Photo courtesy of ADAH*

JOHN HOLLIS
BANKHEAD
copy print

After "seeing the elephant" at Shiloh and Murfreesboro, Capt. John Bankhead of the 16th Alabama Infantry might have thought nothing could exceed the horror of those battles. Chickamauga proved otherwise. The twenty-one-year-old son of a planter from Marion County, whose family ancestry was steeped in Revolutionary War heritage, Bankhead enlisted without hesitation shortly after the outbreak of hostilities. In April 1862 he assumed command of Company K. At dusk on 19 September, Captain Bankhead entered the already raging battle of Chickamauga; Company K aligned on the left side of the regiment, which itself composed the left center of Wood's Brigade. Groping forward in the diminishing sunlight, the 16th was still crossing Winfrey Field when Union musketry erupted. The Alabamians charged and seemed poised to overrun the enemy position. Unfortunately, confusion ensued when the regimental commander shouted an ambiguous order to "march in retreat." Bankhead and a couple of other captains ignored it long enough to bag a few dozen prisoners before falling back. After rallying, the unit returned to the fight and helped secure the field.

Late the following morning, the 16th Alabama participated in a general attack on strongly entrenched Union forces near the Brotherton Farmhouse. Under a seemingly incessant barrage of artillery, the regiment slowly closed in on the bluecoat lines, the Alabamians alternating maneuver with long periods of volley fire. Around 1:00 P.M. Bankhead led his company in a perfunctory charge across a stretch of road, but after suffering 240 casualties in two days of fighting, the regiment was too weak to exploit the meager gains. Bankhead, with one of his arms broken by a shell fragment, withdrew his exhausted command toward cover. On the way he noticed a wounded private lying dangerously close to a rapidly burning section of the battlefield. With his one good arm, Bankhead hoisted the man onto his back and carried him to safety. *Photo courtesy of ADAH*

JOHN OWEN LEONARD
copy print

On the morning of 20 September, the men of the 22nd Alabama Infantry prepared to enter the fight at Chickamauga, a battle that had already reached titanic proportions. Among them was 2nd Lt. John Leonard, a twenty-one-year-old farmer from Montgomery County. In the autumn of 1861, he enlisted in what became Company K, 22nd Alabama. Like most of his fellow soldiers, Leonard was a veteran, having fought at Shiloh and, shortly after receiving his commission, at Murfreesboro. At Chickamauga Company K marched near the center of the regiment, whose 371 men deployed as the left flank of Zachariah Deas's big brigade of almost 2,000 Alabamians. Shortly after 11:00 A.M., with the crescendo of battle reverberating across the landscape to the north, the 22nd Alabama was advancing quickly westward about 300 yards through a section of woods when it came under fire from Union forces behind improvised breastworks on a small hill just south of Dyer Field. "Without halting to exchange fire," acting commander Capt. Harry Toulmin recounted, "the regiment most gallantly charged the works, capturing some 250 prisoners and a piece of artillery, and putting to flight the remainder of the line." Success came at a steep price, however. The assault was reckless and resulted in several casualties among the Alabamians. One of the wounded was Leonard, who after grabbing the regimental colors from a fallen sergeant, rushed forward into the thick of the fray, where he briefly waved the flag before also getting shot down. As the lieutenant departed the battlefield to receive medical attention, his company went on to help overrun other enemy positions, all part of a stunning breakthrough against the Union right flank. Before the day was over, he gained plenty of company in the field hospital. The 22nd Alabama suffered over 200 casualties in the battle.[29]

Photo courtesy of John Lloyd and Craig T. Sheldon

JOHN NICHOLSON
SLAUGHTER
copy print

Maj. John Slaughter of the 34th Alabama Infantry had plenty to worry about on the morning of 20 September. The thirty-five-year-old schoolteacher from Coosa County had served as an officer in the regiment since March 1862, but at Chickamauga he was leading the 34th into battle for the first time as its acting commander. Moreover, the major was fretting the absence of a long-overdue canteen detail. When the order to advance came down at 10:00 A.M., Slaughter conceded that his men would have to go into action without water. Deployed on the left flank of Manigault's Brigade, the 34th Alabama was a small part of the Confederate army's signal breakthrough on the Union right. After driving a Yankee skirmish line back several hundred yards over terrain interspersed with woods and cornfields, the brigade pummeled Union forces that desperately clung to the high ground around the Widow Glenn House. As the fighting intensified, Slaughter realized that he guarded not only the brigade flank but also the flank of the entire army. Shortly before noon, a large contingent of Spencer-wielding bluecoats appeared, commenced a rapid fire, and then

attempted to get behind the 34th Alabama. Slaughter deftly positioned his regiment in a shallow ravine, "over which the men could rise and fire and be protected while loading," and temporarily checked the enemy counterattack. The volume of Yankee lead, however, was too great; after sustaining fifty-eight casualties, the Alabamians fell back to safer ground.

With the arrival of Confederate reinforcements, the 34th Alabama was soon on the offensive again. Late in the afternoon, Manigault's Brigade participated in a massive assault against the Union rear guard along Horseshoe Ridge. Slaughter maneuvered his regiment with difficulty over the spur-encrusted terrain and was never able to press home an attack. His formation did, unfortunately, get caught in an exposed position, and for two minutes endured galling canister fire that killed and wounded another thirty-eight men. Recognizing the futility of further action, Slaughter withdrew his exhausted boys and took up flank security until nightfall. The major may not have known it at the time, but he and the whole Rebel army had achieved a great victory.[30] *Photo courtesy of ADAH*

BOLLING HALL III
copy print

As the Alabamians in Hilliard's Legion approached the smoky air around Snodgrass Hill in the late afternoon of 20 September, remnants of the Army of the Cumberland frantically orchestrated a rearguard action on its slopes. The Battle of Chickamauga was reaching its conclusion, and these Yellowhammers in Gracie's Brigade understood that their efforts might do more than simply complete an improbable Confederate victory; seizure of the hill might well precipitate the destruction of the whole Yankee horde. Commanding the 230 men in the legion's 2nd Battalion was Lt. Col. Bolling Hall III, the oldest son of a prominent planter family from Autauga County. The twenty-six-year-old Hall had been with the battalion since its formation in June 1862, but like most of his men, including two younger brothers who served as junior officers, he was untested in combat. Nevertheless, the planter-colonel would exhibit fearless leadership at Chickamauga. Marching up Snodgrass

Hill as part of the brigade's right wing, Hall guided the battalion to within 250 yards of the summit before enemy guns opened fire. After taking a few casualties from this barrage, Hall's inexperienced soldiers became noticeably apprehensive. The lieutenant colonel ordered the battalion back toward a sheltered part of the field, took a few moments to calm his men, and then resumed the advance. Minutes later he ordered the battalion to charge. As the Alabamians stormed the enemy breastworks, Hall went down with a bullet wound, but he had the satisfaction of watching his boys breach the Yankee lines and briefly hold the high ground. In the end, the 2nd Battalion retreated, its flag in tatters from numerous bullet holes and its strength reduced by ninety-one men. The following day, however, the survivors occupied the hill, quietly abandoned by the bluecoats during the night.
Photo courtesy of ADAH

RICHARD N. MOORE AND JOSEPH WYATT WILSON
copy prints

At the very center of Gracie's Brigade marched the 1st Battalion of Hilliard's Legion. Among the approximately 250 men who fought with that unit at Chickamauga were Capt. Richard Moore of Company D and Pvt. Joseph Wilson of Company A. Moore was a thirty-four-year-old married farmer from Lowndes County; Wilson was an eighteen-year-old florist from Montgomery. The two men shared little in common save their devotion to the Confederacy. Late on the afternoon of 20 September, Moore and Wilson advanced with the rest of their comrades against entrenched Union forces on Snodgrass Hill. En route they passed by wounded and exhausted men from other units who had hurled themselves up the slopes in earlier, failed assaults. Several hundred yards from the enemy breastworks, the 1st Battalion recoiled under a well-aimed volley of musketry, but the Alabamians responded with "a rousing cheer, which rose high above the din of conflict." For the next ninety minutes, officers such as

Moore strived to maintain linear cohesion, while enlisted men such as Wilson loaded and fired until their faces were stained with black powder. No one in the battalion got closer than a few yards to the summit, but no one shirked his duty until the supply of ammunition gave out. Only then did the Alabamians retreat, having suffered an appalling 168 casualties in a hurricane of flying lead. Private Wilson sustained a slight wound to his shoulder, but Captain Moore received a mortal wound. That night the captain slept fitfully in a makeshift field hospital. A sergeant in the battalion vividly remembered the scene: "a lurid glare was cast by scores of flaming rail fires upon the pale, agonized features of the many victims of the battle. There was no canopy for the sufferers save the heavens—no couch save the uneven earth—and no pillow save billets of wood."[31] *Photos courtesy of Clint Johnson Collection, U.S.A.M.H.I., and ADAH*

"On examination of the ground," Zachariah Deas said of the breastworks at the base of Missionary Ridge, "I became satisfied that this position was very disadvantageous." Thus, he questioned his orders to "hold this position to the last." Responsible for the first line of defense at the center of the besieging lines of the Army of Tennessee at Chattanooga, Deas was convinced that if the Union army attacked in strength, then his men would never be able to escape up the steep slope before they were wiped out. He requested that in such an eventuality, he simply deliver a few delaying volleys and then withdraw to the main battle line on the crest. Headquarters responded curtly, "remain as you are."

Originally from South Carolina, in 1835 the thirty-four-year-old Deas moved to Mobile, where he worked with his father in amassing a fortune in the cotton business. A veteran of the Mexican War, he spent the first few months of the Civil War on the staff of Gen. Joseph Johnston. In October 1861 he helped raise the 22nd Alabama Infantry and then won election as colonel, in no small part because he spent $28,000 of his own money for top-of-the-line Enfield rifles and other regimental equipment. Deas fought well at Shiloh, where he was wounded, and at Murfreesboro, after which he gained promotion to brigadier general. The five Alabama infantry regiments—19th, 22nd, 25th, 39th, and 50th—that he ably led at Chickamauga he now worried about at Chattanooga. On the morning of 25 November, Union forces massed into four lines to Deas's front. In the early afternoon the brigadier received welcome instructions to fall back at his discretion. Unfortunately, the lateness of these new orders prevented adequate dissemination. When the Yankees struck at 3:00 P.M., several units held their ground while others skedaddled prematurely. Deas withdrew with what units he could and prepared to help defend the summit of Missionary Ridge. "In a few minutes the firing along the whole front became very heavy," he observed, "and at one point the enemy were advancing against me in solid columns." To his left Deas saw Federal flags burst over the crest at numerous points. To his right he watched as a bluecoats charged

ZACHARIAH CANTEY DEAS
carte de visite

some of his own regiments. "Resistance now had ceased to be a virtue," Deas concluded. After falling back 300 yards, the general tried to mount a counterattack but "found that my ammunition was exhausted and my ordnance train had retired across the Chickamauga." Conceding defeat, he and his Alabamians joined the rest of the Confederate army in its headlong retreat.[32] *Photo courtesy of ADAH*

WILLIAM JACKSON PHILLIPS
copy print from Confederate Veteran

On 21 November 1863, Pvt. William Phillips of the 19th Alabama Infantry quietly celebrated his twenty-third birthday in a rifle pit on Missionary Ridge. Four days later he and his comrades in Company H strived in vain to repel a massive Union onslaught against the entire Rebel line southeast of Chattanooga. A poor boy from Cherokee County, Phillips had worked odd jobs throughout the 1850s to help feed his widowed mother and three younger siblings. Yet with the outbreak of war, he was one of the first to enlist in the 19th Alabama.

With combat experience at Shiloh, Murfreesboro, and Chickamauga, Phillips was a veteran to the core, though one with a somber demeanor. He had watched his brother die at Chickamauga, a battle in which he himself was wounded. At Missionary Ridge Phillips and the rest of the Confederate army held a seemingly impregnable position. His regiment anchored the right flank of Deas's Brigade, which occupied a portion of army's right center. To Phillips's immediate left stood Water's Battery, and to his right the sturdy structure of the Carroll House. Unfortunately, the private could not see down the slope to his front; his regiment had entrenched itself too far back. On the afternoon of 25 November, the staccato of artillery and musketry filled the air as the Union army commenced its attack from Chattanooga. Phillips gripped his rifle as the sounds came closer, the scampering retreat of the regiment's skirmish line presaging the imminent arrival of bluecoats. Pandemonium erupted off to the left as Manigault's Brigade broke and fled, taking half of Deas's Brigade with it. Then a howling pack of Minnesota boys burst over the rocks a mere two dozen yards away. With a target to shoot at, Phillips and the rest of the 19th Alabama unleashed a volley that stymied the enemy long enough for the nearby gun crews to attempt an escape. But a swarm of fresh midwestern regiments soon appeared, overran both the battery and the Carroll House, and pushed the 19th back. Amid the panic and chaos, Brig. Gen. Alfred J. Vaughan commandeered the 150 remaining men in the regiment, including Phillips, added them to his Tennessee brigade, and led a desperate counterattack. The ensuing hand-to-hand fighting around the Carroll House was brief and futile; Phillips and hundreds of other Rebels fell captive to the surging Yankees. In the days that followed, Phillips was sent to the Union prison camp at Rock Island, Illinois. En route the private may have pondered with some irony a stanza from a poem authored by Joseph High, a lieutenant from Company H who was killed at Chickamauga: "Freedom or Death, our song shall be / From land to land, from sea to sea / And when you hear from us again / You'll hear of lots of Yankees slain." For Phillips, the poem's glorious sentiment belied an ignoble reality.[33]

WILLIAM ARMSTRONG MIDDLETON
copy print

For many Rebels who marched with James Longstreet into East Tennessee, the winter of 1863–64 reminded them of Valley Forge. The attack on Knoxville in late November had gone badly awry, and after the Union victory at Chattanooga and subsequent arrival of enemy reinforcements, the putative Confederate offensive had turned into a desultory campaign of evasive maneuvers across the state's snow-covered mountain counties. On 29 January 1864, Capt. William Armstrong of the 23rd Alabama Sharpshooter Battalion gulped down some coffee before leading Company G in a task it had performed numerous times over the preceding weeks—skirmish duty. The thirty-five-year-old Middleton hailed from Montgomery County. He was the son of a veteran of the War of 1812 and a seasoned fighter himself, having fought at Chickamauga with Hilliard's Legion, an organization out of which his sharpshooter battalion was formed. This particular winter day, however, would be anything but mundane for the blue-eyed captain. On the outskirts of the small town of Dandridge, the Confederate army prepared to ford the shallow but frigid French Broad River. Middleton and his company waded across to secure the far side. Toward sunset the captain flushed a party of Yankee scouts, but in the ensuing exchange of gunfire, he took a bullet in the stomach. One of the war's trifling incidents had produced a life-threatening wound. Happily, Middleton survived. *Photo courtesy of ADAH*

Retreat and Defeat in the East

In the spring of 1864, the Army of Northern Virginia braced for the North's most powerful drive of the war. Gen. Robert E. Lee had repelled four previous invasions, but he now faced the Union's best commander, Lt. Gen. Ulysses S. Grant. As the new general in chief, Grant implemented a grand strategy that called for simultaneous offensives on multiple fronts, a plan that promised to stretch Confederate resources to the breaking point. While an army group under Maj. Gen. William T. Sherman advanced toward Atlanta in the western theater, Grant would personally supervise the Army of the Potomac's ongoing confrontation with the Army of Northern Virginia. Augmenting these efforts were two supplementary operations: a sweep down the Shenandoah Valley to cut Confederate supply lines and a thrust westward along the James River against Richmond. By May some 160,000 Union soldiers were in action in Virginia alone. Rebel defenders in the area amounted to 85,000 men, with slightly more than 60,000 serving directly under Lee.

Numerical inferiority was nothing new to the Army of Northern Virginia, but mathematically speaking, the Rebels simply could not afford further heavy losses. Alabamians still answered the morning roll call in sixteen infantry regiments that boasted proud combat histories, although the men looked weary after more than two years of grueling warfare. While the 13th Alabama continued to fight in James Archer's mostly Tennessee brigade, the other regiments were divided among three brigades: the 3rd, 5th, 6th, 12th, and 61st Alabama, under Brig. Gen. Cullen Battle, served in Lt. Gen. Richard Ewell's II Corps; the 8th, 9th, 10th, 11th, and 14th Alabama, under Brig. Gen. Abner Perrin of South Carolina, served in Lt. Gen. Ambrose P. Hill's III Corps; and the 4th, 15th, 44th, 47th, and 48th Alabama, under Col. William Perry (temporarily replacing General Law), served in Lieutenant General Longstreet's I Corps. The three brigade commanders were new to their positions, but their men were mostly veterans. Only the 61st Alabama, a conscript regiment that replaced the transferred 26th Alabama, was untested in battle.

Toward the end of April, Lee conducted a grand review of his forces and came away satisfied with their state of readiness. Morale was high: a majority of the rank and file had recently reenlisted for the duration of the war, many out of a devotion to their beloved commander that rivaled their patriotism for the Confederacy. Nonetheless, the government specifically honored the Alabama brigades of Battle and Perrin, whose reenlistments en masse displayed "a spirit undaunted, a heroic determination to battle ever until the independence of their country is established, and a consecration to the cause of liberty worthy of imitation."[1] Their mission in the upcoming campaign, along with the rest of Lee's army, was straightforward: hold on and bleed the Federal army until defeatism in the North brought down the Lincoln administration in the November elections.

On 4 May nearly 100,000 bluecoats crossed the Rapidan River and commenced marching through an area known as the Wilderness, a dense forest due west of Chancellorsville, where the two sides had clashed exactly a year earlier. Lee immediately sought an opportunity to attack. Two Confederate corps, each moving eastward down two parallel roads, made contact with Union forces late on the morning of 5 May. By early afternoon, fierce fighting erupted along a line of battle more than three miles long. Despite the dense foliage, the Yankees pitched into their adversaries. The Confederate left wing on Orange Turnpike was especially hard pressed. At a small clearing called Saunders' Field, Battle's Brigade reached the scene just as a Union division routed a brigade of Virginians to its front. With terrified soldiers fleeing through their formation, the Alabamians momentarily buckled, "each man appearing as if to halt between two opinions," one private wryly noted.[2] Bellowing commands to stand firm, Battle peremptorily resolved the dilemma and then lived up to his surname by conducting a vigorous holding action that helped thwart any further enemy penetration. With the arrival of additional Confederate units, Battle's Brigade participated in a large counterattack that stabilized the line. For their part,

the Alabamians smashed up several New York regiments. Well into the evening the staccato of gunfire reverberated throughout the forest as the combatants jockeyed for improved positions.

At dawn on 6 May, a reinforced Union army resumed its attack. Hammering the Confederate right flank along Orange Plank Road, Federal units steadily gained ground; by midmorning the Rebel line started to crumble. Fortuitously, Longstreet's corps arrived to save the day. Despite marching thirty-six miles in twenty-five hours, the Rebels plunged into action without pause. General Lee himself supervised the counterattack, one where the Confederates charged in echelon. The first two waves failed to break the Yankee lines, but a third, which included 1,200 men in Law's (Perry's) Brigade, achieved decisive results. While lining up near the Widow Tapp House, the ranks swelled with emotion as General Lee rode among them exclaiming, "God bless the Alabamians!"[3] The 4th and 47th Alabama Regiments followed the road and soon found themselves engaged in a fierce seesaw struggle among dense foliage. The other three regiments executed an impressive turning movement around the immediate Yankee right flank. The 15th Alabama, on the brigade's extreme left, enjoyed the greatest success. After scattering an opposing regiment of raw recruits from New York, the regiment resupplied itself with captured ordnance, then delivered enfilading fire into the enemy flank that drove the bluecoats off in disorder. Overall, Perry's Alabamians helped destroy an entire Union division and regain the ground lost during the morning combat. While Longstreet shifted the bulk of his corps against Union forces farther east, Perry consolidated Confederate control over the immediate battlefield. To this end, he was assisted by Perrin's fresh brigade.

For the next few hours, the two Alabama brigades, reinforced by a brigade of Floridians, fortified their position. With Perrin on the right, the Floridians on the left, and Perry just behind both in reserve, the corpse-strewn northern edge of Orange Plank Road had become a relatively quiet sector. Around 4:00 P.M., however, a full Union corps unexpectedly barreled through the woods and slammed into the formation's left flank. Perry immediately swung over to the left of the Floridians as all three brigades alternated between desperate holding actions and wild counterattacks through the smoke of a now-burning forest. Tired and bloodied from a full day of fighting, Perry's Alabamians (and the Floridians) crumpled under the Federal onslaught and ultimately fled the woods in disorder, having sustained 268 casualties on the day. "It was the first time since its organization," their commander glumly noted, "that the brigade ever was broken on the battlefield."[4] Other Confederate units, including Perrin's Alabamians, eventually contained the enemy breakthrough. Thereafter, the Battle of the Wilderness petered out. In two days of savage fighting, the Union army suffered over 17,000 casualties. Precise losses for the Confederates vary, but Lee's army lost around 10,000 men.

Tactically, the Confederates could chalk the Wilderness as a victory, but strategically it marked the beginning of a gruesome and grueling campaign of attrition. Rather than retreat, as the Army of the Potomac usually did after taking such a beating, Grant ordered his generals to keep advancing. On 8 May Federal forces maneuvered around the right of the Confederate army. Their objective was the crossroads at Spotsylvania, a small town southeast of the Wilderness, possession of which would interpose Grant's army between Lee and Richmond. Lee anticipated the move and, in one of the great races of the war, the Confederates beat the Federals to the key terrain literally by seconds. With Rebel cavalrymen buying time with harassing fire, infantrymen rushed to the scene. Among the first to arrive were Perry's Alabamians, who hastily fortified their position on an eminence named Laurel Hill even as they fended off enemy attacks. Throughout the day, both sides attempted to overlap the other by extending their lines eastward. By late afternoon Battle's Brigade

reached the scene after what one officer in the 6th Alabama described as "the hardest march of the war."[5] Moving past Laurel Hill, Battle's regiments clashed with the enemy in hand-to-hand fighting. Despite heavy losses, the Alabamians helped stave off the last Union effort of the day. During the night (and subsequent days), the Confederates improved their defensive lines, transforming the landscape into an interlocking field of trenches and breastworks; the spade and the axe had become as valuable as the rifle as instruments of modern warfare.

After a day of probing, the Federals unleashed a series of assaults on the afternoon of 10 May against the western portion of the Confederate position. On the Rebel left, Perry's Alabamians easily repulsed an attack against their portion of the line. A concentrated Yankee assault on a salient dubbed the Mule Shoe, however, achieved a breakthrough near the Rebel center. Held in reserve for just such an event, Battle's Brigade rushed forward and helped seal the breach with well-aimed rifle volleys.

Two days later Grant launched a more-massive assault against the northern tip of the Mule Shoe. Coming in fast under cover of early morning rain, a full corps swarmed over the breastworks. An Alabama battery under Capt. William Reese barely discharged two shots of canister before being engulfed by waves of bluecoats. Most of the gunners surrendered, along with hundreds of other Rebels who were simply too exhausted to offer effective resistance. Once again Battle's Brigade strived to repel the attackers, but a week of constant fighting left it too depleted to do much good. At this moment of crisis, the relatively fresh Alabama regiments in Perrin's Brigade conducted a vigorous if somewhat chaotic counterattack that helped finally halt the enemy penetration. After a bullet killed General Perrin, his five regiments basically acted on their own initiative, moving in whichever direction their officers thought they might encounter the enemy. "The cannon's roar was continuous," Capt. George W. Clark of the 11th Alabama vividly recalled of the confusing melee that ensued, "and many of the brave boys with us were killed."[6] Before it was over, some of the Alabamians had participated in the savage hand-to-hand combat around the Bloody Angle. In the end, the Confederates did stave off disaster, and for the next week the two sides mostly glared at one another. Like the Wilderness, Spotsylvania was a bloodbath: Union losses exceeded 18,000 men, while Confederates losses came to 12,000.

While Grant battered Lee's lines around Spotsylvania, a serious development unfolded to the south of Richmond. There Union general Benjamin Butler was advancing on the Confederate capital from his river base at Bermuda Hundred. In actuality, the Federal advance was more of a lurch given Butler's operational ineptitude. Still, because the general had 30,000 men at his disposal, his proximity constituted a genuine threat to the capital. The garrison around Richmond consisted of about 20,000 soldiers and militia under Gen. P. G. T. Beauregard. Among this force were five recently arrived Alabama infantry units under Brig. Gen. Archibald Gracie: the 41st, 43rd, 59th, and 60th Regiments plus the 23rd Battalion of sharpshooters. For about a week, these units had patrolled the Richmond environs, chasing off Yankee scouting parties and mounted enemy raiders. But on 16 May they participated in a pitched battle near Drewry's Bluff, just south of the capital. While Butler dithered in his efforts to strike toward the city, Beauregard managed to concentrate the bulk of his force (18,000 men) against about half of his foe's army (15,000 troops). Gracie's Brigade anchored the Rebel left flank, and at dawn it moved slowly through some low-lying fog before slamming into the enemy right. For about an hour, the Alabamians and neighboring units grappled with the Yankees before the defenders finally gave way. Confederate attacks elsewhere stalled, however, while Gracie's men were too shot up—the brigade suffered 314 casualties—and too low on ammunition to exploit

their success. Fortunately for the Rebels, Butler lost his nerve and withdrew his army back to Bermuda Hundred, where Beauregard was able to contain him with a minimal force.

Disgusted by Butler's failure to accomplish anything of significance, Grant pressed on with his Overland Campaign. Abandoning his efforts to crack Lee's entrenched army, the Union commander resumed his southeastward maneuvering. For the rest of May, the Army of the Potomac sidled its way ever closer to Richmond. But at every turn, the Army of Northern Virginia barred the way with earthen fortifications that Rebel infantrymen seemed capable of erecting in a matter of hours. Along the North Anna River, for instance, Federal forces aggressively probed the Confederate line, but after several days of sparring, they could find no weakness. For their part, Alabamians under Col. J. C. C. Sanders, who succeeded the slain Perrin, executed a successful spoiling attack near Ox Ford on the evening of 24 May. In this action the 8th and 11th Alabama bagged several dozen prisoners.

By the beginning of June, Grant's army had reached the site of the Seven Days' battleground of two years previous. Impatient for something decisive and convinced that the casualty tally of the previous month must have hurt Lee more than it hurt him, the general decided to launch a full-scale frontal attack against the Confederate defensive line at Cold Harbor. The Rebels were certainly exhausted, but their position was formidable. Not quite 1,000 men under Evander Law (who after a lengthy absence had just resumed command of the brigade from William Perry) occupied an eastward facing position just left of the Confederate center. As Union forces approached on the morning of 3 June, the Alabamians marveled at the enemy's audacity. The incredulous men of the 15th Alabama did not even load their muskets until the Yankees were less than fifty yards away. Within minutes, however, the Federal attack was bloodily repulsed at all points. For their part, Law's Brigade shredded advancing bluecoats with pointblank volleys of rifle fire, while an attached artillery section blasted away with double canister. Union casualties exceeded 7,000 troops. An Alabama officer ruefully observed that "the dead covered more than five acres of ground about as thickly as they could be laid."[7] Cold Harbor was the most lopsided Confederate victory of the war, one that many Rebels thought would surely undermine Northern popular support for the war.

Grant admitted the folly of his attack at Cold Harbor, but he persevered with the offensive. Shifting back to maneuver warfare, he deftly transported much of his army across the James River in an effort to capture Petersburg, an important railhead twenty-five miles south of Richmond. The movement caught Lee off guard, but the Union attempt to take the city misfired. From 15 to 18 June, Gracie's Brigade helped the scratch force of Rebel defenders under Beauregard thwart every enemy attack (though it should be noted that Union officers displayed inexcusable clumsiness and that many Yankee enlisted men simply balked at further orders to charge fortified positions). By the end of June, with Lee's army now firmly entrenched, Grant opted to lay siege to the Richmond-Petersburg area. It was a situation neither commanding general liked—for Grant a siege might prove too time consuming under the political circumstances; for Lee a siege pinned his army in a purely defensive posture that made defeat only a matter of time.

In July the two adversaries tried to break the pending deadlock. Despite his numerical inferiority, Lee ordered 10,000 men (including Battle's Brigade) under Lt. Gen. Jubal Early to drive Union forces out of the Shenandoah Valley. This successful operation culminated in a daring raid on Washington, D.C., on 12 July, during which the men of the 5th and 12th Alabama Regiments, among others, engaged in some sharp skirmishing within sight of the Capitol dome. The next day Early withdrew his troops back toward the Virginia mountains, but the whole affair produced a panic throughout the city and compelled Grant to dispatch an entire corps to defend his nation's capital even as he strived to capture another one a hundred miles away.

Back around Petersburg, Grant monitored the progress of a promising engineering endeavor. For several weeks Union miners had dug a tunnel under enemy lines just east of the city and then packed the shaft with four tons of black powder. At first light on 30 July, a gargantuan explosion rocked the countryside and produced a deluge of dirt and body parts that left behind a thirty-foot-deep crater; the Union army had just blown a massive hole in the Confederate defenses. The ensuing attack, however, was poorly executed. Rather than pouring through and beyond the gap, many bluecoats tumbled down into the "Crater" itself while others simply occupied nearby fortifications. Conversely, the Confederates shook off their initial daze and reacted with ferocity. In the counterattacks that followed, perhaps the most impressive was that of the Alabama brigade under John Sanders (now a brigadier general). The last of the reinforcements to arrive, Sanders and his men momentarily paused, taken aback by the smoke-filled lunar-like landscape and by the black faces of African American soldiers shooting at them. Then, with the general leading the way, they hurled themselves against the Yankees holding the southern edge of the Crater. In a quarter hour of hand-to-hand fighting, the Alabamians won the contest, taking nearly 500 prisoners, including 140 blacks. It had been the Alabamians first encounter with the U.S. Colored Troops, and while most displayed outrage, a few admitted that the former slaves gave as good as they got. In any event, Confederate success at the Crater ruined Grant's best opportunity to carry the works around Petersburg in 1864.

Thus far, Lee's skillful defense against a formidable adversary preserved a slim hope of victory. After three months of combat, the Rebels had inflicted over 60,000 casualties on the Army of the Potomac. "Grant is the most obstinate fighter we have ever met," noted Maj. Eugene Blackford of the 5th Alabama. "He has resolved to lose every man rather than retreat, which he knows is equivalent to our independence."[8] A turn of events in the Shenandoah Valley, however, combined with misfortune for the Confederacy in Georgia, doomed the cause for Blackford and his comrades.

Determined to eliminate the Shenandoah Valley as both a food source and a staging area for the Confederacy, Grant assembled an army of 40,000 under Maj. Gen. Phil Sheridan and ordered it to establish control over the region once and for all. After sparring for a few weeks, Sheridan moved aggressively against Early's main army of 11,000 graybacks just east of Winchester. Enjoying a manpower ratio of nearly 4:1, Sheridan envisioned a complete victory. On the morning of 19 September, a strong contingent of Union cavalry armed with repeating rifles pressed in from the north, while 30,000 Federal infantrymen approached from the east (with a second group of Yankee horsemen poised to cut off any retreat to the south). Ignoring the cavalry threats, Early hurled his veterans against the Union foot soldiers, and when this initial counterattack faltered, he threw in his reserve—Battle's Brigade. The Alabamians tore through a gap in the enemy formation and briefly stymied the entire Union advance. A jubilant Capt. Robert Park of the 12th Alabama remembered the moment: "We actually ran, at our greatest speed, after the disordered host in our front. We could see that they had a much larger force than ours, but we cared not for numbers."[9] Nevertheless, numbers eventually decided the day. The Yankees rallied and steadily drove the Rebels from Winchester. Early, however, credited the Alabama brigade with sparing his army total destruction.

After Winchester, Sheridan relentlessly pursued his Rebel quarry and within a month had cleared Early out of the valley, razing hundreds of farms and granaries in the process. On 19 October the Virginian lashed out one final time at the Battle of Cedar Creek. Sneaking through surrounding mountain passes, the Confederates caught the bluecoats unaware with a nasty surprise attack that routed elements of three corps. Alabamians in Battle's Brigade helped deliver a series of stinging blows throughout the morning hours. Gloating prematurely, Early failed to consolidate his victory, instead allowing his famished soldiers to pilfer the abandoned Union commissariat. Sheridan rallied his forces, counterattacked, and soundly whipped the Rebels. With the valley forever lost to the Confederacy, the remnants of Early's army limped back to Richmond to help man the defenses there. In November Abraham Lincoln won reelection. Not even the redoubtable Robert E. Lee could stave off defeat for another four years. Still, the Davis administration stubbornly clung to its delusion of nationhood.

For the rest of 1864, military activity in the Richmond-Petersburg area took on the monotony of static warfare. The diurnal task of digging and extending the lines was punctuated by constant skirmishing and probes that sometimes turned into small-scale battles. And, of course, there were the seemingly incessant artillery barrages. Crenshaw Hall, an adjutant in the 59th Alabama, came to take the shelling for granted. "The mortars are thrown up a great height," he explained, "and fall down in the trenches like throwing a ball over a house—we have become very perfect in dodging them."[10] The disposition of Alabama troops varied little during this time: Law's Brigade was stationed generally to the southeast of Richmond, where it periodically clashed with Yankees along Darbeytown Road; Gracie's Brigade held the line due east of Petersburg, where it endured frequent artillery fire; Sanders's Brigade defended the Weldon Railroad south of Petersburg and found itself involved in several scraps with Yankee raiders striving to cut that line of communication; and Battle's worn-out brigade served in a reserve capacity. Although the Rebels maintained a contiguous line of defense, the price of attrition was manifest to all. Lee's Army of

Northern Virginia was a gaunt specter of its once seemingly invincible self. With all commands hemorrhaging deserters, many already depleted regiments had to consolidate with others to achieve even company-size strength. Going into 1865, only the diehards remained, but even they knew that the death of the Confederacy was imminent.

When the end came, it was fast. As the weather improved toward the end of March 1865, Grant unleashed the final offensive of the war—the Appomattox Campaign. Lee saw it coming and launched a few spoiling attacks, but the weight of the enemy advance crushed everything before it. Thanks to a steady infusion of replacements, the Army of the Potomac still numbered over 100,000 men against less than 50,000 emaciated Confederates. Moreover, the Yankees were relatively fresh and could sense victory. In a series of running battles, Grant's army boxed the Rebels out of Richmond and Petersburg and drove them into south-central Virginia. Like many other Confederate units, Alabama regiments offered brave but futile resistance. Union forces ravaged Gracie's Brigade (now under Brig. Gen. Young Moody) at Hatcher's Run on 25 March, an engagement that wrecked the 59th Alabama as an effective regiment. At Fort Mahone on 2 April, a Yankee attack nearly obliterated Cullen Battle's proud brigade. A crestfallen Pvt. Joel McDiarmid of the 5th Alabama recalled the scene: "The men were posted at the distance of ten paces apart in the works and could offer but feeble resistance to the dense columns of Yanks that was opposing us. Our brave little Regiment continued till the last but was finally overpowered."[11] Finally, at Appomattox Court House, Grant trapped Lee's army and forced it to surrender on 9 April. Among the 27,000 graybacks who stacked arms and furled flags on that unhappy day were some 1,800 Alabamians; hundreds of others had already been captured in the preceding days.

The war in the East was over. Immediately paroled after taking the required oath of allegiance, the surviving Alabamians joined their comrades from other Rebel states in a long trek by foot back to their homes. In the course of the war, over 25,000 sons of Alabama had served in the Army of Northern Virginia. Of that number, 9,000 never saw their loved ones again. Five thousand died from battle wounds, 4,000 from disease. In a war where more men died from illness than gunfire, it is a testament to their hardiness and courage that these particular Alabamians reversed the ratio, though they died all the same. For thousands of other Alabama veterans, a missing arm or leg indicated a less-mortal sacrifice to the cause. Maj. Jemison Mims of the 43rd Alabama Infantry tried to elicit some hope from such a destructive war. Toward the end he prayed: "God grant these arduous struggles, and the vast heckatombs, which have been piled upon the altar of our newborn Confederacy, may result in good to the young republick and of civilized nations everywhere."[12] Certainly, such a sentiment was shared by all Americans in 1865.

WILLIAM COWAN
MCCLELLAN
copy print

An important but overlooked component of all Civil War armies was the provost guard. Comprised of men drawn from the line, the provost guard operated much like the modern-day military police; it was responsible for order and security in the war zone behind the battle front. Pvt. William McClellan of the 9th Alabama Infantry performed such duty for the Army of Northern Virginia. The son of a well-to-do slave-holder from Limestone County, McClellan was twenty-two years old when he enlisted in Company F (the Limestone Troopers) in the summer of 1861. Though his father voted against secession at the Alabama convention, young William eagerly fought for the Confederacy. He saw plenty of action throughout the Peninsula Campaign, receiving a flesh wound at Seven Pines, and was also present with his regiment at

Salem Church. Thereafter, McClellan served mostly in the provost guard. "We go where we pleas pretty much," he once commented on his new duties, "hunting Stragglers, deserters, conscripts & whiskey." McClellan arrested many men, a few of whom were later shot for their delinquency, but overall he enjoyed the provost guard, calling it a "very good position to save my bacon in times of Perile." Confederates on the line both envied and resented such men, but the provost played a crucial function in minimizing "absenteeism," a term used to describe the all-too-common wartime reality that at any given moment, hundreds of soldiers were somewhere other than where they were supposed to be.[13] *Photo courtesy of John C. Carter*

JAMES MADISON CONAWAY
ambrotype

With two nearby Alabama regiments buckling under the pressure of strong Union forces tearing through the trees of the Wilderness in May 1864, Pvt. James Conaway of the 61st Alabama Infantry likely contemplated running away. A thirty-one-year-old farmer from Coosa County, Conaway was a late recruit to the Confederate army, enlisting in Company I in May 1863, perhaps to avoid the shame of being drafted. Indeed, most of the rank and file in the 61st Alabama were conscripts, a fact that brought their fighting quality and patriotic commitment into question. In December 1863 several men from the regiment were severely punished for inciting a mutiny, one in which Conaway was not involved. When the 61st replaced the seasoned 26th Alabama as part of Cullen Battle's brigade, the general was dubious of the new regiment's worth. Private Conaway and his comrades, however, soon erased all

doubts about their combat mettle. With the situation deteriorating early on the afternoon of 5 May, the 61st Alabama held fast under the direct supervision of General Battle. After breaking an enemy charge, the regiment joined the brigade in a counterattack across Saunders Field. Conaway and his mates shot their way through a formation of New York Zouaves and helped overrun a section of Yankee guns. "The 61st loomed up in magnificent proportions," Battle exulted. "It was twice as large as any other regiment in the brigade, and its men were the first to place their hands on the captured guns." Though Conaway escaped his baptism of fire unscathed, the regiment reportedly suffered heavy losses. In any event, the performance of men such as Conaway atoned for the unit's defeatist reputation.[14]
Photo courtesy of Rayford L. Cannon

ISAAC HENRY TATE
tintype

For Pvt. Isaac Tate of the 15th Alabama Infantry, his regiment's early morning flanking maneuver near the Widow Tapp House on 6 May was a most satisfying tactical operation. The whole regiment maintained perfect alignment as it wheeled across a small open patch of land before executing a charge that routed a numerically superior foe, with negligible loss to the attacker, thereby clearing the enemy presence on the left of Colonel Perry's brigade. Col. William Oates chalked up the success to "the rapidity and boldness of my movement, and the accuracy of the fire of my men." Tate was one of those men, a true veteran. Nineteen years old at the time, he was a farm boy from Chambers County. The 15th was not his first unit. In the spring of 1862, Tate enlisted in the 34th Alabama Infantry, but after a prolonged illness, he was discharged. After recuperating, he reenlisted, this time into Company A, 15th Alabama, serving alongside his older brother, James. Having fought at Gettysburg and Chickamauga, the Wilderness would seemingly offer Isaac Tate few surprises. In actuality, the battle nearly

killed him. The early morning heroics were merely part one of a long day for the young soldier. Rejoining the main body of the brigade along Orange Plank Road, Tate and Company A helped repel a strong Union thrust. At the height of the attack, Colonel Oates moved the regiment to an optimal firing position: "One volley in the enemy's flank stopped their racket and caused them to retreat." Part two of Tate's Wilderness experience had ended well. After resting for a few hours, the men of the 15th Alabama pushed deeper into the woods as part of a large reconnaissance that soon turned into a violent meeting engagement. "When we turned the hill," Oates said of a particularly tense moment, "we caught it." A Union ambush decimated the Alabamians, although the regiment briefly held its ground and returned fire for several minutes. It was probably at this point that Tate went down with a serious wound. Evacuated by ambulance men, the private spent the next six months in a hospital.[15]
Photo courtesy of Steven R. Butler

170

WILLIAM McKENDREE
ROBBINS
copy print

Maj. "Mack" Robbins of the 4th Alabama Infantry cus-
tomarily led his men in prayer before going into any
battle. As he rushed them into the raging melee of the
Wilderness on the morning of 6 May, the major and
his fellow Alabamians would need every blessing they
could get. A thirty-six-year-old lawyer from Barbour
County, Robbins commanded Company G until his
promotion in October 1863. On the second day of
fighting at the Wilderness, the 4th Alabama anchored
the extreme right flank of Law's (Perry's) Brigade.
Due to the dense forest, Col. Pinckney Bowles relied
heavily on Robbins to help maintain linear cohesion.
Advancing into the fray along Orange Plank Road, the
regiment soon encountered the enemy in strength. All
the while waving his sword, Major Robbins helped
orchestrate volley fire and then led a charge that
momentarily pushed back the Federals. Moving
beyond the support of friendly units, the 4th soon

came under flanking fire that compelled a retreat.
The Alabamians rallied and charged again, only to be
driven back again. Hunkering down behind a plenti-
tude of tree trunks, Robbins and his boys withstood a
powerful Union assault. "It was a terrible moment,"
Colonel Bowles recalled. "On they came, again and
again, to meet a fearful slaughter, . . . their ranks were
decimated at every advance." Nevertheless, the bluecoats still delivered a few well-aimed volleys of their
own. While pacing the line encouraging his men,
Robbins reeled from a bullet that sliced through his
scalp. The major spun around from the blow, lost the
grip on his sword, and then crashed face down to the
earth. Soldiers nearby thought Robbins was dead, but
the officer soon blinked his eyes through a film of wet
blood dripping down his face. Mack Robbins had survived, though he remained dazed and useless for the
rest of the battle.[16] *Photo courtesy of ADAH*

HENRY STOKES
FIGURES
left, with an
unidentified friend
copy print

The men of the 48th Alabama Infantry were weary from a morning of bitter fighting, but their adjutant, Lt. Henry Figures, seemed the embodiment of energy. The regiment was going back into action at the Wilderness that afternoon, and the lieutenant was doing his part to reinvigorate combat morale. The twenty-one-year-old son of a newspaperman from Madison County, Figures shunned the War Department clerkship his father had secured for him, insisting instead on military service. After a stint as a private in the 4th Alabama Infantry, he accepted an adjutancy in the 48th. With his new regiment, the young officer displayed courage under fire at Gettysburg and Chickamauga. He did so again at the Wilderness. On the afternoon of 6 May, the 48th Alabama deployed at the center of Law's (Perry's) Brigade, which then conducted a reconnaissance in force toward an overgrown

creek bed about a half mile north of Orange Plank Road. After exchanging sporadic musketry with various Federal units similarly groping through the woods, the Alabamians reeled under the pressure of a more concentrated Union attack. Perry's left flank disintegrated as a brigade of Floridians on his right also broke. As the panic spread to the 48th, Adjutant Figures bounded through the trees on horseback, shouting words of encouragement. Unfortunately, an enemy bullet crashed into the side of his head, killing him instantly. Some of the soldiers had the wherewithal to carry the lieutenant's body with them as they fled the field. After the battle the men of the 48th wrapped Figures in a blanket, buried him under a peach tree, and erected a simple wooden cross.
Photo courtesy of ADAH

DUCALION NALL
ambrotype

Late on the morning of 6 May, Maj. "Duke" Nall of the 8th Alabama Infantry commanded his regiment for maybe five minutes before suffering a mortal wound. Part of Perrin's Brigade, the 8th had just arrived to reinforce the right flank of the hard-pressed Alabamians in Law's (Perry's) Brigade. To this end, the major thrashed about in the woods north of Orange Plank Road, getting the companies properly positioned to resist an attack; and a big one was on the way. A thirty-four-year-old planter from Perry County, Nall had been with the 8th Alabama since its organization in May 1861. As captain of Company K, he never missed a battle and earned the respect of the whole regiment with wounds from Frayser's Farm and Sharpsburg. At the Wilderness Nall was still awaiting the paperwork that would make his promotion official, but no one questioned his field-grade authority. As sounds of an approaching Federal brigade grew louder, Major Nall listened as Col. Hilary Herbert instructed the regiment to hold its fire until the bluecoats reached point-blank range. Moments later Herbert went down with a serious wound; Yankee skirmishers had just appeared. Nall immediately assumed command, disseminated the colonel's directions, and ordered the men to lie still. Within a few minutes a wall of blue loomed through the foliage. As he rose to shout "fire," the major was hit in the chest and went down. But his intention was clear: the Alabamians blasted the Union ranks with a deadly fusillade. Though incapacitated, Nall watched with satisfaction as his regiment then rushed forward as part of a brigade-level counterattack. *Photo courtesy of ADAH*

173

W. A. PATE
copy print

One of Nall's charging Alabamians was Pvt. W. A. Pate of Company C. Drafted into military service, the private joined the regiment in August 1862. As a conscript from Coosa County, Pate's personal views of the Confederate cause were probably not favorable. Still, he did his duty with courage. At some point during the counterattack, Pate was badly wounded but tried to keep fighting. In the regimental history of the 8th Alabama, the private is described as "a good soldier." He certainly was at the Wilderness. While Major Nall eventually died from his wound, Pate would survive his.[17]
Photo courtesy of ADAH

SAMUEL W. VANCE
daguerreotype from
Confederate Veteran

Late on the afternoon of 6 May 1864, Sgt. Samuel Vance of the 11th Alabama Infantry crouched behind a tree on a little ridge deep in the woods of northern Virginia. The Battle of the Wilderness was fast coming to an end, but for Vance and his regiment, there was still one more firefight to go. A nineteen-year-old student from Tuscaloosa, Vance joined the 11th Alabama in June 1861, serving in Company G through all of the regiment's engagements since Seven Pines. He became a sergeant after the fight at Salem Church. Now at the Wilderness, Vance participated in some of the war's most chaotic fighting. Part of Perrin's Brigade, the 11th Alabama defended a patch of forest north of Orange Plank Road. For much of the afternoon, the Alabamians skirmished sporadically with enemy units looming in and out of the dense foliage. Sometime after 4:00 P.M., however, they encountered a strong Union column that was attacking on a broad front. Although the Yankees routed Confederate forces off to the left,

they failed to dislodge Vance and his comrades. "We knew the bluecoats were coming," the sergeant recollected years later, "and every man did his duty bravely." Despite poor visibility, the Alabamians delivered repeated volleys that staggered the opposing formations. After about fifteen minutes of firing, Vance heard the order to charge and was soon lumbering wildly through the surrounding thickets; the sergeant later claimed that he ran three miles before halting. An exaggeration to be sure, Perrin's brigade did, in fact, help stabilize the Confederate line. In all, the 11th Alabama suffered twenty-six casualties that day. Sergeant Vance proudly declared that he was among the wounded: "The badge of honor was bestowed on me at the battle of the Wilderness." Though regimental records do not list him among the eight confirmed casualties in Company G, perhaps Vance received only a slight flesh wound, one that did not require medical attention.[18]

175

CULLEN ANDREWS BATTLE
copy print

For a man who once considered himself useless after missing the glorious fight at Chancellorsville due to a stupid horse-riding injury, Cullen Battle was fast developing into one of Lee's most reliable troubleshooters in 1864. Case in point: the brigadier's timely arrival and vigorous attack at Spotsylvania on the afternoon of 8 May. A thirty-four-year-old lawyer from Macon County, Battle was one of Alabama's leading citizens at the outbreak of the war. A political protégé of the fire-eater William Yancey, Battle strongly supported secession. Upon hearing the news of John Brown's raid on Harper's Ferry, he raised a militia company, keeping it active for over a year until it merged into the 3rd Alabama Infantry. After Seven Pines, where he was wounded, Battle took over the regiment. As a colonel he performed competently enough, but it was not until Gettysburg that his true military abilities shined forth. When the other Alabama regiments in O'Neal's Brigade broke on the first day of that engagement, Battle kept the 3rd in the fight, reinforcing other Rebel attacks on his own initiative. Elevated to brigade command, he exhibited coolness in a crisis on the first day of fighting in the Wilderness when a Union attack nearly pierced the Confederate left wing. Now during the race for Spotsylvania, Battle drove his men eastward over dust-choked roads, arriving near the county courthouse around 5:00 P.M. Immediately, the general hurled his brigade against a large concentration of bluecoats lapping around the Rebel right. Battle reported that his men "charged the enemy and drove him rapidly for about 600 yards." In the process the Alabama brigade moved well beyond the support of friendly units. In savage hand-to-hand fighting, the 6th and 61st Alabama Regiments lost their colors. Overcome by martial rage, Battle seemed determined to win the war then and there. "I took the colors of the Third Alabama in my hand," he explained, "went forward, and asked the men to follow." Although the soldiers in his old command rallied behind their leader, this final surge gained no further ground, "a result no doubt greatly attributable to physical exhaustion from long marching, constant labor, and their rapid advance." Nevertheless, his temerity disrupted what had been a serious Union turning movement that might have cost Lee control over the area's key terrain. Only when the fighting was over did Battle feel the throbbing pain in his right foot, the product of a spent round striking his boot. Over the next few days, the general led his men into fierce action inside what would become known as the Mule Shoe salient.[19] *Photo courtesy of ADAH*

176

WILLIAM JASPER BUNN
copy print

Along the eastern tip of the Bloody Angle, Pvt. William Bunn of the 14th Alabama Infantry scrambled over muddy entrenchments before closing with the enemy in hand-to-hand fighting. A resident of Talladega County, the twenty-eight-year-old Bunn had seen plenty of action since joining Company I—the Hillabee Rifles—in July 1861. He was wounded at Gaines' Mill and Frayser's Farm, grieving the death of his brother Marcus in the latter. Spotsylvania would be William's last battle. On the morning of 12 May, the 14th Alabama rushed forward as part of the right wing of Perrin's Brigade, which was trying to seal an enemy breach at the center of the Confederate line. As the regiment moved past the McCoull House, General Perrin went down with a mortal wound, and the brigade split into two independent forces. Bunn's 14th, along with the 11th Alabama, veered right, crossed an open swath of ground, and slammed into a body of bluecoats. The Alabamians lodged themselves behind some earthworks, but a Union counterattack threatened to engulf them. "We were in the middle of a bad fix," an officer in the 11th recalled. "The fire of the enemy never ceased during the entire day, and I could not undertake to say how many assaults were made upon us by the enemy." As ammunition ran low, Bunn and his comrades made effective use of the bayonet. At some point, however, the private received a disabling wound. When his regiment withdrew later that night, Bunn fell into enemy hands.[20] *Photo courtesy of Roy H. Bunn*

ALFRED LEWIS SCOTT
copy print

For Lt. Alfred Scott of the 9th Alabama Infantry, the fighting in the Mule Shoe salient on 12 May was a literal defense of hearth and home. Born in Spotsylvania County in 1838, the young officer spent much of his childhood roaming the bucolic woods and fields that had now become a scarred landscape of military earthworks. While slogging over muddy roads, under an early morning drizzle, toward the clangor of combat, he perhaps reminisced about happier days. Upon graduation from the University of Virginia, Scott moved to Butler County, where he started his bid to become a cotton planter. Then the war broke out. Scott enlisted as a private in the Jeff Davis Rangers, an outfit that soon became Company G, 9th Alabama. He saw action during the Peninsula Campaign, but in November 1862 Scott joined Brig. Gen. Edward Perry's Florida brigade as a staff officer (Perry was Scott's brother-in-law). After the Wilderness, where the Florida brigade was nearly obliterated and Perry badly wounded, Lieutenant Scott rejoined his former comrades in the 9th Alabama just in time to participate in the great counterattack against the Union breakthrough at Spotsylvania. Part of Perrin's reserve brigade, the 9th advanced as the left-center regiment. Around 7:00 A.M. the Alabamians reached the McCoull House, mere yards from the furious hand-to-hand fighting raging to the northwest around the Bloody Angle. Scott remembered everyone lying prone amid a racket of incessant gunfire, then General Perrin barking brusque orders to charge into the maelstrom. The ensuing melee alternated between the surreal and the savage. "As I passed under a heavy cherry tree," Scott recalled, as the regiment hurried through a nearby garden, "I distinctly remember the shower of the bits of leaves floating to the ground in the still sultry air." Moments later, as the lieutenant leaped over a stretch of breastworks, something more sinister filled the air—Yankee projectiles. "If the bullets had been sweeping closer to the ground," Scott observed, "I don't see how many of us could have gotten through." Nevertheless, the close-quarters fighting proved deadly enough. Scott watched three color bearers go down in quick succession, then heard the news that Perrin was mortally wounded. As brigade cohesion unraveled, Scott and other officers from the now-intermingled ranks of the 8th and 9th Alabama Regiments pushed clusters of men toward the nearest enemy target. In the smoky confusion the Alabamians managed to recapture a fifty-yard section of entrenchments. There they grimly held on until after midnight, when all of the Confederate units in the area fell back to a stronger, shorter defensive line. Despite the heavy casualties on both sides, Scott came through the fray unharmed.[21] *Photo courtesy of ADAH*

WILLIAM JEMISON MIMS
copy print

On 12 May 1864 Capt. Jemison Mims of the 43rd Alabama Infantry deployed his Company G as part of a skirmish line for Gracie's Brigade, then advanced north up Meadow Bridge Road toward a large body of mounted Union raiders under Maj. Gen. Phil Sheridan. With the bridge across the nearby Chickahominy River partially destroyed and Rebel artillery posted on the opposite bank, Mims and his men believed that they had their foe trapped. A thirty-year-old lawyer and slaveholder from Jefferson County, Mims fancied himself a country squire. He considered secession an overly rash act but dedicated himself to the Confederate cause nonetheless. After making arrangements for the welfare of his family and farm, including the selection of a trustworthy overseer, Mims organized a company of infantrymen from among his neighbors and joined the army in May 1862. A capable officer, he earned special praise for his conduct at Chickamauga, where he was wounded. At the long-forgotten engagement of Meadow Bridge, Mims would be wounded once again. Never one to be passive, Sheridan simultaneously sent a strike force across

the river to secure the far side and executed an aggressive rearguard action. The latter hit Mims and his company head on. The captain tried to stem the Yankee charge but quickly found himself outmatched on the open roadway. "I was entirely unprotected," he recalled, "as was also many of my Company in full view & point blank range of the enemy." A hail of bullets killed a soldier next to Mims and snapped the radius bone in the captain's left forearm. Grimacing in pain, Mims ushered his men toward the safety of a ravine. Shortly thereafter the whole brigade withdrew under heavy fire; Sheridan then made his escape. As for Mims, the frustration and agony were just beginning. Doctors did not set his bone until the following day, allowing infection to set in. Fortunately, the captain convalesced in a Richmond hospital, where he could receive the best medical care. "The Surgeon removed me to another room," Mims explained, "painted my arm with iron for several days and promptly subdued all Erysypilictic tendences."[22]
Photo courtesy of Birmingham Public Library Department of Archives and Manuscripts

YOUNG MARSHALL MOODY
copy print

For several hours in the early morning of 16 May 1864, Col. Young Moody of the 43rd Alabama Infantry stared into a thick fog that blanketed the farms and woods southwest of Drewry's Bluff. At 4:45 A.M., the persistent fog notwithstanding, he received the order to advance and soon found himself in a hotly contested battle. A forty-one-year-old merchant, Moody had been living in Marengo County for almost twenty years when the Civil War broke out. For the first year of the conflict, he served as a company commander in the 11th Alabama Infantry. Then, in May 1862 he helped organize the 43rd Alabama, serving as that regiment's lieutenant colonel. A genial man by nature, Moody won the admiration of his men less through strict discipline and more through battlefield example. Promoted to full colonel in 1863, he led his regiment into the savagery of Chickamauga as part of Gracie's Brigade. At Drewry's Bluff, Moody led his Alabamians into battle once again. Marching on the extreme right of Gracie's Brigade, which itself composed the extreme left of the Confederate attack, the 43rd slowly crossed an open field still shrouded in mist. The regiment covered a quarter mile of ground, scattering Yankee skirmishers all the way, before it encountered the main Union line entrenched within a patch of woods. At this point a general exchange of volleys ensued. "After a little over one hour's stubborn fighting," Moody's division commander related, "the enemy's rifle-pits and breastworks were carried about 100 yards inside the woods." The 43rd Alabama had helped overrun the Union right flank, but in doing so had both exhausted its supply of ammunition and become tangled with other regiments in the brigade. Moreover, the regiment lost its commander. In the final charge Moody went down with a severe bullet wound to one of his ankles. Though carried away by an ambulance team, he gained satisfaction when he later learned that his regiment held the hard-won ground until the battle petered out later that morning.[23] *Photo courtesy of Library of Congress*

EVANDER MCIVOR LAW
carte de visite
A. B. Avery, Tuskegee

On the morning of 2 June 1864, Evander Law deployed his brigade along a previously occupied section near the center of the Confederate defensive line at Cold Harbor. The general considered the entrenchments he inherited unsatisfactory: "The works were in open ground and were ill-adapted to resist an attack." In rectifying these shortcomings, the general personally staked out new locations for his five regiments and then ordered the men to dig through the night. Law was an able brigadier, but his aloof personality some-times alienated those around him. A native of South

Carolina, the twenty-seven-year-old Law was a gradu-ate of what later became the Citadel. In 1860 he moved to Macon County, where he earned a living as a teacher while he studied law. With the outbreak of war, Law won election as lieutenant colonel in the 4th Alabama Infantry; he was seriously wounded while helping lead the regiment at First Manassas. As full colonel he led the 4th at Seven Pines and thereafter served as an act-ing brigade commander until his official promotion in October 1862. In 1863 his Alabamians would garner a well-deserved reputation as fierce fighters, in no small part because of Law's cool leadership. Unfortunately, the general experienced a frustrating relationship with two of the Army of Northern Virginia's most presti-gious officers, John Bell Hood and James Longstreet. At both Gettysburg and Chickamauga, Law assumed command of Hood's Division when its commander went down with disabling wounds early in each battle, yet Hood received much of the credit for leading the troops in each fight. During the siege of Chattanooga and the Confederate invasion of East Tennessee, Law increasingly found himself the scapegoat for Longstreet's blunders. He successfully defended him-self before a court-martial but forever resented his shabby treatment.

Cold Harbor offered Law a chance at redemption. At dawn on 3 June, Union soldiers charged against the Alabama brigade. Law observed that the Federal attack quickly degenerated into "a mass of writhing human-ity, upon which our artillery and musketry played with cruel effect." The speed with which the Alabamians expended their cartridges compelled the general to submit an urgent request for more ammunition. He need not have worried. "I found the men in fine spir-its, laughing and talking as they fired," Law noted as he paced among his regiments, "more than a thousand men lay in front of our works either killed or too badly wounded to leave the field." Conversely, Law's brigade suffered a mere twenty casualties. Among them, though, was Law himself, struck in the head by a shell fragment toward the end of the day, a wound that damaged his left eye and knocked him out of action for some time.[24] *Photo courtesy of ADAH*

GEORGE WHITFIELD
HUGULEY
copy print

It was nearly dark on 17 June 1864, when Lt. Col. George Huguley of the 59th Alabama Infantry arrived on the eastern outskirts of Petersburg at the head of Gracie's Brigade. Large Union forces had nearly unhinged the Confederate defensive perimeter around the city; desperate action was required to restore the line. For Huguley, it was a moment that promised much glory. The twenty-six-year-old owned one of the biggest plantations in Chambers County, so he fully understood what was at stake should the Confederacy fail. Beginning the war as a captain in Hilliard's Legion, the young planter became a major in the 59th when the Legion became Gracie's Brigade in the autumn of 1863. Soon thereafter, Huguley won praise for his solid performance at Chickamauga. And after the regiment's highest-ranking officers went down at Drewry's Bluff in May 1864, he took command. The 59th Alabama still occupied a position near that battlefield when the crisis around Petersburg occurred. For several days, over 60,000 bluecoats had

been blundering around the city, but on 17 June they seemed on the verge of finally capturing it when Gracie's Brigade rushed to the scene. Lieutenant Colonel Huguley led the brigade vanguard—600 men, including those in the 59th—on a ten-mile forced march. He then honed in on a Union breakthrough near the Shands House and charged. According to a staff officer, the Alabamians "gallantly leaped over the works and drove the assailants back." Huguley's attack stopped the enemy cold; his men inflicted over 1,000 casualties (including hundreds of prisoners taken). Along with the rest of Gracie's Brigade, which soon reached the field, the Alabamians repelled other Union attacks until nearly midnight. The next morning reinforcements from the Army of Northern Virginia poured in and manned the fortifications that Huguley had helped secure. For his dramatic role in defending Petersburg, Huguley received a brevet colonelcy.[25]
Photo courtesy of Al Zachry

183

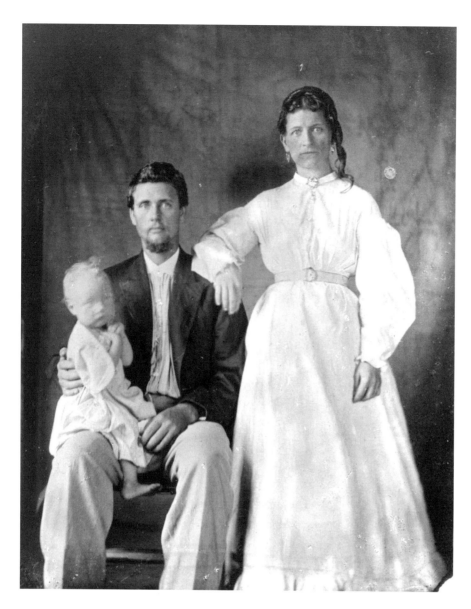

WILLIAM PLEASANT LOYD
(with Margaret Loyd and child)
copy print

If he thought serving in the ambulance corps would keep him out of harm's way, then William Loyd of the 11th Alabama Infantry thought wrong. The private became one of five casualties in the regiment during a skirmish at Ream's Station in late June 1864. A twenty-two-year-old store clerk from Greene County, Loyd enlisted in June 1861 into what became Company B, serving for a time as a regimental musician. The private missed direct involvement in most of the 11th's engagements, either because of frequent spates of illness or because of his assignment to various details, such as ambulance duty. On 23 June 1864 the 11th

Alabama participated in an attack against a Vermont brigade that was trying to destroy a section of the Weldon Railroad near Ream's Station. As the action unfolded, Loyd scurried about as needed, carrying wounded men to the rear. During one of his runs, the private collapsed to the ground in agony; a stray shot had passed through his ankle. The Confederates won the skirmish that day, but Loyd's military service was over. Whether he kept his foot or lost it to amputation is unknown. *Photo courtesy of Mrs. Michelle Orlando Collection, U.S.A.M.H.I.*

MORGAN SMITH CLEVELAND
copy print

As a hot July sun beat down, Adj. Morgan Cleveland of the 8th Alabama Infantry leaned against the side of a ravine waiting for the order to counterattack; Union forces were swarming in and around the newly created "Crater," a serious breach in the Confederate defenses due south of Petersburg. A thirty-two-year-old planter from Dallas County, Cleveland spent the first two years of the war as his regiment's quartermaster sergeant— a rather lowly rank for a big slaveholder. But in the summer of 1863, he became adjutant, and though he was present for most the 8th Alabama's important battles, it was at the Crater where he became recognized as a hero. Around noon on 30 July, Cleveland reiterated instructions for the men to fix bayonets and hold their fire until they had closed with the Yankees. At approximately 1:30 P.M., the men of the 8th (along with four other Alabama regiments in Sanders's Brigade) rose up and charged a Union brigade defending a patch of breastworks near the Crater. "With the fury of a whirlwind," recalled an Alabama captain, "they rushed upon the line." The 8th Alabama slammed into the 2nd Michigan and, after a few minutes of desperate fighting, captured its flag and most of its men. Soon the Alabama brigade completed the Confederate encirclement of the Crater. In the course of the melee, Adjutant Cleveland shot at random enemy targets swirling in the smoke, but once the outer rim was secure, he paused to gaze at the throng of bluecoats still struggling inside the Crater itself— "a dance of death" he called it. At this point Cleveland switched from brandishing a weapon to proffering a canteen: he dragged helpless foes out of the pit and gave them water. While tending to a white officer and a black soldier, both mortally wounded, Cleveland remembered the two men getting into an altercation. Evidently, the "burly negro" blamed the officer for their capture: "Death soon ended the suffering of one and the hatred of the other." In the battle's aftermath, Cleveland, who was slightly wounded in the affair, received praise for his courage in battle and his compassion toward prisoners.[26] *Photo courtesy of ADAH*

185

RICHARD CHANNING JONES
copy print

Lt. Richard Jones, a staff officer in Law's Brigade, had passed through some of the war's biggest battles with nary a scratch until August 1864, when he finally got hit while defending his nation's capital. A twenty-three-year-old lawyer from Wilcox County, Jones began the war as part of the garrison at Fort Morgan. Then in May 1862, he accepted a commission in Company C, 44th Alabama Infantry, rising to the rank of first lieutenant in November 1863. With that regiment, Jones fought at Second Manassas, Sharpsburg, Gettysburg, and Chickamauga. Declining company command in early 1864, he instead became an assistant adjutant general in Law's Brigade. After a summer of busy staff duty, Lieutenant Jones found himself under intense fire at the largely forgotten clash of New Market Heights on 14 August. That morning the

Union army began a rather large operation against Confederate defenses just southeast of Richmond. Law's Alabama veterans were on hand to resist this latest enemy advance. For much of the morning, the Alabamians, dug in on high ground, exchanged a brisk fire with their Yankee adversaries. Throughout, Jones ostensibly acted as a courier between the brigade's regiments. At some point during the contest, the staff officer suffered a painful bullet wound to his shoulder. In the end, though, his brigade helped stymie the Union attack around New Market Heights in a week-long engagement. Thankfully, Jones's wound was not especially serious, but it did knock him out of the war for several weeks. *Photo courtesy of W. S. Hoole Special Collections Library, The University of Alabama*

At 2:00 A.M. on 21 August 1864, Brig. Gen. John Sanders, the "boy brigadier," formed his five Alabama regiments into line of battle. Nearby, Yankee forces were once again trying to break Confederate control of the Weldon Railroad, this time at Globe Tavern. Sanders was eager to do his part in stopping them. Only twenty-four years old at the time, the young general was a military prodigy. The son of a slaveholder from Greene County, Sanders grew into a Southern zealot. With the outbreak of war, he quit his senior year at the University of Alabama (over his parents' objection) and raised what became Company B, 11th Alabama Infantry. As a captain Sanders fought bravely in numerous battles, receiving a leg wound at Frayser's Farm and a facial wound at Sharpsburg. Although he often displayed a social elitism that incensed many of his soldiers, Sanders nevertheless proved a natural warrior whom the men came to respect, even worship. Promoted colonel in December 1862, the youth suffered yet another wound at Gettysburg but recovered in time to lead the regiment at the Wilderness and Spotsylvania. Elevated to brigade command in May 1864, Sanders brought fresh spirit and energy to an army showing signs of war weariness. Throughout the summer, the "boy brigadier" responded to several crises throughout the Petersburg area, including his timely arrival at the Crater to the south of the city and his reinforcement of the hard-pressed Rebel line around Deep Bottom to the north of it. His morning attack at Globe Tavern seemed like more of the same. With the dawn, Sanders advanced his brigade through some woods. Then, after making contact with the enemy, his men waded into a strong Union skirmish line. Scooping up some prisoners, the Alabamians pursued their foe onto the open fields of the Davis Farm. About a half mile on the other side, Union batteries commenced fire. Riding back and forth on a jet-black steed, Sanders quickly realigned the brigade before ordering a charge across the field. By this time a muggy heat added to everyone's misery, but the "boy brigadier" seemed unaffected by it all. Having dismounted, Sanders moved among his regiments, urging

JOHN CALDWELL CALHOUN SANDERS
copy print

the men onward despite the growing discharge of canister. One hundred yards from the Yankee breastworks, though, Sanders wobbled as a projectile passed through both thighs. "I heard a bullet hit the General," Capt. George Clark, a staff officer, recalled. "As I was quite close to him I saw him reel, and grasping him around the waist I helped him up and asked him if I should go on, but he said, 'No, stay with me,' and immediately lapsed into unconsciousness." Clark and a few others carried Sanders to a shady tree, where the general rapidly bled to death from a severed femoral artery. The attack failed; Sanders was dead; and the war taught its redundant lesson that all men are mortal.[27]
Photo courtesy of W. S. Hoole Special Collections Library, The University of Alabama

EDWIN LAFAYETTE HOBSON
copy print
Homeier and Clark, Richmond, Va.

many combat heroics was a conspicuous charge at Gaines' Mill, a valiant effort to hold the Bloody Lane at Sharpsburg, a refusal to leave the field at Chancellorsville even as he nearly bled to death, and a timely counterattack near the Mule Shoe at Spotsylvania, where he was again wounded. But his greatest feat at arms came at Cedar Creek.

At 6:30 A.M. Battle's Brigade initiated the Rebel attack. The Alabamians overwhelmed a Union encampment, but in the process General Battle suffered a severe leg wound. Lieutenant Colonel Hobson immediately took over and realigned the brigade perpendicular to a roadway leading into the village of Middletown. For several minutes, Hobson and his men endured cannon fire while other Confederate brigades came in line. Finally, the lieutenant colonel moved against the battery that had been bombarding his location. "Men bounded forward with a yell," he later recounted in a letter to his fiancé. "In a few minutes they were in the midst of artillery, calling upon the yankees to surrender and, when [they failed] to do so, cutting them down with their swords or shooting them down." The Alabama brigade captured at least five guns. Exploiting his tactical success, Hobson next focused his regiments against a large contingent of bluecoats deployed in a square formation. "My brave men attacked it so vigorously," the lieutenant colonel continued, "that we drove it back and scattered it in every direction until we encaptured [*sic*] many." Maintaining the momentum, Hobson pushed his men past the western outskirts of Middletown and crashed into another hapless grouping of Federals: "in less than ten minutes we routed them as completely as troops ever were." Over the course of three hours, the Alabamians advanced nearly two miles and helped maul three Union corps.

Unfortunately for them, a vicious late-afternoon counterattack led by Sheridan himself dramatically reversed the situation. With the graybacks now fleeing, Hobson managed to preserve order within his own brigade but strived in vain to mount an effective rearguard resistance. "Humiliated beyond expression," the furious lieutenant colonel concluded, "we retired to Fishers Hill to tell all of our disgrace." Cedar Creek was a signal defeat for the Confederacy, but Hobson personally considered it his finest performance of the war.[28] *Photo courtesy of ADAH*

After an all-night march over mountainous trails, Lt. Col. Edwin Hobson of the 5th Alabama Infantry waited impatiently for the commencement of Lt. Gen. Jubal Early's dawn attack at Cedar Creek. As part of Battle's Brigade, the 5th would be among the first units to strike the unsuspecting Yankees that chilly autumn morning of 19 October. It was an exciting moment for men such as Hobson, who for the past month had endured one defeat after another in the Shenandoah Valley at the hands of Phil Sheridan. A wealthy, twenty-nine-year-old planter from Greene County, Hobson epitomized the Southern warrior ideal with his fearlessness in battle. After raising Company I in May 1861, he soon rose to field-grade rank and, more often than not, served as acting regimental commander whenever real fighting approached. Among his

On the first day of December 1864, Archibald Gracie escorted Robert E. Lee through his brigade's sector of the defensive line around Petersburg. Because the Rebel fortifications there formed a salient protruding outward, they tended to draw heavier-than-usual sniper and artillery fire. The defending Alabamians dubbed their position "Gracie's Mortar-Hell." As such, the general was concerned for his commander's safety. Gracie turned thirty-one the day Lee visited, yet he presented the bearing of a much older man, perhaps due to his social and military credentials, which placed him solidly in the South's patrician class. He was the heir to a family fortune—he and his father managed the Mobile office of the London-based Barings Bank. Moreover, he attended West Point, graduating fourteenth in the class of 1854. During the secession crisis, Gracie personally commanded the Alabama militia forces that seized the Mount Vernon Arsenal. An ambitious officer, he gained promotion rapidly: captain in the 3rd Alabama Infantry, major in the 11th Alabama Infantry, colonel of the 43rd Alabama Infantry, and by the end of 1862, brigadier general. Oddly, his rise occurred despite not seeing any real combat. But Gracie proved that he was every bit the warrior of his peers when he finally did see significant action. At Chickamauga he led his brigade in the final assault on Snodgrass Hill. At Bean's Station he suffered a wound. At Drewry's Bluff he skillfully handled his men in a difficult fight. And at Petersburg his timely arrival on 17 June helped save the city from capture. But thereafter, Gracie and his Alabama boys endured the drudgery of trench warfare. So it was that Lee's visit afforded Gracie both pleasant relief and unsolicited anxiety. At one point the commanding general stopped to observe the Federal lines from a spot where an Alabama private had recently been shot dead. Gracie indulged his superior for only a few seconds before gently nudging Lee out of harm's way. "It is better," he reportedly told the general, "that I should be killed than you." Evidently, Lee appreciated the gesture and soon departed. This inspired a poem by Frank O. Tichnor that included two stanzas that immortalized the moment: "And then the glass was lowered, / And

ARCHIBALD GRACIE
carte de visite
E. and T. Anthony, New York

voice that faltered not / Said in its measured cadence: / 'Why, Gracie, you'll be shot!' / And Alabama answered: / 'The South will pardon me / If the ball that goes through Gracie / Comes short of Robert Lee." Naturally, there was an ironic ending to all of this chivalry. The day after Lee's inspection, Gracie returned to the spot and, as he viewed the enemy positions through a telescope, dropped dead from a shell burst directly over his head. "I do not know how to replace him," Lee wrote after receiving the news. "He was an excellent officer and a Christian gentleman."[29] *Photo courtesy of ADAH*

HARVEY ELLIS JONES AND SIMON CONNELL BAGBY
copy print

He knew the war was essentially over, but for Capt. Harvey Jones, a staff officer in Moody's Brigade, any chance to sting the Yankee foe one more time was worth the effort. On 31 March 1865 at the Battle of White Oak Road, Jones and his Alabama compatriots did just that. A twenty-two-year-old college student from Tuscaloosa County, Jones quit his studies after Fort Sumter and accompanied his friend Simon Bagby to Mobile, where the two enlisted in the 3rd Alabama Infantry. The following year Jones accepted a commission in Company K of the newly raised 43rd Alabama Infantry and bid Bagby farewell. The new assignment allowed Jones to serve alongside kin and neighbors from Tuscaloosa. He soon became the assistant adjutant general in Gracie's Brigade, and by the time Young Moody took command in late 1864, Jones had become a captain. He also learned about the fate of his friend Bagby, who as a lieutenant in Company E, 3rd Alabama Infantry was killed in action on 22 September 1864 at Fisher's Hill in the Shenandoah Valley.

At the end of March 1865, the Army of Northern Virginia commenced its westward trek, abandoning the Richmond-Petersburg area. With Union forces harassing the whole movement, Moody's Brigade was tasked with holding open White Oak Road for the evacuating Rebel wagon train. On the damp morning of 31 March, a Union division attempted to disrupt this line of transportation. Captain Jones first disseminated warning orders to the brigade's four Alabama infantry regiments. He then rode alongside Col. Martin Stansel, acting brigade commander, throughout the ensuing clash. Rather than simply defend the road, the Alabamians participated in a division-level counterattack. A sergeant in the 60th Alabama Infantry described a scene that Jones witnessed for the last time: "With that peculiar, liver-quaking cheer, which ever preceded a Confederate onset," the soldier related, "the Confederate line rose from the ground, poured a volley into the blue masses, and rushed forward upon them, loading and firing as they rushed." The Rebel onslaught unnerved the Federals and drove them back several hundred yards before reinforcements arrived and steadily pushed the Alabamians across the road. However gratifying the charge had been, the brigade lost perhaps two hundred men and failed in its mission. Jones was among the casualties, shot through a thigh, a wound that required amputation of a leg a mere ten days before the final capitulation at Appomattox.[30] *Photo courtesy of ADAH*

FLAG OF THE 41ST ALABAMA
INFANTRY
copy print

One of the last Confederate flags lost in combat was the banner of the 41st Alabama Infantry. Part of Gracie's Brigade, the men of the 41st hailed mostly from Pickens and Tuscaloosa counties. After participating in several campaigns in the western theater, including Chickamauga, the regiment (with its brigade) was transferred to Richmond. Prior to its arrival in April 1864, the 41st Alabama received a special battle flag, one that reflected the pattern of others in the Army of Northern Virginia—blue St. Andrew's Cross, woven with thirteen white stars, on a red background. Curiously, the regiment's flag contained no unit designation and inexplicably had a red pole sleeve, a feature usually reserved for artillery units.

Regardless, the 41st Alabama fought with distinction under its new flag at Drewry's Bluff and throughout the siege of Petersburg. During the Union army's final offensive against the Confederate capital, the 41st Alabama lost its colors while conducting a spoiling attack on 31 March 1865; Cpl. Franklin Lutes of the 111th New York Infantry claimed the prize. Forty years later, after the flag was returned to Alabama, two veterans of the 41st Infantry disputed the circumstances under which the flag was captured, arguing in fact that their regiment never lost its colors in battle, but rather surrendered them at Appomattox. The historical record, however, quite clearly substantiates the original version of events. *Photo courtesy of ADAH*

192

Bullets zipped past the galloping Maj. Thomas Jones as he raced across a field shrouded in light smoke, all the while waving frantically a large white napkin affixed to his sword. The rider was trying to reach Appomattox Court House; he was trying to surrender, trying to end the war. Though only twenty years of age, Jones had already lived a full life. The son of a civil engineer from Montgomery, he was a cadet at the Virginia Military Institute when the war broke out. Jones briefly served as a drillmaster for the mobilizing Confederate army and then served unofficially with Stonewall Jackson during the 1862 Valley Campaign. Toward the end of that year, he became the first sergeant of Company K, 53rd Alabama Infantry (Partisan Rangers). A few months later his purported administrative acumen came to the attention of John B. Gordon, a rising star in the Army of Northern Virginia. Jones became a staff officer under Gordon, and by 1864 was that general's aide-de-camp. As a courier, the youth often relayed battlefield communications, risking his life on many occasions; he was wounded in action four times. At Appomattox, when General Lee asked Gordon to request a truce from the enemy, the latter could think of no one more trustworthy than Major Jones for such an important task. On 9 April 1865 (Palm Sunday), Jones put on a dress uniform, mounted "a good-looking bay horse," and trotted toward the Union line some two hundred yards distant. When Yankee skirmishers opened fire, the major performed some impressive acrobatics. "A horse was seen to dart," observed a Confederate soldier on the picket line, "and from his side hung a man clinging to the saddle with his legs while his body hung down after the fashion of a cowboy." Thankfully, the bluecoats saw the white cloth, stopped shooting, and soon directed Jones toward Maj. Gen. Joshua Chamberlain, the most senior Federal officer on the field. The major dismounted, saluted, and conveyed his message: "General Lee desires a cessation of hostilities until he can hear from General Grant as to the proposed surrender." Shortly thereafter, Philip Sheridan arrived to verify and legit-

THOMAS GOODE JONES
copy print

imize the major's message; evidently, other flags of truce were being simultaneously presented elsewhere. After a few more minutes of protocol, Jones returned and related his encounter to Generals Gordon and Lee. That afternoon the Confederate commander formally surrendered the Army of Northern Virginia. Just like that, the war in Virginia was over.[31]
Photo courtesy of ADAH

Chapter 7

Retreat and Defeat in the West

One week into May 1864, William T. Sherman set in motion his army group of more than 100,000 blue-coats in three armies; the second great Union offensive of the season was underway. Like Grant, who was clashing at that moment with Lee in the Wilderness, Sherman's mission was to aim for a high profile city—Atlanta in this instance—and destroy all Confederate forces and military resources in his path. Opposing this juggernaut was the proud but ill-fated Army of Tennessee, initially 45,000 strong but soon reinforced to a peak strength of 62,000 troops. Of its 170 infantry regiments, thirty-four came from Alabama. Of the 187 guns in the artillery component, a dozen Alabama batteries comprised more than 50 of them. Of the approximately fifty contingents of cavalry, Alabama horsemen made up eight regiments' worth. All in all, these fifty-four combat units amounted to well over 8,000 men—the largest concentration of Alabama soldiery at any point in the war.

Most of the men in the ranks had experienced the gamut of military triumph and tragedy over the previous three years. As they marked time in makeshift shelters "chinked" out of the red clay of northern Georgia, a sense of apathy pervaded the ranks. That all changed on 27 December 1863, when Gen. Joseph Johnston replaced the much-despised Braxton Bragg at the helm. A capable and prudent officer, Johnston's manifest concern for the welfare of his men immediately raised morale. Recognizing that even the veterans had grown lackadaisical, he instituted an intense regimen of training that revitalized confidence in the ranks. For weeks, the units rotated through various firing ranges to improve their marksmanship or marched about in formation to hone their tactical movements. Furthermore, Johnston granted generous furloughs and encouraged a religious awakening that swept through the army's camps. In just about every regiment, chaplains led a remarkable series of bible-thumping revivals. Finally, the Rebels played a lot of baseball, particularly the 24th Alabama Infantry, which purportedly fielded one of the best teams in the whole army.

At the outset of the campaign, Johnston deployed his army along Rocky Face Ridge, an 800-foot escarpment that shielded the small town of Dalton, Georgia. Sherman had no intention of storming that height. Instead, on 5–9 May, he distracted the defenders with a strong demonstration, while a force of 40,000 slipped southwestward to turn the Confederate army's left flank. Discovering this maneuver just in time, Johnston hastily repositioned his forces around Resaca, where the Rebels quickly established a strong defensive line. On 14–15 May Union forces attempted in vain to punch through. Four all-Alabama brigades under Brig. Gens. Zachariah Deas, Edmund Pettus, Alpheus Baker, and Henry Clayton anchored the Confederate right flank, where they conducted a series of piecemeal counterattacks throughout the battle. Clayton's experience typified the nature of the fighting in that area. On the afternoon of 14 May, his four regiments —the 18th, 32nd/58th (consolidated), 36th, and 38th Infantry—overran an advanced Union position. From there they launched a more ambitious assault the following afternoon. The first two Yellow-hammer regiments made good progress under cover of some woods, but the other two, advancing across open ground, came under heavy fire. Rushing from the prone position in short bursts, these Alabamians still managed to get off a few volleys before falling back. Clayton's Brigade suffered over 350 casualties at Resaca but helped inflict an estimated 500 on the enemy to its front. Overall, both sides lost about 2,800 men each.

Convinced that the Confederate position at Resaca was too strong, Sherman executed another southwestward turning movement. Johnston deftly countered and, though fumbling an opportunity to strike the enemy columns around Cassville, blocked his adversary's progress at Dallas. On 25 May Union forces tried to bludgeon their way forward at nearby New Hope Church, but Rebel defenders stopped them cold. Clayton's Brigade played a key role once again. The Alabamians had just felled enough trees for breastworks when enemy batteries opened fire and a Yankee division charged. Backed by effective artillery, Clayton's men beat back three successive waves over a period of two hours before sunset, and a massive thunderstorm, ended the battle. The attackers labeled the blood-soaked terrain in front of the Alabama brigade a "hell hole."[1] Two days later the Yankees attempted to turn the Rebel right with an assault at Pickett's Mill, where three Alabama regiments—the 16th, 33rd, and 45th —under Brig. Gen. Mark Lowery helped repulse the attack. Sherman's failures around Dallas cost his army 425 casualties and compelled him to sidle southwestward yet again.

For the first three weeks of June, seemingly interminable rain showers turned northern Georgia into a muddy morass. Still, Sherman crept closer to Atlanta. The inclement weather, however, gave Johnston time to establish another formidable defense centered on Kennesaw Mountain. While Sherman described the countryside as "one vast fort," his soldiers joked that "the Rebels must carry their breastworks with them."[2] The kidding stopped when the Union commander, impatient for success, aggressively probed the Kennesaw line for several days before ordering a full-scale frontal assault on 27 June. While Alabama infantrymen mostly played a supporting role, Yellowhammer batteries delivered galling canister fire in several instances; the Union attack utterly failed. Returning to maneuver warfare, Sherman shifted his forces southeastward around Kennesaw. In early July Johnston briefly held a line along the Chattahoochee River, a mere twelve miles from Atlanta, but believing the position untenable, he withdrew the Army of Tennessee into the outer defenses around the prize city. As the Yankees crossed the Chattahoochee at multiple points, an exasperated Jefferson Davis decided to replace the overly cautious Johnston with a more combative leader, Gen. John Bell Hood, who assumed command on 17 July. One of Johnston's three corps commanders, Hood had earned a reputation as a fearless and reckless warrior. On hearing the news, many Confederate soldiers expressed their misgivings. Capt. E. D. Willett of the 40th Alabama Infantry did not mince words: "It came like a thunderbolt to the army, so unexpected, so undeserved."[3] Everyone knew that with Hood in charge, the Army of Tennessee would go over to the offensive.

Sure enough, on the afternoon of 20 July, Hood launched an all-out attack. On that date nearly half of Sherman's forces were operating several miles east of Atlanta, while the remainder under Maj. Gen. George Thomas, commanding the Army of the Cumberland, endeavored to cross Peach Tree Creek just north of the city. Recognizing that Sherman had divided his strength, Hood decided to pounce on Thomas's troops. The numerical odds were about even, but Hood's subordinates botched the plan, one that envisioned a seriated oblique attack that was to unfold from east to west against the Union lines. Confusion on the Rebel right wing under General Hardee caused delays, while the Rebel left wing under Lt. Gen. Alexander Stewart charged prematurely. In this latter action, two Alabama brigades played a conspicuous role. Five regiments—the 27th, 35th, 49th, 55th, and 57th—under Brig. Gen. Thomas Scott got off to a promising start. Advancing rapidly, they overwhelmed a regiment of New Jersey boys in an advanced position and captured that unit's flag. As they proceeded toward the main Yankee line along Collier Ridge, however, the brigade came under intense rifle fire from front and flank. The brigade managed to reach the works and briefly silence a Union battery, but the volume of lead from nearby infantry smothered the Alabamians and compelled them to retreat. Attacking some distance to the left of Scott's Brigade were three more Alabama regiments—the 17th, 26th, and 29th—under Col. Edward O'Neal. Hampered by uneven terrain and thick underbrush, this Yellowhammer assault lacked linear cohesion, but it compensated with fury. Ordered to hold their fire until virtually on top of the enemy, O'Neal's boys charged several hundred yards straight up Collier Ridge and then unleashed a point-blank volley, shattering three Yankee regiments that had neglected to entrench themselves properly. Union artillerymen, however, concentrated their guns on this breakthrough and were soon bombarding O'Neal's troops with merciless canister fire. By 6:00 P.M. the whole Rebel assault had ended in failure. Casualties at Peach Tree Creek amounted to 2,500 Confederates and 1,700 Federals.

Undaunted, General Hood ordered another attack only two days later against Union forces approaching Atlanta from the east. According to his plan, one corps under Maj. Gen. Benjamin Cheatham was to block Union access to the city, while a second under Hardee was to swing southeast and then strike north to roll up the presumably exposed Union left flank. After an all-night march to get into position, Hardee's men, still fatigued from their fight at Peach Tree Creek, attacked in the early afternoon under a scorching summer sun. Much of the combat revolved around Bald Hill, a piece of key terrain at the apex of the Union line of battle. For several hours, the Rebels grappled in vain for control of this eminence. At one point Pettus's Alabama brigade struck the hill from the east while Alabamians in Lowrey's Brigade conducted one of the last desperate charges of the day—all for naught. As the fighting raged around Bald Hill, Cheatham conducted a general attack farther north, his divisions marching perpendicular to the east–west running Georgia Railroad. Sixteen Alabama infantry regiments, distributed among four brigades, participated, but the three in Manigault's Brigade (the 24th, 28th, 34th Alabama, plus two South Carolina regiments) achieved the greatest success in this sector. Enduring artillery fire all the way, the Yellowhammers and their Gamecock brethren carried a Union strongpoint at the Troup Hurt House, a brick edifice that protected a Yankee battery. "Altho the line staggered and reeled for a moment," Manigault later explained, "it quickly recovered and went forward."[4] In a fierce seesaw battle, his men seized the enemy cannon, then with the help of four more recently arrived Alabama regiments—the 18th, 36th, 38th, and 32nd/58th—resisted determined counterattacks for about an hour before finally retreating under mounting pressure. Like Peach Tree Creek, the so-called Battle of Atlanta resulted in another Confederate defeat. At a cost of over 5,000 of his own men, Hood inflicted about 3,700 casualties on his adversary.

Toward the end of July, Hood tried once again to thwart Sherman's efforts to invest Atlanta. Federal artillery now shelled the city daily while cavalry roamed the countryside tearing up railroad track. Impressed by Atlanta's elaborate defenses, Sherman decided to move his army to the south of the city and sever its last significant line of communication—the Macon and Western Railroad. Accordingly, a Union corps under Maj. Gen. Oliver Howard commenced marching around Atlanta on its western side. Hood countered by dispatching the corps of Lt. Gen. Stephen D. Lee (newly promoted) and Stewart to intercept this movement. On 28 July the two sides clashed at the Battle of Ezra Church. This engagement proved short and one sided. Anticipating Hood's reaction, Howard deliberately halted his army at Ezra Church and entrenched. Coming up Lick Skillet Road, Lee's Corps made first contact, and rather than wait for Stewart's Corps to arrive, the headstrong Lee committed to battle, sending his brigades (including six with Alabamians) forward one at a time as they reached the battlefield. Union firepower shredded these haphazard assaults. Henry Clayton, now a division commander, recognized the futility of further charges and called off the action on the Rebel right. The piecemeal fighting on the left eventually subsided as well, but not before some 3,000 Confederates had been killed or wounded. Union losses were less than 600 men. "A few more such affairs as this," complained Pvt. Hiram Williams of the 40th Alabama, "and we will have no army left."[5]

Ezra Church only encouraged Sherman to press on. His army's pattern of strategic offense and tactical defense was both bleeding the Rebel army and allowing the Yankees to gain ground. In early August, however, the Confederates briefly reversed the trend. From 5 to 7 August, Union forces tried to push their way through a strong grayback position at Utoy Creek, southwest of Atlanta. Clayton's division anchored the Rebel right and repelled every attack. Only the 36th Alabama, which manned the picket line, suffered any appreciable loss after it was driven back in the initial Yankee assault; Union casualties approached 1,000. For the next three weeks, the opponents mostly probed or conducted cavalry raids. From the Confederate perspective, however, the situation seemed to be deteriorating. Atlanta civilians suffered intensified bombardment, while morale waned in the ranks. Not surprisingly, desertion rates increased. Approximately 100 Alabamians slipped off from Baker's Brigade over the course of a week. Then toward the end of the month, Union forces went in motion again with a bold thrust toward Jonesboro, an important railhead about twenty miles south of Atlanta.

Uncertain of where all the Federal units were, Hood belatedly dispatched first Hardee's Corps, then Lee's to check this latest enemy movement. As three Union corps fortified themselves on high ground just west of Jonesboro, the ever-aggressive Hood ordered his men to storm the heights and push the Yankees into the nearby Flint River. The ensuing assault was a fiasco. The action against the Union right flank foundered immediately as several Confederate units, including the 16th, 33rd, and 45th Alabama Infantry, wasted time and energy chasing dismounted Yankee troopers on the periphery of the battlefield. The attack on the Union left made no headway at all. Four brigades of Alabamians participated, but no unit got closer than sixty yards; the intervening cornfields permitted the Yankees a fabulous field of fire. Psychologically broken by a summer of futile and costly assaults, many regiments simply refused to go forward. Col. Bushrod Jones of the 32nd/58th Alabama inanely commented that "the men seemed possessed of some great horror of charging breastworks, which no power, persuasion, or example could dispel."[6] Union losses amounted to less than 200 men, while the Confederates suffered an appalling 1,700 casualties. The next day the Yankees went over to the offensive and ripped through the Rebel lines at several points. Jonesboro was the climax of the Atlanta Campaign, compelling Hood to evacuate the city, which surrendered to Sherman on 2 September.

Losing Atlanta greatly hurt the Southern cause, primarily because defeat there enhanced Lincoln's chances of reelection, an outcome that spelled doom for the Confederacy. Nevertheless, the Army of Tennessee remained a viable force, and after reorganizing in southwestern Georgia, Hood went back on the offensive. Throughout September and October, the general conducted various forays against Sherman's line of communications north of Atlanta. Thus, for several weeks the war in the West featured the bluecoats defending many of the same spots that the graybacks had defended earlier in the year. But Hood never seriously threatened Union control over the Chattanooga–Atlanta corridor. Moreover, Sherman tired of the cat-and-mouse game and decided to pursue his ultimate goal—a march to the Atlantic Ocean that would disembowel the Confederate interior. Toward the end of October, Hood similarly switched gears and embarked on the war's great forlorn hope—an invasion of Tennessee, with the capture of Nashville the grand objective. For this mission, the Rebel commander mustered about 39,000 soldiers, including twenty-five regiments of Alabama infantrymen and ten Alabama batteries. (In actuality, there were twenty-nine infantry regimental designations, but due to insufficient strength, four were consolidated with other units.) Using the Tennessee River as a staging area, which had the salutary effect of liberating northern Alabama once again, the Army of Tennessee crossed the state line during the first days of November. For the last time, the rank and file displayed a boisterous spirit. As Pvt. J. W. Harmon of the 35th Alabama Infantry noted in a letter home, "the army left Florence with bright hopes for victory and success."7

Despite some delays, Hood's invasion got off to an auspicious start. Although Federal forces in Tennessee exceeded 70,000 troops under George

Thomas's competent leadership, many of these men were scattered about the state in small detachments. In late November the Rebel army outflanked a Union blocking force of 30,000 at Pulaski, Tennessee, forcing it to retreat, and then outflanked it again at Columbia. As the Yankees beat another hasty retreat northward toward Franklin, Hood attempted to trap his quarry at Spring Hill. But in one of the war's great controversies, a seemingly surefire success miscarried due to confusion and lethargy among Confederate generals; the Union column escaped virtually unscathed and fortified itself at Franklin. Enraged by the missed opportunity, Hood ordered his corps commanders to pursue and attack no matter the circumstances. On 30 November they did just that.

The Union position at Franklin was virtually impregnable. Two lines of breastworks backed by more than thirty cannon all situated on elevated ground overlooking several square miles of cleared farmland. Against this Hood ordered an immediate late-afternoon strike before much of his army had even arrived on the field. The ordeal of General Scott's Alabama brigade (27th/35th/49th Consolidated, 55th, and 57th Regiments) exemplified the futility of the whole assault. Constrained by the Harpeth River on their right flank, the Alabamians advanced up Lewisburg Pike in a tight cluster. One thousand yards from the enemy works, they came under artillery fire; at two hundred yards they began receiving canister; and at seventy-five yards sheets of rifle fire tore through the ranks. With those officers still standing urging them on, the Yellowhammers emitted a Rebel yell and charged through a pastoral scene of Osage orange trees, where they briefly clashed with the defenders before reeling back under relentless enemy fire. The brigade suffered 187 casualties, including General Scott, who was severely wounded. Hitting the Union lines a few hundred yards to the left of Scott's Alabamians was Brig. Gen. Charles Shelley's brigade (the 17th, 26th, and 29th Alabama). In a similar melee, it lost 190 men to no avail. At dusk Hood threw in more units,

199

including eight Alabama regiments under Generals Deas and Manigault. Blundering about in the darkness, the efforts of these reinforcements only succeeded in raising the Confederate body count. The next morning Pvt. Sam Vann of the 19th Alabama literally cried over the carnage he witnessed: "Oh! You cannot have the slightest imagination of how many men were killed. They were lying heaped up all over the battleground. Such a slaughter of men never was seen on neither side."[8] In all Hood's army lost 6,300 men, 4,000 more than the number it inflicted on the Federals. That the Union army crossed the river the following day, thereby conceding the field, came as small comfort.

Franklin was the quintessence of a pyrrhic victory, and it badly undermined morale in the Army of Tennessee. Only a stoic sense of duty enabled the soldiers to push on toward the outskirts of Nashville. During the first week of December, the Rebels erected a chain of redoubts along a stretch of high ground southeast of the state capital. Lee's Corps, including seventeen Alabama infantry regiments and three batteries, manned the trenches on the right; Stewart's Corps, including seven Alabama infantry regiments and four batteries, held the left; one consolidated Alabama regiment and a battery served in the reserve corps under Cheatham. Single-digit temperatures and heavy sleet made life miserable for Hood's largely barefoot army. By mid-month the Confederates presented an effective strength of less than 25,000 men. Conversely, the Union army numbered over 50,000 men, many of whom were enjoying the comforts of warm barracks and hot food. While the badly outnumbered Rebels shivered in their slushy rifle pits along a line that was overextended to begin with, their commander seemed to have run out of ideas. It was a pitiful scene that General Thomas prepared to exploit once the spate of ice storms passed.

On 15 December Thomas and his men delivered one of the most perfectly executed attacks of the war. While one division demonstrated against the Rebel right, some 40,000 Yankees smashed into the Confederate left. Overwhelmed at every point, the Confederate flank collapsed. In desperation Hood pulled troops from his unthreatened right and rushed them to his disintegrating left. Arriving amid a scene of panic and confusion, eight Alabama regiments under Deas and Manigault attempted to align behind a stone wall running along Hillsboro Pike. Hurrahing bluecoats, however, swarmed over and sent the Yellowhammers packing. Alabama gunners offered feeble resistance and soon joined the general flight, many leaving their fieldpieces behind. At the end of the day, Hood's army had been driven south almost two miles. There the Confederates managed to establish a more compact defensive line cased between Shy's Hill on the left and Overton Hill on the right.

On 16 December Thomas resumed his offensive, with the primary effort once again targeting the Confederate left. Like the previous day, the Yankees opened with a strong demonstration against the Rebel right at Overton Hill. Incorrectly assuming that the position must be weak, Union generals there actually initiated a full-scale assault. Several contingents of U.S. Colored Troops rushed forward and soon ran into a blizzard of shot and shell. Clambering up Franklin Pike, one regiment of black soldiers came under murderous fire from Brig. Gen. James Holtzclaw's Alabama brigade (the 18th, 36th, 38th, and 32nd/58th). While many of his men expressed disgust at having to fight "negroes," Holtzclaw confessed a certain grim admiration: "they gallantly dashed up to the abatis, forty feet in front, but were killed in the hundreds. Pressed on by their white brethren in the rear they continued to come up in masses to the abatis, but they came only to die."[9] Although the Rebel right stood strong, the left around Shy's Hill utterly failed to hold, and by evening Hood's whole army was in complete retreat. Fortunately for the Army of Tennessee, Henry Clayton helped orchestrate a skillful rearguard action that prevented a total rout. In any event, Hood's invasion was over. Confederate casualties at Nashville exceeded 6,000 men, compared to losses of about 3,000 for the Federals. By the end of the month, remnants of the Confederate army huddled around Tupelo, Mississippi.

To any rational observer, the war was essentially over going into 1865. Grant had pinned Lee outside Richmond, Thomas had wrecked the Army of Tennessee at Nashville, and Sherman had burned a swath of destruction through central Georgia. But the war persisted; delusion and inertia kept the Confederacy going. In January 1865 Hood resigned. The following month the Davis administration appointed Joseph Johnston command over the Department of North Carolina with orders to stop Sherman's continued advance into the Carolinas—though with what was the question. Over the course of several weeks, surviving units of the Army of Tennessee arrived in rivulets. By March Johnston had assembled a decent fighting force of about 21,000 men. Among these stalwarts were composites of some twenty Alabama infantry regiments, loosely organized into six brigades. For several weeks, this army shadowed Sherman's progress through North Carolina. Months of relatively easy conquest fostered carelessness on the part of some Federal units. At Kinston on 8 March, Deas's old Alabama brigade, now under Lt. Col. Harry Toulmin, slashed into a Union foray out of New Bern. During this engagement, the 45 veterans that made up the 50th Alabama captured over 300 Yankees, mostly new recruits.

Such engagements were but prelude to the war's last great open-field battle—Bentonville. In mid-March Sherman sought to concentrate his scattered columns around Goldsboro. One of these, some 17,000 men under Maj. Gen. Henry Slocum, became the target of opportunity for Joe Johnston; on 19 March the Rebels went on the offensive. While one Confederate corps blocked the Union column from the east, two more attacked from the north. All of Johnston's Alabamians fought in the left wing of the flank attack. Initially the Rebels rolled over several unsuspecting enemy units, the gentle hills and sylvan countryside belying the imminent blood fest. Union counterattacks, however, soon produced a confusing back-and-forth struggle in which Yellowhammers battled Buckeyes and Hoosiers in vicious close-quarters fighting. Around 4:00 P.M. a gap appeared in the Union lines just south of Goldsboro Road. Three Alabama brigades under Brig. Gen. Alpheus Baker, Lt. Col. John Carter, and Toulmin rushed headlong into the opening, wheeled left (east), and attempted to hit a Yankee division in the rear. But here the terrain turned swampy and unit cohesion unraveled amid drifting clouds of thick smoke. Disoriented Alabamians began operating in disconnected groups, many without any officers, on a part of the battlefield thereafter dubbed the "bull pen." Before long the supposed gap became a trap as rapidly arriving Union reinforcements chopped to pieces the disorganized Alabama brigades. Realizing that he had overplayed his hand, Johnston went over to the defense. At dusk three other Alabama brigades helped repel additional Union counterattacks, but the battle was lost. After a couple more days of skirmishing, Johnston withdrew his army, having lost 2,600 men against 1,700 Union casualties.

Over the next month the bloodied Rebel army watched Sherman's "bummers" from afar. News of Lee's surrender at Appomattox presaged a similar act on the part of Johnston. On 26 April 1865 the Confederate commander capitulated to his Union counterpart at Bennett Place outside Durham. On paper, twenty-eight regiments of Alabamians surrendered, but in reality they had been consolidated into a handful of regiments comprising little more than 1,200 men. Three Alabama cavalry regiments numbering another 300 men also surrendered. Thus, some 1,500 Yellowhammers were still standing as the flags furled for the last time. Years later Henry Clayton could find only one redeeming quality about his country's military defeat: "He who has once commanded brave soldiers should give sleepless vigils to their honor," he reminisced, "since it was all that was left from their heroic struggle to the living, and all the dead secured in dying."[10]

FLAG OF THE 33RD
ALABAMA INFANTRY
copy print

By 1864 the 33rd Alabama Infantry had established a reputation as one of the hardest-fighting regiments in the Army of Tennessee. Organized in April 1862, the 33rd consisted of tough yeoman from the southeastern part of the state. At Perryville, Murfreesboro, and Chickamauga, the regiment (part of Maj. Gen. Pat Cleburne's renowned division) found itself in the thick of each battle, enduring heavy losses in all three. The Alabamians in the 33rd, however, always considered their performance in the lesser known engagement at Ringgold Gap, Georgia, among their best. With the Army of Tennessee in full retreat following the Union victory at Missionary Ridge, Cleburne conducted a skillful rearguard action that included a nasty ambush of pursuing Yankees at Ringgold on 27 November 1863. For its part, the 33rd Alabama participated in a slashing attack against the enemy's left flank. The Alabamians, many of whom were fighting barefooted,

delivered several well-aimed volleys that helped drive back the Federals. "My men have never gone into a fight so eagerly as they did in this," noted Col. Samuel Adams. "They moved with the greatest promptness to any position that they were ordered. They fired with the greatest deliberation." Unlike previous engagements, the 33rd Alabama suffered only eleven casualties. In March 1864 the regiment received a banner that reflected its many feats at arms—a "Hardee pattern" battle flag with a white, full moon on a royal blue background. Standing out for all to see were the painted words "Ringgold Gap." The 33rd went on to further glory during both the Atlanta Campaign and Hood's invasion of Tennessee, but during the latter, the colors fell into Union hands during an ill-fated charge at Franklin that virtually wrecked the regiment as an independent combat unit.[11] *Photo courtesy of ADAH*

202

JOHN CLARK FRANCIS
copy print

One of the first Confederate fatalities of the Atlanta Campaign was Maj. John Francis of the 30th Alabama Infantry. The son of a respected physician and slaveholder from Calhoun County, Francis was still a teenager when he joined the regiment in March 1862. The youth evidently showed an aptitude for tactics, rising quickly through the ranks from commanding Company B to acting executive officer at only twenty-two years of age. But he would never see his twenty-third birthday. In early May powerful Union columns conducted an aggressive demonstration against the Rebel lines along Rocky Face Ridge. The 30th Alabama, one of five Alabama regiments in the brigade of Edmund Pettus, occupied a crest on the northern edge of the ridge. On 8–9 May it helped fend off a number of Union attacks that had Francis and everyone else in his regiment thinking they faced Sherman's main effort instead of a mere diversionary operation. The fighting on the morning of 9 May was especially fierce. Placing his regiment behind boulders and felled trees, Major Francis helped the brigade inflict hundreds of casualties on the enemy. The 30th Alabama suffered only ten losses, but one of them was the major, who received a mortal wound despite carrying a lucky gold coin sewn into his collar by his mother. Although a Union turning movement farther south ultimately compelled the Army of Tennessee to abandon its hold on Rocky Face Ridge, Maj. Gen. Carter Stevenson, the division commander, commented that "the fight was obstinate and bloody, but resulted in a complete success for us." Francis never learned of these laudatory words; he died on 11 May.[12] *Photo courtesy of ADAH*

JOHN FRANCIS CONOLEY
tintype

On 14 May 1864 Col. John Conoley of the 29th Alabama Infantry entrenched his regiment on the western outskirts of Resaca and braced for a possible Union attack. A fifty-three-year-old merchant and lawyer from Dallas County, Conoley was a longstanding civic leader. He commanded a militia company during the Creek War of 1836 and served as county sheriff in the mid-1840s. After secession Conoley traveled throughout the state to help recruit and equip volunteer companies. In the autumn of 1862, he received command of the 29th Alabama and for the next year was part of the garrison around Pollard. Ordered to reinforce the Army of Tennessee in the spring of 1864, Conoley brought with him one of the few full-strength regiments anywhere in the Confederacy. (Among the ranks was the colonel's oldest son, 2nd Lt. Louis Alexander Conoley.) Part of Brig. Gen.

James Cantey's brigade, the 29th helped anchor the Rebel left flank at Resaca; from his position Colonel Conoley could watch the gentle current of the Oostanaula River just to his south. The attack he feared, however, never came. The Yankees probed, but the main action took place farther north. Nevertheless, Union batteries bombarded the Alabamians all day, and with astonishing accuracy. Casualties in the regiment approached one hundred before the fighting subsided. Among those wounded was Conoley himself, struck by a cannonball at some point during the barrage. Fortunately, he was soon back in command and stayed there for the duration of the Atlanta Campaign. The brush with death during the little Battle of Resaca had made him and his men instant veterans.
Photo courtesy of ADAH

JOHN HUNT HIGLEY
copy print

After exiting a grove of oak trees, Col. John Higley of the 40th Alabama Infantry prepared to seize a Union battery some twenty yards in front of his skirmish line. It was late on the afternoon of 14 May 1864, but the colonel was confident his regiment could achieve something worthwhile from the inconclusive, daylong fighting north of Resaca. Abruptly, Alpheus Baker, the brigade commander, ordered Higley to halt and have his men lie down—"a very foolish command at this time," observed Sgt. John Curry of Company B. Evidently the general was drunk and wasted time and personnel dragging furniture from a burning planta-tion house nearby. Among the salvaged items was a piano, which Baker proceeded to play to an audience of stupefied soldiers. Minutes later Alexander Stewart, the division commander, arrived in a fury, relieved Baker on the spot, and placed Higley in command of the brigade. He proved a capable officer at such a bizarre moment. A thirty-four-year-old merchant from Mobile, Higley became lieutenant colonel of the 40th at its formation in May 1862. As full colonel he led the regiment at Vicksburg, where he and his men were taken prisoner. Upon taking command at Resaca, he immediately resumed the brigade's westerly advance, deploying his four Alabama regiments, from left to right: the 37th, 40th, 42nd, and 54th. The combined Yellowhammer attack drove the Yankee lines back over a mile before sunset forced a cessation of combat. "I never saw a prettier movement executed on the battle-field," noted Lt. Sam Sprott of the 40th. During the night, Higley withdrew the brigade to a more defensi-ble position. The next day he handed command back over to a presumably sober Baker.[13] *Photo courtesy of ADAH*

JAMES M. STEDHAM
ambrotype

Pvt. James Stedham had served in the 25th Alabama Infantry for over two years when he was captured at Resaca. A thirty-three-year-old ditcher from Talladega County, Stedham enlisted in Company F (the Heflin Highlanders) in October 1861. Other than a spell of sickness in the autumn of 1862, he appears to have fought in all of the Army of Tennessee's major battles.

At Resaca the 25th was part of Deas's Brigade, which was positioned on the right flank of Maj. Gen. Thomas Hindman's division at the apex of the Confederate defensive line. On 15 May Stedham and his fellow Alabamians withstood repeated assaults. Somehow during one of these attacks, Stedham was taken prisoner. *Photo courtesy of David Wynn Vaughan*

May 1864 was a busy month for Col. Lewis Woodruff and his 36th Alabama Infantry. The forty-eight-year-old merchant from Mobile had seen plenty of combat in the war, mostly notably while leading his regiment at Chickamauga and on Missionary Ridge, but the Atlanta Campaign proved a stern test of his leadership. From 8 May until a disabling wound on 25 May, Woodruff was seemingly in constant action. A bona fide Connecticut Yankee, Woodruff immigrated to Alabama in 1839, settled in Mobile, worked his way up the business ladder in one of the city's auction and commission houses, and basically fell in love with the Deep South. Prior to the war, he served a few terms on the city's municipal board; right after secession, he gained a commission in the 3rd Alabama Infantry. A year later he helped raise the 36th Alabama, whose companies came from the southwestern portion of the state, and promptly won election to lieutenant colonel.

Going into the Atlanta Campaign, Woodruff and his men composed one of four Alabama regiments in Clayton's Brigade. At Rocky Face Ridge on 8–9 May, Woodruff helped repulse a Union probe against the northeastern tip of the Rebel line; his regiment suffered only eight casualties. On 14–15 May the colonel led the regiment in a series of flank attacks against the Union left at Resaca. The second day's fighting was especially challenging. After erecting a strong line of breastworks on ground the regiment had seized a day earlier, the men of the 36th advanced on the extreme left of the brigade. Upon entering an open field, the Alabamians came under "a fatal and scathing fire." Woodruff ordered his companies to rush forward in short bursts, dropping to the ground and delivering a volley of musketry between each advance. On the third lunge the Alabamians closed in on their quarry, but the brigade attack had already faltered. After losing ninety-two men, Woodruff executed an orderly retreat back to his starting point. Ten days later the 36th and its fellow Alabama regiments bore the brunt of a massive Union assault against the center of the Rebel line at New Hope Church. Occupying a hastily constructed, though quite strong, line of felled logs, the 36th blazed away at charging Yankees for over two hours, repelling

LEWIS THOMPSON WOODRUFF
copy print

three successive waves while sustaining only thirty-two casualties. Unfortunately, one of those was Woodruff. About 4:00 P.M., during the enemy's second assault, the colonel was shot through the thigh, the ball lodging dangerously close to his femoral artery. Initially, surgeons thought the wound mortal, but Woodruff pulled through, though his fighting days were over. Described by Henry Clayton as "a zealous and faithful officer," Woodruff's departure was lamented by the men of the 36th Alabama, who had come to regard their colonel as a father figure.[14] *Photo courtesy of ADAH*

JAMES ROBERT MAXWELL
copy print

On the morning of 20 June 1864, Sgt. James Maxwell of Lumsden's Battery munched on a plate of "hot cush"—cornmeal fried in bacon grease. He and his section had just finished entrenching their guns on the southwestern crest of Little Kennesaw Mountain and were taking a well-earned break. Though only twenty years old, Maxwell was an accomplished soldier: a military cadet at the University of Alabama; a private in the 34th Alabama Infantry, with whom he was captured at Murfreesboro; and after his prisoner exchange, a noncommissioned officer in Lumsden's Battery, with all its combat since Chickamauga under his belt. On the afternoon of 20 June, Capt. Charles Lumsden decided he wanted to determine the number of Union guns opposite his front. When Maxwell and the other crews lobbed a few shells, two dozen rifled cannon returned fire. A few minutes into the lopsided duel, an enemy shell plowed into one of Maxwell's caissons, detonating the ordnance. "How those Yanks did yell," the sergeant noted, adding sarcastically, "we found out, what the enemy had over there, and we did not stir up that hornet's nest again."

On 27 June General Sherman ordered a massive frontal assault against the whole Confederate line at Kennesaw. The biggest clash occurred a mile south of Maxwell's position, but the artilleryman saw plenty of action nonetheless. As the bluecoats came out of the not-too-distant woods, Maxwell and his fellow gunners "swept the earth with canister and over their line of infantry made every bullet count, so that in our immediate front, they did not get nearer than 150 yards." In all, Lumsden's Battery helped inflict 600 casualties in repelling the attack in their sector; none of Maxwell's comrades was hurt. Still miffed by the previous week's incident, the young sergeant commented on the day's success with obvious satisfaction: "we more than evened up on the Yanks."[15]
Photo courtesy of ADAH

FREDERICK ELIJAH DUGGAR
copy print

The Confederate attack at Peach Tree Creek enjoyed the artillery support of at least two dozen batteries. One of those was Selden's Battery of four Napoleon smooth-bores. Working one of the guns was Cpl. Frederick Duggar, a twenty-five-year-old Episcopal seminarian from Marengo County. He served alongside one brother, William, and under another, Luke, the section leader. A graduate of the University of Alabama (class of 1859), Frederick presumably received some of that institution's military education. In any event, he learned his specific wartime trade while stationed for two years with the battery at Mobile. Sent to reinforce Johnston's army in northern Georgia in early 1864, Duggar gained combat experience in the fighting around Resaca and Kennesaw. On the afternoon of 20 July, Selden's Battery received orders to support an Arkansas brigade as it advanced as part of the general assault against the Union right. To this end, Duggar unlimbered his field-piece on elevated, open ground overlooking the lines of gray infantrymen. Throughout the battle, he alternated between loading and firing his cannon and displacing so as to avoid Union counterbattery fire. Unfortunately, the young gunner apparently moved too slow during one barrage and suffered a fatal hit. Selden's Battery continued to fire until it expended all of its rounds. Only then could the surviving Duggar boys reflect on the death of their brother, a man whose ambition in life had been to become a priest. *Photo courtesy of W. S. Hoole Special Collections Library, The University of Alabama*

RICHARD HUEY SMITH
copy print

On the afternoon of 20 July 1864, color bearer Dick Smith of the 29th Alabama Infantry stared across an undulating, wooded landscape that separated the Army of Tennessee from Union forces gathering on the south bank of Peach Tree Creek. While doing so, he undoubtedly gripped his flagstaff a bit tighter in anticipation of the imminent orders to attack. A twenty-eight-year-old farmer from Blount County, Smith was not new to the Confederate army, but he was untried combat. As a corporal in Company C— the Avalanche Company—Smith and his unit had spent the first half of the war on garrison duty in southern Alabama. During this time, he became a member of the regimental color guard, and in September 1863 he got married to his childhood sweetheart, Malinda Long, while on furlough. Then in mid-April 1864, the 29th was transferred to the Army of Tennessee and brigaded with two other Alabama regiments and one from Mississippi, all under Edward O'Neal. Within weeks the whole brigade was in action, first at Resaca, where Smith received his baptism of fire, and again at Kennesaw Mountain, where he experienced the fear of enduring an enemy artillery barrage.

Smith's initial military encounters paled in comparison to his involvement at Peach Tree Creek. Deployed on the brigade's extreme left, the 29th Alabama was one of the more sizeable regiments at just under 500 men. Corporal Smith stood front and center, flag in hand. At about 3:00 P.M. the regiment stepped off, with Smith navigating through thick underbrush. After marching several hundred yards, the line officers realized that the regiment had drifted too far to the left and had lost contact with the main body. Smith helped guide the Alabamians back into proper alignment just as the skirmish line began to pop with small-arms fire. As the rest of the brigade engaged the enemy works at close range, the 29th moved through a nearby ravine, which provided cover and concealment. Emerging suddenly on the right flank of a regiment of Buckeyes, the Alabamians poured in a deadly enfilade volley. For the next few minutes, both sides became intertwined in hand-to-hand combat before the Yankees gave way and fled. O'Neal tried to exploit the momentum, but Federal batteries rained down a heavy concentration of shot and shell. One salvo tore into Smith's left arm, tearing the staff from his now-mangled left hand. While one comrade grabbed the blood-spattered flag, another assisted Smith off the field. Everyone else soon followed; the assault had failed. Approximately 150 men fell in the 29th Alabama alone. And for Dick Smith, the war was over. *Photo courtesy of ADAH*

BAILEY
MONTGOMERY
TALBOT
copy print

The hardest hit Alabama regiment at Peach Tree Creek was the 57th Infantry. Charging up Collier Ridge as part of Scott's Brigade, it lost 157 men out of 330 engaged. One of the casualties was Bailey Talbot, captain of Company H. A thirty-year-old merchant from Pike County, Talbot was an officer plagued by bad luck. First, headquarters cancelled his furlough to see his wife of five years, Mary Ann, and their two little children. Then, just before the battle, Talbot somehow lost his horse. He revealed some of his exasperation in a last-minute letter home to his young son. "Should I fall fighting," he wrote, "my boy avenge the blood of your father." Once in action, Talbot performed with courage. Leading his men into the fray, he helped capture some hapless New Jersey pickets, then kept the company together as it reached the main enemy works on Collier Ridge. After a few minutes of close-quarters fighting, during which Talbot's men briefly captured an enemy gun, galling crossfire compelled the whole regiment to fall back. During the retreat, the captain suffered multiple wounds as his men ran across an open field. At the time, he was in the rear of his company, ensuring that as many made it to safety as possible. Last seen crawling for some cover, Talbot was initially listed as missing but later declared killed in action. In actuality, he turned up in a hospital in Atlanta, where he subsequently died anyway from complications arising from having one of his legs amputated. In a summary report of the engagement by Capt. Augustus Milligan, a fellow company commander, Talbot's death received special meaning. "The long list of casualties in this regiment," Milligan averred, "will be sufficient evidence of its deep devotion to the cause of Southern liberty and independence."[16] *Photo courtesy of ADAH*

SAMUEL ADAMS
ambrotype

The day prior to the Battle of Atlanta, a Confederate division under Patrick Cleburne sparred with the Yankees in a sharp, preliminary fight for control over Bald Hill, a piece of key terrain due east of the city. Participating in this struggle was the 33rd Alabama Infantry's Col. Samuel Adams, one of Cleburne's favorite regimental commanders. A South Carolinian by birth, Adams came to Alabama in 1851 at the age of twenty-two and settled in Butler County, where he practiced law and engaged in politics; from 1857 to 1861 he served two terms in the state legislature as a Whig. For the first year of the war, he served as a junior officer in the 9th Alabama, but in April 1862 he gained appointment as colonel of the newly raised 33rd, whose recruits came from Butler and surrounding counties. A stern exterior belied Adams's amiable nature; over time, his men came to love him. Leading the regiment at Perryville, Adams suffered a painful foot wound. Recovering in time for Murfreesboro, he performed well in that fierce contest, as he did later at Chickamauga, where his regiment was part of Cleburne's wild night-time assault on 19 September 1863.

During the Atlanta Campaign of 1864, Adams once again ably led his regiment as part of Lowery's Brigade.

At Pickett's Mill on 27 May, his regiment helped repel a Union thrust. A month later at Peach Tree Creek, the 33rd was part of the reserve force and saw little action. Instead, it was ordered eastward to seize Bald Hill as a prelude to Hood's second major sortie around Atlanta. On the morning of 21 July, Adams and his men encountered stiff enemy opposition around the hill. In the face of enemy shelling and sniper fire, the colonel attempted to probe the Union position. At 9:30 A.M. a bullet pierced Adams's heart. The colonel grabbed his chest, slumped next to a small oak tree, and died. His demoralized men fell back. The next day the 33rd hurled itself against Bald Hill as part of the larger Battle of Atlanta, but the boys from southern Alabama failed to avenge the death of their commander. Brig. Gen. Mark Lowery expressed his own grief by praising Adams: "this true patriot and Christian hero—a perfect specimen of a soldier and a gentleman—who distinguished himself on many well-fought fields, fell at his post, leaving his gallant regiment to feel as orphans, and many other friends and comrades in arms to mourn an irreparable loss." Also in mourning was Dora Eliza Adams, the colonel's wife of more than ten years.[17] *Photo courtesy of ADAH*

CHARLES HARRIS D. LAMPLEY
copy print

By the late afternoon of 22 July, the Battle for Atlanta was reaching its climax. For several hours, the Rebel tide had been crashing around Bald Hill with steady, though intermittent, waves of troops rolling up the western, southern, and eastern slopes. At 5:00 P.M. Patrick Cleburne sent in his reserves, including the 45th Alabama Infantry of Lowery's Brigade. In command of that regiment was Col. Harris Lampley, a thirty-one-year-old merchant and slaveholder from Barbour County. A veteran of all of the Army of Tennessee's campaigns, Lampley was confident that his men would prevail where so many others had failed—never mind that neither he nor his men had slept in two days. Advancing as part of the brigade's left wing, the 45th passed through some woods, then some 500 yards away from the enemy lines, the Alabamians picked up their pace. Uneven terrain interspersed by trees prevented Lampley from maintaining contact with the brigade's right wing, but he urged his men forward nonetheless. The regiment routed a company of Yankee skirmishers, then hit a portion of the main Union line defended by a brigade of Iowans dug in behind a parapet. With the colonel out front, he and his men came within arm's reach of the earthworks when hundreds of Yankee muzzles flashed in unison. The 45th Alabama literally crumpled under the volley. It rallied and attacked again with similar results. As the regimental color bearer went down in this last charge, Lampley himself reeled from a deep bullet wound to his right shoulder. Delirious from pain and fatigue, the colonel cursed his fallen and retreating men as cowards and then leaped alone onto the parapet. His counterpart on the Union side, Col. William Belknap, grabbed Lampley by the collar, spun him around, and shouted: "Look at your men! They are dead! What are you cursing them for?" Badly wounded and now a prisoner of war, a crestfallen Lampley spent the next month in a Union field hospital before finally dying on 24 August.[18] *Photo courtesy of ADAH*

213

SAMUEL N. MCINNIS
copy print

Whether Pvt. Samuel McInnis heard his colonel's wild shouting along the enemy parapet at Bald Hill, his own conduct proves that few in the 45th Alabama Infantry acted cowardly on 22 July. Like Harris Lampley, McInnis was from Barbour County, and he too was a veteran of all the regiment's major engagements. The private also demonstrated his commitment to the cause when earlier in the year he reenlisted for the duration of the war (his acceptance of a fifty-dollar bounty notwithstanding). Marching with his comrades in Company A, a unit dubbed the Barbour Yankee Hunters, it is unclear how close the thirty-five-year-old McInnis came to the enemy works before going down with a wound. Unlike Lampley, the private avoided capture and fell back with the rest of the regiment. The final tally for the 45th Alabama was grim: 27 killed, 72 wounded, and 32 missing. The regiment's 131 losses were the highest in the brigade, which suffered 578 total casualties. "I never saw a greater display of gallantry," General Lowery declared in recounting the performance of all his regiments, though he added, "the thing attempted was impossible for a thin line of exhausted men to accomplish."[19]
Photo courtesy of ADAH

JOHN HENRY
DOLLAR
copy print

After tramping more than a thousand yards over uneven, wooded terrain on a sweltering July afternoon, Pvt. John Dollar of the 34th Alabama Infantry gratefully complied with an order to rest prior to participating in a general attack on Union forces due east of Atlanta. A twenty-five-year-old subsistence farmer from Tallapoosa County, Dollar enlisted in Company D of the regiment in March 1862. Leaving behind a young wife and an infant daughter, he passed unharmed through such ordeals as Murfreesboro and Chickamauga. But at Atlanta his good fortune ran out. About 3:00 P.M. on 22 July, the 34th Alabama advanced as part of the left wing of Manigault's Brigade. Halting for five minutes to rest and realign, the Alabamians resumed their march under increasing enemy fire, especially from a Union battery entrenched around the Troup Hurt House. One hundred yards from the enemy position, Dollar heard the order to charge. Sprinting across the tracks of the Georgia Railroad, he helped overrun the ground just left of the house. Dollar then jumped into a nearby trench and added his rifle fire to the volleys aimed at counterattacking bluecoats. It was probably about this time that a Minié ball tore a deep gash into the top of his skull. The private became one of the 112 casualties sustained by the regiment during this action. His next memory was of lying in a field hospital, wondering if he would die. Apparently, Dollar always carried a silver coin with him, and according to family lore, a surgeon did something "to sterilize the piece of money, which was then placed over the wound and thus saved his life."[20]
Photo courtesy of ADAH

THOMAS HOARD HERNDON
copy print from Confederate Veteran

had been an active Democrat before the war. As his county's representative at the secession convention, he had voted for independence and then had helped raise the 36th Alabama, serving first as major, then as lieutenant colonel. In late May 1864 he took over the regiment from the beloved Lewis Woodruff, whose wounding at New Hope Church permanently disabled him. Increased responsibility during the campaign weighed heavily on Herndon. "I would never do for a colonel," he once ruminated. "I cannot divest myself of sympathy for the men, nor look upon them as mere machines." Herndon need not have worried. Having shed blood at Chickamauga, he enjoyed the respect of his soldiers. Prior to the Battle of Atlanta, one of his captains assuaged his doubts: "in our darkest moments, you have been with us, exhibiting the calm composure that has distinguished you as a commander." Exiting the woods at 5:00 P.M., the 36th Alabama rushed forward to help reinforce Manigault's beleaguered brigade around the Troup Hurt House. Tying in on that brigade's left flank, Herndon's men hugged the ground as enemy shot and shell whistled overhead. After nearly fifteen minutes, the colonel realized the danger of remaining motionless under such a barrage. In conjunction with an advance by the 38th Alabama, Herndon ordered his regiment to charge. "The men promptly sprang to their feet and went forward with alacrity," he recounted, "passing through the field in the face of a raking fire of grape and canister from six and perhaps more pieces of artillery and not halting or faltering until they reached the works of the enemy." The temerity of the assault unnerved the Yankee artillerymen, who broke and ran, leaving behind four guns. "My men poured repeated volleys into them as they fled," the colonel added with satisfaction. Falling back to some breastworks northwest of the Troup Hurt House, Herndon aligned his companies just in time to blunt a powerful Union counterattack. He and Maj. Shep Ruffin of the 38th Alabama were initially confident that they could hold their position, but when Manigault's Brigade abruptly withdrew, the colonel was forced to execute an awkward retreat. During this movement, Herndon sustained a grievous wound yet extricated his regiment in relative good order. Nonetheless, out of 150 men Herndon led into the battle, 61 were killed, wounded, or captured.[21]

He could hear the thunder of combat off to the east of Atlanta, but Col. Thomas Herndon of the 36th Alabama Infantry was having difficulty reaching the battlefield. Commanding one of the four Alabama regiments in Bushrod Jones's brigade, he was endeavoring to navigate an unfamiliar patch of woods on the blazing hot afternoon of 22 July 1864. A thirty-six-year-old lawyer and family man from Greene County, Herndon

JAMES HENRY BICKERSTAFF
copy print

At high noon on 28 July, Lt. James Bickerstaff licked his parched lips as he put the boys of Company I, 34th Alabama Infantry into line of battle. Peremptory orders earlier that morning to move forward immediately and attack the Yankees at Ezra Church dissuaded the regimental officers from dispatching any water details. Though only twenty years old, Bickerstaff was a veteran. In 1861 he enlisted in the 6th Alabama Infantry and was present at First Manassas. In May 1862 he returned home to Russell County to join a company raised by his father, Company I, 34th Alabama. With that unit, Bickerstaff participated in Bragg's Kentucky Campaign, watched his father fall at Murfreesboro, and fought at Chickamauga and Missionary Ridge as well as the recent Battle of Atlanta. At Ezra Church the 34th Alabama advanced on the extreme left flank of Manigault's Brigade; two other Alabama regiments— the 28th and 24th—tied in on the 34th's right. Like everyone else in his regiment, Bickerstaff quickly realized that there were no friendly forces on their left; the brigade was attacking unsupported. Nevertheless, they trudged across a stretch of boggy ground, all the while under artillery fire, before reaching a thin copse of trees. Here the Alabamians commenced firing on an enemy hilltop position, but like every other Rebel unit that hit the Union lines that day, the 34th found itself pummeled by Yankee lead. At one point the men tried to charge but made no headway as their exposed left flank came under especially severe enfilade fire. Speaking for the men, Maj. John Slaughter later asserted that "this was by far the most destructive fire they ever had been under." Among the sixty-nine Alabamians cut down was Bickerstaff, whose left elbow was shattered. As the sound of retreat echoed over the crimsoned landscape, exhausted men wandered the woods in search of water while ambulance stewards hurried Bickerstaff to a makeshift hospital. The surgeon took one look at the lieutenant's mangled arm and took out his saw. James Bickerstaff lived, and he received explicit praise for his bravery from Major Slaughter, but he would never fight again.[22]
Photo courtesy of ADAH

217

WILLIAM A. McLEOD
ambrotype

Also participating in the assault at Ezra Church was Capt. William McLeod of the 28th Alabama Infantry. The twenty-seven-year-old farmer from Jefferson County had commanded Company H since the beginning of the Atlanta Campaign. Ezra Church, however, marked the end of McLeod's tenure. Advancing as part of Manigault's left wing, the regiment marched between two other Alabama formations (the 34th and 24th). In the course of the attack, the 28th appears to have moved slightly ahead of the other units in the brigade—doing so only apprised them of the folly of their course that much sooner. Sprawled over the ground that McLeod and his company now traversed were the dead and wounded of a brigade of Mississippians that had just been repulsed. As the defenders' musketry intensified, Col. William Butler ordered his companies to lie down a mere 30 yards from the Federal works and return fire from the prone position until the rest of the brigade caught up. It was probably at this point that Captain McLeod died, killed by one of the thousands of projectiles whizzing through the air; perhaps his final, abrupt thoughts were of Elizabeth, his wife of four years. Twenty-nine other Alabamians in the regiment also fell. The men endured this predicament for no more than five minutes before the survivors fell back to the safety of some woods 150 yards to the rear. The officers tried to rally the men for another attempt, but no one really wanted to move past the tree line; the battle was lost. But all of that was now irrelevant to William McLeod.
Photo courtesy of ADAH

STARKE HUNTER OLIVER
copy print

Less than a week after fighting desperately around the Troup Hurt House during the Battle of Atlanta, Capt. Starke Oliver went into action again at Ezra Church. This time, however, the line officer was acting commander of the 24th Alabama Infantry. A twenty-seven-year-old civil servant from Mobile, Oliver originally enlisted in the 3rd Alabama, but in the spring of 1862, he gained permission to seek a commission in the newly raised 24th. Elected captain of Company D, whose recruits all came from Mobile, Oliver led that unit through some of the fiercest battles in the western theater—Murfreesboro, Chickamauga, Chattanooga, and the Battle for Atlanta, where he was slightly wounded. Now at the head of the regiment, Oliver faced his toughest challenge on the afternoon of 28 July: a frontal assault against an entrenched enemy. The 24th Alabama deployed as the center regiment in Manigault's Brigade. Two South Carolina regiments marched on its right, while two Alabama regiments marched on its left. At 12:30 P.M. the men of the 24th advanced, not knowing that their corps commander, Stephen Lee was sending in his brigades one at a time. As Oliver led his men from the sanctuary of nearby woods into an open field, the regiment came under enemy fire from strong fortifications about five hundred yards away. Moments later the captain ordered a charge, but his men got no closer than thirty yards before severe fire from front and flank broke the assault. Thankfully for the 24th, the Yankees had concentrated most of their volleys against the regiments to its left. Nevertheless, the Alabamians fled for several hundred yards in some confusion before Oliver restored order. The captain reported only twenty casualties in the regiment. All in all, he had done as well as he could under the circumstances. *Photo courtesy of Historic Mobile Preservation Society Archives*

219

JAMES HENRY HEARN
copy print

Sgt. James Hearn of the 46th Alabama Infantry was exhausted as his regiment deployed into line of battle due west of Jonesboro. It was the afternoon of 31 August, a stifling hot day, and the sergeant, who had been marching since midnight, was now expected to help capture a strongly fortified Union position. A struggling yeoman farmer, the twenty-eight-year-old Hearn and his family were living in Coosa County when the war broke out. In February 1862 he enlisted in Company A, 46th Alabama and did his duty, fighting throughout the Vicksburg Campaign and seeing action around Chattanooga in the fall of 1863. For unspecified reasons, Hearn was reduced to the ranks in January 1864 but by that summer was the first sergeant of his company. At Jonesboro the 46th was one of five Alabama regiments in Pettus's Brigade, a unit ordered to strike the central apex of the Federal line as part of the initial Confederate attack. Launched around 3:00 P.M., the assault went nowhere fast. The Union commander there described the ease with which his blue-coats repulsed the Yellowhammer onslaught: "None of the charging parties came nearer than 150 yards, being unable to stand the withering fire that greeted them to hospitable graves." While steering his men toward the safety of a shallow ravine, Hearn sustained a terrible wound: a Minié ball tore through his right arm, entered his body, and then exited out the back mere inches from his spine. Although the sergeant eventually recovered, his fighting days were over.[23]
Photo courtesy of Roy H. Bunn

JOSEPH BENAJAH BIBB
copy print from Confederate Veteran

The situation called for boldness, so Edmund Pettus selected his best regimental commander—Joseph Bibb of the 23rd Alabama Infantry—to spearhead the river crossing at Columbia, Tennessee, on 28 November 1864. A planter from Montgomery County, the forty-two-year-old Bibb was an ardent Confederate from one of the state's wealthiest families. During the secession crisis, Bibb raised a unit of so-called Minute Men, whom he later merged into the 23rd. As lieutenant colonel, Bibb ably served as the regiment's executive officer under the intrepid Franklin Beck, until assuming command outright during Hood's invasion of

Tennessee. At Columbia, the plan was not only to cross the Duck River as quickly as possible, but trap the sizeable enemy contingent on the other side. During the afternoon, engineers ferried the 23rd over the river, where Bibb positioned his men in line of battle. Then, immediately after the 31st and 46th Alabama Regiments joined him, Bibb led a charge up the steep embankments. The Yellowhammers routed two regiments of Kentucky Federals, with Bibb's men also capturing a Yankee battery. Although their foe ultimately slipped away, Bibb had "nobly won his spurs" in the eyes of higher headquarters.[24]

VIRGIL S. MURPHEY
copy print

At 4:00 P.M. on 30 November, Col. Virgil Murphey led the 17th Alabama Infantry toward a cotton gin just east of the Carter House, the center of the Union position at Franklin. An accomplished lawyer from Montgomery, the twenty-seven-year-old Murphey was a staunch secessionist who helped organize some of the city's first companies for war. Having led the 17th Alabama throughout the Atlanta Campaign, the colonel was a seasoned regimental commander, but the fighting at Franklin proved his most difficult, and final, challenge. Advancing as part of Shelley's Brigade (which included the 26th and 29th Alabama), the 17th made good initial progress. The Alabamians quickly routed an outer line of Yankee pickets, but then came under brutal artillery fire. On reaching the main line of breastworks, Murphey's men encountered a ditch. Immobilized by this obstacle yet suffering under enemy musketry, the Alabamians jumped into the ditch and pressed against the inner walls of dirt. Murphey knew that his men could not remain in such a vulnerable position, and when a cannon blast killed nine of them, he went into a berserker rage. Screaming "forward," the colonel and his surviving Yellow-hammers clambered up the parapet "like infuriated demons." The Yankees, however, easily repulsed this desperate charge and captured Murphey.[25]
Photo courtesy of ADAH

Robert Phillip Owens
copy print

It is unclear whether Pvt. Robert Owens was part of the 17th Alabama's final, forlorn charge at Franklin, but given the mortal wound he received in that battle, there is no doubt that he was part of the day's savagery. Just seventeen years old when he enlisted in September 1861, Owens hailed from Montgomery. From the beginning, the war was not kind to him. As a soldier in Company B, the teenager was severely wounded at Shiloh. After recovering, he was appointed regimental musician but soon went on sick leave for extended periods, first with odontalgia (that is, a toothache) and then with acute diarrhea. By the time Hood commenced his invasion of Tennessee, however, Private Owens was healthy again and ready for action. He

cheated death at Shiloh, but not at Franklin. At some point during the 17th Alabama's ill-fated charge, Owens went down. "The field was strewn with the dead and the Columbia turnpike ran with the purest blood of our heroic land," Col. Virgil Murphey later described, "the works was wet with human gore, and men disfigured mutilated and dying lay upon them while the carnage raged around them." Stretcher bearers managed to carry Owens to safety, but before surgeons could operate, he died, one of the nearly 1,800 Confederates who perished that autumn afternoon.[26]
Photo courtesy of Mrs. Robert L. Kerr Collection, U.S.A.M.H.I.

ROBERT HADEN ABERCROMBIE
copy print

It was dusk on 30 November when Col. Robert Abercrombie of the 45th Alabama Infantry led his 290 soldiers uncertainly toward a distant gin house south of Franklin. A twenty-seven-year-old attorney from Macon County, Abercrombie joined the regiment at its inception in May 1862, rising steadily in rank from captain of Company H, to major, lieutenant colonel, and finally full colonel after the Battle of Atlanta. Miraculously, he fought unscathed through the regiment's many battles—that is, until Hood's invasion of Tennessee. At Spring Hill on 29 November, a bullet grazed his scalp during a sharp skirmish with retreating Federals. At Franklin he was wounded again. Part of Lowrey's Brigade, the 45th Alabama advanced as the reserve for Cleburne's divisional assault. When called forward, Abercrombie initially thought his regiment might help exploit a temporary breakthrough around

the Carter House, but on encountering one shattered Confederate unit after the next, he knew his boys could do little more than offer some relief. Seeing the flag of the nearby 33rd Alabama flapping pathetically among the enemy breastworks, the colonel tried to lay down a volley of supporting fire, but a section of Union guns raked his line. Within minutes his regiment sustained over 150 casualties, including Abercrombie himself, struck in the breast. Somehow the colonel stayed on his feet and began issuing orders for everyone to fall back. Roll call the next morning revealed that the brigade had lost about half its complement. The 16th and 33rd Alabama Infantry Regiments merged with the 45th Alabama, all under Abercrombie, whose second wound in as many days actually proved relatively minor. *Photo courtesy of ADAH*

224

After spending the first half of December 1864 digging up the frozen earth just south of Nashville, Capt. Charles Lumsden concluded that, under the circumstances, the position afforded his battery decent protection and a clear field of fire. When the Union army actually attacked, however, the artillery officer discovered that his so-called Redoubt No. 4 was pitifully untenable. A Virginian who was teaching military tactics at the University of Alabama when the war broke out, the thirty-year-old Lumsden offered his services to his adopted state. In November 1861 he issued a call for volunteers: "Alabama is about to be invaded by a mercenary foe! Her soil to be desecrated by the tread of Lincoln's myrmidons! Will you not rise up and defend her?" Over two hundred men responded, most coming from Tuscaloosa, many of whom were Lumsden's own students. For the next three years, Lumsden's Battery participated in the Army of Tennessee's fiercest battles —Perryville, Murfreesboro, Chickamauga, and the Atlanta Campaign. At Nashville Lumsden's four 12-pounder smoothbores covered nearly six hundred yards of Hood's left flank. Unfortunately, the Confederate line in general was thinly manned; infantry support for the battery consisted of a mere 100-man detachment from the 29th Alabama Infantry. As the fog lifted late on the morning of 15 December, Redoubt No. 4 came under an intense artillery barrage from as many as two dozen enemy cannon. One of Lumsden's gunners recalled the scene: "Above our heads was a net work of shrieking shells." Miraculously, the battery suffered negligible damage, but the onrush of an entire Union corps presented an impossible challenge. When dismounted Yankee cavalrymen overran Redoubt No. 5, several hundred yards to Lumsden's left, the captain deftly repositioned two of his pieces and bombarded the enemy troopers. Soon swarms of bluecoats descended on Redoubt No. 4. Although virtually every nearby Rebel infantry unit was falling back in confusion, Lumsden received a peremptory order "to hold the enemy in check to the last minute regardless of losses." In compliance, his artillerymen rammed their barrels with canister and

CHARLES L. LUMSDEN
copy print

blasted an approaching regiment of Missouri Federals. As he prepared another charge, however, Lumsden realized that the gunner holding the friction primers had fled, to which the captain turned to the others and shouted, "Take care of yourselves boys!" Lumsden escaped, but eighteen of his men were killed or captured and all of his guns were in enemy hands; after three hours of fighting, the battery was gone. To his demoralized men who now considered the war lost, Lumsden replied that no matter the outcome, "we all of us want to be conscious that we have done our duty from start to finish."[27] *Photo courtesy of W. S. Hoole Special Collections Library, The University of Alabama*

WILLIAM FLETCHER LOWERY
ambrotype

Looking down at the blue-coated corpses strewn along the slopes of Overton Hill on the afternoon of 16 December 1864, 2nd Lt. William Lowery of the 20th Alabama Infantry was convinced that the Army of Tennessee had won a great victory at Nashville. A thirty-two-year-old resident of Bibb County, Lowery joined the 20th in September 1861 and soon won election to the second lieutenancy in Company D, the Bibb Rangers. As far as the records indicate, he participated in all of the regiment's major battles from the Vicksburg Campaign through the Atlanta Campaign. At Nashville the 20th Alabama was part of Pettus's Brigade. A strong Union attack on 15 December pushed the Rebel siege lines back a mile or more in places. Lowery and his unit saw little action that day, but on 16 December they were hotly engaged. The regiment was dug in on the western side of Overton Hill, a formidable position that protected the Rebel right flank. Throughout the afternoon, Lowery helped orchestrate a stout defense against the renewed enemy advance. "They rushed forward with great spirit," Maj. Gen. Carter Stevenson wrote of the Yankee assault, "only to be driven back with dreadful slaughter." Lieutenant Lowery was among the many graybacks feeling "perfectly cool and confident" by the propitious course of events. Toward dusk, however, alarming reports of disaster on the Rebel left shattered the jubilant mood. While Confederates such as Lowery had been repulsing the enemy around Overton Hill, the rest of the Army of Tennessee had disintegrated under a massive Yankee juggernaut. In the face of an enveloping Union tide, the 20th Alabama attempted to redeploy, but fleeing soldiers from other units spread their panic. "It was impossible to withdraw the command in order," Stevenson explained in his report, "and it became considerably broken and confused." Lieutenant Lowery and other officers tried to stem the rout, but dozens of Alabamians either ran off or surrendered to the onrushing Yankees. At some point during the chaos, Lowery suffered a wound. He did manage to avoid capture, but whether he participated in the rearguard actions later that night and the following day is unclear. What he did participate in, however, was an inglorious retreat mere hours after he had thought his side had won the battle.[28]
Photo courtesy of ADAH

For nearly three weeks since mid-November 1864, Col. Joseph Hodgson of the 7th Alabama Cavalry had been riding hard virtually every day, screening Hood's advance into Middle Tennessee and sparring with Yankee forces all the way. Originally from Virginia, the twenty-six-year-old Hodgson settled in Montgomery as a lawyer just before the secession crisis. For the first two years of the war, he served as a company commander in the 1st Alabama Cavalry but resigned in July 1863 to raise the 7th Cavalry. After a year patrolling the Alabama-Florida border, Hodgson received orders to join the brigade of Col. Edmund Rucker in preparation for the invasion of Tennessee. On 7 December Hodgson and his 300 troopers occupied a position overlooking the Cumberland River less than three miles west of Nashville. For the next few days, they harassed Union water traffic while guarding the extreme, rather far-flung left flank of Hood's besieging army. When the Federals attacked on 15 December, Hodgson's troopers helped defeat a local strike against Rucker's Brigade, but the main enemy body bypassed the cavalrymen. Lest his brigade be cut off, Rucker withdrew most of his regiments during the night, leaving behind only the 7th Alabama, whose men were to divert the attention of a sizeable contingent of Yankee cavalry. The ruse worked, and the following morning Hodgson slipped away down Charlotte Pike and eventually established flank security farther south near the outlying town of Brentwood.

On 16 December the Union offensive again overwhelmed the Rebel left wing. Fighting dismounted, Hodgson and his men skirmished intermittently until dusk, when they realized Hood's army was in full retreat. The colonel decided that the best way to escape was to attack the nearest Union formation. For the next several hours, his Alabama troopers engaged in a wild night fight, where the woods flashed and crackled with steady carbine fire. In the confusion Hodgson lost track of his companies' whereabouts. Fortunately, capable subordinate officers kept the scattered troops

JOSEPH HODGSON
copy print

moving until the regiment reached the safety of friendly lines. First reports suggested that Hodgson's command lost over 200 men at Nashville, but as more and more missing troopers showed up, the final tally of killed, wounded, and captured came to about 50, which was bad enough. The 7th Alabama Cavalry participated in various rearguard actions for the rest of December. *Photo courtesy of Historic Mobile Preservation Society Archives*

JOHN F. GAINES
ambrotype

For more than a week in November 1864, Lt. Col. John Gaines of the 53rd Alabama (Mounted) Infantry sparred with Union troopers around the small Georgia town of Waynesboro. General Sherman had recently commenced his destructive march to the sea, and men such as Gaines were determined to hinder his progress. A thirty-three-year-old Montgomerian, Gaines initially served as a junior officer in the 1st Alabama Cavalry, but in November 1862 he accepted appointment as executive officer in the 53rd Alabama, a regiment of mounted infantry under the designation "Partisan Ranger." As part of Joseph Wheeler's cavalry corps during the Atlanta Campaign, Gaines and the 53rd were constantly reconnoitering or raiding, with the lieutenant colonel often commanding the regiment. By late 1864 Gaines was an acting brigade commander in charge of both his own regiment and the 24th Alabama Cavalry Battalion. Toward the end of November, he and his troopers participated in a series of running fights with enemy cavalry outside of Waynesboro. For several days, the Rebel horsemen got the best of their mounted adversaries. Upon the arrival of several thousand Federal infantrymen, however, the tide quickly turned. The climax came on 4 December, when Lieutenant Colonel Gaines orchestrated an impressive, albeit short-lived, defense against superior numbers. Fighting dismounted behind breastworks made from fence rails, the graybacks held their ground for most of the morning. "Every charge of the enemy was repulsed by volleys and countercharges," reported a local correspondent. Nevertheless, the position was eventually outflanked, and the Rebel horsemen forced to retreat. "Our loss was between 70 and 80 men," the correspondent added, whereas "the enemy's loss is reported officially as 'very heavy.'" In fact, the Yankees suffered nearly 200 casualties. Among the Confederate casualties, though, was Lieutenant Colonel Gaines, who at some point during the fray was shot through his right leg. "He bore his misfortune with manly resignation," observed an Alabama trooper. Unfortunately, the wound would require amputation.[29]
Photo courtesy of ADAH

JAMES ALFORD
THOMPSON
copy print

It was really a forgettable skirmish that had no bearing on the outcome of the war, but for Pvt. James Thompson of the 17th Alabama Infantry, the scrap at Egypt, Mississippi, in December 1864 brought a pathetic end to a most unhappy wartime ordeal. A twenty-six-year-old overseer from Butler County, Thompson was an ambivalent Confederate. In May 1862 he enlisted in the Butler Rifles, which became Company C, 17th Alabama, yet he spent most of the next year trying to raise money to hire a substitute. Indifferent to military life and often sick with diarrhea, Thompson expressed growing homesickness in his infrequent correspondence. The Atlanta Campaign, in which the 17th saw continuous action week after week, pushed the private to the threshold of despair. "I wish I had died when I was little," he wrote his wife, Mary, in August. "It don't seem to me that I care much to live. If it was not for you and the children, I would not want to live another day longer for I have been pulled and hauled about until I don't care for nothing much." He concluded this morose letter with, "Kiss the babes for me," the last words Mary would ever receive from her husband of five years. That autumn Thompson came down with another bad case of diarrhea. When the Army of Tennessee commenced its offensive toward Nashville, the disconsolate private was left behind in Tuscumbia, too unfit for the rigors of a campaign. Soon, however, he was sent to northeastern Mississippi as part of a detail assigned to repair and guard those sections of the Mobile and Ohio Railroad still of value to the Confederacy. In late December Union cavalry raided the line. Thompson was part of a small force ordered to protect the station at Egypt. On 28 December Yankee troopers swept aside the ineffectual Rebel skirmish line, galloped through the town, and then stormed the stockade near the track, where Private Thompson and a few hundred ill-equipped comrades offered feeble resistance before capitulating. Ten days later Thompson arrived at Alton Prison in Illinois. Now suffering from pneumonia, he immediately went to the infirmary. On 22 January 1865, James Thompson breathed his last.[30] *Photo courtesy of Wilbur and Illene Thompson*

229

EDMUND WINSTON PETTUS
copy print

For Brig. Gen. Edmund Pettus, the Battle of Benton-ville was the coda to an exemplary career in the Confederate army. The forty-three-year-old lawyer from Dallas County was a dedicated citizen-soldier of the South. Born into a slaveholding family, Pettus fought in large measure to protect the peculiar institution, serving first as a secession commissioner to Mississippi (where his brother was governor at the time), then as an officer in the 20th Alabama, an infantry regiment he helped raise in September 1861. His battlefield heroics earned him rapid promotion. At Champion Hill it was Pettus who discovered the turning movement that threatened to destroy Pemberton's army, giving the Confederates time to redeploy. During the subsequent siege of Vicksburg, he led a daring, commando-style sortie on 22 May that recaptured an important redoubt. Promoted to brigadier general in September 1863, he commanded five Alabama regiments—the 20th, 23rd, 30th, 31st, and 46th—for the duration of the war. He ably led this brigade at Lookout Mountain and throughout the Atlanta Campaign. As the vanguard of Hood's invasion of Tennessee, Pettus seized control of the Duck River crossings and later helped stem the tide of retreat at Nashville with a skillful rearguard action.

On the afternoon of 19 March 1865, Pettus faced his last military challenge. His brigade marched in the sec-ond echelon of Joseph Johnston's flank attack at Bentonville, North Carolina. His 400 men were rest-less, but Pettus maintained a disciplined advance, all the while keeping his formation safely away from the artillery fire that peppered Confederate units in the first wave. As the action developed to his front, the general patiently determined how best to deploy his command. He first shored up the flank of a hard-pressed neighboring brigade, then routed a careless assault by an Indiana regiment. While three other Alabama brigades stormed into the "bull pen," Pettus took up an over watch position astride Goldsboro Road. When surviving Rebels came streaming back, he smartly aligned his regiments in the prone position behind good cover. The setting sun provided just enough light for his Alabamians to deliver a nasty surprise to pursuing Yankees. As the bluecoats burst through the haze of smoke, Pettus's regiments opened fire simultaneously with deadly effect. Staggering back, the Federals reorganized and charged again, but the Alabamians repulsed every attack until nightfall brought the clash to an end. This tactical success did come at a cost. Pettus was one of sixty-seven casualties in the brigade; he suffered a flesh wound to one of his legs. The general also witnessed the death of E. W. Pettus, his nephew and aide-de-camp, who was killed by an enemy volley. *Photo courtesy of ADAH*

Alabama Home Front

A year after secession, the war for independence seemed a distant affair to many Alabamians. To be sure, economic hardships were nascent, but the Confederacy's capital had moved from Montgomery to Richmond, and most of the volunteer regiments were on battlefields hundreds of miles away. John Shorter, the new governor, tried to press home a sense of urgency, but his inaugural address in December 1861 seemed overly dramatic: "Our coasts may be ravaged, our cities and towns reduced to ashes," he thundered, "but the sacred right of self-government . . . Alabamians never will surrender."[1] Suddenly, in early February 1862 three Union gunboats steamed up the Tennessee River as the vanguard of a Yankee invasion. On 8 February the little flotilla reached Florence, where it captured or destroyed several commercial steamers. This incident produced wild excitement throughout the valley region. Many residents fled, while others hastily mustered local militia units. A considerable number, however, actually welcomed the enemy, thereby revealing a long-dormant unionist sentiment that belied the secessionist euphoria of the previous

year. War had come to Alabama at last, and the state was largely unprepared.

Over the next several weeks, Union armies overran the western half of Tennessee, winning the great battle of Shiloh in early April. That same month 8,000 bluecoats under Brig. Gen. Ormsby Mitchel swept into northern Alabama. On 11 April Mitchel's strike force occupied Huntsville, Stevenson, and Decatur, towns that connected a one-hundred-mile section of the Memphis and Charleston Railroad. In the process the Yankees captured dozens of locomotives and seized intact several bridges crossing the Tennessee River. These aggressive operations also foreshadowed an emerging hard-war policy. On 2 May a brigade of midwesterners sacked the small town of Athens in retaliation for mounting Rebel guerrilla attacks. Desperate to repel the invaders, Governor Shorter accelerated the formation of numerous homegrown mounted units. These fought under such renowned Confederate raiders as Nathan Bedford Forrest and Joe Wheeler, but it was a contingent of Alabama horsemen under Capt. Philip Roddey that proved the most consistent defenders of the valley region. A major Rebel offensive into Kentucky that autumn helped drive out the Union occupiers, but residents along the Tennessee would not experience peace for another three years.

In the meantime, Alabama offered its manifold fruits to the Confederacy. The state's central location made it a vital transportation and communication link despite its limited rail system (less than 800 miles of track). But of equal importance were the state's invaluable material assets: iron, food, and manpower (both free and slave). In maximizing these resources, however, Alabama's governing authorities faced unexpected challenges, most notably famine and political dissent, both of which eroded popular support for the overall war effort.

Though not apparent at the outset, Alabama became a major supplier of war material. The state possessed rich deposits of iron ore and coal, primarily in its hill counties. Going into the war, there were seven small-scale ironworks in operation. Governor Shorter negotiated generous state contracts with each to produce pig iron for the military. Beginning in early 1862, however, the Confederate government asserted despotic control over this crucial enterprise. Under Josiah Gorgas, head of the Confederacy's Ordnance Department, Alabama became a military-industrial complex. The Nitre and Mining Bureau expanded the existing ironworks and supervised the construction of ten more, all of which were privately owned in name only. Between January 1863 and September 1864, these facilities, with the Shelby Ironworks being the largest, produced over 12,350 tons of iron. Though a seemingly modest quantity, historian Joseph Woodward points out that "the blast furnaces of Alabama produced more pig iron for the Confederacy than all the other Confederate states combined."[2]

In addition to providing raw materials, Alabama also became the Confederacy's principal manufacturer of arms and munitions. Recognizing that the Union blockade would eventually eliminate foreign sources of weaponry, authorities in Richmond expanded the South's inchoate industrial base, particularly in Alabama. For example, the incipient textile industry in Prattville became a center for making cloth for uniforms, while artisans in Tallassee specialized in small arms, producing over 6,000 carbines by the end of 1864. The most important factory city, however, was Selma. Ideally situated near the state's ironworks and along the navigable Alabama River, Selma quickly developed into one of the most diversified industrial locations anywhere in the Confederacy. "By 1863 did our little city present one scene of skill and labor," recorded longtime resident John Hardy, "employing, at least, ten thousand men and women within our limits." These laborers worked in the navy yard, in one of two arsenals, or in the various foundries and machine shops. They made armor plating, boilers, and engines for the navy; cartridges, canteens, and knapsacks for the army; and the famous rifled Brooke cannons for both. "There is nothing," Hardy further commented, "but what could be produced at Selma." Indeed, during the last half of the war, a plurality of the Confederacy's artillery and ammunition came out of Selma.[3]

Alabama also served the Confederacy as a breadbasket. Well known for its cash-crop plantations, the state was also abundant in grain. As an indication of how well Alabama could feed its people, farmers in 1860 harvested over 33 million bushels of corn (12 percent of the South's entire yield).[4] Unfortunately, the exigencies of war steadily impaired the state's agriculture. Most army volunteers were yeoman, whose absence from the family farm inevitably reduced local productivity. Moreover, the dearth of railroad mileage coupled with the incompetence of the Confederate commissariat inhibited efficient distribution. Finally, grain production competed against cotton and whiskey. Planters often persisted in growing cotton despite the official embargo, while many small farmers pursued the greater profits of distilled spirits. As a consequence, food shortages inflated prices and gradually pushed the state to the brink of starvation. In November 1863 a government survey classified 30 percent of Alabamians as "indigent." Not surprisingly, cities such as Mobile experienced bread riots, while throughout the state thousands of "corn women" trudged to and from home carrying sacks of donated foodstuffs. Determined to ameliorate their plight, Governor Shorter initiated public-relief programs, imposed a tax on cotton production above so many bales, and cracked down on distilleries. Nonetheless, Alabama's food crisis only worsened.

Closely connected to food production was the availability of salt, an indispensable preservative. Prior to secession, Southerners imported this commodity cheaply; the blockade, however, created an alarming "salt famine" throughout the Confederacy. Fortunately, Alabama possessed a natural source—the saline-rich soil along the Tombigbee River in the southwestern part of the state. Although several small, private salt makers had worked the region for years, Governor Shorter subsidized the construction of two large saltworks in Clarke County. By the end of 1862, the state-managed sites employed over 1,000 laborers. Pumping up brine and then boiling it during round-the-clock shifts, both facilities combined to produce 100,000 pounds of pure salt every month (only Saltville, Virginia, manufactured more). To be sure, this output was a pittance of what the South enjoyed before the war, but it was a vital contribution to Confederate society all the same.

Undoubtedly, Alabama's most significant contribution to the Confederacy was its fighting men. About 96,000 Alabamians wore the Confederate uniform. The vast majority of these men were volunteers who joined during the first year of the conflict, but officially 14,875 were conscripts. Beginning in April 1862, the Confederate Congress passed a series of controversial enrollment acts. Men in the eighteen-to-thirty-five age range (later expanded to seventeen to fifty) were subject to military service. Moreover, soldiers already on active duty had their terms extended until the end of the war. There were some exemptions, such as war-industry-related occupations, but the "Twenty-Negro Law" angered many Southerners. This measure permitted planters to retain an adult white man, perhaps a son or the master himself, on the plantation for slave control. However sensible this provision seemed to a society obsessed with race order, it prompted the oft-quoted outcry "rich man's war, poor man's fight." Governor Shorter personally disliked the idea of conscription, seeing it as a violation of individual liberty and an insult to real patriotism; nevertheless, he vigorously enforced the new law. Unfortunately, state and national authorities often clashed over how best to implement it. Maj. William T. Walthall, a native conscript officer at Talladega, understood that to be drafted carried with it a stigma of inferiority. Therefore, he sought to cosset a potential conscript, "gradually infusing into him a soldierly pride and consciousness of being on a footing of equality."[5] Most Confederate agents, however, impatient for results, usually preferred more-coercive measures of enrollment.

Almost immediately, conscription in Alabama spawned resistance, especially in the hill counties of the north and wiregrass region in the south, areas that exhibited lukewarm support for secession. For the most part, draft dodging took the form of "lying out," whereby men simply evaded, with the aide of local sympathizers, conscript agents whenever they appeared. But in some instances resistance became quite violent. In Randolph County, for example, a band of vigilantes, reportedly numbering 400 men, rendered conscription virtually impossible in that part of the state. To combat such lawlessness, the Conscription Bureau in Alabama formed twenty-five companies of militia, ironically consisting of at least 2,000 conscripts, though all to no avail.

Confederate difficulties with conscription were closely related to the growing problem of desertion. Not all conscripts deserted and not all deserters were conscripts, but enforcing one invariably entailed punishing the other, for draft dodgers and deserters often helped one another. Officially, 104,000 graybacks quit the ranks during the course of the war; at least 10,000 of these men were Alabamians. Reasons varied, but the most common explanation was domestic pressure to return to families hardest hit by the ravages of war. In some cases, though, plain defeatism was the culprit. At Pollard in January 1864, a mutiny erupted within a brigade made up primarily of conscripts from the wiregrass counties. The uprising failed, and while the ringleaders faced courts-martial, most of the other conscripts were sent to the Army of Northern Virginia, where they fought in the 61st Alabama Infantry.

If many white Alabamians chose to stop serving as the war dragged on, black Alabamians had no choice. It did not take long for the Confederacy to tap into its greatest labor resource—slavery—for noncombat military duties, such as building fortifications, hauling supplies, repairing railroad tracks, and serving as common workers at industrial sites. Because slaves were private property, however, state legislatures had to pass laws authorizing their governors to impress specific quotas of slaves for set periods of time. Even before the requisite law passed in Alabama in October 1862, Governor Shorter invoked emergency power, impressing thousands of slaves for various projects throughout the state, most notably work on the defenses around Mobile. Although he genuinely tried to minimize the economic inconvenience of the policy, he failed to placate planters who objected to his putative abuse of power and to the army's disregard for the well-being of slaves (some five hundred died during their impressments). Though vital to the war effort, such actions cost Shorter a great deal of political capital.

And then there were the women. "Hurray for the ladies!" exclaimed Pvt. Robert Bliss of the 27th Alabama Infantry in letter home in 1863: "They are the soul of the war." Like their male counterparts, most Alabama women supported the Confederacy. Disallowed by social convention from fighting them-selves, women showed their patriotism in other ways: pressuring hesitant youths to uphold community honor and join the army, hosting dances to boost morale, and most importantly running the farm or plantation in the absence of their men. Another prominent display of female patriotism were the ubiquitous "ladies' aid societies," volunteer county organizations that both augmented government and church efforts to provide famine relief and supervised the production, collection, and distribution of homespun clothes for soldiers in the field. Finally, women played an increasing role in the state's expanding hospital system (by 1864 there were twenty-eight military hospitals in Alabama). Besides providing nurses, the aid societies were instrumental in raising money for upkeep. The Ladies Hospital of Montgomery, for instance, was a 265-bed facility maintained almost exclusively by charitable donations from the city's women. Their dedication notwithstanding, Alabama women found belief in the cause increasingly difficult to maintain. "We were working and fasting and praying that victory might reward all our sacrifices and sufferings," noted Parthenia Hague of Eufaula in 1864, but "day by day the conviction strengthened with us that, struggle as we would, we were on the losing side."[6]

Internal troubles alone could not prevent the Shorter administration from pushing the war effort, but in conjunction with the Union army's incessant advance, the state's domestic fissures grew more and more deleterious. At the end of April 1863, the Federals launched a new incursion into northern Alabama. As a column of some 8,000 bluecoats marched on Tuscumbia, a mounted force of nearly 2,000 more, led by Col. Abel Streight, raced across the state en route to the Western and Atlanta railhead at Rome, Georgia. (Both operations were ancillary components of two larger, concomitant campaigns to capture Chattanooga and Vicksburg.) Against this threat, Colonel Roddey defended Tuscumbia, eventually driving off the enemy column, while General Forrest pursued

Streight in one of the war's most exciting cavalry engagements. In a series of running gunfights from 29 April to 3 May, Forrest overhauled and captured Streight's command at the Georgia border. Overlooked in the immediate wake of this drama was both the Union infantry's razing of over one million bushels of Confederate corn in the vicinity of Tuscumbia and Streight's destruction of the newly opened Round Mountain Furnace in Cherokee County.

Streight's Raid also highlighted the significance of unionism in Alabama. Perhaps a quarter of the colonel's troopers came from the very hill counties through which he passed. In all, about 2,600 Alabamians served in the Union army, a majority in the 1st Alabama Cavalry (Union), a regiment that began forming in October 1862. Most of these "Alabama Yankees" came from the northern part of the state and, in the words of a Northern captain who commanded a company of them, "their love and devotion for the union and the old flag, was not excelled by any who wore the blue."[7] In addition to fighting the rebellion in its home state, the 1st Alabama participated in Sherman's march through Georgia and the Carolinas, earning distinction in numerous engagements.

Recent scholarship has determined that slightly more than one in ten white Alabamians at the beginning of the Civil War could be described as overtly unionist. Unlike the cooperationists of the secession crisis, these were citizens who utterly rejected the Confederacy. Winston County best represents this defiant mindset. A sparsely populated region in the state's northwest corner, Winston was the poorest county in Alabama, but most of its people saw the Union as a sacred trust passed down from their Revolutionary forebears. In the spring of 1862, local leaders held a special meeting a Looney's Tavern, during which several hundred unionists from the surrounding countryside debunked secession. "We agree with [Andrew] Jackson that no state can legally get out of the Union," one resolution read. "But if we

are mistaken in this," it added, "then a county, any county, being a part of the state, by the same process of reasoning could cease to be a part of the state." With that said, those gathered declared their neutrality: "we are not going to shoot at the flag of our fathers, 'Old Glory.'"[8] Given that almost 240 residents from the county served in the Federal army, quite a few evidently had no reservations about shooting at the flag of the Confederacy.

Not surprisingly, unionism infuriated Confederate authorities in Alabama. Governor Shorter rightly attributed his headaches with conscription, desertion, and lawlessness in no small part to unionism, which he damned as treason. His attempt to put on trial the captured Alabamians who rode with Streight came to naught due to the prisoner-exchange policy, while his aggressive use of sheriffs and home-guard units against unionist communities, such as Winston County, exacerbated a burgeoning guerrilla conflict in the state. Derided as "Tories" by their Confederate neighbors, unionists invariably found themselves the target of persecution, official or otherwise. Untold numbers on both sides of the issue died in this civil war within the Civil War.

In the summer of 1863, a growing number of Alabamians expressed disfavor with the war. The twin defeats at Gettysburg and Vicksburg convinced them that independence was no longer possible and therefore that further privation at home was not only unnecessary but inhumane. This sentiment manifested itself through the so-called Peace Society, a clandestine antiwar movement that exercised varying influence throughout the Deep South. In Alabama disaffected Confederates allied politically with the unionist minority against the unpopular Shorter administration. Heading into the statewide election in August, the Peace Society campaigned on a platform of "Reconstruction," meaning that its candidates would seek to repeal wartime legislation and cooperate with Lincoln in bringing Alabama back into the Union. The gubernatorial contest pitted the incumbent Shorter against Thomas Watts, admittedly a secessionist but one whom the electorate believed might adopt a more moderate and realistic approach to the war. Whereas in 1861 Watts lost to Shorter (28,127 to 37,849), in 1863 he trounced his opponent, 28,221 to 9,664. Furthermore, Peace Society candidates won two of nine congressional races and picked up several dozen seats in the state legislature.

At first glance these returns suggest a startling repudiation of the Confederacy by many Alabama voters, but the results are misleading. Under the state constitution, one of the requirements for voting stipulated that a citizen had to reside physically in his home district for three months prior to an election. Yet tens of thousands of eligible voters were away in the army, so therefore the election of 1863 does not reflect an accurate view of the state's political outlook. Nevertheless, it clearly exposed a very real loss of will on the part of many Alabamians after two years of grueling warfare.

Despite the outcome of the voting, peace and reconstruction did not soon come to Alabama. In a widely circulated "fast day" sermon on 21 August, Isaac Tichenor, a Baptist minister from Montgomery, confessed that Alabama's misery was the inevitable product of vanity and avarice by those who thought independence would come easy and without sacrifice. "It may be that God has for the South a world mission," he nevertheless averred, "and that by these sufferings he is preparing them for that trust." Thomas Watts was less abstract. During a speaking tour in September, the new governor stunned the Peace Society with his bellicosity: "If I had the power, I would build up a *wall of fire* between Yankeedom and the Confederate states, there to burn, for ages, as a monument of the folly, wickedness, and vandalism of the puritanic race!" Far from pursuing reconstruction, Watts declared himself "a war man all over." The dissension between the state government and defeatist Alabamians only intensified.[9]

Despite a determined effort, Governor Watts could not rectify the interminable problems plaguing his state. He continued to impress slaves and other property much like his predecessor had done, though he too failed to prevent Confederate authorities from abusing the system. He remonstrated against, yet still upheld, the odious Tax-in-Kind Law, a Confederate measure passed in early 1863 that required all farmers to give 10 percent of their produce to the government. And he ran afoul of antiwar legislators in his attempt to mobilize more Alabamians to fight. In September 1864 the governor sought to circumvent the faulty Confederate conscription policy by enrolling the state's dwindling manpower pool into the state militia for use as a supersized constabulary under his control. To this end, he recommended that this new militia include nonexempt citizens between sixteen and fifty-five years of age. Opponents in the capital balked: "Will you force the sires and striplings of the land to fight your battles?"[10] They preferred the awkward home-guard system that restricted most militiamen to their home counties and instead challenged Watts to round up deserters and put them back in the ranks. On this matter the governor encountered only frustration. By the end of 1864, the northern half of the state (where most of the deserters dwelt) was teeming with brigands and bushwhackers, rendering law enforcement there virtually impossible. Even Confederate units sent to police the region often only aggravated the situation by despoiling civilians of their meager food supplies.

Amid internal collapse, Alabamians confronted newer and more-destructive Union incursions into their homeland. With Sherman's army preparing for its offensive against Atlanta and RAdm. David Farragut's fleet gathering to attack Mobile Bay, the state faced its most serious threats of the war. In a fiery speech in mid-February 1864, Governor Watts tried to galvanize resistance. "Your property, your firesides, your wives and children are in danger," he warned his listeners. "Alabama *must,* Alabama *shall* be defended."[11] When the enemy came this time, however, Rebel forces in the state completely failed to stop them. For instance, in mid-July 1864 a cavalry column of 2,500 bluecoats under Maj. Gen. Lovell Rousseau blitzed through the northeastern portion of Alabama, burning granaries and tearing up a thirty-mile stretch of the Montgomery and West Point Railroad, a vital supply artery for the Confederate army defending Atlanta. The ease with which these Yankees passed through the state demonstrated the Confederacy's growing military incapacity. Philip Roddey, the usual guardian of northern Alabama, was off fighting in northern Mississippi, while most of the regular infantry regiments were either in Georgia or around Mobile. The only forces available to contest Rousseau's march were a hodgepodge of understrength cavalry regiments, home-guard units, and a small contingent of cadets from the University of Alabama; they offered mostly token resistance.

Alabama gained a respite in the late autumn of 1864, when John Bell Hood's invasion of Middle Tennessee briefly carried the conventional struggle out of the state. In the interim the Confederate Congress moved toward its most revolutionary decision of the war—the creation of black infantry regiments. Leading newspapers in Alabama, most notably John Forsyth's *Mobile Register,* had been urging such a policy since 1863. After weeks of rancorous debate, the government in Richmond enacted the controversial legislation on 13 March 1865. But the white South's hope that its chattel would rally around the Confederate flag was desperate delusion. To be sure, blacks generally continued to submit to white authority, but they were not ignorant of the war's inevitable outcome— emancipation. Slaves fled plantations in droves whenever a Union army approached. Nancy Jones, a teenager from Madison County, aptly explained the prevailing black attitude in Alabama: "I got free after both set of soldiers had been in our country,

but it was the Yankee soldiers who told us we was free."[12] For many slaves, liberation also provided an opportunity to strike back at the peculiar institution. Almost 5,000 black Alabamians joined the Union army during the last two years of the war, many of them serving as garrison troops along the Tennessee River.

Along with the rest of the Confederacy, the end for Alabama came in the spring of 1865. After Hood's defeat in Tennessee, Union forces moved at will through the state. In late March Union cavalry commander James Wilson delivered the mortal blow with a devastating raid through the state's interior. Operating in conjunction with a Union offensive against Mobile, General Wilson set out from Gravelly Springs at the head of 13,000 troopers, all veterans. The horsemen moved rapidly toward their main target, Selma. Along the way Wilson gutted several ironworks and dispatched a brigade to raze Tuscaloosa. Against this juggernaut General Forrest fielded a paltry few thousand cavalrymen, including the Alabamians of Roddey's Brigade. The Rebels made courageous stands at Montevallo (31 March) and Ebenezer's Church (1 April), but the Yankees shoved them out of the way with ease. On 2 April Wilson's columns reached the outskirts of Selma. Forrest hastily assembled somewhere between 4,000 and 7,000 defenders (over half of whom are unreliable militia). Had they been adequately manned, Selma's defenses might have been impregnable: an outer ring of entrenchments running in a four-mile arc around the northern half of city (the river protected the southern side) backed by an inner ring of redoubts equipped with thirty-two pieces of artillery. General Roddey defended the right, or eastern, section of the line with five regiments of dismounted Alabama horsemen, local militia manned the center, and Tennesseans under Forrest himself held the left. Around 5:00 P.M. the Yankees commenced their attack. One column stormed the Rebel left and carried that position after twenty-five minutes of frenzied combat. A second column assaulted the right-center defenses, quickly breaking through and silencing several batteries. With darkness falling, Wilson then personally led a full-scale mounted charge that routed the remaining Rebels and captured the city. Though suffering slightly more than 300 casualties, the Yankees captured over 2,700 graybacks. Over the next week, Wilson's men torched every building of military value and confiscated vast quantities of armaments; one of the Confederacy's greatest arsenals was no more.

After destroying Selma, Wilson moved on to Montgomery. Until this moment the former capital of the Confederacy had been a place of relative calm in a land of turmoil. Far removed from the main theaters of war, the city had served as an important logistical center and medical facility, hosting six hospitals. Though still dedicated to their dying nation, Montgomerians went about their daily tasks more from a sense of duty than passion for a cause. Care for the wounded became their highest priority. "An appreciation of the soldier," remarked an observer, "has been nowhere more strikingly manifested than in the little city of Montgomery." Following Rousseau's raid and the fall of Mobile Bay, however, residents watched in trepidation for the imminent appearance of Federal invaders. In mid-April 1865 Wilson's raiders arrived. Confederate general Daniel Adams, the district commander, initially vowed "to make [a] full defense of the city," but this was pure bombast.[13] Serious fortification had only recently started, and the garrison was a pitiful collection of reservists and last-minute volunteers. On 11 April Adams abruptly ordered Montgomery abandoned and withdrew his command. In their haste to depart, Confederate soldiers nearly razed whole sections of the city in a clumsy effort to burn some 88,000 bales of cotton stored there. Fortunately, local firefighters, including a company of African Americans, doused the blaze. The next day Mayor Walter Coleman met Wilson's vanguard and formally surrendered the city, thus sparing it from the enemy's wrath. The Stars and Stripes soon flew over the state capitol, an unmistakable sign that the Cradle of the Confederacy had now become a deathbed for the Lost Cause.

WILLIAM PARISH
CHILTON
copy print

On 20 May 1861 Congressman William Chilton of Montgomery tried in vain to garner the votes necessary to keep the Confederate capital in Alabama. Defeat on this matter did not dampen his ardor for the Confederacy; he dutifully packed his bags and headed for Richmond. Fifty years old at the time, Chilton was a prominent Alabama politico, having served as a Whig in the state legislature before accepting an appointment as chief justice of the state supreme court (1852–56). A lawyer in Montgomery during the secession crisis, he initially objected to disunion but devoted himself to the cause once the convention rendered its decision. Chilton served in all three sessions of the Confederate Congress, where he established a pro-war voting record. For instance, he enthusiastically supported conscription, though he did worry that the law provided inadequate exemptions for the South's limited pool of mechanics. He also attended public rallies back home in Montgomery, where he exhorted the citizenry to make greater sacrifices. At times Chilton's ultrapatriotism reached inane proportions. In opposing a pay raise for soldiers in 1863, the congressman averred that true Southerners fought not for wages, "but for freedom and glory." Generally an admirer of Jefferson Davis, Chilton both denounced the president's critics and approved the administration's periodic resort to martial law.[14]
Photo courtesy of ADAH

JOHN GILL SHORTER
copy print
Blackshear Studio, Macon, Ga.

Much like Jefferson Davis at the national level, Alabama governor John Shorter personified at the state level the Confederacy's triple paradox: as a States' Rights Democrat, Shorter did not hesitate to invoke emergency power to enforce such authoritarian policies as conscription; as a slaveholder, he showed little compunction in impressing chattel for military projects; and as a cash-crop agrarian, he not only insisted that planters shift their production from cotton to grain but also encouraged efforts at industrialization. Forty-three years old at the time of his inauguration in December 1861, Shorter possessed impressive credentials: lawyer, state legislator, circuit-court judge, and member of the Eufaula Regency, an influential party of political fire-eaters from Barbour County. In January 1861 he served as Alabama's secession commissioner to Georgia. As governor, Shorter frankly acknowledged the controversy of his executive decisions. He understood perfectly how the exigencies of a revolutionary war contradicted the principles that motivated secession. But he came to realize that victory required pragmatic flexibility and a total commitment. "Let the entire resources and energies of the people be devoted to the one great purpose of the war," the governor proclaimed in March 1862, "war stern and unrelenting— such a war, as in the providence of God we may be compelled to wage in order to vindicate the inalienable right of self-government." His reference to the Almighty was no mere rhetorical flourish, for Shorter was a Baptist with a profound belief in predestination and the sovereignty of God. Such faith enabled him to implement tough policies with a remarkable equanimity. During his two-year term, Shorter cooperated more fully with the Davis administration than any other war governor in the South. He was no petty despot, however, and Alabama remained a democracy, so much so that in August 1863 Shorter lost his bid for reelection. "The very excellent manner in which you have discharged the duties of Executive have made you enemies," one supporter wrote just prior to the outcome, adding that "it is an unpleasant reflection that you have done your *whole* duty and done it well, yet our people find fault. . . . They would be enemies of [George] Washington in similar circumstances."[15]
Photo courtesy of ADAH

242

JULIET OPIE HOPKINS
copy print
Merriett and Ward,
Washington, D.C.

In the summer of 1861, Juliet Hopkins petitioned friends and politicians back home in Alabama for aid in providing medical care for the state's soldiers then serving in northern Virginia. Inexplicably, authorities in Richmond were slow to develop a medical department, and so it was left to the enterprising efforts of individuals such as Hopkins to help get a military-hospital system up and running. The forty-four-year-old daughter of a wealthy planter from Virginia and the wife of Arthur Hopkins, a retired judge from Mobile, Juliet certainly lived the life of a Southern aristocrat, but she also sacrificed as a Southern patriot. Drawing on her family's private fortune, she established three hospitals in the Richmond area for Alabama soldiers. In December 1861 Governor Shorter appointed her superintendent of all three facilities, even though they were technically part of a vast Confederate complex at Chimborazo, one that included other state hospitals. Blessed with a capacity for organization, Hopkins brought efficiency to her task. She demanded cleanliness, maintained good relations with the surgeons, hired and supervised a large staff of female nurses, and ensured that the personal belongings of deceased soldiers were returned to loved ones back home. Hopkins also kept the books. Working without pay, she disbursed over $263,000, of which $50,000 came from the Alabama treasury, $13,000 from private donors, and the rest from her own personal wealth. Hopkins even found time to succor soldiers at the front. In fact, while tending to a wounded officer during the Battle of Seven Pines, she suffered a wound of her own, a shell fragment to the left leg, that resulted in a permanent limp. For good reason was she known as the "Florence Nightingale of the Confederacy." Toward the end of 1863, Hopkins resigned her position and returned to Alabama. Not only were funds drying up, but Confederate authorities were centralizing control over the Chimborazo complex. Nevertheless, Hopkins had done her part for the war effort. From August 1861 to September 1863, almost 7,400 Alabamians received medical care under her tenure; less than 8 percent (538) died of either their wounds or some illness. In a resolution honoring Hopkins, residents from Dallas County offered their "cordial and warmest thanks for her noble and generous devotion to the interest of the soldiers of Alabama." It was a sentiment shared by everyone throughout the state.[16] *Photo courtesy of ADAH*

KATE CUMMING
tintype

While tending to wounded soldiers at a hospital in Corinth, Mississippi, Kate Cumming reflected on her new role as Confederate nurse: "The war is certainly ours as well as that of the men," she wrote in her journal on 23 May 1862. "We can not fight, so must take care of those who do." It was a novel outlook in an age and in a society that considered wartime hospital care unsuitable for ladies. A thirty-four-year-old resident of Mobile, Cumming emigrated with her family from Scotland to Alabama in the 1840s. As a young woman, she grew to love her new home and approved the South's secession from the Union. Anxious to contribute something to the cause, Cumming joined a

group of women who traveled to Mississippi in the aftermath of the Battle of Shiloh. There she volunteered for service as a nurse; there she saw the carnage of war up close. "Three men have just had limbs amputated," Cumming noted during one of her first nursing experiences. "How my heart sickens in contemplating the horrors with which I am surrounded!" Still, she remained committed to her calling, even when critics objected to the idea of women working in field hospitals. "It is useless to say the surgeons will not allow us," she penned with undisguised frustration. "This is our right, and ours alone." Fortunately, the medical patriarchy came both to accept the need and to respect the ability of women such as Cumming. Dr. Samuel Stout, a physician who operated a mobile hospital for the Army of Tennessee, was among the first to recognize the value of his female nurses, one of whom was Cumming. Through his and similar efforts, the Confederate Congress formally created the position of hospital "matron" in September 1862. The official title may have given Cumming some satisfaction, but it did nothing to change the grueling nature of hospital care. The new matron was taken aback by the volume of casualties her side sustained at the Battle of Murfreesboro. "The wounded kept coming in last night, till 12 o'clock," she recorded in early January 1863. "Every corner of the hospital is filled with patients. . . . Many have to be carried from the ambulances, as they are unable to walk. . . . [H]ave been up for two or three nights in succession." And so her entries ran for over a week, much like they did after Chickamauga and every other battle whose human wreckage she dutifully attended to as best she could.

When Atlanta fell in September 1864, Cumming accompanied Stout's mobile hospital in its frequent movements back and forth over the Alabama-Georgia state line. In December, after ten months on the go, she took leave to visit family and friends in Mobile. When she returned to duty the following March, the war was nearly over, and in its aftermath she spent several weeks comforting paroled wounded prisoners.[17]
Photo courtesy of ADAH

244

EDWARD HAWTHORNE
MOREN
carte de visite

As a circulating surgeon among the military hospitals in Montgomery, Dr. Edward Moren regularly saw the bleaker side of the Civil War. A thirty-six-year-old physician from Bibb County when the conflict broke out, Moren immediately proffered his medical talents. He initially performed his duties as the chief surgeon of the 29th Alabama Infantry, but frequent bouts of angina pectoris compelled him to resign. Thereafter, the doctor held a senate seat in the state legislature but also volunteered in a civilian capacity when his health permitted. He had glimpsed blood-stained field hospitals before during his brief service in the Mexican War, but nothing could prepare him for the omnipresence of death during his three years of work in Mont-gomery's hospitals (and briefly those in Greenville). Dozens of soldiers died every month, some from their wounds, most from any number of maladies. After watching one patient die of disease after a prolonged struggle, Moren concluded ruefully that instant death on the battlefield was one of war's few mercies. Another mercy was the caring presence of female nurses, whom he compared to mother figures.

Besides the misery of the hospitals, Moren observed the deleterious effect of the war on Montgomery's economy. Growing scarcity and inflation, along with battlefield setbacks, seemed to be the only constants. Thoroughly depressed, he awaited the final days of the war with stoic resignation. *Photo courtesy of ADAH*

JOHN BASIL TURCHIN
copy print

Long before Sherman became the face of Northern aggression to white Southerners, there was Col. John Turchin. On 2 May 1862, Turchin committed one of the Civil War's first atrocities when he sacked Athens, Alabama. A Russian immigrant whose real name was Ivan Vasilevitch Turchininoff, he served many years in the tsar's army before coming to America in 1856,; settling in Chicago. Turchin initially commanded an Illinois regiment in Missouri, where he helped wage counterinsurgency warfare against secessionist guerrillas, then took over a brigade of midwesterners in November 1861, leading it during the Union invasion of northern Alabama the following spring. The forty-year-old colonel was popular with his men, rowdy farm boys and factory workers who loved his impetuous leadership. Based on personal experience in both Europe and Missouri, Turchin considered civilians as much a threat to his men as enemy soldiers. His was an attitude at odds with the army's conciliatory occupation policy at the time, an attitude guaranteed to produce controversy. On 1 May Rebel cavalrymen waylaid one of Turchin's advance regiments at Athens, a town with a population of less than 1,000. Casualties were light, but the colonel was incensed by reports that the people of the town not only applauded his men's defeat but also may well have provided the Confederates with military intelligence. In a fury the Russian expatriate marched his entire brigade into the streets the next day. "Colonel Turchin allowed us to take our revenge," recalled one of his subordinates, "although it was not his orders, still he winked at our proceedings." As he trotted about the town square, Turchin watched as his men looted and vandalized numerous buildings and homes, but it should be noted that no one was killed and nothing was burned. Nevertheless, this conduct violated standing orders to treat civilians with respect. A subsequent court-martial found the colonel guilty and cashiered him from the service. The Lincoln administration (along with a growing number of Union officers), however, was beginning to share Turchin's hard-war outlook; the War Department soon afterward not only reinstated the Russian but also promoted him to brigadier general.[18] *Photo courtesy of U.S.A.M.H.I.*

Mary Jane Chadick never expected to see her world literally come crashing down around her, yet that is exactly was happened when the Union army occupied her hometown of Huntsville in April 1862. The forty-two-year-old wife of the Rev. William Chadick, a Presbyterian minister and colonel in the Confederate army, Mary Jane was a native of New England, but having spent her adult life first in Tennessee and then in Alabama, she was as true a Southerner as anyone. When the Yankees came Chadick was managing the household, which included five slaves, while her husband was off fighting at Shiloh. She resented the rude behavior of the enlisted men, especially their periodic searches for contraband, which Chadick considered nothing more than a guise for trespassing and theft. She also worried that these patrols would arrest her husband whenever he returned from the front. What most disturbed her, however, was the effect Union occupation had on the family slaves. Over the summer Chadick discovered that her domestic, Corinna, was consorting with the enemy. "They are playing the mischief with the Negroes," she observed. "The Yankees can be seen at the corners, in the alleys, in confidential chats with them." She endured Corinna's growing defiance and frequent absences throughout the summer. "Had to cook for the entire family," she complained toward the end of August, writing in her journal that the occupation was "a foretaste of what we will have to go through when the rebellion is quashed, and the wonderful 'Yankee nation' gets possession of 'Niggerdom.'" After Lincoln issued the Emancipation Proclamation, Chadick noticed the speed with which race order unraveled in Huntsville. To her, Union soldiers seemed to delight in "telling [blacks] that they are free *now* and *here*." In February 1864 Federal authorities started a school open to the freedmen. Corinna enrolled her son, "against my positive commands," fumed Chadick. In the ensuing months, she rarely saw Corinna, who had left to find work elsewhere in the city. She spoke with her former slave only one more time, in November 1864, when Corinna was preparing to leave for Nashville with the Union army as it with-

MARY JANE CHADICK
copy print

drew ahead of Hood's offensive into Tennessee. "She was at first inclined to be important and impolite," Chadick said of Corinna, "but when I talked kindly to her, she changed her tone." The freedwoman, however, ignored her former master's advice that she stay in Huntsville. Evidently, Corinna was not the only former slave leaving town. "A large proportion of Africa is collected at the depot tonight," Chadick snorted, "awaiting transportation." Although she came to respect a Union officer who quartered his family in her home during the early months of 1864, Chadick never fully came to terms with the war's reality: "We cannot believe that a just God will suffer such an enemy to triumph over us." By April 1865 the objection was moot.[19]
Photo courtesy of ADAH

247

CHARLES CHRISTOPHER
SHEATS
copy print

When Union forces under Col. Abel Streight entered Morgan County in the summer of 1862, no one was more delighted to see them than Chris Sheats. A twenty-three-year-old schoolteacher and politician from neighboring Winston County, Sheats hated the rebellion and wanted to let the Yankees know that Alabamians such as he were ready and willing to fight for the Union. Just eighteen months earlier, he had represented Winston County at the state's secession convention, where he voted with the minority against the final ordinance. Since then he had won election to the state legislature but had gone into hiding after refusing to take an oath of allegiance to the new government and for his treasonous role in organizing the meeting at Looney's Tavern, where residents of Winston County declared their neutrality. In mid-July 1862 Sheats greatly assisted Streight in his efforts to enlist local unionists as soldiers. "Tomorrow morning I am going to the Union army," he shouted to a gathering of prospective recruits. "I am going to expose this fiendish villainy before the world." Vowing to fight the Confederates "to hell and back again," the young schoolteacher urged his listeners to join him: "I will stay here no longer till I am enabled to dwell in quiet at home." Over the next few days, Sheats helped persuade no fewer than 150 men to volunteer for service, some of whom formed the nucleus of the 1st Alabama Cavalry (Union). Unfortunately, a lame leg prevented Sheats from serving as well, but he continued his role as recruiter and propagandist. Later that autumn, however, Confederate authorities captured the unionist and incarcerated him for several months. To add insult to injury, the state legislature expelled him for his disloyalty. Released in early 1863, Sheats was soon re-arrested for his apparent connection with the Peace Society; he remained imprisoned for the duration of the war.[20] *Photo courtesy of Reita Jones Burress, Daughters of Union Veterans of the Civil War, Major Bell Reynolds, Tennessee Tent No. 4*

248

CASWELL CAMPBELL
HUCKABEE
carte de visite
F. A. Gerrish,
Montgomery

C. C. Huckabee was a patriot, but he was also a capitalist. In 1861 the forty-four-year-old Tennessee native built a blast furnace in Bibb County, one that became known as the Brierfield Ironworks, and served as the installation's president. Though partnered with Jonathan N. Smith, Huckabee provided most of the money and slave labor. Understandably, he grew protective of his private enterprise and avoided signing contracts with the Confederate government, preferring instead to sell his iron and assorted finished products to the highest bidder. For about a year and a half, Huckabee earned a profit from local buyers, including Confederate agents who purchased limited quantities of cannon and ordnance manufactured at the ironworks. But in 1863 the Nitre and Mining Bureau pressured him to enter a contract that restricted his market to the Confederate military. The industrialist twice refused, so in September 1863 the army took over the complex and the bureau transacted a "forced sale" for $600,000 in Confederate currency. Huckabee was furious at this display of wartime socialism but acceded to the nonnegotiable terms. His Brierfield Ironworks soon became a major supplier of pig iron for the arsenal at Selma. *Photo courtesy of ADAH*

JOSIAH GORGAS
copy print

For all of its logistical shortcomings, the Confederate army rarely lacked firepower. Credit for this belongs primarily to Josiah Gorgas, Alabama's adopted son from Pennsylvania. As chief of the Ordnance Bureau, Gorgas almost miraculously transformed the agrarian South into an arms producer. He brought to the Confederacy extensive military expertise in ordnance going back to his days at West Point (class of 1841). His many prewar duty assignments included a stint in the early 1850s at the Mount Vernon Arsenal just north of Mobile. When he was not expanding and improving the grounds of that facility, Gorgas was courting Amelia Gayle of Mobile, the daughter of former Alabama governor John Gayle. In 1853 the Northern-born Gorgas became a Southerner through marriage.

Early on in the war, Gorgas pursued various strategies to compensate for the South's dearth in industry. He imported war material from Europe, until the Union blockade choked off that source, and deployed teams to scavenge battlefields and campgrounds for expended lead and discarded weapons. His most vital contribution to the war effort, however, was the establishment of an impressive array of home-grown man-ufactures. Initially, he planned to centralize the bulk of Confederate ordnance production in Georgia, with factories in Atlanta, Macon, and Columbus. But Gorgas eventually recognized that the encroaching threat of Union invasion made concentration in one place too risky. Therefore, in March 1863 he officially dispersed these operations throughout the Deep South. As a result, Selma, Alabama, became increasingly important. In fact, Gorgas periodically fantasized about making Selma the "Pittsburgh of the South." The city never quite achieved that lofty status, but it did emerge as a vital manufacturer of weapons and ammunition. Moreover, during the course of Sherman's conquest of Georgia in 1864, Selma became the principal supplier of military hardware to the Army of Tennessee, a testament to the wisdom and foresight of the decentralization order. In November 1864 the forty-six-year-old Gorgas received a long-overdue promotion to brigadier general. In a war known for its combat heroes, it is easy to overlook the less glamorous, but no less monumental, achievements of a military bureaucrat such as Josiah Gorgas.[21]
Photo courtesy of Library of Congress

In early 1863 Col. Philip Roddey successfully battled an opponent three times the size of his forces along the Big Bear Creek in northwestern Alabama. At the time the colonel was new to his command, but his performance that spring helped establish his reputation as "the swamp fox of the Tennessee Valley." A self-made man from Lawrence County, the thirty-seven-year-old Roddey had made a living first as a tailor and then as a steamboat captain, with a stint as sheriff in between. Right after secession he raised a cavalry company, which he led with gallantry at Shiloh. In October 1862 Roddey became colonel of the 4th Alabama Cavalry, though within a few months he was commanding a brigade that included his own regiment and the 5th and 53rd Alabama Cavalry Regiments. In mid-April 1863 he led this force (about 2,000 men) against a Union thrust designed to both capture Tuscumbia and divert attention away from Streight's Raid across northern Alabama. On 17 April the colonel stymied a column of nearly 6,000 bluecoats around a place called Buzzard's Roost. In series of quick skirmishes, Roddey's men bagged an unwary section of Yankees artillerymen, repulsed a reckless charge by a unit of Alabama unionists, and deftly avoided an enemy attempt to trap the Rebels. Two days later Roddey struck again. Upon learning of the arrival at nearby Eastport, Mississippi, of a herd of mules for Streight's planned raid, the colonel moved swiftly against the inviting target. On the night of 19 April, the "swamp fox" and his men instigated what they forever after recalled as one of the war's more hilarious moments. Carrying two cats and several sacks filled with hornets and yellow jackets, the Alabamians slipped past the sentries and approached the mule corral. "Then with rebel yells and the firing of pistols, they let the cats out of their bags and threw their hornets nests. The mules were stampeded into ice cold Tuscumbia Spring, and those that were not drowned or died of insect stings took to the countryside." In all, some 400 mules bolted, of which only about half were recovered. Over the next week the weight of the Union advance managed to reach Tuscumbia, but it was too bloodied to press farther. As a result, Roddey felt confident to merely shadow his adversary with a scratch force while he himself joined the pursuit of Streight's raiders with the bulk of his command.[22] *Photo courtesy of Library of Congress*

PHILIP DALE RODDEY
copy print
C. M. Bell

ABEL D. STREIGHT
copy print

252

As his men left Moulton, Alabama, on the morning of 29 April 1863, Col. Abel Streight was brimming with confidence. His raid across northern Alabama was off to a good start, and as far as he knew, his operation still enjoyed the element of surprise. A thirty-four-year-old publisher from Indianapolis, Streight accepted command of an infantry regiment in September 1861. Though present at Shiloh and Murfreesboro, the colonel spent most of the early war on various occupation duties. While recruiting Alabama unionists in the Tennessee Valley in 1862, the restless Streight conceived an idea for a destructive raid in the region. Essentially, the colonel persuaded his superiors that with a relatively small strike force, he could slice across northern Alabama, relying on the region's loyalty for aid and comfort, until he reached the Western and Atlanta, a vital Confederate rail line just over the Georgia border, and destroy it. His was a bold plan that unfortunately suffered from poor preparation and bad luck. Rather than defer to an experienced cavalry commander, the untried Streight personally led the operation with 2,000 mounted infantrymen. Instead of riding horses, he agreed to use more readily available mules, thereby instantly earning for his command the sobriquet "Jackass Cavalry." These deficiencies aside, the raid might well have achieved success had the Indianan maintained the initiative. But on the very day—29 April—that Streight

blithely resumed his trek, Col. Nathan Bedford Forrest was bearing down on him with veteran cavalrymen. Startled by this unexpected development, Streight responded with impressive resourcefulness. On 30 April he launched a series of rearguard counter-attacks that bought time. Given enough distance from his opponent, he believed that his raiders could still destroy the Western and Atlanta and make good their escape. Haste, however, resulted in carelessness on 1 May, when much of the bluecoats' ammunition supply got wet as they splashed across Big Willis Creek. Now constrained in his firepower and unable to shake the enemy pursuit, the Union commander ordered an all-night march on 2 May. Passing along Shinbone Ridge in Cherokee County, the raiders finally paused at Cedar Bluff. Streight was a mere dozen miles from the state line, but his odyssey came to an abrupt end when he learned that Forrest had also arrived, evidently in greater numbers with fresher troops. Streight glumly assessed his situation: "our ammunition was worthless, our horses and mules in a desperate condition, the men were overcome with fatigue and loss of sleep, and we were confronted by fully three times our number, in the heart of the enemy's country." The colonel did not know it at the time, but Forrest had only 600 men on hand, whereas the Yankees numbered 1,400. Nonetheless, at noon on 3 May, Streight surrendered.[23]
Photo courtesy of Library of Congress

ANDREW LOGAN
copy print

The period from 27 April to 3 May 1863 was one of the most exciting times in Andrew Logan's life. During that week, he fought in Company K, 1st Alabama Cavalry (Union) as part of Abel Streight's ill-fated raid. A farmer from Fayette County, the thirty-one-year-old Logan rejected the Confederacy and, along with six other brothers, enlisted in the Union army in the summer of 1862. After surviving typhoid fever the following winter, Logan rejoined his company in time for Streight's Raid. Led by Capt. David Smith, he and his comrades rode through a pouring rain on 27 April, evading enemy patrols, until they reached the outskirts of Moulton. The next day the Alabama cavalrymen quickly occupied the undefended town and liberated a jailhouse filled with "Tories" who had resisted conscription into the Confederate army. From there the raiders moved into Morgan County, where Logan basked in a friendly reception by local unionists. On 30 April the joyride suddenly turned deadly. That morning Logan was helping guard the rear of Streight's column as it passed through Day's Gap when he noticed a fast-approaching band of Rebel horsemen

—Forrest had arrived. While Streight deployed his men for battle, Logan helped buy time with a delaying action. As the Confederates executed a full-scale attack, he and his fellow Alabamians retreated as part of a successful plan to draw the enemy into an ambush. The Alabamians performed the same task again that afternoon at nearby Hog Mountain. Each time Streight's force both bloodied its pursuers and continued its eastward progress. Another two days of such skirmishing, however, took a physical toll on the raiders and their mules. Because Logan's mount was evidently still in good condition, he became part of a select group led by Capt. Milton Russell whose mission was to secure the bridges across the Coosa and Oostanaula Rivers outside Rome, Georgia, the raid's final destination. Reaching that town on 3 May, Russell determined that Confederate defenses were too strong; he turned back only to learn that Streight had surrendered. Russell also surrendered, thus sending Logan into captivity. Within a few weeks, however, the private was paroled and soon returned to the 1st Alabama Cavalry (USA).
Photo courtesy of Barry Lee Collins

254

EMMA SANSOM
copy print

On 2 May 1863, a fifteen-year-old farm girl named Emma Sansom became a proud heroine of the Lost Cause. That morning Emma, her sister Jennie, and their widowed mother were doing chores when a column of Union cavalry—Streight's command—burst upon the scene. En route for Gadsden, the bluecoats were agitated, their mounts foaming from hard riding. The troopers from one unit demanded that Emma bring them water, while those from another hastily rifled through the Sansom household. All the while the Yankees interrogated the women, one even supposedly asking Emma what she thought of the South's prospects in the war. "I think God is on our side," she later claimed to have replied, "and we will win." Suddenly, the enemy rode off, crossed a small bridge spanning nearby Black Creek, and set the structure on fire. Moments later Colonel Forrest appeared at the head of several hundred Rebel horsemen. Frustrated by the destroyed bridge yet determined to maintain hot pursuit of the raiders, the Confederate commander queried Emma whether there was any other expedi-

tious way across the creek. "I told him there was an unsafe bridge about two miles farther down stream," Sansom recalled, "but that I knew of a trail about two hundred yards above the bridge on our farm, where our cows used to cross in low water, and I believed he could get his men over there." Complying with a request to show the way, the teen hopped behind Forrest in his saddle and, despite enemy rearguard fire from the opposite bank, she directed him to the precise spot. Within thirty minutes the Rebels forded Black Creek and resumed the chase. According to the mythology that developed around this whole affair, Forrest allegedly asked Emma for a lock of her hair to commemorate the occasion and then left her a note of thanks: "My highest regards to Miss Emma Sansom for her gallant conduct." Although the Sansom story has been embellished by varying accounts, the woman undoubtedly rendered invaluable service to Forrest and justly deserves the accolades of posterity.[24]
Photo courtesy of ADAH

255

JABEZ LAFAYETTE MONROE CURRY
carte de visite

member of the U.S. House from 1857 to 1861, Curry displayed his states' rights philosophy. To him, the fulcrum of liberty and order within the Republic lay with the individual states, which theoretically kept in check the anarchy of mass democracy on the one hand and the tyranny of executive power on the other. Given this mindset, Curry fiercely defended the institution of slavery against the threat posed by the Republican Party. When Alabama seceded in 1861, Curry, who had served as secession commissioner to Maryland, promptly resigned from the U.S. House and immediately won election to the Confederate House. As speaker pro tempore, he supported the controversial policy of conscription but opposed the decision to finance the war primarily through paper currency. All the while he privately objected to the increasing power of Jefferson Davis, complaining at one point that the president "gave Congress little information" and "apparently expected [it] to put into statute what he deemed best for the interests of the Confederacy." Nonetheless, Curry castigated as "demagogues and malcontents" those who publicly criticized the government.

Returning to Talladega in May 1863, he ran for reelection "as a secessionist in favor of a vigorous prosecution of the war." But the mood in the four counties of his district had grown noticeably defeatist. Antiwar voters supported Marcus Cruikshank, a local newspaperman who declared the rebellion a failure and supposedly enjoyed the backing of the Peace Society. When Curry questioned the patriotism of his opponent during a stump speech, a disgruntled listener broke through the crowd and shot him, inflicting a minor wound. He may have survived the assassination attempt, but Curry managed to win only one county— Calhoun—while losing in Randolph, Shelby, and even his native Talladega. He attributed this defeat in large part to the absence of men who shared his convictions, namely the thousands of soldiers from his district who either had already been killed in action or were then fighting at the front.[25] *Photo courtesy of ADAH*

Jabez Curry was disgusted by the outcome of the 1863 election. He was one of the strongest supporters of the war effort, yet he had lost his bid for reelection to the Confederate Congress. A thirty-eight-year-old planter from Talladega, Curry was a longtime defender of Southern rights who regarded John C. Calhoun as his political role model. A graduate of Harvard (class of 1845), Curry eagerly went into politics, aligning himself with the Yancey wing of the Democratic Party. As a state legislator in the 1850s, he focused mainly on railroad development and education reform, but as a

ALFRED FLOURNEY
ZACHRY

Over the winter of 1863–64, Capt. Alfred Zachry of the 61st Alabama Infantry witnessed firsthand the loss of will that often plagued those regiments that formed later in the war. In January 1864 he helped suppress the infamous Pollard Mutiny. An educator and business-man from Chambers County, the forty-four-year-old Zachry was both director of a female college in West Point and vice president of a textile mill near the Chattahoochee River. Though dedicated to the Confederacy, he perhaps hoped that he might avoid military service. Manpower demands, however, prompted him to organize a company of recruits. On 30 July 1863, Zachry mustered in about forty of his neighbors, some of whom evidently joined to avoid the opprobrium of being conscripted. The new captain and his men became Company F, 61st Alabama, a regiment whose complement was a fifty-fifty mixture of volunteers and conscripts. Stationed at Pollard, both to protect the town's rail connection to Mobile and to monitor Union activities in the Florida Panhandle, Zachry soon discovered the multifarious nature of gar-rison duty. Company F alternated between guarding bridges over the Escambia River, impressing local slaves for hard labor, processing prisoners of war, rounding up deserters, and enforcing conscription policies. It was unglamorous work in a dreary climate.

Out of this setting emerged a "spirit of mutiny," one exacerbated by higher authorities abrupt cancelling of all furloughs in December 1863. On 5 January 1864, sixty men from the regiment laid down their arms, apparently as part of a preconceived plan, and refused to report for duty. Dozens more followed suit over the next few days. Company F remained loyal, but some of the men expressed sympathy for the mutineers. Captain Zachry's sentiment is not known, but he did follow orders to help quell the trouble. There was no violence, and the ringleaders were soon in custody. Nevertheless, Confederate authorities decided to trans-fer the 61st Alabama to the Army of Northern Virginia, far away from the treasonous miasma that seemed to permeate the region around Pollard.
Photo courtesy of Al Zachry

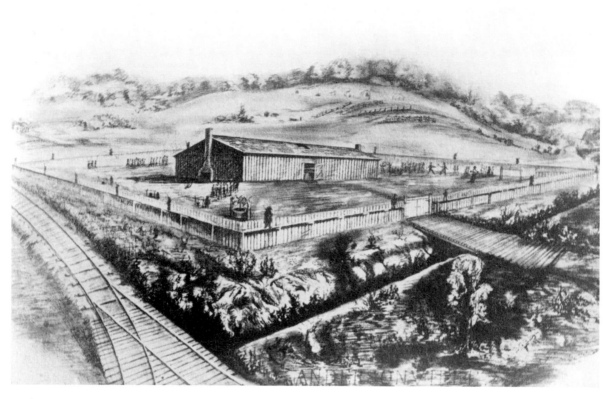

CAHABA PRISON/CASTLE MORGAN
copy print

In a war known for its notorious prison camps, Alabama's facility at Cahaba in Dallas County stands as an exception to the rule. Following the North's suspension of prisoner exchanges in late 1863, the Confederacy improvised a prison system whereby every state shouldered responsibility for holding captured Yankees. In early 1864, authorities in Alabama selected Cahaba as the state's principal containment area. Situated on the west bank of the Alabama River, Cahaba Prison consisted of an old cotton warehouse made of thick brick walls with an open-air cook yard, in all about 15,000 square feet of space. Around the perimeter ran a twelve-foot-high wooden plank fence with elevated walkways for sentries. The facility was designed to hold 500 inmates, but numbers quickly surpassed capacity: 660 in March 1864; 2,151 in October; and nearly 3,000 by the spring of 1865. The prisoners called the place Castle Morgan (after the famed Confederate raider John Hunt Morgan) and greatly disliked it. Water, though plentiful, was usually dirty, while plain cornmeal and bacon made up a typical day's rations. The prisoners were responsible for cooking their own food, cleaning the grounds, and constructing their own furnishings; most simply slept on the bare floors of the warehouse. Not surprisingly, poor hygiene and squalor contributed to disease, most notably scurvy and dysentery. Fortunately, the prisoners enjoyed the medical services of Dr. R. H. Whitfield, a physician from Demopolis who reported no more than 147 fatalities, a remarkable achievement compared to such infamous hellholes as Andersonville.

Another factor in the low mortality rate was the benign wardenship of Capt. H. A. M. Henderson, a veteran of the 28th Alabama Infantry and a devout Methodist who insisted on humane, albeit Spartan, treatment. Henderson still found it a challenge to maintain order, particularly as the prison population grew while his guard remained constant at a mere 180 men and a few bloodhounds. To forestall any trouble, the warden kept a vigilant watch. According to one prisoner, "two or three pieces of artillery pushed their forbidding noses through little openings in the stockade surrounding the cook-yard, and other pieces were said to command the prison from another side." Nevertheless, the inmates displayed growing unrest during the winter of 1864–65. Living conditions became intolerable as heavy seasonal rains flooded the compound with several feet of frigid water. On 20 January 1865, while Captain Henderson apparently was away on business, a group of prisoners launched an uprising. After subduing the guards, the inmates attempted to escape. Foul weather and a swift response by local Confederate forces, however, thwarted their plans. Upon his return, Henderson called for leniency given the circumstances behind the riot, and so punished only the ringleaders. Thereafter nothing of note occurred at Cahaba until Union cavalry destroyed nearby Selma in April. As the guards fled across the river, the Cahaba Town Council voted to close the prison and cooperate with Federal authorities. Sadly, many of the former prisoners died on the homeward trek when their transport, the steamer *Sultana*, exploded on the Mississippi River.[26]
Photo courtesy of Library of Congress

LOVELL HARRISON ROUSSEAU
copy print

In June 1864 Maj. Gen. Lovell Rousseau, Union commander of the District of Middle Tennessee, requested permission from General Sherman to lead a raid against Selma. Sherman approved the idea but changed the target to the Montgomery and West Point Railroad, the main artery carrying war material produced in Selma to the Confederate army defending Atlanta—Sherman's strategic objective at the time. On 19 July Rousseau set out from Decatur, Alabama, with 2,500 veterans and orders to head directly southeast toward the Opelika station. Physically quite large,

Rousseau was a forty-five-year-old criminal lawyer and state legislator from Kentucky. A veteran of the Mexican War, the political general gained further military seasoning as a brigadier in the Battles of Shiloh and Perryville and as a division commander at Chickamauga. The raid on Opelika was a bit outside of his area of expertise, but Rousseau brought to the mission daring and common sense. His command traveled light, which enabled it to average forty miles a day, but it also traveled well armed, the troopers toting Spencer carbines and two pieces of rifled artillery. For the most part, Rousseau avoided engagements, but on 14 July he encountered opposition along the Coosa River. A small band of Rebel horsemen—the 6th and 8th Alabama Cavalry Regiments under Brig. Gen. James Clanton—contested his crossing at Ten Islands Ford. In an exemplary display of fire and maneuver, the Yankees pushed across the river at multiple points and routed the Confederates, inflicting sixty-three casualties for the loss of but one man. Pressing on, Rousseau reached the Loachapoka station on 17 July. From there he sent demolition teams west toward Chehaw and east toward Opelika. The next day a 500-man contingent of home-guard units and cadets from the University of Alabama attacked the raiding party at Chehaw; Rousseau's men easily defeated this threat. By 19 July the Yankees had ripped up a thirty-mile stretch of the Montgomery and West Point, including the depots and bridges in between. Three days later the raiders linked with friendly forces at Marietta, Georgia. Although Confederate authorities worked fast on repairs, Rousseau's operation rendered the Montgomery and West Point unserviceable as a supply line for almost six weeks, during which time Sherman's army achieved the capture of Atlanta. Historian Edwin Bearss considers Rousseau's raid "one of the most successful cavalry strikes of the entire Civil War" in large part because "so much damage was inflicted upon the adversary, at such a small cost to the side undertaking the raid."[27] *Photo courtesy of Library of Congress*

For several days during the latter half of September 1864, a contingent of Alabama cavalrymen under Col. William Johnson helped reduce Federal blockhouses along the Tennessee River. The colonel and his men were part of General Forrest's autumn expedition against Sherman's overextended supply lines in northern Alabama and Middle Tennessee. A former steamboat pilot from Lauderdale County, Johnson knew the river-valley region well. In October 1862 he accepted a commission in Colonel Roddey's newly raised 4th Alabama Cavalry, serving first as major, then lieutenant colonel, and finally colonel of the regiment. Though officially a part of Roddey's command, Johnson often fought under Forrest in an attached capacity. And after distinguishing himself in June 1864 at Brice's Cross Roads, where he ably commanded Forrest's right wing in that upset victory, the colonel became a favorite subordinate of the great Confederate general.

In the fall of 1864, Johnson was at his tactical best. On 24 September the colonel completed the investment of a Federal garrison at Athens when he sealed off the western side of the town. After some desultory skirmishing, Forrest persuaded the now trapped bluecoats, some of whom were African Americans, to surrender. The next day the Rebel force (4,500 strong) moved against the Sulphur Springs Trestle, just two miles north of Athens. The Union position here consisted of two strong blockhouses that guarded the 300-foot-long bridge. Forrest methodically deployed his batteries for bombardment, then conducted a dismounted attack. "Colonel Johnson and his brave troops," the general later reported, "acted with conspicuous gallantry in marching up and assaulting the enemy's works." After a two-hour battle, the Yankees capitulated; Johnson and his boys helped raze both the bridge and the blockhouses. As the raiders moved north toward the state line, Johnson celebrated his thirty-seventh birthday on 26 September, but events the following day almost made it his last. As the graybacks approached Pulaski, Tennessee, on 27 September, they encountered stiff resistance. Forrest placed his command into line of battle, with Johnson's

WILLIAM ARTHUR JOHNSON
copy print

Alabamians in the center, and launched a general attack. For his part, Johnson made slow but steady progress and by noon seemed poised to break through to the town. Suddenly, the colonel and his men came under enfilade fire on their left flank. Johnson, who according to Forrest had "displayed every soldierly virtue" in the assault, sustained a severe wound. Confederate artillery soon eliminated the danger, but after seven hours of combat, Forrest called off the attack as futile. The Rebel raid continued for another week, but for Colonel Johnson, the war was essentially over.[28] *Photo courtesy of ADAH*

WILLIAMSON ROBERT
WINFIELD COBB
copy print

Had he known in November 1864 that the Confederate Congress was in the process of expelling him from that body, Williamson Cobb would not have cared one bit. Since winning his congressional seat in August 1863, the fifty-seven-year-old former clock peddler from Jackson County had not bothered going to Richmond and evidently had no intention of ever doing so. Such insouciance was typical of Cobb's long political career. From 1847 to 1861, he served seven terms in the U.S. House, an impressive tenure made all the more unusual for its lack of any noteworthy accomplishment. A poorly educated man, Cobb was a contrarian who despised Alabama's aristocratic class and may well have engaged in politics simply to spite his supposed social betters. "He was the perfect type of demagogue," observed one critic, "and was singularly popular with the humble and unlearned, whose devotion to him was most ardent, and defied reason itself." Throw in his skill with the banjo, and Cobb was a man who entertained his way from victory to victory among the hill folk of northeastern Alabama. During the secession crisis, however, he took a principled stand in favor of

the Union. "I see a country, greater than any other the sun ever shone upon, distracted, and perhaps severed forever," Cobb lamented. "I feel deeply; and I am not ashamed to confess it." He eventually resigned from the U.S. House but waited until after the rest of Alabama's secessionist delegation had already left. On returning to Alabama, Cobb ran unsuccessfully as a unionist for the Confederate Congress, losing to the pro-war candidate, John P. Ralls. Two years later, though, Cobb beat Ralls in a landslide that reflected the pronounced antiwar sentiment sweeping the district. Depriving the Confederate government of a diehard Rebel seemed enough for Cobb, who spent the next year working on his farm. Because of his frequent liaisons with Federal authorities in the Tennessee Valley, not to mention his failure to report for duty, the Confederate Congress brought forth charges of disloyalty in the autumn of 1864. Oblivious to these proceedings, Cobb was mending a fence on 1 November when he dropped a pistol he always carried; the weapon's accidental discharge fatally wounded the congressman.[29] *Photo courtesy of ADAH*

262

JOSEPH PINSON
BYERS
copy print

On 10 March 1864, Joe Byers entered the Federal compound at Decatur and volunteered for service in Company G, 1st Alabama Cavalry (Union). A twenty-seven-year-old farmer from Jefferson County, Byers's ostensible loyalty to the Union belied his erstwhile devotion to the Confederacy. Back in heady days of July 1861, he had enlisted in Company C, 18th Alabama Infantry. With that regiment Byers "saw the elephant" at Shiloh and saw further action at Chickamauga. Something in him snapped in the latter battle, though. After the action on 19 September 1863, when the 18th Alabama participated in one of the many bloody see-saw frays that day, Byers deserted. For the next six months, he presumably hid among the hills of northern Alabama until his decision to return to the war as a soldier for the other side. Whether he was officially a "galvanized Yankee"—that is, a former Confederate who took an oath of allegiance to the United States and then served in the Federal army—is unclear. In any event, Byers became a sergeant soon after joining the 1st Alabama Cavalry (Union) and fought with that unit for the duration of the war. *Photo courtesy of Mrs. Norma Y. Garbert Collection, U.S.A.M.H.I.*

JONATHAN MILTON STEWART
copy print

During the rainy predawn hours of 10 March 1865, Pvt. Jonathan Stewart of the 1st Alabama Cavalry (Union) snoozed fitfully under his poncho. Suddenly, shouts and gunfire erupted—the Battle of Monroe's Crossroads was underway. Stewart was a twenty-nine-year-old farmer from Lawrence County. When the war broke out nearly four years earlier, he was living in Randolph County and incurred the wrath of his siblings by proclaiming his loyalty to the Union. While his two brothers joined the Confederate infantry, Jonathan moved his family to northern Alabama. In May 1863 he belatedly entered the struggle, enlisting in Company K, 1st Alabama Cavalry (Union). Stewart saw plenty of action, particularly during Sherman's march through Georgia and the Carolinas, when his regiment served in a brigade that included troopers from Kentucky and Ohio. The Alabama Yankees proved themselves to be good fighters but were notorious plunderers as well, a predilection for all of the "Bummers" under Sherman's command.

During the first week of March 1865, the 1st Alabama helped screen a Union advance on Fayetteville, North Carolina. On the evening of 9 March, the regiment occupied a copse of pine trees on swampy ground due west of Monroe's Crossroads. Brigade headquarters insisted that the area was safe, so the exhausted Alabamians went to sleep without posting any security. At dawn the next day, three divisions of Confederate cavalry attacked the Union position from the west and the north. As a whooping band of Texas horsemen galloped through his encampment, Stewart joined one of several clusters of Alabamians who offered resistance. "Our boys fought Indian style," remembered a fellow private, "getting behind trees and other objects, without order of battle, at first, so complete was the surprise." Cracking off shots with their carbines, the unionists refused to retreat, and their determined stand finally repelled the enemy assault. The rest of the brigade, however, was in flight, so the 1st Alabama also fell back in good order until reinforcements arrived. Later in the morning the regiment participated in a dismounted counterattack that regained the lost ground. Somewhere in the course of this three-hour fight, Stewart went down with a bullet wound through both of his thighs. He was one of twelve casualties in Company K (the regiment as a whole suffered eighty-two losses, mostly captured).[30] *Photo courtesy of Carl S. Smith*

JOHN TYLER MORGAN
copy print

As he crisscrossed the state line between Alabama and Mississippi, Brig. Gen. John Morgan must have known his mission was a fool's errand. It was mid-March 1865, and the general was trying to recruit slaves for the Rebel army. A thirty-nine-year-old lawyer from Dallas County, Morgan was a rising fire-eater in the late 1850s. At the Alabama convention in 1860, he urged immediate secession. Morgan spent the first year of the war serving as a field-grade officer in the 5th Alabama Infantry, a detachment of which he led at First Manassas. In August 1862 he returned to Alabama to raise the 51st Alabama Mounted Infantry (or Partisan Rangers). For the next year, he conducted cavalry raids for the Army of Tennessee. In November 1863 he received promotion to brigadier general and led five Alabama cavalry regiments during the Atlanta Campaign. Morgan's performance throughout the struggle was competent but lacking in laurels; he never fought directly in any of the war's big battles. So per-

haps he believed that leading black soldiers into combat was his last chance to do something great for the dying Confederacy. Beginning in his hometown of Selma, Morgan called on Alabama planters to send forth able-bodied African Americans to serve. "This contribution to the strength of our armies," he announced, "will change our reverses into assured victory and ultimate independence." In clarifying a misunderstanding that black military service meant emancipation, Morgan added further that participation in the policy "[would] not affect the title of the owner." For the most part, slaveholders greeted the appeal with a mixture of curiosity and pessimism; as far as the record indicates, Morgan received no volunteers. When the war came to an end, the general was making his pitch to the residents of Meridian, Mississippi. He may as well have made it to the wind.[31]
Photo courtesy of ADAH

JEFFERSON ELISHA
BOZEMAN
copy print

The Rebel stand near Montevallo, Alabama, on 31 March 1865 was a pitiful affair. Against a full division of veteran Union cavalry, an outnumbered collection of Alabama militiamen and mounted infantry conducted a short-lived, hasty defense just south of the town. For Cadet Jeff Bozeman, however, the engagement provided one of his last opportunities to fight the Yankee invader. A twenty-year-old farmer from Autauga County, Bozeman had some military experience, having served a spell in Lumsden's Battery in 1862, but he does not appear to have seen any combat. In 1863 he entered the University of Alabama, where he helped the Corps of Cadets drill new recruits for the Confederate army. Toward the end of 1864, Alabama authorities increasingly called on the corps to augment the efforts of the home guard. So it was that Bozeman found himself at Montevallo in March 1865, presumably as part of Brig. Gen. Daniel Adams's contingent of state militia, all under Philip Roddey. In the early afternoon, the bluecoats laid into Roddey's position. Bozeman and his comrades exchanged a brisk fire but rapidly gave way, falling back through a thicket of pine trees to a new line of defense along Six Mile Creek. Reinforced by about 300 men, the graybacks then launched an unexpected counterattack that momentarily stymied the Union onslaught. But the outcome was never really in doubt; the Yankees still carried the field. Casualties for both sides were minimal.

Photo courtesy of W. S. Hoole Special Collections Library, The University of Alabama

266

It was barely past midnight on the morning of 4 April 1865 when alarum drums rudely yanked Greene Labuzan from his slumber. The previous day he and his fellow cadets at the University of Alabama had blithely gone about their academic routines; now the boys were hastily preparing to resist a brigade of Union cavalry. A nineteen-year-old lad from Mobile, Labuzan entered the university in 1863. On 4 April 1865, he was serving as a lieutenant in Company C of the Corps of Cadets. After fumbling into his uniform, Labuzan assembled outside with his unit and awaited instructions as a light rain gently bathed the parade ground. Capt. John H. Murfee, instructor of tactics, explained the situation: enemy forces were reported at the nearby bridge over the Black Warrior River and some had entered the outskirts of Tuscaloosa. Accordingly, the cadets were to conduct a reconnaissance in strength. Labuzan commanded the skirmish line and carefully guided it through the wet darkness into the center of town. At that point he encountered shadowy figures, one of whom called out, "Who comes there?" Captain Murfee yelled back, "Alabama Corps of Cadets!" The cadets then came under fire. As Captain Murfee fell wounded, Labuzan and his skirmishers dropped to the ground and returned several volleys that killed three Union troopers and chased away the rest. Soon the main body of cadets arrived and the whole force advanced to River Hill, which overlooked the bridge crossing. From there the two sides exchanged sporadic gunfire, shooting by sound rather than by sight. Although Labuzan and his mates had thus far held their own, inflicting about two dozen casualties, the cadre was dubious of continued success. The cadets were outnumbered, and they had no artillery. Shortly before 2:00 A.M., therefore, school president Landon Garland reasoned that his boys would be no match for Yankee veterans in a daytime fight and ordered the university evacuated. By dawn the whole corps, laden with as many supplies as the students could carry, was posted some eight miles away at Hurricane Creek, where the cadets restlessly awaited developments.[32]
Photo courtesy of W. S. Hoole Special Collections Library, The University of Alabama

GREENE MARSHALL LABUZAN
copy print

ANDRE DELOFFRE
copy print

Aroused by the excitement of the early morning skirmishes, Prof. Andre DeLoffre gathered with other members of the university faculty on the steps of the school's rotunda. From there they watched mounted bluecoats occupy the campus shortly after dawn on 4 April 1865. A modern-language instructor and veteran of the 1848 Revolution in France, DeLoffre had been teaching at the University of Alabama since 1855. By the time of the Civil War, he had also become custodian of the library housed inside the rotunda. Disgusted by the ongoing destruction of public buildings in Tuscaloosa, DeLoffre was stunned to learn that the enemy intended to raze the university as well. As a party of Yankees approached the rotunda, the Frenchman beseeched the officer in charge—

Col. Thomas M. Johnston—to spare the library. Johnston seemed inclined to comply but dispatched a courier to his commanding officer for clarification. The response left no room for clemency; the university was a military school and therefore the colonel's orders were to burn everything down. Before torching the rotunda, however, Johnston went inside to save at least one book. (DeLoffre likely accompanied him to help with the selection.) The lucky tome was a rare 1853 English translation of the Koran. Moments later the rotunda was ablaze, the flames eventually consuming more than 5,000 books and leaving the building a charred ruin. *Photo courtesy of W. S. Hoole Special Collections Library, The University of Alabama*

JOHN LEONARD WEEKS
copy print

As he awaited the Union assault on Selma, Pvt. John Weeks of the 4th Alabama Cavalry perhaps reflected on the unusual course of events that brought him there. A twenty-six-year-old volunteer from Marion County, Weeks originally joined Company K, 16th Alabama Infantry in August 1861. With that unit he fought at Mill Springs and Shiloh, witnessing the death of his uncle in the latter battle. During the retreat from Shiloh, Weeks somehow became separated from his company. Inexplicably, he did not rejoin his parent organization and was listed as a deserter. In actuality, he had enlisted in the 1st Mississippi Cavalry in June 1862. In October 1863 he was wounded and captured during a clash around Ripley, Mississippi. For the next year, Weeks languished first at Alton Prison, then at Fort Delaware, bedridden for much of his captivity

with smallpox. For reasons of poor health, Weeks gained his parole in October 1864 and returned home. Desperate for manpower, however, Confederate authorities soon had Weeks back in uniform with the 4th Alabama Cavalry, part of Roddey's command in northern Alabama. After participating in the skirmish at Montevallo, Weeks helped man the right flank of the defensive perimeter around Selma. The enemy action began against the Rebel left but quickly enveloped the right at well. Exactly what Weeks did in the fight is not known, but the Yankees soon pierced his section of the line and captured a battery. Bedlam ensued as the Rebels alternately ran, fought, or surrendered. Weeks may well have been captured, but the record is unclear. *Photo courtesy of J. D. Weeks*

JAMES HARRISON WILSON
copy print
Mathew Brady

With the Battle of Selma in full fury, Union general James Wilson decided it was time to stop watching the combat and start participating in it. Astride Sheridan, his favorite mount, the general charged into the fray. A twenty-seven-year-old Illinoisan who had finished sixth in the West Point class of 1860, Wilson was one of the many "boy generals" of the Civil War. Although an engineer by training, he developed into a formidable cavalry commander, garnering favorable attention for his performances at Vicksburg, Chattanooga, and especially Nashville, where he led his troopers in helping rout the entire left flank of the Army of Tennessee.

At the head of 13,500 veterans, General Wilson had set out from Eastport, Mississippi, on 22 March 1865 to disembowel the state of Alabama with one of the largest cavalry operations of the war. Dispersed into three columns, both to confuse the enemy as well as to strike more of the state's ironworks, the Yankee horsemen closed on Selma after ten days of hard riding. Wilson wasted little time in launching his assault on the afternoon of 2 April. In a sharp fight the general and his men carried the Rebel lines, defended by the renowned General Forrest, and won a complete victory. The bluecoats went on to occupy Montgomery

(12 April) and cross into Georgia (16 April), where they wreaked more havoc, but it was the clash at Selma that exemplified the superiority of the Union war machine in 1865. "I regard the capture of Selma the most remarkable achievement in the history of modern cavalry," Wilson exclaimed shortly after the battle, "and one admirably illustrative of its new powers and tendencies." Viewed from the perspective of the whole campaign, the general's rhetoric is not overblown. In less than two months, Wilson's raiders galloped more than 500 miles, prevailed in at least six pitched engagements, destroyed what was left of the South's industrial and railroad capacity, and even captured Confederate president Jefferson Davis, whose flight from Richmond came to an end at Irwinville, Georgia, on 10 May 1865. The price in blood was remarkably low by Civil War standards: 700 Union casualties against 8,000 Confederate (6,800 of whom were taken prisoner). With good reason did Wilson come to regard his men as "invincible." To be sure, the raid highlighted as much as it caused the collapse of the Confederacy, but that in no way diminishes what Wilson and his troopers accomplished in the dying days of the rebellion.[33]
Photo courtesy of Library of Congress

THOMAS HILL WATTS
carte de visite
Shackell Studios, New York

Despite the approaching hoof beats of Wilson's cavalry, Alabama governor Thomas Watts vowed to put up a fight. "With my consent," he exhorted the residents of Montgomery on 4 April 1865, "the seat of government shall not be surrendered as long there is a reasonable hope of defending it." Evidently, there was no reasonable hope, for Watts and his staff fled the city only a few days before the Yankees arrived. The governor then abruptly decided to move the state capital to Eufaula and continue waging the war from there.

Having long coveted the governorship, and having won it at last in August 1863, "Big Tom" Watts refused to admit that both his career and his country were no more. A forty-six-year-old planter from Montgomery County, Watts was one of the biggest slaveholders in the state, with nearly 200 bondsmen. Until the secession crisis, he was a voice of moderation, serving many years as a Whig politician and then in 1860 as a supporter of the Constitutional Union party. The election of Lincoln, however, turned Watts into a fire-eater. Although he lost to John Shorter in the gubernatorial race of 1861, he sought other venues of service. He raised the 17th Alabama Infantry, winning election to colonel of that regiment. Then in April 1862 he accepted an appointment as attorney general of the Confederacy. In his new capacity Watts demonstrated centralist tendencies, particularly in his declaration that the Conscription Act of 1862 was fully constitutional. Yet the attorney general yearned for outright executive power of his own. Sensing Governor Shorter's unpopularity back home, he signaled his intention to run for the office again in 1863. Determined to win, Watts betrayed political opportunism. While his surrogates criticized the Shorter administration, Big Tom disingenuously intimated that he sympathized with Alabama's Peace Society. After prevailing, however, Watts dropped all pretenses at bringing the conflict to an end. Instead, he pursued the war as vigorously as his predecessor. Unfortunately for Watts, manifold internal and external pressures proved too much for him to overcome; the state was literally disintegrating. Nonetheless, Big Tom put on a brave face. "We hold more territory now than we did twelve months ago," he nonsensically declared at the end of February 1865. Perhaps Watts was bereft of his grip on reality; more likely he was disguising his frustration at having no control over events. Regardless, he never reached Eufaula, never established a new base of operations. Instead, he fell into Union hands on 1 May.[34] *Photo courtesy of ADAH*

Some historians consider the engagement at Columbus, Georgia, on 16 April 1865 the last "true" battle of the Civil War. Among the participants was Capt. Nathaniel Clanton of Macon County. Originally a lieutenant in the 6th Alabama Infantry, Clanton transferred to the artillery in early 1863 and raised a battery that bore his name. For the most part, Clanton's Battery protected the railhead at Pollard, Alabama. In early 1865, however, Confederate authorities redeployed the unit to Girard, a small town opposite Columbus on the Alabama side of the Chattahoochee River. There Clanton commanded Fort 2, a crescent-shaped earthwork on high ground just north of the town. With his two 12-pounder howitzers and two 10-pounder Parrott guns well placed, the captain occupied a strong position. Clanton's Battery was part of a 3,300-man force whose purpose was to prevent Wilson's raiding cavalry from crossing the river into Georgia. But that mission would be a failure.

On the afternoon of 16 April, 2,900 Yankee troopers tried to enter Girard from the south. Thwarted, they shifted their main effort against the northern outskirts and waited until nightfall to commence their attack. Shortly after 8:00 P.M., an anxious Captain Clanton peered into the darkness toward Summerville Road, which led directly into the Alabama town. Knowing that the Yankees were on the move but unable to gauge their precise location, the captain ordered his gunners to start firing anyway. The battery's initial salvoes landed more than a thousand yards behind the fast approaching cavalrymen. But by the time the Yankees began assailing Fort 3, an outpost due west of Fort 2, Clanton's sections had found the range and poured on the cannon fire. On the receiving end of this barrage were several regiments of dismounted Iowans, who after overrunning Fort 3, wisely decided to bypass Clanton's position and push on toward the bridges connecting Girard and Columbus. With the local fight ending abruptly and the Yankees disappearing into the night, Clanton and his men found themselves isolated from friendly forces and ignorant of the battle's further course. For a little while longer, the gunners lobbed a few shells at presumptive targets, but they were really at a loss for what to do next. At last Captain Clanton called his lieutenants together and issued his

NATHANIEL HOLT CLANTON
copy print

final orders: "Spike guns and disband." In small squads the Alabamians abandoned the fort. A small, nearby party of Union soldiers, who had lain in quiet, then rushed in and captured all four guns along with a few stragglers. The fall of Fort 2 coincided with the Union seizure of the river bridges and subsequent capture of Columbus. Battlefield casualties were slight for both sides—sixty-two for Union forces; eighty (none from Clanton's Battery) for the Confederates—but two-thirds of the Rebel army either deserted (essentially what Clanton and his men did) or fell captive. The artillery captain did not know it at the time, but he had fired some of the final shots of the war.[35]
Photo courtesy of ADAH

273

Chapter 9

Mobile:
A City under Blockade

On 26 May 1861, the USS *Powhatan* appeared on the horizon outside Mobile Bay and initiated what became a three-year blockade of Alabama's famous port city. With a multiethnic population of 29,000 (including 8,000 slaves), Mobile was the largest and wealthiest city in the state. It was also an important commercial hub for the infant Confederacy. About the time Alabama seceded, cotton factors in the city were processing over 100,000 of bales for export. One Federal warship did not seem to pose a serious threat to Alabama's maritime trade, but before the year was out, dozens of enemy naval vessels prowled the waters along the state's coastline. And with the Confederate evacuation of Pensacola and the Union capture of New Orleans, both in early 1862, Mobile stood alone as the Confederacy's principal Gulf port. As a result the 150-year-old city found itself cut off from the sea that gave it life.

Alabamians understandably worried about their coastal city, but the Davis administration was concerned as well. Besides providing the Confederacy a vital outlet to foreign markets, Mobile was the nexus of some important railroads in the Deep South; therefore it was also a crucial transportation link between the eastern and western portions of the Southern nation. After shuffling through an array of army generals, the War Department appointed Maj. Gen. Dabney Maury in May 1863 to command what became known as the District of the Gulf, with Mobile as its centerpiece. Amiable as well as capable, Maury came to believe that the city was indispensable to the survival of the Confederacy. As he said after the war, "Mobile was to our western armies what Richmond was to the army of Virginia."[1] Thus, the general strived to augment the city's defenses, though he understood that Confederate priorities beyond his district would constrain any such effort. Furthermore, Maury confronted interservice rivalries that produced intense competition for the limited resources at his disposal. The army wanted to ring Mobile Bay with forts, while the navy wanted to construct a fleet that could challenge the U.S. Navy. Fortunately, the Federals neglected to launch a serious bid to capture Mobile until the summer of 1864. In the meantime, Confederate military authorities transformed the city and its surroundings into a citadel, displaying in the process a remarkable degree of Southern industry and ingenuity.

At the beginning of the war, Mobile's only real defenses were Forts Morgan and Gaines, both of which guarded the main entrance to the bay, thirty miles south of the city. Located on the western tip of the promontory named Mobile Point, Fort Morgan protected the eastern side; on small Dauphin Island, Fort Gaines blocked the western side. In the spring of 1861, Danville Leadbetter, who soon became chief engineer for the District of the Gulf, began bolstering the city's fortifications. Despite a persistent lack of resources, Leadbetter pursued an ambitious plan for an all-around perimeter defense of the entire bay region. First, he ordered upgrades for the two bay forts and supplemented them with a third stronghold—Fort Powell—to cover shallow Grant's Pass to the west of Dauphin Island. Second, worried about the possibility of a Union thrust from Mississippi, the chief engineer devoted considerable energy to erecting an extensive line of entrenchments around the western and northern outskirts of Mobile. Third, in order to secure a lifeline with the state's interior, he erected numerous strong points along the Tombigbee and Alabama Rivers, some of them more than thirty miles north of Mobile. Finally, to strengthen the eastern side of the bay and protect the various tributaries that flowed in from the Alabama River, Confederate engineers in 1864 revamped the old Spanish Fort and constructed a new strongpoint—Fort Blakely.

In all of these endeavors, Leadbetter was ably assisted by a number of talented subordinates, including Samuel Lockett and Viktor von Sheliha, the latter arriving to take charge in the autumn of 1863. This team of engineers relied heavily on impressed slave laborers, particularly the Mobile Negro Force, whose number of workers fluctuated from as few as 450 to as many as 2,300 depending on availability. When he departed for a new assignment

in October 1863, Leadbetter had markedly improved Mobile's military readiness. Boasting that its city enjoyed "the best engineering that has anywhere been put in requisition during the war," the *Mobile Advertiser and Register* declared that "the land defenses are so constructed that it would require a powerful army to carry them against even a feeble garrison."[2] Unfortunately, the fortifications were still vulnerable at many points, while the garrison was indeed feeble. Lockett and von Sheliha constantly agonized over the inadequacy of the forts. There was simply insufficient time, money, and labor to acquire and place all of the guns deemed necessary to cover every possible angle of attack, nor sufficient resources to shore up brick-masonry walls with earthworks or to erect obstacles, let alone establish secondary positions in the event of an enemy breakthrough. Similarly, General Maury and his predecessors complained that they rarely had more than a few thousand regular soldiers (plus some state militia) to man the vast network of defenses. The most reliable force was the 1st Alabama Artillery Battalion. Raised at the outset, this unit generally manned the guns of the bay forts, with detachments frequently assigned to other parts of the lengthy defense system. The only consistent infantry presence came from the 2nd Alabama during the first year and thereafter from the 21st Alabama. Confederate army leaders, in trying to defend everywhere, reluctantly left Mobile weak.

For all the activity on land, the safety of Mobile ultimately rested with the tiny Confederate flotilla in Mobile Bay. Historians have noted that the Davis administration failed both to develop a joint army-navy policy for defending Mobile and to weigh such a policy in favor of building armor-plated steamships instead of extraneous fortifications. For most of 1861, Confederate naval forces in the bay consisted of a handful of small, makeshift gunboats and the *Baltic*, a clunky, barely seaworthy ironclad. In February 1862 Henry D. Bassett, a Mobile shipbuilder, completed construction of the *Gaines* and the *Morgan,* wooden sidewheelers with six guns apiece. These two vessels became the nuclcus of a motley collection of boats dubbed the Mobile Squadron. Also in February Capt. Victor Randolph, a native Alabamian, arrived with orders from the Navy Department to break the Union blockade. On the morning of 3 April 1862, Randolph conducted an ineffectual raid against the two Union warships then on duty outside the bay. The Mobile Squadron hastily fired about a dozen shots, hitting nothing but water, before speedily withdrawing. Thus ended the Confederate navy's lone bid to disperse the blockading vessels outside Mobile.

Captain Randolph's failed sortie hardly mattered, for the Union blockade proved a sieve at best. To be sure, access to the bay could be tricky. The waters west of Dauphin Island were too shallow for easy maneuver, while Union warships concentrated most of their patrols along the main shipping channel flowing between Forts Gaines and Morgan. The best point of entry for a runner was Swash Channel, which followed the eastern shoreline, much of it under the protective guns of Fort Morgan. This became the favored route, though only swift, light-draft ships could hope to outrun a vigilant Union vessel. "Blockade running goes on very regularly," observed visiting British officer James Freemantle, "the steamers nearly always succeed, but the schooners are generally captured."[3] Throughout 1862 and for most of 1863, scores of enterprising blockade runners slipped in and out of Mobile, bringing much-needed war material (and quite a few luxury items) and departing with cargoes of cotton (over 30,000 bales during the course of the war). The most dramatic passage came on 4 September 1862, when the CSS *Florida,* a commerce raider under Capt. John N. Maffit, zipped into Mobile Bay past three Union warships via the main channel in broad daylight. After resting and refitting his vessel, Maffit then exited the bay on 16 January 1863 under cover of darkness and rain, evading seven warships in reaching the high seas. The blockade stiffened toward the

end of that year, but until the bay fell into Union hands, Mobile served as an invaluable Confederate lifeline to the outside world. The last successful runner was the *Red Gauntlet,* which entered the bay on 4 August 1864, bringing with it 25,000 pounds of lead. According to historian Arthur Bergeron, nearly 170 ships of all types, a plurality being steamers, successfully breached the Union naval cordon, giving runners in to or out of Mobile an 80-percent success rate, the highest at any port in the Confederacy.[4]

In August 1862 Adm. Franklin Buchanan took over as naval commander in Mobile. Having skippered the CSS *Virginia* during that ironclad's destructive sortie at Hampton Roads in Chesapeake Bay earlier in the year, "Old Buck" was far more aggressive than Randolph, though he also realized that the Mobile Squadron needed ships with real punch. To that end Buchanan patiently waited until his squadron was furnished with proper ironclads. Furthermore, the admiral came to understand that the mission was no longer to break the blockade, which was not a feasible objective anyway, but rather to keep Mobile Bay open to blockade runners. In short, the Mobile Squadron was to act primarily as a deterrent, fighting the Union fleet only if and when it tried to enter the bay.

In 1862 the Navy Department negotiated lucrative contracts with shipbuilders in Mobile, Montgomery, and Selma to construct as many as seven ironclads. Through the vigorous organizing efforts of Colin J. McRae, a businessman and state politician, Selma soon emerged as the state's principal navy yard and ordnance facility. Its proximity to the Alabama River, to nearby iron deposits, and to the already established foundries in neighboring Bibb and Shelby Counties made the town a seemingly ideal and safe location for a military-industrial complex. Under the supervision of Cmdr. Ebenezer Farrand, the city's shipyard launched two ironclads in early 1863—the *Tuscaloosa* and the *Huntsville.* Admiral Buchanan, however, was disappointed by these ships' lack of speed (barely two knots at full steam) and decided not to use them on the bay. Instead, he placed his hopes in a third ironclad—the *Tennessee*—whose keel was laid in October 1862.

A legion of problems plagued completion of the *Tennessee* specifically and the Mobile Squadron in general: dwindling supplies of iron ore, mounting competition for skilled mechanics, and frustrating disagreements with contractors. To top it off, production of appropriate armaments fell behind schedule. When Cmdr. Catesby R. Jones took over the Selma Foundry Works in the summer of 1863, not one cannon had been manufactured. Within a few months, though, this efficient naval officer had the factory in high gear; his workers cast 133 guns in 1864, primarily 6.4-inch and 7-inch Brooke rifles. In the meantime, Buchanan cracked heads to get everything else he needed. In February 1864 the *Tennessee* was commissioned at last.

That May the admiral conducted naval maneuvers in the bay. With the formidable *Tennessee* as his flagship, Buchanan's operational force also included the *Gaines*, the *Morgan*, and the *Selma*, the last a partially armored, 4-gun steamship. In addition to some 130 officers, there were about 800 sailors in the whole squadron. The quality of the enlisted men evidently left much to be desired: some were infantrymen drawn from the city's garrison, many more were foreigners. "There are on board," Buchanan complained to the Navy Department, "these vessels some of the greatest vagabonds you will ever read of." An officer aboard the *Morgan* expressed a similar assessment: "Out of a hundred and fifty," he claimed, "not one is even an *American*, much less a Southerner. We have Irish, Dutch, Norwegian, Danes, French, Spanish, Italian, Mexican, Indians, and Mutezos—a set of desperate cut throats."[5] These unflattering observations aside, the Mobile Squadron was as ready as it was ever going to be when it finally went into action in the summer of 1864.

Amid all these military preparations, civilians tried to maintain their city's traditional, cosmopolitan lifestyle. For the first year or so, parties and parades abounded, with everyone dining on the bay's famous and seemingly plentiful oysters. One proud resident declared that Mobile had become "the Paris of the Confederacy."[6] To outside critics who found these festivities unbecoming of a nation at war, Mobilians countered that their behavior actually reflected true patriotism. Given that some 5,000 male residents from the city served in the Confederate army, Mobile undeniably did its part. The city also provided as many as a dozen first-rate hospitals for military use. Under the overall supervision of Dr. Josiah Nott, these facilities provided quality care to thousands of convalescing Confederate soldiers throughout the war.

The city's boisterous nature notwithstanding, the war eventually took its toll. The blockade crippled the port's prewar trade and thereby ruined many of the city's businessmen. Moreover, military exigencies and governmental price controls reduced the availability of food, thereby pushing Mobile County to the brink of starvation. On 4 September 1863, the city experienced a full-blown bread riot. Hundreds of poor women, some armed with farm tools and others carrying banners reading "Bread or Blood," rampaged through the streets, looting stores and warehouses. Called on to suppress the riot, the soldiers of the 17th Alabama Infantry, temporarily stationed in the city, sympathized with the rioters and flatly refused to intervene. Rushing to the scene, Mayor Robert Slough beseeched the women to desist. Only after he repeatedly promised to ameliorate their plight did "the Amazonian phalanx" peacefully disband.[7]

Despite troubles within the city and fears of invasion from without, the people of Mobile rarely wavered in their devotion to the Southern cause. They read with delight the propaganda literature of hometown author Augusta Jane Evans, whose wartime novel *Macaria* savagely denounced "Lincolndom" as nothing more than "shameless, hideous Abolitionism" and lavishly praised Confederate soldiers as "the bodyguard for the liberty

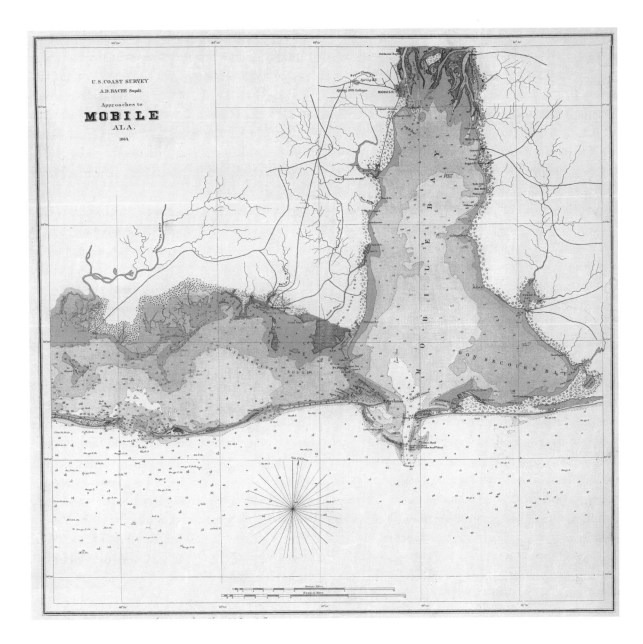

of the Republic."[8] Mobilians also closely followed the exploits of their favorite local hero, Adm. Raphael Semmes, captain of the CSS *Alabama*. Starting in the summer of 1862, Semmes terrorized Northern merchantmen all over the globe, destroying or capturing sixty-five vessels before losing a ship-to-ship action with the USS *Kearsarge* off the coast of France in June 1864. In the wake of the *Alabama's* demise, residents in the city braced for a military showdown closer to home.

During the first half of 1864, a large Union fleet under RAdm. David Farragut prepared to attack Mobile. Farragut had long wanted to capture the bay, but "brown water" priorities on the Mississippi River postponed such an operation. The appearance of the CSS *Tennessee* only prompted further delays as the Union admiral waited for ironclads (monitors) of his own. Assisting the U.S. Navy was a Union army corps under Maj. Gen. Gordon Granger, whose mission was to neutralize the bay forts. On 3 August

1,500 bluecoats landed on Dauphin Island and invested Fort Gaines. The next evening the ironclad USS *Tecumseh* arrived, bringing Farragut's fleet to four ironclads and fourteen wooden warships; he was now ready to go. Watching and waiting were the artillerymen in Fort Morgan and the sailors of the Mobile Squadron. General Maury was confident that his land batteries would pulverize anything that tried to enter the bay: "No vessel yet built could pass through that channel in daylight." Admiral Buchanan, however, was less optimistic. "Everybody has taken it into their heads that one ship [the *Tennessee*] can whip a dozen," he opined a few months earlier, "and if the trial is not made, we who are in her are damned for life. Consequently, the trial must be made."[9] On 5 August the two sides fought the greatest naval battle of the Civil War.

Shortly before 7:00 A.M., Farragut launched his attack. The Union commander deployed his fleet in column, with the wooden ships lashed together in pairs and the monitors acting as a shield on the starboard side facing Fort Morgan. Lying in wait just north of the fort was the Mobile Squadron, which hoped to intercept the Union ships in detail as they ran a gauntlet that included water obstacles of wood pilings and torpedoes (floating mines). Over the next hour, Fort Morgan belched nearly 500 projectiles, yet this hurricane of shot and shell did surprisingly little damage. Ignoring the land-based batteries, the *Tecumseh* steamed through the channel and, on sighting the *Tennessee*, recklessly veered into a torpedo field. Rocked by an explosion, the *Tecumseh* sank in a matter of minutes, taking over ninety crewmen down with her. Horrified, the commander of the leading wooden ship wavered at further advance. Knowing that hesitation invited defeat, Farragut decisively bellowed, "Damn the torpedoes, full speed ahead!" Regardless of the authenticity of this famous quote, the admiral led his flagship *Hartford* into the bay.

At this time the Mobile Squadron attacked. With the three Rebel gunboats inflicting dozens of casualties aboard several Union vessels, the *Tennessee*

attempted to ram the *Hartford,* but at six knots she simply could not close fast enough. As Farragut's ships cleared the channel, Union numbers and firepower soon turned the tide of battle. The *Gaines* foundered after taking a shot below the waterline; her captain ran the vessel aground and then abandoned ship. The *Selma* fled northeast, with the *Metacomet* in hot pursuit; after a brief chase, the Confederate ship surrendered. The *Morgan* managed to maneuver under the safety of its namesake fort's guns, but in doing so effectively took herself out of the action. The *Tennessee* now fought alone. After a brief lull, Old Buck steered his warship into the heart of Farragut's formation; it was a glorious but futile charge. Pummeled and buffeted from all sides, the *Tennessee* sustained one debilitating blow after another. Yankee fire toppled her smokestack, jammed her gun portals, and finally snapped her steering chain. Around 10:00 A.M. the helpless behemoth struck her colors. "The destruction of our fleet at Mobile creates no surprise," Alabama's Josiah Gorgas sardonically noted, "nothing but disaster comes from that unfortunate branch of the service."[10]

With the Confederate navy subdued, Farragut and Granger moved rapidly to reduce the bay's forts. Forts Powell and Gaines fell quickly. Assailed from the bay side as well as from the Gulf, the defending Alabamians evacuated the former on 5 August and surrendered the latter three days later. Dabney Maury was stultified by what he considered a lackluster defense on the part of the two garrisons. Richard L. Page, commander at Fort Morgan, was similarly irate. When Farragut petitioned Page on 9 August to also surrender, the Confederate general replied, "I am prepared to sacrifice life, and will only surrender when I have no means of defense."[11] Within a fortnight, however, Fort Morgan also fell. The paltry 600 Rebel defenders simply could not withstand the combined strength of Farragut's ships and Granger's soldiers.

Having captured the lower bay, thereby eliminating Mobile as a source of blockade running, Farragut was in no hurry to move against the city itself. Besides, the waters of the upper bay were shallow and strewn with manmade obstacles. Furthermore, the Mobile Squadron, now under Capt. Ebenezer Farrand, still posed something of a threat. The new Confederate commander's force consisted of the *Morgan,* which had slipped past the Union fleet the night after the battle; the *Tuscaloosa* and *Huntsville,* both of which would serve as floating batteries; and the recently commissioned CSS *Nashville,* an ironclad built in Montgomery that was even larger than the *Tennessee,* though only partially armored. Dismissing any thoughts of a naval engagement, Farrand opted to deploy his warships within the river system, where they could support Spanish Fort and Fort Blakely.

Although the Rebel navy was no longer inclined to give battle, military authorities in Mobile did pursue a fascinating alternative. For over two years, the city was the site of an erratic and revolutionary experiment in underwater warfare. The famous submarine CSS *Hunley* was built in Mobile and tested in the bay before the Navy Department sent it to Charleston in August 1863. Skippered by George Dixon, a former lieutenant in the 21st Alabama Infantry, the submarine sank the USS *Housatonic* in February 1864, though Dixon and his crew also perished. By the autumn of 1864, local entrepreneurs working in the Selma Navy Yard completed another submarine, the *St. Patrick.* This time the new technology was aimed at Union vessels in Mobile Bay. In the predawn hours of 28 January 1865, the partially submerged *St. Patrick* glided silently toward the gunboat USS *Octorara* and attempted to ram a spar torpedo into her hull. The weapon, however, failed to detonate, and the submarine hastily retreated under a barrage of gunfire. The *St. Patrick* never went into action again and was evidently scrapped during the closing days of the war.

In mid-March 1865, 45,000 bluecoats under Maj. Gen. Edward R. S. Canby advanced up the eastern side of Mobile Bay as the southern prong of a grand Union pincer operation designed to knock Alabama out of the war. (James Wilson's 13,000 troopers constituted the northern prong.) To oppose this force, General Maury possessed barely 9,000 men. Moreover, the Rebel commander had to contend with the panicked citizenry of Mobile, even though the city itself was not the primary Union objective. While exercising quasi–martial law over the locals, Maury reinforced his two garrisons on the opposite side of the bay. At Spanish Fort about 2,100 Confederate soldiers feverishly prepared for battle. Five miles farther north, a few thousand more did the same at Fort Blakely. Small contingents of Rebel cavalry, including the 6th and 8th Alabama Regiments, tried in vain to stymie the Union juggernaut. Pvt. Robert Posey of the 8th Alabama Cavalry humorously described a failed attempt to prevent an enemy river crossing on 25 March: "We made a good run instead of a bad stand."[12] Seasonal rains and marshy terrain did more to hinder Canby's advance than mounted graybacks. Nonetheless, by 27 March, 32,000 Yankees had closed in on Spanish Fort from the east. Less than a week later, another 13,000 invested Fort Blakely. The war in Alabama had reached its climax.

Spanish Fort was essentially a massive earthwork that stretched almost 3,000 yards between Bay Minette to the north and the Apalachee River to the south. In command was Brig. Gen. Randall L. Gibson of Louisiana, a seasoned officer who was determined to mount a vigorous defense. Unfortunately, the bulk of his force at the outset consisted of the Alabama Reserves—950 boys in their midteens recently organized into the 62nd and 63rd Alabama Infantry Regiments. These poorly trained and excitable adolescents wildly expended thousands of cartridges and often exposed themselves needlessly to enemy fire. On 30 March General Maury transferred the youngsters to Fort Blakely, replacing them with a veteran unit: James T. Holtzclaw's brigade of Alabama infantrymen (18th, 36th, 38th, and 32nd/58th Regiments, with the surviving companies of the 21st Alabama attached). Holtzclaw's Brigade held the center of the line at

Spanish Fort, with Lumsden's Battery of four guns and three coehorn mortars in support. For the next week, the Alabamians alternated digging with skirmishing. Then on the afternoon of 8 April, ninety Union guns commenced a terrific bombardment that could be heard and felt distinctly in the streets of Mobile. Toward dusk, Union infantry stormed through the shell-shocked left wing of the fort, scattering its Texas and North Carolina defenders. Realizing a counterattack was pointless, General Holtzclaw instead mounted a holding action until nightfall, after which the garrison evacuated the fort, some by steamer, others on foot through the swamps. Confederate casualties during the siege came to at least 600 men, including 110 Alabamians. But the little garrison had held out for two weeks against vast numbers, in the process inflicting 650 casualties on the Federals. Pvt. G. T. Cullins of the 18th Alabama considered Spanish Fort "one of the hardest fights of our great war."[13]

Fort Blakely survived one day longer than Spanish Fort. Starting on 1 April, the 3,400-man garrison under Brig. Gen. St. John Liddell of Mississippi confronted a Union force that grew to nearly 30,000 within a week. Located on the eastern bank of the Tensa River, Fort Blakely was mostly a long trench line (about 4,000 yards) connecting nine artillery redoubts. A battle-hardened brigade of Missourians defended the left half of the fort, but on the right stood the unreliable boy soldiers of the Alabama Reserves, which apparently now included a few geriatric volunteers from the surrounding counties. Nevertheless, Liddell tried in vain to disrupt Union siege operations. On the night of 7 April, the 63rd Alabama conducted a half-hearted sortie under the glow of blue flares; Yankee pickets easily repulsed the effort, inflicting three dozen casualties and greatly demoralizing the boys in that regiment. By the afternoon of 9 April, General Canby was ready to storm the fort. At 5:30 P.M., under cover of an intense artillery barrage, 16,000 bluecoats in thirty-five regiments executed a general attack that shattered the entire Confederate line. Obstacles of abatis and land mines did little to slow the Union assault. The Missouri brigade offered stout, albeit brief, resistance, but the Alabama Reserves disintegrated immediately. Most of the boys simply fired one shot, typically too high, and then fled, leaving battery crews to fend for themselves. Escape, however, proved impossible; within twenty minutes the Union onslaught overpowered the whole garrison. One bewildered Alabama private asked his captors, "Where did you Yanks all come from?"[14] The attackers did suffer 750 casualties, but most of those losses came at the hands of the Missourians. Despite being one sided, Fort Blakely was arguably the last full-scale battle of the Civil War.

With the east-bay forts gone, the backdoor to Mobile was wide open. For a couple of days, controlled bedlam reined in the city as General Maury hastily withdrew the remainder of his army—about 4,500 men—to Meridian, Mississippi. Simultaneously, Commodore Farrand guided the *Nashville* and a motley flotilla of gunboats and blockade runners up the Tombigbee River. When General Granger and two Union divisions (which included several regiments of black soldiers) reached the outskirts of the city on 12 April, they were greeted by Mayor Robert Slough, who formally and unconditionally declared Mobile an open city. After conducting a triumphant march through the streets, Granger deployed his troops as an army of occupation. It was a hollow victory, however: Lee's army in Virginia had already surrendered, while Confederate forces elsewhere posed no further threat. Had the Federals captured Mobile even a year earlier, its loss to the Confederacy might have been quite significant. But by 1865 its fall only highlighted the pitiful and complete collapse of the rebellion. "The city is a sad picture to contemplate," observed a Northern newspaperman toward the end of April, "the people look sad and sorry."[15] Perhaps so, but Mobile's four-year ordeal was over at last.

In the early years of the war, garrison duty at Fort Morgan fostered a sense of ennui among the soldiers stationed there. The tedium of diurnal drill and sentry duty was broken only by periodic excursions into nearby Mobile or onto the surrounding beaches. For Pvt. Tom Black of the 2nd Alabama Infantry, this routine made the war seem an unreality. Immediately after the commencement of hostilities, the twenty-year-old Black joined Company C, formerly the "Claiborne Guards" of Monroe County. He then spent most of his twelve-month enlistment gazing at the Gulf waters from the ramparts of Fort Morgan. Instead of fighting, the private wrote poetry. One of his pieces, likely penned sometime in September 1861, captured the simple serenity of the Alabama coastline even as it acknowledged the menacing forces that lurked offshore.

THOMAS D. BLACK
copy print

On the cold white sand, Of a war washed strand
    A weary soldier was dreaming
    While pearly light, Of moonbeams bright
    Was over the soldier beaming

The diamond spray, Of Mobile Bay
    Dashed wildly at his feet
    His thoughts were far, From cares of war
    Where voices of loved ones meet

The joyous thrill, The words that fill
    The heart of the soldier dreaming
    The soft white arm, The love kiss warm
    Are all too real for dreaming

In dreams of joy, The soldier boy
    Cares naught for the morrow coming
    Yet the booming guns, Of the morning sun
    May usher a day of sorrow

On the cold white sands, Of a wave washed strand
    A soldier there may be sleeping
    While around the bed, Of the soldier dead
    Nor sorrowing friends be weeping

Yet Angel's eyes, From azure skies
    Far over the moonlit wave
    Their tears of dew, Will softly strew
    On the sleeping soldier's grave

In early 1862 the 2nd Alabama disbanded. Many of the men from Company C volunteered for service in the newly raised 42nd Alabama Infantry. It is unclear whether Private Black joined them or went home. *Photo and poem courtesy of Fort Morgan State Historic Museum, T. D. Black Collection*

DANVILLE LEADBETTER
from Confederate Military
History, *by Joseph Wheeler*

Few things demonstrated the military value of slavery to the Confederacy than Brig. Gen. Danville Leadbetter's use of the Mobile Negro Force to help construct the fortifications around Mobile Bay. As chief engineer of the District of the Gulf, Leadbetter played a key role in preparing Mobile for invasion. To this end, he relied heavily on thousands of impressed slaves to perform the bulk of those tasks requiring unskilled labor, such as digging entrenchments and hauling building material. Leadbetter's upbringing, however, made his conduct as a grand army overseer rather ironic. Raised in Maine, he initially considered a career in law before attending West Point. Graduating in 1836, third in his class, Leadbetter possessed exemplary engineering talent and spent the next twenty years in the regular army. He did not set foot in Alabama until 1852, when he began repair work on Forts Morgan and Gaines. Evidently, Leadbetter came to love the state, for in 1857 he resigned his commission, took up residence in Mobile, got married, and acquired at least six slaves. When Alabama seceded, this fifty-year-old "southern gentleman" offered his services to the Confederate army. Not surprisingly,

Leadbetter resumed his work on the bay area's defenses, though he also served for a time in the Army of Tennessee. Envisioning an all-around defense in depth, the engineer lobbied constantly for money and labor. The latter eventually became an obsession. "We need many more negroes than we have," Leadbetter petitioned the state government in 1863, "and I am sure that all good citizens would prefer to suffer some inconvenience [rather than] permit the defense of important points to be neglected." With the Mobile Negro Force comprising 750 blacks as a rough average, Leadbetter micromanaged its employment, often calling for harsher means of discipline when the slaves malingered. Whenever planters demanded the return of their chattel after the prescribed impressment period, the engineer usually delayed compliance for as long as possible. Desperate for workers, he even lured some free blacks to work for meager wages drawn from his bureau's strapped budget. In the end Leadbetter's efforts failed to stop the Union army and navy from shutting down Mobile, but by then the engineer had returned to the Army of Tennessee.[16]

284

Though suffering from yellow fever, a malady that also afflicted half his crew, and in spite of the menacing presence of four Union warships, Capt. John Maffit of the CSS *Florida* was determined to enter the sanctuary of Mobile Bay. A forty-three-year-old career navy man from North Carolina, Maffitt spent the antebellum years patrolling the West Indies in search of illicit slavers. "Being a jaunty, handsome fellow," Raphael Semmes once said of his brother officer, "he was a great favorite with the ladies." He was also an out-standing sailor and fearless fighter. Thus, when he cast his lot with the Confederacy, Maffitt was a natural choice to skipper the *Florida*. Built in England, the *Florida* was designed to be a commerce raider. A sleek vessel that could make eleven knots on steam and more under sail, she also packed a wallop, with two pivoting 7-inch rifles and six 32-pounders. Unfortunately, in the late summer of 1862, Captain Maffitt lacked sufficient naval stores, and while enlist-ing additional seaman at Havana, he contracted yellow fever. The old salt needed to get to a friendly port; he needed to get to Mobile. On 4 September the *Florida* came within sight of Fort Morgan. Waving off sugges-tions that he wait until nightfall, Maffitt ordered a day-time approach largely because he was unfamiliar with the main ship channel and feared running aground. Hoisting a Union Jack, he gambled that the blockading vessels would not fire on one of Her Majesty's Ships. The ruse worked; the Yankees realized too late that they had been fooled. Still, in discharging a few desper-ate broadsides, they inflicted damage to the *Florida's* rigging and boiler room. But Maffitt's boldness had paid off, and the captain became an instant hero.[17]

After a fortnight under quarantine, Maffitt rounded out his crew with volunteers from Mobile, fully repaired his ship, and stocked up on ordnance. There was, however, the matter of putting to sea again. Seven Union warships now stood vigil, and this time trickery would not work. In the predawn hours of 16 January 1863, the *Florida* commenced her breakout. Heavy rain combined with gale-force winds blowing in from the north enhanced the ship's chances. Maffitt stealthily

JOHN NEWLAND MAFFITT
carte de visite
S. T. Blessing, New Orleans

navigated past most of the enemy squadron before being spotted. As the Union ships signaled each other, the Rebel captain raised his sails and let Mother Nature blow the *Florida* beyond reach at fourteen knots. He had deftly eluded his adversaries once again. Ship and crew then embarked on a year-long voyage of destruc-tion, sinking or capturing two dozen U.S. merchant-men. *Photo courtesy of ADAH*

RAPHAEL SEMMES
from The Photographic History of the Civil War
by Francis T. Miller

On the morning of 19 June 1864, Capt. Raphael Semmes of the CSS *Alabama* sailed his vessel out of Cherbourg, France, and engaged the USS *Kearsarge*, a sloop that had arrived offshore just a few days earlier. It did not matter that the *Alabama* was badly in need of an overhaul or that the *Kearsarge* was a formidable warship mounting 11-inch guns. "I am tired of running from that flaunting rag," Semmes explained to his executive officer. A fifty-four-year-old seadog, Semmes had been in the navy since 1832. Though born in Maryland, he had long made Mobile his home of record. When Alabama seceded, Semmes eagerly joined the new Confederate navy and received command of the CSS *Sumter.* During a six-month cruise, he captured eighteen merchant ships before having to scuttle his vessel off Gibraltar after Union warships trapped him.

In August 1862 Semmes took command of the *Alabama,* a state-of-the-art commerce raider that the Confederate government clandestinely purchased from Laird Shipyard in Liverpool. She was a magnificent vessel, capable of fifteen knots and equipped with eight cannon, including a 100-pounder Blakely rifle. While all of the ship's officers were Southerners, most of the crewmen were British volunteers. Still, the sailors came to love their skipper, whom they called "Old Beeswax," and embraced the cause of the Confederacy. From 5 September 1862 to 27 April 1864, Semmes prowled the Atlantic and Indian Oceans, seizing sixty-four U.S. merchant ships and sinking the USS *Hatteras,* inflicting a total of $6.75 million in damages. But after twenty-two months at sea, the *Alabama* had lost some of her fighting trim. While replenishing his supply of coal in Cherbourg, Semmes espied the *Kearsarge* on 14 June. The captain could either admit his voyage was over or he could attack; he chose the latter option.

As he steered the *Alabama* beyond French waters, Old Beeswax issued a fiery exhortation. "The flag that floats over you is that of a young republic," Semmes shouted to the crew, "who bids defiance to her enemies, whenever, and wherever found!" At 11:00 A.M. the *Alabama* opened fire at a distance of one mile. For the next hour, the two adversaries circled each other, seven times in all, drawing closer and closer with each revolution. In their enthusiasm the Rebel seamen fired fast but inaccurately. Out of 300 shots, fewer than 30 hit the *Kearsarge,* none of them doing any serious damage. Union gunnery, in contrast, was patient and deadly. Toward noon the *Alabama* had lost her rudder, most of her guns were disabled, and she was taking on water through gaping holes in her hull. Semmes struck his colors, then jumped overboard. As he treaded water, the Alabama sank to her doom. Of the 149 who served aboard her, 9 died in battle, 20 others were wounded, and 12 drowned. As for Captain Semmes, he was rescued by a private yacht that carried him and several of his crewmen to England. Little did Old Beeswax know that he had participated in the last ship-to-ship engagement between wooden vessels in naval history.[18]

Atop the ramparts of Fort Morgan, Capt. Julian Whiting of the 1st Alabama Battalion of Artillery had an excellent view of a fast-approaching Union fleet. As officer of the day on 5 August 1864, Whiting was responsible for warning the garrison in the event of an attack. Shortly before 6:00 A.M., the captain initiated the Long Roll, calling everyone to battle stations; the Battle of Mobile Bay was about to begin. A twenty-six-year-old resident of Montgomery, Whiting came to Alabama after graduating from the University of Virginia. Finding the martial spirit of the Deep South to his liking, he joined the Metropolitan Guards during the secession crisis. In the spring of 1861, Whiting accepted a commission in the 1st Alabama Battalion of Artillery, rising to the captaincy of Company E. Stationed at Fort Morgan since the summer of 1861, he commanded a battery along the southwest bastion, close to the bay's lighthouse. At 7:06 A.M. Whiting fired the first Rebel shot of the battle in response to a salvo from the lead monitor, the USS *Tecumseh*. As the cannonade became general, the captain concentrated his guns on the *Tecumseh*. When that vessel went down, Whiting believed that either his men or some other battery had sunk her; only later did he concede that a torpedo was the real killer. In any event, the captain continued to fight. "The roar of the guns was terrific," he recalled, "so much so that orders had to be screamed to the gunners who were within three feet." Dense smoke made accuracy difficult, but Whiting managed to direct well-aimed fire into the USS *Oneida*. An 8-inch round hit that vessel's boiler, unleashing steam that killed or wounded thirty sailors. Later in the day Whiting's battery helped disable the USS *Philippi*, a small gunboat that then ran aground. (A Confederate raiding party subsequently destroyed this ship.)[19]

Whiting's robust gunnery notwithstanding, the Union fleet still secured the lower bay. Thereafter, the artillery captain and the rest of the fort's garrison endured a two-week siege. Whiting spent most of this time supervising efforts to improve overhead cover from plunging enemy mortar fire. Only rarely was he able to shoot back, his crews coming under intense counter battery fire whenever they did so. On 23 August the fort surrendered, and Whiting became a prisoner. *Photo courtesy of David Wynn Vaughan*

JULIAN WYTHE WHITING
copy print

287

FRANKLIN BUCHANAN
carte de visite

U.S. Navy in 1815, Buchanan served as the first superintendent of the U.S. Naval Academy and also accompanied Commodore Matthew Perry on his famous expedition to the Far East. While commanding the Washington Navy Yard during the secession crisis, Buchanan assumed his native Maryland would join the nascent Confederacy and resigned accordingly. When his state did not secede, a disappointed Buchanan later accepted a commission in the Confederate navy, where he became a zealot for the Southern cause. As captain of the ironclad CSS *Virginia,* Old Buck destroyed two enemy frigates at Hampton Roads on 8 March 1862. Though badly wounded in the action, his exploits foretold the end of wooden ships at sea.

After recovering, Buchanan received promotion to admiral and took over the Mobile Squadron in August 1862. Two years later, while aboard the ironclad CSS *Tennessee,* he attempted to thwart David Farragut's passage into the bay. During the opening phase of the battle, Buchanan tried to ram his adversary's ships, but the painfully slow *Tennessee* missed on four attempts. When the rest of his squadron was put out of action, Buchanan withdrew his vessel to the sanctuary of Fort Morgan. After fuming for about half an hour, Old Buck abruptly turned to Capt. James Johnston, commander of the *Tennessee,* and curtly ordered, "Follow them up, Johnston, we can't let them off that way." With the admiral personally supervising the cannon fire, the ironclad lumbered into the midst of more than a dozen Union warships. Although he had point-blank targets, Buchanan discovered that many of the ship's fuse primers were defective. Still, he fought on until a casemate, whose portal he was trying to help unjam, received a direct hit. Two sailors literally disintegrated under the blast, while Buchanan suffered a broken leg from flying metal debris. Shortly thereafter, the *Tennessee* struck her colors.

Old Buck proved cantankerous in defeat. He initially refused to surrender his sword and then verbally abused his captors. Buchanan's officers, however, expressed only the highest praise for their admiral: "Had he been enabled by any means in his power to change the fortunes of the day," Captain Johnston later speculated, "he would certainly have been justly hailed by the civilized world as the greatest naval commander who had ever lived." Instead, Buchanan had to settle for the fleeting celebrity of being a high-profile prisoner.[20] *Photo courtesy of ADAH*

As the Union fleet approached the entrance to Mobile Bay on the morning of 5 August, Adm. Franklin Buchanan addressed the crew of his four-ship squadron with a fiery oration. "Whip and sink the Yankees," he exhorted, "or fight until you sink yourselves, but do not surrender." For the sixty-three-year-old Buchanan—known throughout both navies as "Old Buck"—the Battle of Mobile Bay was the coda to a storied career as an American sailor. Entering the

CSS *Tennessee*
copy print

On 7 February 1863, Confederate naval authorities in Selma launched the CSS *Tennessee* from her platform astride the Alabama River. Weighing nearly 1,300 tons, the huge ironclad displaced so much water upon entering that her crew temporarily lost control. The vessel careened into a brick warehouse along the shore, completely demolishing the building. The *Tennessee's* captain, James D. Johnston, facetiously commented later, "This was her first and only experience as a ram." This awkward incident notwithstanding, everyone was impressed by the Confederacy's latest warship. The *Tennessee* was 209 feet long and 48 feet wide. With six inches of armor plating protecting the prow and four inches the sides and stern, she was literally a metal monster. After her arrival in Mobile, the *Tennessee* received her armament: two powerful 7-inch Brooke rifles fore and aft and four 6.4-inch Brooke rifles, two each port and starboard. Deemed ready for action, the ironclad was commissioned on 16 February 1864. Unfortunately, before she could reach the lower bay, the *Tennessee* had to negotiate the Dog River Bar, only nine feet deep at high tide, whereas the ironclad's draft was thirteen feet. After a series of mishaps, Confederate engineers floated the warship over the barrier using wooden caissons filled with water that they attached to the vessel's hull and then pumped of their ballast to provide the necessary lift—barely.[21]

Once in the lower bay, the *Tennessee* became the flagship of the Mobile Squadron. Trial runs and an aborted sortie into the Gulf revealed both the ironclad's poor speed—six knots—and lack of maneuverability in choppy water. Still, its crew of 170 officers and sailors were eager to test her in battle. That moment came on 5 August, when Farragut's fleet stormed into the bay. The ensuing clash displayed the strengths and weaknesses of the *Tennessee*. The vessel's armor was virtually impenetrable. Out of hundreds of enemy rounds fired into her, most at point-blank range, only one shot (from the USS *Manhattan's* massive 15-inch gun) punched through the ironclad's exterior. Casualties aboard the *Tennessee* for the entire engagement were a mere two killed and nine wounded. The ironclad's speed and design, however, rendered the vessel incapable of doing much damage herself. Captain Johnston tried in vain to ram the Union warships, which actually did themselves more harm through numerous collisions in vying to close with the *Tennessee*. Moreover, Rebel sailors struggled with faulty primers and jammed gun portals, all the while enduring the suffocating heat and smoke of their ship's interior, where the temperature eventually exceeded 140 degrees. When the *Tennessee's* exposed steering cable was shot away, the iron beast drifted helplessly, and Johnston hoisted a white flag. Although the *Tennessee* lost the battle, she had wrestled alone for over an hour against fourteen wooden warships and three ironclads.

Union mechanics quickly repaired the captured vessel and added her to Farragut's fleet. Toward the end of August, the newly christened "USS" *Tennessee* participated in the general bombardment of Fort Morgan. Later in the year she joined the Union fleet patrolling the Mississippi River. Decommissioned shortly after the war, the great ironclad was sold for scrap at an auction in New Orleans in 1867. *Photo courtesy of Naval History and Heritage Command*

JAMES MADISON WILLIAMS
copy print

young man fell in love with the South, married a local girl, and moved to Mobile to take a job as a bookkeeper in a jewelry firm. Williams supported Alabama's secession, but family matters prevented him from enlisting until October 1861, when he joined the 21st Alabama Infantry. Rising to company command, he fought well at Shiloh and by the end of 1862 had become lieutenant colonel of the regiment. Stationed at Fort Powell in January 1864, Williams commanded a small garrison of two companies from the 21st Alabama and a contingent of artillerymen from South Carolina—140 men in all. Though not especially thrilled with garrison duty, Williams was proud of his "pet fort" and frequently indulged in the region's famous cuisine—oysters and crab gumbo. On 16 February ten small Union gunboats entered Grant's Pass and attempted to destroy Fort Powell. Though ill at the time, Williams conducted an enthusiastic defense. "I am never too sick to fight the Yanks," he wrote his wife. For two weeks, the Union navy sporadically bombed the post, but Williams and his men withstood every attack. The most serious moment occurred on 23 February, when a shell exploded near the lieutenant colonel, momentarily stunning him and badly bruising his ribs. Williams laughed off this brush with death: "They fired today 304 shells—I shot 35 times—I like the fun finely so far." On 1 March the Union ships withdrew.[22]

Praised for his successful resistance, Williams's luck ran out on 5 August. That morning, as the opposing navies grappled farther east in the lower bay, the lieutenant colonel exchanged fire with a group of gunboats in the Gulf. With the defeat of the Mobile Squadron, however, Fort Powell came under attack from the bay side too. At 2:30 P.M. the monitor *Chickasaw* moved to within 700 yards and pummeled the little fort. Williams could manage only three shots, one of which did damage the ironclad's smokestack, before his battery was knocked out. By nightfall the fort's interior was a shambles; the lieutenant colonel was convinced he could not endure another such drubbing. With permission from his superior at Fort Gaines, Williams evacuated his "pet fort," detonating the magazine at 10:30 P.M. *Photo courtesy of John K. Folmar I*

While the Battle of Mobile Bay raged, a smaller but still important clash unfolded around nearby Fort Powell in Grant's Pass. There Lt. Col. James Williams of the 21st Alabama Infantry strived in vain to defend his post against a flotilla of small Union gunboats. A midwesterner, the twenty-six-year-old Williams migrated to Georgia in 1859 in pursuit of clerical employment. The

MALACHI LAMAR
STABLER
copy print

As he watched the destruction of the Mobile Squadron from the ramparts of Fort Gaines, Pvt. Malachi Stabler of the 21st Alabama Infantry lost all hope of repelling the Yankee invasion. A Union landing force had already occupied the western portion of Dauphin Island, and on 4 August it commenced a regular bombardment; it was only a matter of time before the now-isolated garrison capitulated. A twenty-one-year-old Mobilian, Stabler had been with the regiment for at least two years, serving in Company G (the Southern Star Guards). During that time, he helped improve the fort's defenses. By the summer of 1864, Fort Gaines was one of the few installations that Confederate engineers deemed fully prepared for a long defense. With twenty-six pieces of artillery and a garrison of about 850 men (including six companies from the 21st Alabama), all of it well provisioned with ordnance

and food, the fort did indeed seem capable of holding out for some time. But morale was low among the ranks. On the evening of 6 August, after enduring a day of heavy fire from enemy land batteries as well as Union warships in the bay, a majority of officers petitioned Col. Charles Anderson, the garrison commander, to negotiate terms of surrender or risk a mutiny. Despite peremptory orders from Brig. Gen. Richard Page at Fort Morgan to "hold on to your fort," Anderson formally surrendered on the morning of 8 August. "Anderson's conduct," Dabney Maury stated, "is officially pronounced inexplicable and shameful." For Stabler, who was mostly a passive observer through these proceedings, six months of incarceration awaited him on Ship Island, Mississippi, where his prison guards were African Americans.[23]
Photo courtesy of ADAH

FORT MORGAN
copy print
McPherson and Oliver

On 15 August 1864, Union monitors in Mobile Bay shelled the seaside walls of Fort Morgan. The ships' 15-inch shells demolished one section of the wall, knocking out at least two pieces of Confederate artillery. The fort's commander, Richard "Ramrod" Page, who only six days prior had defiantly refused to surrender, privately admitted that he could not hold out for much longer: "Our brick walls were easily penetrable by the heavy missiles of the enemy," he explained, "a systematic concentrated fire would soon breach them." Completed in 1834 after fifteen years of construction, Fort Morgan was one of many installations composing America's coastal-defense system in the early years of the Republic. Made of 500 million bricks reinforced by sandbags and earthworks, it was virtually impregnable to smoothbore cannon fire from 8-inch guns or smaller. Unfortunately for the Confederacy, the Union besiegers possessed rifled cannon of heavier caliber.

Nonetheless, the pentagonal Fort Morgan was the centerpiece of Mobile's defense. The fort's garrison consisted of slightly more than 600 men, including two companies from the 21st Alabama Infantry and most of the 1st Alabama Battalion of Artillery, which manned forty-six guns of varying size. Confronting this force were the Union fleet under Admiral Farragut and 5,500 Union soldiers under General Granger, who landed at Mobile Point on 9 August. Although the Rebels knew their fate was sealed, their morale generally remained high. A special detail of sharpshooters made up of Alabamians occasionally harassed the landward approach of the Union soldiers, dubbed "Granger's Sand Crabs" because of their ceaseless work on advancing parallel lines. Nothing, however, slowed the enemy's progress. Beginning on 15 August, naval gunfire became a regular feature of daily life for the defenders. Several officers chafed at Page's reluctance to fire back, apparently because he feared exposing his guns to counterbattery fire. "Perhaps this policy has been a wise one," Alabama artilleryman Hurieosco Austill mused, "but it does seem to me we should have offered more resistance to the enemy before he came so near and entrenched." Instead, the garrison mostly stayed under cover and held prayer vigils. On 21 August Granger had forty-one cannon and mortars in position only a few hundred yards from the fort. The next morning the Union forces unleashed a massive all-day bombardment. Over 3,000 shells pounded Fort Morgan, disabling all but two of the garrison's guns. At 8:30 P.M. the fort's citadel, located in the central quad, caught fire and burned to the ground. With the walls themselves beginning to collapse, General Page ordered the magazine, with its 80,000 pounds of gunpowder, flooded lest it ignite and blow up the whole fort. Further resistance being pointless, the general spiked those guns still serviceable and ran up the white flag of surrender at daybreak on 23 August. Miraculously, only three Rebels died during the siege; the rest went into captivity. Now a prisoner, Lieutenant Austill remembered watching his foes hoist the U.S. flag, "emblem of tyranny," over the fort. "Men shed tears at the sight," he observed. What had taken more than fifteen years to build had fallen in less than fifteen days. The Union now enjoyed uncontested control of Mobile Bay.[24] *Photo courtesy of Library of Congress*

DAVID GLASGOW FARRAGUT
AND GORDON GRANGER
copy print

294

The Union victory at Mobile Bay was a paragon of interservice cooperation. By working together, the U.S. Navy under RAdm. David Farragut and the army under Maj. Gen. Gordon Granger simultaneously defeated a Confederate naval squadron and captured the lower bay's three forts in a campaign that lasted just eighteen days. Though born in Tennessee, the sixty-three-year-old Farragut was a man of the sea, having served in the navy since the age of nine. A veteran of the War of 1812 and the Mexican War, he was a captain when the Civil War broke out. Assigned to the Gulf, Farragut captured New Orleans in April 1862, earning promotion to rear admiral. In 1863 he ably facilitated army operations against Port Hudson, Louisiana, farther up the Mississippi River. Once the mighty river was secure, Farragut received orders to attack Mobile, a port he had long wanted to close off to the rebellion.

Twenty-one years junior to Farragut, Gordon Granger of New York was no less a professional. Although he finished near the bottom of his West Point class in 1845, Granger earned brevets for bravery during the Mexican War and later spent many years fighting Indians on the frontier. His performance in the Civil War was undistinguished until Chickamauga, where on his own initiative Granger rushed his reserve corps to the aid of hard-pressed Union forces on Snodgrass Hill and thereby helped prevent a rout.

Brought together in early 1864, Farragut and Granger made a good team. The admiral masterminded the overall offensive against Mobile Bay, while the general, who was known for his independent streak, dutifully deferred. When Farragut recommended that Granger make Fort Gaines the army's first priority instead of Fort Morgan, the general complied with celerity. And during the siege of Fort Morgan, Granger diligently deployed his heavy ordnance while Farragut provided support with naval gunfire. Only after their joint victory did disharmony surface. Evidently, Granger felt that the navy claimed too much credit for winning the battles around Mobile. Moreover, he complained that Farragut's ships rendered the captured forts indefensible due to excessive damage on the seaward sides, damage that required months of repair. Perhaps further souring Granger's mood was Farragut's promotion to vice admiral in December 1864, while he in turn was made subordinate to Maj. Gen. Edward Canby during the final phase of the Mobile Campaign in 1865. Nonetheless, while it lasted, the Farragut-Granger partnership displayed combined-arms warfare at its best. *Photo courtesy of the University of South Alabama Archives*

JOHN FORSYTH
copy print

With a Union fleet poised to strike in August 1864, John Forsyth of the *Mobile Register* prophesied that "Mobile Bay will be strewed with the wreckage of many a Yankee man-of-war." Such gasconade was typical of Rebel propaganda at the time, perpetuating false hopes with wanton irresponsibility. Although he was an ardent Confederate throughout the war, the forty-one-year-old Forsyth was actually a political moderate in the years prior to secession. The son of a Georgia planter, he came to Mobile in 1836 and soon began his career as a newspaperman. As a Democratic editor of the *Register* (which he purchased outright in 1854), he defended Southern rights yet stressed the importance of party unity in the face of antislavery politics. After a term as ambassador to Mexico (1856–58), Forsyth won a seat in the U.S. House, where he made clear his support of popular sovereignty as the only peaceful solution to the discord over slavery in the territories. Accordingly, he endorsed the centrist Stephen Douglas for president in 1860, even though most Southerners voted for hardliner John C. Breckinridge. After Lincoln's election, however, Forsyth wholeheartedly supported secession and the subsequent Confederate war effort. As mayor of Mobile in 1861, he helped supervise the city's defense. As correspondent with the Army of Tennessee in 1862–63, he provided detailed coverage of the military campaigns. And as full-time editor of the *Register* from 1864 until the end, he exhorted his readers to persevere against all odds. "Let it not be said that Mobile is craven," he wrote after the Union navy captured the bay, "when we have the illustrious examples of Richmond, Petersburg, and Charleston looking us in the face." In spite of the facts, Forsyth seemed to relish his role as cheerleader, printing nonsense about Sherman's defeat in one issue and Lee's triumph over Grant in another. On one occasion, however, the editor expressed his private desperation when in December 1864 he recommended that the Confederacy enroll slaves into the army. Returning to form the following year, Forsyth was still promising a "splendid victory" just a week before Mobile surrendered. In the end, though, the pen was no mightier than the sword in winning Southern independence.[25]
Photo courtesy of Library of Congress

JOSIAH CLARK NOTT
copy print

Countless Confederate soldiers in the western theater greatly benefited from the medical talents of Dr. Josiah Nott of Mobile. Born and educated in South Carolina, Nott came to Mobile in the mid-1830s. Thereafter he emerged as one of the state's most prominent citizens, founding the Medical College of Alabama in 1859. Nott was among the first scientists to identify insect vectors as a causative factor in the spread of yellow fever and malaria (he had lost four children to a yellow fever epidemic in 1853). He was also at the forefront of using science to legitimize notions of white supremacy. In his various publications Nott argued that Caucasians were a separate species of humanity manifestly superior to Negroes and Indians. Thus, Nott defended the institution of slavery as a natural social relationship between whites and blacks. When it came to secession, the doctor displayed regional chauvinism. "The southern people would rise up as one man," he said of the Lincoln administration's resort to military force, "and resist it with the old spirit of '76." Early in the war, Nott served as a surgeon in the Army of Tennessee, but in 1863 he became superintendent of hospitals in the District of the Gulf. He immersed himself in his new duties, inspecting hospital facilities to ensure cleanliness even as he readily operated on those most seriously wounded in battle. Dr. Nott's active daily regimen disguised a profound inner grief. He lost two more children to the war: one son died at Shiloh, and another was killed in action at Chickamauga. Moreover, by the end of 1864, the then-sixty-year-old physician knew that the Confederacy itself was on its last legs. When U.S. Colored Troops occupied Mobile in April 1865, Nott came face to face with the full consequences of emancipation. "God Almighty made the Nigger," Nott privately fumed, "and no dam'd Yankee on top of the earth can bleach him." One of the fundamental outcomes of the war had produced a visceral reaction in a man who prided himself on his scientific reason. Nevertheless, as a surgeon Nott brought genuine relief to many young men ravaged by a long, terrible war.[26] *Photo courtesy of Erik Overbey Collection, the University of South Alabama Archives*

RICHARD HOOKER WILMER
copy print

The Rev. Richard Wilmer of Mobile was not especially fond of his unofficial title, "Rebel Bishop," but he appreciated the circumstances under which it arose. Consecrated in November 1861 as the Episcopal Bishop of the Diocese of Alabama, the Virginia-born Wilmer accepted his call amid the turmoil of the Civil War. In doing so he became the only Southern bishop elected under the Confederacy. Educated at Yale, Wilmer was an erudite theologian who strived to keep his message Christ-centered even as his ministry occasionally revealed a Southern bias. "We confess before thee, with sorrow and shame, our manifold offences against thy Divine Majesty," he exclaimed in a prayer delivered in Mobile in 1862, but qualified his petition, "we cannot reproach ourselves with any wrong done to our enemies, wherefore they should invade our land, and our continual prayer is, that thou, Lord, wouldst judge between us and them." In this spirit Wilmer defended the obligation of clergymen in occupied northern Alabama to pray publicly for their lawful government, the Confederate States of America, and urged them to

remain steadfast against mounting Federal pressure to desist. But the Rebel Bishop preferred pastoral care over institutional defiance. He continued to evangelize and baptize, and as the war dragged on, Wilmer organized statewide efforts to succor the conflict's overlooked casualties—orphans. While military exigencies postponed construction of an orphanage in Mobile, the bishop secured $50,000 in charitable donations to build a temporary one in Tuscaloosa. At the close of the war, Wilmer tried in vain to avoid the politics of Reconstruction. When Union authorities ordered him in 1865 to begin issuing prayers in behalf of the United States, the bishop refused on the grounds that Alabama had not yet been restored to its proper civil relationship within the Union. Wilmer did, however, instruct his church to cease its prayers for the now-defunct Confederacy. All in all, the Rebel Bishop did a commendable job of upholding the sacred over the secular.[27] *Photo courtesy of Erik Overbey Collection, the University of South Alabama Archives*

Throughout the Mobile Campaign in the spring of 1865, Union general Edward Canby held the strategic initiative. His invasion of southern Alabama, however, would pit the forty-seven-year-old Kentuckian against a close friend from his prewar days, Dabney Maury. A bland, doctrinaire army officer, Canby elicits little interest among Civil War scholars. Having finished next to last in the West Point Class of 1839, a colleague described Canby's career in the regular army as "the faithful cultivation of rather mediocre gifts." Nonetheless, Canby served honorably in the Seminole War and the Mexican War. Known for his administrative ability, he governed the Territory of New Mexico, which he successfully defended against a small-scale Confederate invasion early in the Civil War. Thereafter, Canby helped police New York City after the draft riots there in July 1863 and also helped pacify Rebel guerrillas in western Mississippi in 1864. Thus, the Mobile Campaign was his first major field command. The U.S. War Department urged speed and boldness, but Canby preferred thorough preparation and methodical execution. From his perspective, the war was obviously drawing to a close, so he hoped to minimize needless casualties. Besides, the rainy weather and swampy terrain militated against any rapid movement.[28]

Toward the end of March, Canby's army of 45,000 men invested Spanish Fort and Fort Blakely, both of which would threaten his supply line if not reduced. The general conducted his sieges with deliberate efficiency. Engineers constructed elaborate parallel saps while artillerymen systematically bombarded the forts. Once everything was set for a general assault, massed formations of Union infantrymen easily carried first Spanish Fort on 8 April, then Fort Blakely on 9 April. Rebel resistance was certainly heroic, but the outcome was never in doubt. After mopping up two nearby Confederate outposts—Battery Tracy and Battery Huger—Canby dispatched a sizeable force to occupy now-defenseless Mobile. Plans to push deeper into Alabama became irrelevant when news arrived of the capitulation of Rebel armies in Virginia and North Carolina. During the first week of May, the general negotiated the final surrender of all Confederate forces east of the Mississippi River. Over the course of his brief campaign, Canby's army sustained relatively modest losses: 190 killed and 1,200 wounded. The supposedly "mediocre" general had delivered a competent performance. *Photo courtesy of Library of Congress*

EDWARD RICHARD SPRIGG CANBY
copy print
Theodore Lilienthal

HICKMAN PIERCE WALKER
copy print

After all the fighting he had experienced, Capt. Hickman Walker of the 18th Alabama Infantry was impressed by the fierce level of combat at Spanish Fort in April 1865. A twenty-five-year-old merchant from Tuscaloosa, Walker had just graduated from the University of Alabama when he joined the 18th Alabama in July 1861. The following year he won election to captain of Company G (the Yancey Guards). Thereafter Walker fought in every major engagement in the western theater. His men held him in high esteem. Pvt. Edgar Jones later said, "We don't now remember that the company ever went into a battle that Capt. Walker did not command it and bore himself with gallantry and courage." At Chickamauga, for instance, the captain led fifty-three men into battle, and only six were still standing when it was over. During the retreat from Nashville, he assumed de facto command of the regiment. Now at Spanish Fort, he shared leadership responsibilities with Capt. Augustus Greene of Butler County. The men of the 18th Alabama, part of Holtzclaw's Brigade, dug in around the "Red Fort," a heap of earthworks guarding the Confederate center. When not dodging mortar fire, Walker supervised the construction of abatis or tried to quash rumors that Lee had surrendered in Virginia. He also maintained vigilant security along his section of the line. "Under cover of darkness the enemy would attempt to remove our obstructions," explained Private Jones, but "we always caught them, for we were on the alert." On 8 April Walker could see that Union sappers had approached to within sixty yards of his position, and when the usual mortar barrage intensified, he knew an assault was imminent. Toward dusk the bluecoats charged, and the Alabamians shot back. The main attack, however, struck Rebel forces to Walker's left and soon threatened to outflank his regiment. A general retreat ensued, with Holtzclaw's Brigade conducting a rearguard action. The 18th Alabama was one of the last units to leave the fort. Consequently, many in the regiment became prisoners, though not Captain Walker.[29] *Photo courtesy of ADAH*

SILAS MATTISON BUNN
copy print

One of the last big battles of the war—at Fort Blakely—happened to be the first for Pvt. Silas Bunn of the 62nd Alabama Infantry. A nineteen-year-old from Talladega County, Bunn was actually one of the older soldiers in a regiment of teenagers. With one brother killed outside Richmond in 1862 and another captured at Spotsylvania in 1864, Bunn was determined to emulate their heroic examples. In 1863 he joined a battalion in the Alabama Reserves, which by 1864 had become the 62nd Alabama, with Bunn serving in Company E. During the last week of March 1865, he and his comrades sat in rifle pits on the perimeter of Spanish Fort, though because of their inexperience they were soon withdrawn to Fort Blakely. When the Union army invested that position during the first week of April, the private was among the last soldiers the Confederate high command had left with which to fight. Deployed on the extreme right of the fort, the 62nd Alabama defended Redoubt Nos. 8 and 9.

For several days, Bunn mostly watched as Union forces methodically dug ever closer. But on the afternoon of 9 April, he endured heavy artillery fire and then trembled as a brigade of midwestern veterans hit his regiment head on. Before the bluecoats even reached the ramparts, however, most of the boy-soldiers were fleeing toward the docks along the Tensa River. In the process they neglected to remove the foot bridges across a lengthy ditch intended to slow the enemy advance. As the Yankees scaled the parapets, a cluster of Alabamians, perhaps including Private Bunn, rallied and briefly resisted. "Young as they were, they fought like devils," commented a Union officer. Nevertheless, the fighting around the two redoubts lasted maybe ten minutes. Bunn became one of more than 3,000 Rebel prisoners. A month later, though, the war was over and the private received his parole.[30] *Photo courtesy of Roy H. Bunn*

301

EDWARD W. TARRANT
copy print

Capt. Edward Tarrant's battery of Alabama artillery-men hold the dubious honor of firing the last Confederate shot in the fighting at Fort Blakely. Though only twenty-two years old, Tarrant had plenty of combat experience. He first served in the 5th Alabama Infantry, with whom he received a minor wound in the skirmishing prior to First Manassas. While on sick furlough that fall in Tuscaloosa County, Tarrant accepted a lieutenancy in Lumsden's Battery, then in June 1863 formed his own battery, which he led throughout the Atlanta Campaign and during Hood's invasion of Tennessee. His command was nearly destroyed at Nashville in December 1864, but within a few months Tarrant reconstituted much of his force and deployed it to Fort Blakely. The captain and seventy-five men occupied Redoubt No. 1 on the extreme left edge of the fort, where they worked eight guns, mostly 3-inch Parrot rifles, and two mortars in support of a brigade of Missourians. For the first week of April 1865, Tarrant's gunners helped repel several probes by U.S. Colored Troops. When the Union army launched its general attack on 9 April, the captain's position was apparently the last to fall. The attacking African Americans had difficulty carrying the redoubt, in part because of the many buried torpedoes (land mines), which accounted for more than a dozen casualties. But Tarrant's Battery also inflicted many dozen more with point-blank fire. The captain vividly recalled the final moments: "Sergt. John J. Gray aimed a twelve-pounder James rifle, charged with canister, directly down the line and sent the contents hurtling through the crowded ranks of the enemy. The resulting casualties were great." Tarrant then waved a white handkerchief in surrender. The black soldiers, however, enraged by their many losses from the torpedoes and by what they considered an unfair cannon blast right at the end, shot one captive and clubbed down another. Captain Tarrant was just ordering his men to pick up their weapons and resume fighting when several white Union officers arrived and restored order.[31]
Photo courtesy of ADAH

During the sieges of Spanish Fort and Fort Blakely, the Mobile Squadron played an invaluable role in aiding the Confederate defenders. The officer responsible for this naval support was sixty-one-year-old Commodore Ebenezer Farrand of New York. A navy man since 1823, Farrand had just attained the rank of commander when he threw in with the Confederacy in 1861. For the first three years of the war, he directed various shipbuilding projects, most notably at the Selma Navy Yard, until the defeat of the Mobile Squadron in August 1864, when he replaced the captured Admiral Buchanan. As a newly appointed flag officer, Farrand exhibited a gruff and lethargic demeanor. He not only seemed disinterested in using his remaining warships for battle but also greatly disliked taking orders from his army rival Dabney Maury. By March 1865, however, the Davis administration reaffirmed the army's authority over all military assets in the Gulf District and ordered the commodore to cooperate. Thereafter Farrand performed creditably both as logistician and as warrior. At both east-bay forts, a steady flow of smaller vessels, including the erstwhile blockade-runner *Red Gauntlet*, ferried arms and supplies to the beleaguered garrisons and also evacuated wounded personnel. Concomitantly, the Mobile Squadron—specifically the *Nashville*, *Huntsville*, and *Morgan*—provided regular barrages. This naval gunfire was especially effective at Fort Blakely, where Rebel ships on the Tensa River pounded the Yankee lines. Union general Frederick Steele attested to the Confederate navy's usefulness at Blakely: "The enemy gunboats," he stated, "kept up a constant fire night and day, which was very harassing and destructive." On 8 April Union batteries managed to drive away the *Morgan*, but their shells bounced off the six-inch armor plating of the *Nashville*, which responded with seventy rounds of its own that day. Federal warships tried to disrupt Farrand's naval operations, but they ran afoul of the river system's numerous torpedo fields; two monitors and one gunboat sank after striking these explosive devices. Thus freed from his worries about enemy warships, Farrand successfully accomplished his part of the mission. The commodore's exploits in the spring of 1865 lacked the drama of the Farragut-Buchanan showdown of the previous summer, but they contributed much more to sustaining the cause in the twilight of the Confederacy.[32] *Photo courtesy of ADAH*

EBENEZER FARRAND
carte de visite
Duffee and Sancier, Mobile

JOHN LAWRENCE RAPIER
copy print

When his gun crews aboard the CSS *Morgan* were not shelling Union positions outside Fort Blakely, Lt. John Rapier perhaps reflected on his rather atypical wartime experience. A twenty-two-year-old bookkeeper from Mobile, Rapier had been working in New Orleans when the Civil War broke out. Rather than return home, he and some local friends joined a battalion of Louisiana Zouaves, with whom Rapier saw extensive action in the Army of Northern Virginia. Shortly after earning promotion to sergeant major, he was nearly blinded by an exploding shell during the Battle of Frayser's Farm. In July 1863 he transferred to the Confederate Marine Corps with a commission as second lieutenant and an assignment back home in Mobile. On 3 August 1864, Rapier received orders to reinforce the garrison at Fort Gaines, which the Union army was preparing to besiege. At a council of war only three days later, the marine lieutenant was stunned to learn that a majority of officers desired to surrender the fort. Rapier voted with the minority against this course of action. Rather than wait to be exchanged, Rapier and a dozen comrades made their escape in October from a Union prison camp in New Orleans. After hiding out in the bayous, the fugitives made their way to Mobile, arriving in November. Early the following year, Rapier became a gunnery officer aboard the *Morgan;* he was responsible for two 32-pounders. At Spanish Fort and again at Fort Blakely, he helped provide offshore artillery support for the beleaguered garrisons. His final combat experience came on 8 April, when he directed fire from the Tensa River into the right flank of the Union army then closing in on Fort Blakely. Unfortunately, a Union battery of Parrott rifles returned fire, quickly finding their range. The *Morgan* sustained seven hits and withdrew, never to see action again. A month later the Mobile Squadron, including Rapier and twenty-three other marines, surrendered. *Photo courtesy of Library of Congress*

DABNEY HERNDON MAURY
carte de visite
E. and H. T. Anthony,
New York

No general ever wants to admit defeat, let alone surrender his army, but in May 1865 Dabney Maury of Virginia did just that. For almost two years, he had defended the region around Mobile Bay against long odds, a thankless task often overlooked in the larger story of the Civil War. As a graduate from West Point (class of 1846) and as a veteran of the Mexican War, the forty-two-year-old Maury attained high rank quickly in the Confederate army. He saw combat at Pea Ridge and Corinth before accepting command of the District of the Gulf in May 1863. Though only five feet, three inches in height, Maury immediately won over the residents of Mobile with his genteel personality. He similarly earned the respect of his men through a genuine concern for their well-being. The soldiers affectionately dubbed their general "Puss in Boots." Maury proved a capable and energetic organizer in his efforts to prepare the bay area for the inevitable Union invasion. Unfortunately, his district rarely enjoyed top pri-

ority for the Confederacy's ever-diminishing resources of men and material. The loss of the bay entrance in August 1864 certainly disappointed Maury, but it hardly dismayed him; resistance would continue. Such tenacity contributed to the general's finest hour in the closing weeks of the war, when as he later said, "scarce a hope was left of that independence for which we had fought four years." At Spanish Fort and Fort Blakely, the Virginian mounted a dogged defense against a foe that outnumbered him better than five to one. Even after he lost those forts and subsequently evacuated Mobile, Maury remained upbeat. But on 4 May he finally surrendered his small army of 4,500 men at Citronelle, Alabama. In looking back on this experience, Maury expressed great pride: "Nothing in the history of those anxious days appears to me more touching and devoted than the conduct of the garrison of Mobile."[33] *Photo courtesy of ADAH*

Reconstruction and Legacy

Throughout the summer of 1865, roads all over Alabama felt the trudge of paroled soldiers returning home. Other than the relieved tears of family members, there was little joy in the occasion—the Heart of Dixie was a defeated land. Of the 96,000 Alabamians who wore gray, upward of one-third perished in the conflict (354 Alabama "Yankees" also died). Another third sustained wounds of varying sorts. All of the surviving veterans faced an uncertain future. "These men have been through tempests of shell, grape and minnie balls," commented a Huntsville newspaperman, who then added that "those who have seen the most of war are the fastest friends of peace, and grumble the least."[1] His was a fine sentiment that proved illusory during the Reconstruction years.

In addition to the human toll, Alabama's economy lay in ruins. Most obvious was the physical destruction of all but one of the state's blast furnaces as well as most of the railways, including depots, trestles, and rolling stock. Less apparent, but perhaps more deleterious, was the war's ramifications on agriculture. Farm production across the state, particularly the "hogs and hominy" staple of small land-holders, had dropped about 50 percent below prewar levels and would remain so for at least the next decade. The Tennessee Valley, which incurred the rampage of both sides' armies since early 1862, was especially hard hit. "In all directions," observed Union general James Wilson in March 1865, "there was almost absolute destitution."[2] And then there was the effect of emancipation, which at a stroke wiped out $200 million worth of chattel property without any compensation. The war had impoverished planter and yeoman alike.

In stark contrast to the saturnine demeanor of Alabama whites was the jubilant mood of the state's black population. Nearly 440,000 slaves were now "freedmen," and for them the immediate aftermath of the war was a time of excitement and hope. Blacks displayed their new freedom most noticeably through their mobility. Throughout the summer of 1865, thousands of freedmen roamed about, in part because they could but more practically because they sought either family members taken away via the interstate slave trade or nonagrarian jobs in urban areas. Discomfited whites believed that this unregulated movement by a formerly enslaved race verged on anarchy. The daughter of a Dale County planter regarded emancipation with paternalistic skepticism. "Morally most of the negroes today are not as good as the slaves were," she matter-of-factly explained, "they are free and can follow their own inclinations and the tendencies of their natures, not being held in restraint by the advice, discipline, and influence of their white owners and friends."[3]

Overseeing the relative chaos of the early postwar years was the Federal garrison. While responsible for hunting down leftover guerrilla bands and, for a time, prosecuting cotton profiteers, the U.S. Army's most important function was facilitating blacks' transition from slavery to freedom. Enter the Freedmen's Bureau (officially the Bureau of Refugees, Freedmen, and Abandoned Lands). Under Maj. Gen. Wager Swayne, who served as assistant commissioner for Alabama from August 1865 to January 1868, the Freedmen's Bureau established a respectable record. Among its many duties, the bureau distributed food rations to tens of thousands of displaced people, white and black; initiated a program of public education for blacks; operated a court system where freedmen could receive impartial justice; and refereed labor disputes between the two races. The last task consumed much of the bureau's time, for Swayne insisted that blacks get back to work as field hands but that white landlords treat them with fairness. Negotiating contracts that satisfied both parties proved a challenge. In Marengo County, for instance, an impatient planter quipped, "the trouble with the freedmen is that they have not yet learned that living is expensive." To which a former slave responded, "if we make contracts we will be branded and made slaves again."[4] Nevertheless, bureau agents persevered in what eventually became a system of sharecropping.

With the cessation of hostilities, Pres. Andrew Johnson implemented his "restoration" policy, one intended to readmit the South as quickly as possible. To this end, he appointed provisional governors for all of the former Rebel states. In Alabama that role

fell to Lewis Parsons of Talladega County. A longtime Democrat but also a Union sympathizer during the war, Parsons readily complied with the president's wishes by encouraging eligible white men to take a prescribed loyalty oath and then register to vote. Some 50,000 Alabamians did so, and in August 1865 they elected delegates to a constitutional convention. Sixty-three of the ninety-nine delegates were classified as "conservatives," meaning that they generally disapproved of secession and reluctantly supported the Confederacy. The other thirty-six delegates were dubbed "anti-Confederates," essentially wartime unionists. The convention met in September and by large majorities speedily accomplished its mission: it declared null and void the 1861 ordinance of secession, acknowledged the emancipation of slavery (though not the equality of the freedmen), and repudiated the state's war debt. Both Johnson and Parsons were pleased with the results. The new state constitution dismantled the old Confederate order yet explicitly maintained a "white man's government."

Ex-Confederates in Alabama were also pleased by the process of "restoration." In statewide elections that fall, they gained controlling influence over the legislature and even elected to Congress former Confederate officers, most notably Cullen Battle. Although they ratified the Thirteenth Amendment, which formally abolished slavery, ex-Confederate legislators also pushed through the Alabama Black Code, a series of laws regulating the economic lives of the freedmen. The broadly defined vagrancy clauses, for example, severely restricted the mobility of blacks and basically compelled them to submit to plantation serfdom.

Ex-Confederate resurgence in Alabama and elsewhere in the South provoked the wrath of Northern Republicans, who feared that the fruits of their victory had already gone rotten in the hands of unrepentant Rebels. Accordingly, they scrapped Johnson's Restoration policy in favor of a more punitive approach to Reconstruction. In December 1865 the Republican majority in Congress refused to seat the entire Southern delegation. Then in the early months of 1866, it moved against the states' Black Codes, a campaign that culminated in the Fourteenth Amendment. Under the congressional plan, former Confederate states could only rejoin the Union upon ratification of this amendment, one that emphasized biracial citizenship, including equality before the law. Alabama's new governor, Robert Patton, a political moderate from Lauderdale County, urged his state to ratify lest the Republicans expand their demands. The political battle between victor and vanquished, however, had become a point of honor to most white Southerners. "It is one thing to be oppressed, wronged and outraged by overwhelming force," bellowed John Forsyth of Mobile, "it is quite another to submit to voluntary debasement."[5] On 7 December 1866, Alabama legislators decisively rejected the Fourteenth Amendment, 96–10. Nine other Southern states did likewise. An angry Congress responded by passing the Reconstruction Acts, laws that remanded the South to military rule.

In March 1867 Alabama became part of the Third Military District (along with Georgia and Florida) under Maj. Gen. John Pope. Within the state itself, General Swayne held all authority; Governor Patton became a bystander. As per congressional decree, Swayne simultaneously disfranchised a considerable number of ex-Confederates (in accordance with the "iron-clad" test oath) and extended the franchise to black men. By the end of the summer, over 100,000 freedmen had registered, bringing the state's total electorate to about 170,000. In October most blacks cast their first ballot in an election for delegates to another constitutional convention, one designed to fulfill congressional expectations for Reconstruction. Of the one hundred delegates, ninety-six, including eighteen blacks, were members of the new Republican Party. In short order the convention drafted a new constitution that officially enfranchised blacks, though it left unresolved matters of racial equality.

Despite a veneer of solidarity, Alabama's Republican Party betrayed the internecine power struggles typical of an organization hastily thrown together. Formed in June 1867, party leadership emerged in inverse proportion to the numerical strength of various factions. The "carpetbaggers" (a pejorative for Northern whites recently settled in the South) numbered only about 5,000 yet wielded enormous influence over the party, due in large part to their extensive business and military connections. In general, these Yankee transplants promoted economic modernization but soon divided between two former Union generals: Willard Warner of Ohio, who sought broad-based policies, and George Spencer of New York, who sponsored initiatives favorable to blacks. A second faction, Southern whites dubbed "scalawags," numbered anywhere from 10,000 to 30,000 of the party's membership. Prominent within this group were upstate unionists, led by Chris Sheats of Winston County, who assumed that wartime loyalty would translate into peacetime privilege. In seeking to dominate their state and their party, Alabama unionists both defended the political proscription of ex-Confederates and opposed black suffrage. A more conservative group of scalawags, banded behind William H. Smith of Randolph County, considered the unionist agenda unrealistic and instead came to regard carpetbagger machinations as the more serious problem to reconstructing the state.

Domineering white members aside, the Republican Party's principal constituency—about 80 percent—was the freedmen. Politically ignorant and inexperienced, blacks initially deferred to white leadership, but they never displayed inferiority. "We are wise enough to know our rights," averred Lawrence Berry of Mobile, "and we are going to claim those rights."[6] An important means to that end was the Union League. Originally designed to rally public support for the Lincoln administration, during Reconstruction the league became an effective grassroots movement in behalf of Republicans. Pennsylvania carpetbagger John C. Keffer served as titular leader in Alabama. Throughout 1867 he supervised for the freedmen what amounted to a crash course in party politics and the democratic process. Not surprisingly, with chapters in virtually every county, the league became an immediate vehicle for black activism at the local level. The cooperative spirit fostered in its meetings empowered blacks to bargain with white landlords for better working arrangements and to vote en masse for Republican candidates, including many of their own, such as James Rapier of Lauderdale County. The son of a free black artisan, Rapier emerged as a champion of labor reform and public education. In the process he unflinchingly challenged white Republicans for control over the direction of the party.

Besides internal divisions, Republicans also faced opposition from the Democrats. Reorganized in the summer of 1867 and led by such prominent ex-Confederate officers as James Clanton and Joseph Hodgson, Alabama's Democratic Party unabashedly touted a platform of race order. "Shall the white man be subordinate to the negro?" asked a party newspaper. "Shall the property classes be robbed by the no property herd?"[7] Socially, Democrats ostracized their Republican neighbors. Politically, they engaged in obstructionist tactics. In February 1868, when the Republican-controlled state convention submitted the new constitution for ratification, Clanton and Hodgson instigated a boycott. The Reconstruction Acts stipulated that a majority of registered voters had to participate in ratification. By staying away from the polls, the Democrats thwarted this requirement even though 70,000 mostly black voters approved the constitution versus a mere 1,000 opposed. Fortunately for the Republicans, Congress intervened with legislation that retroactively validated the outcome. Moreover, because state elections were held in tandem with ratification, the Republicans swept virtually every office.

In July William H. Smith took the inaugural oath as Alabama's first Republican governor. And in November the party delivered the state's electoral votes to Pres. Ulysses S. Grant. (In 1869 the Republican-controlled legislature also ratified the Fifteenth Amendment by a vote of 101–17.) Factionalism, however, spoiled these victories. Scalawags

enjoyed a plurality in the legislature, but carpetbaggers won most of the national offices, including both U.S. Senate seats (Warner and Spencer), which gave them control over federal patronage. Blacks found themselves marginalized. They held twenty-seven seats in the state house but only one in the senate, while the executive and judicial branches remained all white. Further complicating Republican governance was the party's divergent priorities. Carpetbaggers and scalawags wrangled over whether to restore fully the political rights of ex-Confederates, but both approved extravagant disbursals for railroad construction. During Smith's administration alone, the state allocated nearly $5 million for new lines yet provided minimal oversight for such a large disbursal of funds. For their part, blacks emphasized civil rights but immediately ran afoul of racism. Scalawags in the state senate killed a common-carriers bill that would have granted blacks equal access to public transportation. On the matter of public education, however, the party achieved some success. The new statewide system was segregated, but in 1870 the Republican-controlled Board of Education proudly announced that its 1,800 schools enrolled nearly 400,000 children. Unfortunately, looming fiscal woes jeopardized this promising start.

Republican rule fomented retaliatory violence by Alabama whites. For a time right after the war, bands of so-called Regulators—a throwback to the slave patrol—occasionally prowled the countryside intimidating blacks, but massive resistance to Reconstruction really began in early 1867, following the establishment of the Republican Party in the state and the proliferation of the Union League. The first major instance of political violence (which invariably was also racial in nature) occurred with the "Pig Iron" Kelley Riot in Mobile. On 14 May 1867, Pennsylvania congressman William Kelley, whose moniker "Pig Iron" derived from his voting record on high protective tariffs, visited Mobile to drum up support for the state's nascent Republican Party. His speech to an audience of 4,000 included many disparaging remarks about the Confederacy. When whites in the crowd began heckling Kelley, a scuffle ensued, followed by gunshots. Within minutes a full-blown race riot enveloped several city blocks, leaving one white and one black dead and another twenty residents wounded.

The spontaneous violence of the "Pig Iron" Kelley Riot gave way to the premeditated terrorism of the Ku Klux Klan. The organization originated in Tennessee but soon spread to Alabama and the rest of the South. In actuality, "Klan" was a generic term for a wide variety of Rebel vigilante organizations. The Klan in Alabama included the Knights of the White Camellia from the Black Belt, the Night Owls of Pickens County, and the Sipsey Swamp Boys of Tuscaloosa. Consequently, the Klan was decentralized in its operations; Democrats and planters tried to coordinate paramilitary activities around political-economic goals, but local den leaders frequently bucked the chain of command. Nevertheless, from 1868 to 1870 the Alabama Klan perpetrated a ruthless guerrilla insurgency against Republicans specifically and the freedmen generally. In the blunt words of newspaperman Ryland Randolph, the grand cyclops of Tuscaloosa, the basic goal of the Klan was "by God's grace, to pitch into scallawags, niggers, and carpetbaggers to the end of recorded time."[8]

Most Klan outlawry occurred in the northern and western counties of the state, where race ratios were close. Through nightriding, Klansmen burned black churches and schools, disrupted Union League meetings, whipped Republican voters on the eve of elections, and meted out summary punishment on freedmen accused of stealing livestock. Of course, they also killed people. In November 1868 a den in Tuscaloosa assassinated M. T. Crossland, a white Republican state legislator from the county. The same fate befell two Greene County Union Leaguers, Alexander Boyd (white) and Jim Martin (black), both gunned down at night by disguised marauders in March 1870. In July 1870 the Klan in Calhoun County committed a particularly grisly crime when a pack of nightriders kidnapped four blacks and their carpetbagger friend and lynched all five. The climax to this reign of terror came on 25 October 1870, when Klansmen attacked a Republican rally in Eutaw (Greene County), inflicting anywhere from three to five dozen casualties. Officially, the Klan perpetrated at least 258 "outrages" in Alabama, including ninety-three homicides. William Figures, a scalawag from Huntsville, aptly explained its influence: "These bands are having a great effect, in inspiring a *nameless terror.* . . . [T]he mischief is taking place daily and nightly—nobody is found out, or arrested, or punished . . . and the thing goes on, and is getting worse."[9]

The Smith administration's response to "Kukluxism" was erratic and at times pusillanimous. The legislature passed anti-Klan laws in December 1868 and authorized the mobilization of the state militia, but the governor vacillated. Smith reasoned that any militia formation would perforce be mostly black in personnel and so only risk a race war. Besides, he often dismissed as exaggerations the numerous petitions on Klan violence. Instead, Smith alternated between urging sheriffs to take charge of the crisis and calling on the army to quell the unrest. Few sheriffs mustered the courage to openly confront the Klan, while army officers lacked both the jurisdiction and the inclination to get involved in state affairs now that Alabama was back in the Union. Still, Maj. Gen. Samuel Crawford, the garrison commander in Alabama, did shuffle small detachments from one trouble spot to the next, though mostly as a show of force. In 1870 and 1871, Congress belatedly passed a series of Enforcement Acts that empowered the War Department and the new Justice Department to crush the Klan. In Alabama, District Attorney John Minnis gathered evidence and issued indictments. Simultaneously, influential state Democrats came out against the Klan, charging that its atrocities had grown barbaric and counterproductive. Sometime in 1871 the organization in Alabama disappeared, the dens disbanding under legal and public censure.

The Klan's demise hardly mattered, for it had

accomplished much of its mission. Through its terror tactics, the group essentially destroyed the Union League movement, which in turn weakened the Republicans' ability to canvass the state. This development, coupled with party factionalism, greatly affected the outcome of the election of 1870. That year William Smith stood for reelection, but black victims of Kukluxism expressed little enthusiasm for him, while carpetbaggers publicly excoriated the incumbent's ineffectual leadership. Moreover, scalawags were appalled by the inclusion of James Rapier on the ticket for secretary of state. Conversely, most white Alabamians rallied around the Democrats' nominee, Robert Lindsay, a political moderate from Colbert County. In a very close election, the Democrats won the gubernatorial contest 77,000 to 75,600 and also captured two of the six congressional seats. Rightly claiming fraud and intimidation in several Klan-wracked counties, Republicans disputed the outcome, and Governor Smith briefly refused to step down, but the courts eventually verified the returns. In December 1870 Lindsay became the new governor.

The Democrats' celebration was short lived, for Lindsey's term coincided with a fiscal meltdown in the state. Mere weeks after taking office, the governor received word that the Alabama and Chattanooga Railroad was defaulting on its multimillion dollar loan from the state. A subsequent investigation exposed not only widespread political bribery and misuse of funds by the owners but also similar skullduggery within the state's other railroad ventures. In a hectic attempt to avoid financial disaster, Lindsey halted virtually all treasury disbursals, not just to the railroads but also to the fledgling school system. When this proved ill advised, he then inexplicably purchased the Alabama and Chattanooga at a bankruptcy sale and thus saddled the state with a capitalistic lemon. Lindsey's missteps notwithstanding, blame for the railroad boondoggles lay primarily with the Republicans, though many Democrats also had their hands in the till. In the end, the taxpayers suffered as the Reconstruction-era debt eventually exceeded $25,000,000.

The election of 1872 produced a dramatic about-face. During the campaign, carpetbagger George Spencer not only persuaded the Republican factions to set aside their differences but also managed to get U.S. troops deployed to some of the more troublesome polling sites. For governor, the party nominated David P. Lewis, an upstate Alabamian who pleased the scalawag element. Though distrustful of their white brethren, blacks came to terms in part because James Rapier secured nomination for Congress, but also because the political alternative demanded unity. The Democrats had set aside caution by nominating Thomas Herndon, a hardline secessionist and former colonel in the Confederate army. Lewis comfortably defeated Herndon (89,000 to 78,500), and Rapier also won his race, but Democrats seemingly prevailed in both houses of the legislature. Through an impressive feat of political legerdemain, however, the Republicans convened a rival legislature, one instantly recognized by the new governor, and then successfully appealed to President Grant for legitimacy. Eventually, enough Democrats were unseated on federal charges of voting fraud to give the Republicans a working majority in the state house.

Alabama Republicans may have remembered how to win, but they still did not know how to govern. George Spencer finagled his reelection to the U.S. Senate in part by intimating that he would collaborate with the Democrats if denied his ambition. Irate scalawags, who still held a plurality of seats, then launched a purge of the carpetbaggers, including impeachment proceedings in some cases. Exacerbating this renewed factionalism was a demand by black legislators that their party pass a civil-rights bill. When white Republicans balked, their black colleagues cursed them as hypocrites. All the while Democrats watched in silent amusement as their political rivals devoured themselves. The self-destructive tendencies of the Republican Party have led one team of scholars to conclude that "Reconstruction in Alabama was a revolution that increasingly lost its cause and became an exercise in holding power."[10]

By 1874, Democrats had suffered enough such Republican power and decided to make the gubernatorial race of that year a final showdown. To this end, they reverted to the politics of force and heightened the tension through a steady barrage of racial propaganda. The Democrats' paramilitary approach, however, was no mere resurrection of the Ku Klux Klan. This time ex-Confederate officers wielded firm control, ensuring that militant activity served specific political goals. Boldly concentrating their efforts in Black Belt counties, gun-toting Democrats disrupted numerous Republican rallies, not through wanton violence, but through carefully orchestrated intimidation. Nevertheless, there were some instances of bloodshed. In August vigilantes in Sumter County murdered two Republican organizers, and on the eve of the election in Barbour County, a band of whites ambushed a parade of black voters, killing seven and wounding dozens more. Nearly 700 U.S. troops patrolled selected precincts, but as in 1870 the army's presence did little to deter white aggression. Interestingly, the Democrats' campaign did more to unify whites than discourage blacks. With disaffected scalawags abandoning the Republican fold, the freedmen took charge of their party and acted with a sense of urgency. "It is the hardest thing in the world to keep a negro away from the polls," admitted Eli Shorter, an ex-Confederate from Eufaula, "that is one thing he will do, to vote."[11] In the end, both races and both parties turned out greater numbers than ever before during Reconstruction. The Democratic candidate for governor, George Houston, garnered a whopping 107,000 votes against Republican incumbent David Lewis's still impressive 94,000. In the legislature Democrats gained solid majorities in both houses, but black Republicans achieved their greatest political success, winning a record thirty-three seats. There was cruel irony in this outcome. Blacks finally dominated their party at a time when their party faced political exile.

The Houston administration moved fast to consolidate white power. Democrats gerrymandered the congressional districts to their advantage and continued the social ostracism of carpetbaggers until Northerners left the state altogether. In the meantime, the governor convened a constitutional convention that reapportioned the state house to give white counties greater representation. Not surprisingly, in 1876 the Democrats crushed their Republican adversaries in the gubernatorial election, 96,000 to 55,600. Ex-Confederate Alabamians could now rejoice over their "Redemption," a self-serving term that meant salvation from the supposed evils of Republican and Negro misrule.

Anyone visiting Alabama in the decades after Reconstruction might well have wondered whether the Confederacy really lost the Civil War. Government in the state was a "who's who" of Rebel war heroes, and planters still dominated a largely agrarian economy (Birmingham's rise as an industrial city notwithstanding). As for blacks, though they may have been free, they were definitely not equal. Sharecropping devolved into debt peonage and a caste system emerged, one that gained legal imprimatur with the 1901 state constitution that disfranchised blacks and codified Jim Crow segregation. All the while veterans held tearful reunions, where the memory of the Civil War increasingly became shrouded in the romance of the Lost Cause. At one such gathering in 1917—a huge ex-Confederate parade through the streets of Washington, D.C.—Sen. John H. Bankhead of Lamar County, erstwhile captain in the 16th Alabama Infantry, delivered a speech that emphasized the notion of a fresh start. Of his aging Rebel compatriots he said, "Today, marching with feeble body and faltering step, on a mission of peace and love, not of hatred and bloodshed, in a spirit of resolute reconciliation and absolute loyalty to our flag, they voice in vibrant tones to all the world, the indissoluble union of the United States."[12] A half century after their failed revolution, white Southerners like Bankhead had finally, psychologically come to terms with defeat and began redefining their still anomalous place in the national fold.

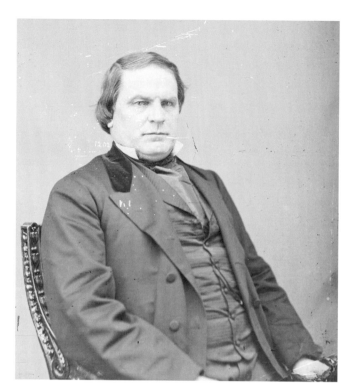

LEWIS ELIPHALET
PARSONS
copy print

As Alabama's first Reconstruction governor, Lewis Parsons faced the challenge of guiding a defeated people back into the national fold. His efforts enjoyed remarkable, if short-lived, success. A New Yorker by birth, the forty-eight-year-old Parsons began practicing law in Talladega County in 1840. Over time he became a wealthy Southern gentleman, though he never owned any slaves. Politically a Whig, he supported economic diversification and believed the South's growing obsession with slavery unhealthy for future progress. Like other political moderates in the state, Parsons voted for Stephen Douglas in 1860 and opposed the secession movement thereafter. During the first two years of the war, he kept a low profile, but in 1863 antiwar voters elected him to the state legislature, where he worked to ameliorate the hardships of the people. Given his unionist credentials, Parsons was a natural choice for provisional governor, a position he assumed on 21 June 1865. A month later he issued a proclamation that reflected President Johnson's restoration policy. The governor dismissed any lingering devotion to the Confederacy—bluntly telling his listeners that slavery was dead and that secession was a failure—and instead spoke urgently of survival, "likening the Union to a steamship and the state of Alabama to a man swimming around in the water, trying to get on board." Accordingly, Parsons called for a special convention and started registering voters. Concomitantly, he helped the federal garrison suppress lawlessness and worked with the Freedmen's Bureau in getting the cash-crop economy functioning again. During the convention, Parsons strongly recommended that blacks be given the right to testify in court. He also hinted that the delegates might want to consider the idea of qualified black suffrage. The governor's motives had less to do with racial egalitarianism and more to do with political expediency; blacks after all composed 45 percent of the state's population. The post-convention legislature did grant the freedmen a conditional right to testify in court but tabled the suffrage issue. When he left office in December 1865, Parsons won election to the U.S. Senate. Unfortunately for him, Congress refused to seat the former governor (along with every other Southern representative) and over the next three years dismantled many of Parsons's gubernatorial achievements.[13] *Photo courtesy of Library of Congress*

ROBERT MILLER PATTON
copy print
Frederick Studio, New York

As Alabama's second postwar governor, Robert Patton confronted a fundamental challenge of Reconstruction—how to reconcile the sudden reality of emancipation with the enduring idea of race order. In his inaugural address on 13 December 1865, he presented his answer: "We shall not only extend to the freedmen all their legitimate rights, but shall throw around them such effectual safeguards as will secure them in their full and complete enjoyment. At the same time it must be understood that politically and socially ours is a white man's government." A fifty-six-year-old planter from Lauderdale County, Patton considered the Civil War a needless disaster for the South. Although a big slaveholder, Patton was a unionist who denounced the fire-eater mentality and voted for Stephen Douglas in 1860 (this following a political career as a Whig). After secession Patton quietly acquiesced to Confederate rule and privately grieved the loss of two sons, both of whom died for the Rebel cause. Following the convention of 1865, he accepted nomination for governor and handily defeated two other unionist candidates. Patton quickly recognized that Alabama's readmission to the Union hinged on placat-

ing basic Northern expectations, particularly those regarding black freedom. To this end, he vetoed much of the state legislature's initial attempts at imposing a harsh Black Code, primarily because it smacked of slavery by another name. Patton also cooperated with the Freedmen's Bureau in pursuing equitable labor arrangements between white landholders and black workers. And he urged legislators in 1866 to ratify the Fourteenth Amendment, believing its provisions for colorblind citizenship a reasonable congressional demand. His political pragmatism notwithstanding, Patton was a typical Southern paternalist who ultimately acceded to the need for a caste system (he approved subsequent Black Code revisions) and anxiously hoped Alabama might steer clear of federally mandated black suffrage. When the latter came in 1867, the governor briefly associated with the Republican Party in the mistaken belief that scalawags such as himself might be able to control black votes. It hardly mattered, for under military reconstruction, the state executive was mostly a political supernumerary.[14]
Photo courtesy of ADAH

WAGER T. SWAYNE
carte de visite
J. H. Lakin, Montgomery

The most important figure in the story of Alabama Reconstruction is arguably Maj. Gen. Wager Swayne of Ohio. As both the longtime head of the Freedmen's Bureau in the state and as de facto military governor in 1867, Swayne exerted immediate and far-reaching influence over all matters of political economy. Just thirty years old when he assumed his postwar duties in July 1865, Swayne brought to Alabama an impressive resume: son of U.S. Supreme Court Justice Noah Swayne; law degree from Yale; distinguished wartime record (he led a regiment at Corinth and Iuka and lost a leg during Sherman's march through South Carolina). According to one biographer, "Swayne personified the ethnocentric Yankee"—in other words, he possessed a self-righteous sense of mission. For Alabama, that meant restoring loyal government and

assimilating the freedmen into free society. The general's reign, however, was really a tale of two temperaments, neither of which formulated a durable policy for success. At the outset Swayne adopted a fairly conservative approach to Reconstruction. Working closely with the state's white leaders, he emphasized economic recovery and political moderation. To this end, through the Freedmen's Bureau, the general not only insisted that blacks sign labor contracts with white planters but also encouraged them to rent homesteads in the hope that tenant farming might lead eventually to land reform. He also permitted ex-Confederates a substantial degree of latitude in managing local affairs. Toward the end of 1866, an optimistic Swayne promoted ratification of the Fourteenth Amendment as a reasonable step toward getting Alabama back into the Union. White rejection of this measure astounded him. "The press, the Legislature, and apparently the people have made up their minds they will do *nothing* towards reconstruction, except stand and take it," he fumed in early 1867.

The ensuing imposition of Radical Reconstruction coincided with the general's change in attitude. Gone was Swayne's erstwhile pragmatism, replaced by a radicalized commitment toward congressional policies. He openly supported the Republican makeover in the state, attending Union League meetings and party rallies. Concomitantly, Swayne summarily abolished the chain-gang system and increased his support for black education, contributing thousands of dollars of his own money. Finally, he enthusiastically supported universal suffrage, viewing unfettered access to the ballot box as "the true corrective" to racial injustice in the state. Swayne played an instrumental role in shaping the 1867 Constitution but would not be around to help implement its provisions. President Johnson considered the general's partisan conduct unprofessional and in December removed him from office. "The only feeling of regret I have in leaving here," he said, "is that of leaving one's command before the fight is over." His intentions had been good, and his accomplishments were real, but by 1868 Wager Swayne had overplayed his role in Reconstruction.[15] *Photo courtesy of ADAH*

316

More so than any other Alabama carpetbagger, Richard Busteed appears to have deserved the opprobrium associated with that epithet. As federal district judge over the entire state from 1864 to 1874, Busteed frequently abused his office for personal gain. A New Yorker of Irish descent, he was a Democrat before the war but became a Republican during it. He briefly held the rank of brigadier general but in late 1863 accepted his judicial appointment in Alabama. It was not until Reconstruction, however, that Busteed's corrupt activities commenced. On several occasions early on, he interfered with the army's prosecution of cotton profiteers, ostensibly in order to uphold the writ of habeas corpus, but quite likely because he was receiving kickbacks from the accused. The judge also became notorious for lining his pockets with a portion of the exorbitant court fees his bench charged. He ignored or quickly dismissed cases where the profits were minimal, such as challenges to the test oath (which he actually thought was unconstitutional), and instead mostly presided over those involving wealthy parties on both sides. Busteed and his staff "judged the case as per purse," according to a Montgomery newspaper, "then they portioned out the spoil." In addition to graft, the judge attempted unsuccessfully to parlay his position into a U.S. Senate seat. Scalawags in the state, however, consistently stymied his political aspirations. In retaliation Busteed started colluding with the Democrats, from whom he allegedly accepted bribes. Not surprisingly, scalawags moved to impeach him, their efforts coming to fruition in 1874, when the U.S. House Judiciary Committee concluded that there was sufficient cause to put the fifty-two-year-old on trial. Realizing that his racket was over, Busteed abruptly resigned and returned to New York with his "carpetbag" filled with Alabama treasure.[16]

Photo courtesy of ADAH

RICHARD BUSTEED
copy print
Mathew Brady

3

BENJAMIN STERLING TURNER
copy print

318

In 1870, blacks in Alabama's First Congressional District, which encompassed nine counties in the southwest corner of the state, nominated Ben Turner to be their representative in Washington, D.C. A Dallas County freedman, Turner's life as a slave was atypical for most African Americans. He received a basic education from indulgent masters, who later entrusted him with the daily management of a family hotel and livery stable in Selma. Consequently, Turner held no grudges toward whites after the war. Moreover, he possessed rare credentials for a Southern black man during Reconstruction. In 1867 Turner joined the Republican Party. As a local politician, he worked to improve economic opportunities for blacks even as he called for amnesty to ex-Confederates. Turner's political style was effective yet unprepossessing; both blacks and whites regarded him as an amiable and honest fellow. Nevertheless, he was part of Reconstruction's revolution in race relations. In the congressional election of 1870, Turner trounced his Democratic rival, 18,200 votes to 13,200. Forty-five years of age at the time, he became Alabama's first black congressman (and among the first in U.S. history).

Turner's record in Congress was unremarkable, in part because Republican leaders largely ignored him, taking for granted his vote on legislation. Still, he persevered in sponsoring various economic bills, including a repeal of the cotton tax on Southern farms and a recommendation that the federal government reexamine the idea of selling land to freedmen; no action was taken on his proposals. In May 1872 a somewhat disillusioned Turner finally gained the floor and defended the contributions of African Americans to the life of the nation: "These people have struggled longer and labored harder, and have made more of the raw material than any people in the world." Unfortunately, in his bid for reelection in 1872, Turner became a casualty in the growing factional struggle within the Republican Party. Carpetbaggers in his district disliked the incumbent's accomodationist views toward ex-Confederates and backed a rival candidate, Philip Joseph, a free black from Mobile. Angered by this unexpected challenge, Turner denounced Joseph as a former spy for the Rebel cause and a current dupe of Yankee outsiders. Nonetheless, the competing Republican tickets wrecked Turner's chances. While he garnered 37 percent of the vote, thereby beating out Joseph, who won 19 percent, he ultimately lost to Democrat Frederick Bromberg, who prevailed with a plurality of 44 percent. Thereafter Turner withdrew from politics, except for a brief participation as delegate to the Republican National Convention in 1880.[17]
Photo courtesy of Library of Congress

JEREMIAH HARALSON
copy print

Among the many active black politicians during Reconstruction, Jeremiah Haralson was one of the most important and arguably the most perplexing. A self-educated freedman and a self-appointed clergyman from Dallas County, Haralson possessed a mercurial, independent streak. For instance, he rejected the Republican-authored 1868 state constitution because it failed to explicate black equality. He then shocked his neighbors by stumping for Horatio Seymour, the overtly racist Democratic candidate for president in 1868. His conduct in this campaign, however, betrayed a sarcastic sense of humor; he whimsically declared his own candidacy, even though he was below the requisite age and often did not seem to care about the outcome at all. In 1869 Haralson formally joined the Republican Party and went on to win election to the state legislature. Local whites came to despise Haralson's cocky personality, physically threatening him from time to time. The former slave expected rough treatment from ex-Confederates, but what he could never tolerate was the indifference of many white Republicans for black initiatives. In February 1873 he successfully steered a civil-rights bill through the state senate only to see it tabled by his white colleagues in the house. By 1874 Haralson was fed up with his party's lackluster approach to Reconstruction and in June helped organize a black caucus, the Equal Rights Association. The twenty-eight-year-old then secured a legitimate nomination as Republican candidate for Congress. In the ensuing election Democrats

endorsed incumbent Frederick Bromberg and campaigned on a platform of overt white supremacy. Haralson gamely countered by flaunting his pure black ancestry. Some white Republicans broke ranks and voted for Bromberg, but blacks flocked enthusiastically to the polls for their man. Haralson won 54 percent of the vote and weathered a failed attempt by Bromberg to contest the outcome.

Haralson's term in Congress was one of frustration. Democrats controlled the House and never allowed him to speak on the floor. Furthermore, his own party neglected his talents, relegating him to a minor seat on the Committee for Public Expenditures. Returning to Alabama in 1876, Haralson wrongly assumed he would receive Republican support for reelection. Instead, party leaders nominated James Rapier, one of the state's leading black politicos who had just moved his residency to Dallas County in order to tap into the district's large black vote. Haralson branded Rapier an opportunist and launched a third-party bolt. Thus, the congressional race of 1876 pitted the two most powerful black Republicans against one another. Democratic nominee Charles Shelley, a former Confederate general, polled just 38 percent of the vote, but it exceeded Haralson's 34 percent and Rapier's 28 percent. Haralson charged Shelley with voter fraud, but when he challenged his Rebel nemesis again in 1878, white vigilantes warned him to leave the district or risk death. This time the usually combative Haralson left Alabama. *Photo courtesy of Library of Congress*

ROBERT POLLARD
GRIGG
carte de visite
I'. A. Gerrish,
Montgomery

Because of the secrecy surrounding the Ku Klux Klan, knowledge of who exactly served in this organization, let alone what they looked like, poses a problem for any researcher. Fortunately, a few photographs, such as this one from 1871 of Robert Grigg, helps put a face to the conspiracy (a handwritten statement on the back attests to his membership). An ex-Confederate from Montgomery, Grigg fought as a private in Company F, 60th Alabama Infantry, seeing action at Chickamauga and sustaining two wounds (18 September 1864 and 24 January 1865) during the siege at Petersburg. Grigg probably joined the Klan in 1868, when he was about twenty-eight years old. He may well have served in a den called the Shrouded Brotherhood. A public circular, posted throughout the state capital in March 1868, conveyed the cryptic and macabre nature of this particular organization: "The dark and dismal hour will soon be. Some live to-day, to-morrow DIE. Be ye ready. The whetted sword—the bullet red and the rights are ours." Although Klansmen elsewhere in Alabama instigated a reign of terror in several counties, those in Montgomery were more ceremonial than violent. There is no indication that Grigg and his "shrouded" brothers committed any lawless acts. Furthermore, it appears that the Montgomery Klan disbanded after 1868.[18] *Photo courtesy of ADAH*

NICHOLAS DAVIS RICHARDSON
carte de visite

Also wearing the white hood in 1868 was Dr. Nicholas Richardson, a thirty-five-year-old physician from Athens, Alabama. In April of that year, he became the grand cyclops of the Ku Klux Klan in Limestone County, where the dens were much more truculent than those in Montgomery. When Richardson was not orchestrating nightriding terrorism, the good doctor enjoyed all of the social respect accorded a Southern gentleman. In 1856 Richardson earned his M.D. from Jefferson Medical College in Philadelphia and opened his practice in Athens the same year. With the outbreak of war, he accepted appointment as the regimental surgeon of the 50th Alabama Infantry. In that capacity Richardson tended to the sick and wounded from Shiloh through Bentonville. After the war the physician returned to Athens, where he and his wife raised six children. For whatever reason, Richardson also came to despise Republican efforts at Reconstruction;

he joined both the Klan and the Democratic Party. Outwardly, the Limestone Klan presented a friendly face, promising to provide protection to whites in a time of racial confusion. But like its brethren throughout the Tennessee Valley, it engaged in murderous depredations against the black populace. During the election of 1868, the Limestone Klan fearlessly patrolled the streets of Athens and even fraternized with a squad of federal troops stationed there to guard the precinct. The following July the den forcibly freed three Klansmen who had been jailed for homicide. Dr. Richardson's exact role in these activities is unclear, but he was the local Klan leader until the end of 1869. To the white community of Limestone, however, the specifics hardly mattered, for they only remembered Richardson as a man who "contributed strong aid to the maintenance of order in that day of civil disorder."[19] *Photo courtesy of ADAH*

In the realm of Reconstruction propaganda, few newspapers surpassed the partisan vitriol of the *Tuscaloosa Independent Monitor*. Owned and edited by Ryland Randolph, an ex-Confederate officer and local Klan leader, the masthead encapsulated the rag's essential message: "White man—right or wrong—still the white man!" When not flagrantly recruiting for the Klan, the *Monitor* mercilessly lambasted Republican rule in Alabama. The U.S. Army briefly curtailed publication in the spring and summer of 1868, when Randolph stood trial for inciting racial violence and for personally knifing a black man. Following his acquittal, however, Randolph resumed his duties and exercised freedom of the press with a vengeance. The *Monitor* specialized in crass political cartoons. Two in particular exemplify the white South's stereotypical hatred for Reconstruction. On 1 September 1868, the *Monitor* published a woodcut that depicted two Ohio carpetbaggers limply hanging by the neck from a tree. Sauntering off from the scene of this lynching is a donkey (the mascot of the Democratic Party) branded with the capital letters "K.K.K." The caption reads, in part, "Hang, curs, hang!" This cartoon gained instant notoriety throughout the country and has since become one that historians frequently use to highlight the terror of the Reconstruction Klan. A couple of months later, on 10 November, the *Monitor* printed another woodcut, one slightly less provocative but just as crude. Specifically, the cartoon depicts a mongrelized American flag, where eleven of the stars are replaced by grinning pick-a-ninny faces. "The niggerheads signify the Southern States, that have been doomed to negro supremacy," the caption explains to its white readers: "Can we ever love such a disgusting piece of bunting? Never." The message was clear: Reconstruction is a travesty that cannot be tolerated. For the next few years, until Randolph sold the newspaper in December 1871, the *Monitor* persisted in its denigration of blacks and Republicans, but the cartoons and editorials never quite reached the same inflammatory level as those from the autumn of 1868; perhaps readers had grown accustomed to its racist satire. Regardless, while it lasted the *Tuscaloosa Independent Monitor* set a benchmark with its unapologetic and polemical defense of white supremacy and home rule.[20]
Photo courtesy of ADAH

TUSCALOOSA INDEPENDENT MONITOR
carte de visite
Voyle Studio, Tuscaloosa

GEORGE ELIPHAZ SPENCER
copy print

when he helped raise the 1st Alabama Cavalry (Union), a regiment comprised of volunteers from the Tennessee River valley. Spencer's initial approach to Reconstruction was extremely radical. "I am in favor of Negro Suffrage," he declared shortly after the war, "or reducing all these states to the position of territories & keeping them so for years to come or until the leaders are all dead." With strong support among both the scalawag element and the freedmen, Spencer won election to the U.S. Senate in 1868. Significantly, he managed to achieve seniority over his carpetbag rival, Willard Warner, who won the other seat. As senator he ingratiated himself with the Grant administration and thereby gained control over most the federal patronage in the state.

In 1870 Spencer's politics became noticeably self-serving. While his anti-Klan speeches earned praise from many Republicans, they also insinuated that scalawag governor William Smith was incapable of stopping the violence. Similarly, his endorsement of Rapier suggested bold progressivism, but it was calculated to alienate those scalawags who found appalling the prospect of a black secretary of state. In short, Spencer deliberately sabotaged the Republican canvass knowing that a Democratic majority in the state house would deny Warner his bid for reelection. After his gamble worked, Spencer emerged as the leading carpetbagger in the state, one who enjoyed a monopoly over patronage. The skullduggery did not end there. In 1872 he used the threat of a party bolt to strong-arm distrustful Republicans into reelecting him to the Senate. His opportunistic successes proved short lived, however, for the Republican Party disintegrated in the mid-1870s, thanks in large part to the very factionalism that Spencer inflamed. In 1879 Democrats happily sent the senator packing with the expiration of his second term. Whatever his real view of Reconstruction, Spencer lacked the political maturity and vision needed to guide a fledgling party through a time of turmoil.[21] *Photo courtesy of National Archives and Records Administration*

At the outset of the campaign of 1870, Sen. George Spencer seemed the epitome of Southern Republican courage. In calling for military force to crush the Klan, he demonstrated a commitment to loyal government. In persuading his party to nominate the black politician James Rapier for secretary of state, he demonstrated a commitment to racial equality. But were these gestures merely a disguise for blatant opportunism? A thirty-four-year-old former Union general from Iowa, Spencer made Tuscaloosa his home in 1865. Actually, his connection to the state started two years earlier,

As he rose to address an outdoor gathering of Republicans in Eutaw (Greene County) on 25 October 1870, Sen. Willard Warner came under a tornado of verbal abuse. "We don't want any damned carpetbaggers around here," whites yelled from the crowd. Warner persevered for nearly an hour before yielding to other guest speakers. The whites, however, had heard enough. Firing pistols randomly into a group of black spectators, they turned the Republican rally into a street riot. Warner escaped to a nearby hotel but had to fend off a group of white pranksters who tried to steal his top hat.

The senator could not know it at the time, but the Eutaw Riot of 1870 presaged the end of his political career. A forty-four-year-old ex-Union general from Ohio, Warner originally came to Alabama to make money. In 1865 he purchased 1,000 acres outside Prattville, where he hired freedmen to help him raise cotton. Apolitical at the time, Warner approved President Johnson's restoration policy as the most sensible approach to bringing former enemies together again in peace. With the advent of Radical Reconstruction, however, Warner joined the state's nascent Republican Party and won election to the U.S. Senate. Under the rules of readmission, his term was truncated to three years. The short term notwithstanding, Warner was elated. "I glory in the progressive spirit which made me a carpet-bagger," he exclaimed to his Senate colleagues in December 1868. Believing that economic prosperity was the key to making Reconstruction succeed, Warner strongly urged Congress to subsidize internal improvements in Alabama and elsewhere in the South. Back home the senator engaged in conciliatory politics that reflected an understanding of both the resentment felt by ex-Confederates and the suspicions held by scalawags. The aspirations of the freedmen rarely figured into Warner's political calculus; his outlook was bipartisan, not biracial. As the Eutaw Riot demonstrated, however, pacific overtures toward ex-Confederates were made in vain. Moreover, Warner succumbed to factionalism within his own party, most notably from fellow carpetbagger George Spencer, who sought unrivaled control over federal patronage. After Democrats gained con-

WILLARD WARNER
copy print

trol of the state house in 1870, Warner did not expect to win reelection to the Senate, but he was disappointed by the small number of Republicans who endorsed his candidacy. "We have in the Southern States as much to fear from bad men in our own ranks as we have from the rebels themselves," he ruminated. In 1872 Warner joined the Liberal Republicans, a high-minded movement that sought to restore integrity to a political process that seemed mired in corruption and backstabbing. The door to higher office in Alabama, however, remained permanently closed to the former senator.[22] *Photo courtesy of Library of Congress*

325

ROBERT BURNS LINDSAY
copy print

On 16 June 1871, Alabama governor Robert Lindsay appeared before a congressional committee that was looking into the outlawry of the Ku Klux Klan. The governor's testimony was a mixture of candor and subterfuge, but overall it exemplified the white South's generally apologetic assessment of Klan terrorism. A forty-six-year-old lawyer from Franklin County, Lindsay immigrated to Alabama from Scotland in the 1840s. A reluctant Rebel during the war, Lindsay briefly served in Roddey's cavalry, but for the most part avoided direct participation. During Reconstruction, he emerged as a moderate leader within the Democratic Party. After winning the governorship in 1870, he spent most of his tenure wrestling with a fiscal crisis brought on by the collapse of the state's reckless railroad ventures. Because his election was tainted by Klan violence, Republicans in Congress interrogated him as part of a huge federal investigation into Southern paramilitary activity. For his part, Lindsay opened by saying that "in regard to the security of life, person, and property, the State of Alabama to-day will compare favorably with its condition in any year or any period since its formation." While he conceded that there was a Klan movement in his state, the governor both denied its political motives and downplayed the extent of its alleged crimes. Instead, he tried to turn the hearing into an indictment of Radical Reconstruction. Lindsay stressed Alabama's "spirit of willing gladness to return to the Union," but then Congress demanded that it ratify the Fourteenth Amendment, "an odious measure of degradation." He then accused Union Leagues of inflaming racial hostility and "that they were banded together for the purpose of committing depredations upon the whites." Finally, he cited black suffrage, "a measure fraught with very unpleasant consequences," as the final act in a social revolution that made "the negro race . . . exceedingly insolent." Therefore, the governor concluded, the rise of the Klan was a perfectly understandable, perhaps even imperative, development. To assuage any skepticism on the part of his listeners, he insisted that he had taken diligent steps toward ferreting out the worst Klan perpetrators, though "the mere bringing of criminals to justice is entirely beyond the duties of the executive." Lindsay's comments helped establish the longstanding mythology of the Klan as a band of heroes in a time of misfortune.[23] *Photo courtesy of ADAH*

ALABAMA STATE SENATE (1872)
copy print

One of the most remarkable features of Reconstruction was the involvement of former slaves in Alabama politics. Case in point, the state senate in 1872, when five freedmen served in that body as Republicans. Clustered together on the right-hand side of a group photograph, the five men exemplify the readiness with which blacks embraced their recently established citizenship. In the back, on the top step, is thirty-year-old John William Jones, a general-store owner from Lowndes County. Standing side by side one step below are Lloyd Leftwich, a thirty-year-old farmer from Greene County, and to his left Benjamin F. Royal, a middle-aged mulatto farmer from Bullock County. Royal was particularly important as a party leader, having organized a 400-member chapter of the Union League. He also served in the state senate longer than any other African American, winning four consecutive elections between 1868 and 1874. Between Leftwich and

Royal, a few steps farther down, is Jeremiah Haralson of Dallas County, who two years later went on to become the third black Alabamian to serve in the U.S. House. Finally, to the right of Haralson is the mulatto Alexander H. Curtis, a forty-one-year-old merchant from Perry County, who gained prominence for his energetic devotion to public education and civil rights. Together these five men belied the longstanding stereotype that defined the freedmen as unfit for full participation in the political life of the South. Unfortunately, the photograph is an anomalous image of short-lived progress. Within a few short years, Democrats gained control of state government and restructured the laws so as to virtually eliminate blacks from public office. African Americans would not serve again in the Alabama state legislature until the late 1960s. *Photo courtesy of ADAH*

ALEXANDER MCKINSTRY
copy print

In February 1873 Alexander McKinstry, the newly elected Republican lieutenant governor, instigated a controversial power grab when he manipulated parliamentary rules to deny Democrats control over the state senate. A forty-nine-year-old jurist from Mobile, McKinstry was one of the more unusual scalawags in the state. Although he strongly opposed secession in 1861, he did serve in the Confederate army, first as the colonel of the 32nd Alabama Infantry and later as provost marshal of the Army of Tennessee. For the first few years of Reconstruction, McKinstry attended to his law practice. By 1869, however, he had joined the Republican Party and was the running mate on David P. Lewis's gubernatorial ticket in 1872. Lewis and McKinstry won the executive race, but both parties

contested the legislative outcome and formed rival state houses. In early December 1872, the Grant administration helped put an end to this nonsense. Under federal supervision, a "fusion" assembly emerged, one where Republicans enjoyed a solid majority in the house and Democrats a tenuous majority of one in the senate. As president of the senate, McKinstry was determined to deny the Democrats their majority, claiming that too many of their candidates had won through fraud and intimidation. When U.S. Attorney General George Williams admonished the lieutenant governor to abide by the settlement, McKinstry vented his exasperation. "We who are natives of the south have been subjected to an ordeal that persons living among civilized people can form no idea or even believe," he explained. "It required rare nerve, bravery, resolution, and self abnegation to be a Republican." On 18 December McKinstry acted on these feelings when he forbade any business on the senate floor until a decision had been rendered in the pending Miller-Martin dispute (State Sen. William Miller was the Republican incumbent representing Butler and Conecuh Counties, Martin his Democratic challenger). On the face of the returns, Martin appeared to have won fair and square, an outcome that gave the Democrats their one-seat majority. But McKinstry dismissed the figures and threw the senate into abeyance until after the Christmas recess. When it reconvened in February, McKinstry took advantage of the absence of one Democratic senator to call a vote on the Miller-Martin case. Naturally, the Republican position prevailed, and Miller took his seat. Democrats cried foul, but the lieutenant governor ignored their protestations, correctly gambling that the federal government would ultimately abide his action. (During the proceedings, McKinstry reportedly kept a pistol stashed in his desk drawer in the event the Democrats caused excessive trouble.) Poetic justice, however, would punish McKinstry for his extralegal tactics. The untimely death of a Republican senator soon after the power play restored the Democrats' one-seat majority. McKinstry ran again for lieutenant governor in 1874, but the Republican ticket went down in defeat.[24] *Photo courtesy of Historic Mobile Preservation Society Archives*

For Charles Hays, Republican congressman from Greene County, the Democrats' "white-liner" campaign in 1874 was the last straw in a spree of political violence going back to the days of the Ku Klux Klan. On 15 September he published a 5,000-word letter that documented, in sensational style, numerous "outrages" against his mostly black constituents in the counties of his western Alabama district. "The killing has all been on one side," he averred. The forty-year-old Hays then called for federal intervention and in February 1875 helped push a Force Bill through the U.S. House. This zealous commitment to Reconstruction belied the congressman's background. Before the war Hays owned a 2,000-acre plantation with 100 slaves. During the war, he served as an aide-de-camp in the Army of Tennessee, seeing action at Shiloh and Chickamauga. But afterward Hays became a scalawag without compunction. To him, emancipation was the new reality, and the Republican Party offered the surest means of modernizing the South. Blacks evidently trusted the former slaveholder (who was apparently a beneficent master), voting for him every time he ran for office; Hays reciprocated by consistently supporting civil-rights legislation. In 1869 he received 17,300 votes in his bid for Congress, easily defeating his two opponents, who together garnered less than 7,000. In 1870 Hays won reelection in a tight race plagued by Klan terrorism, including the disruption of one of his rallies during the Eutaw Riot in October. In 1872 he won again, this time by more than 4,000 votes. And in 1874, the year he wrote his letter condemning racial violence, he prevailed a fourth time against determined opposition. During each campaign, Democratic newspapers vilified Hays, while Rebel vigilantes threatened his life. "I do not know how long it will be before you will hear of my assassination," he once wrote Senator Warner, "but one thing you may count on with certainty and that is that I shall die *game*." After 1874, Democrats did not have to kill Hays. Having gained control of the state government, they simply gerrymandered his district. Hays sensed the imminent demise of Reconstruction

CHARLES HAYS
copy print

during his final term in Congress. He voted for the national Civil Rights Act of 1875, but the new law proved a dead letter. As for the Force Bill he helped sponsor in the House, it never reached the floor of the Senate. Weary and disappointed, Hays retired from politics in 1876, having served in Congress longer than any other Southern Republican during Reconstruction.[25] *Photo courtesy of Library of Congress*

GEORGE SMITH HOUSTON
copy print

In 1874, Democrats nominated George Houston for governor. For most of the Civil War era, Houston had deliberately avoided politics, but pressure to help end the power struggles of Reconstruction compelled him to throw his hat into the ring. A sixty-three-year-old lawyer and railroad investor from Limestone County, Houston's main attraction as a candidate was that he had not alienated anyone. He opposed secession yet remained neutral during the war, even as his two sons served in the Confederate army. He supported early efforts at Reconstruction but carefully steered clear of Republicans, who sought to convert him into a scalawag. Finally, his reputation for business probity, as well as his obvious reluctance to run, suggested to Democrats that he was precisely the man Alabama could trust with gubernatorial power. In a campaign rife with paramilitary intimidation and racist propaganda, Houston navigated above the fray, pledging to rectify the state's financial crisis if elected. And he won (107,000 to 94,000).

While Democrats passed laws (and a new constitution) that essentially neutralized their Republican adversaries for the next century, the governor concentrated on ameliorating the state's credit. When Houston took office, Alabama's debt stood somewhere between $25,000,000 and $30,000,000. He implemented a draconian program of retrenchment. Public salaries were cut, the budget for the school system was reduced, and a line item for public health went unfunded. Also the convict-lease system was reinstituted at a profit. Finally, Houston created a special commission to address the ongoing railroad scandals. Employing some complicated math, the commissioners readjusted downward much of the railroad debt. Furthermore, they transferred holdings from the troubled Alabama and Chattanooga (a Republican-owned railroad in receivership) to companies run by Democrats, including cronies of the governor. The commission's occasionally questionable actions notwithstanding, most Alabamians applauded the Houston administration's dramatic results: Alabama's debt had been reduced to just over $12,000,000. Nominated again in 1876, Houston easily won reelection (95,800 to 55,600), an outcome that markedly demonstrated the Democrats' impregnable hold over the state's election machinery. Thus, George Houston can be seen as both Alabama's last Reconstruction governor and its first Redeemer governor.
Photo courtesy of Library of Congress

With fellow ex-Confederates having already "redeemed" most of the state in 1874, Charles Shelley was determined to prevail in the congressional election of 1876. His district (five Black Belt counties) remained one of the last Republican strongholds in Alabama. Fortunately for the former general, its mostly black electorate was torn between two rival candidates: Jeremiah Haralson, the incumbent, and James Rapier, the most prominent African American in the state. Even so, Shelley was not certain he could corral enough white Democrats to win; the time had come for another round of paramilitary politics. A forty-year-old building contractor from Dallas County, Shelley was best known for his sterling combat record in the western theater during the Civil War. After briefly serving as a captain in the 5th Alabama Infantry, he organized the 30th Alabama Infantry in January 1862, became its colonel, and led it through a gauntlet of savage battles: Port Gibson, Champion Hill, the Vicksburg siege, Chattanooga, and the many engagements around Atlanta. Promoted to brigadier general in September 1864, he saw further action at Franklin and Nashville. After the war Shelley contemplated immigrating to South America but instead devoted himself to revitalizing the Democratic Party. In 1874 he received an appointment as sheriff of Dallas County, having apparently deceived Republican governor David Lewis as to his true political affiliation. Shelley used his position as law enforcer to great advantage in the political campaign of 1876. His deputies constantly harassed black voters and politicos, while surrogates did the same in the other counties of the district. By August the general concluded that Haralson enjoyed greater popularity among black voters, and so he targeted the congressman for special treatment. Shadowing Haralson's movements, Shelley abruptly arrested his opponent after a Republican rally in Cahaba. In a closed room the former Rebel demanded that Haralson sign a statement declaring his intention to withdraw from the race and urging his followers to vote for Shelley. Haralson refused. "You God damned black son of a bitch," Shelley growled as he thrust a Derringer pistol in the congressman's face,

CHARLES MILLER SHELLEY
copy print

"I'll murder you right here." Under duress, Haralson signed. Whether this bogus statement influenced the election is unclear, for the face of the returns left Shelley, with 10,453 votes, about 100 below Haralson's tally of 10,557 (Rapier garnered 7,340). Immediately, Sheriff Shelley persuaded the county canvassing board to toss the votes from eleven precincts on the grounds of unspecified voting irregularities. As a result, the new totals dramatically altered the outcome: Shelley, 9,655; Haralson, 8,675; Rapier, 7,236. The politics of force had worked once again; Shelley took his seat in the U.S. House. He won the next three elections as well.[26]
Photo courtesy of Library of Congress

331

WILLIS JULIAN MILNER
copy print

Overshadowed by the political struggle of Reconstruction in Alabama was the economic rise of Birmingham as the quintessential New South metropolis. Among the pioneers in this phenomenon was Willis Milner, a civil engineer from Butler County. A former major in the 33rd Alabama Infantry, with which he fought and was wounded at both Murfreesboro and Chickamauga, Milner followed the path of capitalism after the war. In this respect he was following in the footsteps of his father, a railroad man and mining entrepreneur. Working for a time as a druggist while completing his education as an engineer, Milner eagerly accepted a job with the South and North Alabama Railroad, an occupation that brought him to Birmingham in early 1871 (the year the city was founded). Milner was twenty-nine years old at the time, and his capacity for organization soon earned him a managerial position with the Elyton Land Company, which was responsible for urban development around the city. "I assumed my new duties and took charge of the books, records and other archives,"

he recollected, "thus beginning business connections and associations which were to continue for more than twenty-five years." During that quarter century, Milner directed numerous projects "of grave importance in the pioneer work" at the time: in 1875 he commenced building Birmingham's water-works system; in 1884 he supervised plans to expand the residential areas; and in 1887 he constructed the Belt Railroad that integrated transportation throughout the city. Although Milner had no direct involvement in the manufacturing of steel, the enterprise for which Birmingham became most famous, he played an indispensable role in creating the infrastructure necessary for industrial success. His youthful dreams of being part of an independent Southern nation may have been shattered by the reality of military defeat, but Milner's no-less-ambitious dream of being part of a modernized New South came much closer to fruition.[27]
Photo courtesy of Birmingham Public Library
Department of Archives and Manuscripts

JEFFERSON MANLY FALKNER
copy print

In 1901 Jefferson Falkner, a fifty-eight-year-old Montgomery lawyer and former Confederate officer, observed that hundreds of Rebel veterans had fallen into poverty and homelessness. He was appalled that men who had served with honor could be so easily cast aside by society. To be sure, Confederate veterans received a small pension from the state, but it was hardly enough to make ends meet. The one-time captain of Company B, 8th Alabama Cavalry decided to rectify this pitiable situation. Donating his own land and money, Falkner erected the Alabama Confederate Soldiers' Home in Chilton County and invited destitute soldiers from all over the state to come and live.

By 1903 he had also persuaded the state legislature to appropriate annual funding for the facility. On the eve of the First World War, the multibuilding Soldiers' Home housed just over one hundred "inmates," as the residents were affectionately called. In addition to room and board, the home provided free medical care with its twenty-five-bed hospital. The facility remained in operation until the last veteran still living there died in 1934. By that time the home's founder had also long since passed away (in 1907), but Captain Falkner's philanthropic vision had enabled many lonely veterans of the Lost Cause to live out their final years in dignity. *Photo courtesy of ADAH*

28th Alabama Infantry Reunion
copy print

On 10 June 1908, veterans of the 28th Alabama Infantry gathered in Birmingham as part of a larger reunion of Civil War units from the state. Thirty-three members of the regiment marked the occasion by posing for a photograph with their old battle flag. Captured at Orchard Knob on 23 November 1863, the flag had been acquired by the state archives in 1905 thanks to the efforts of Director Thomas Owen. Whereas the obverse exhibited the St. Andrew's Cross common to many Confederate banners, the reverse (as displayed in the photograph) presented a unique pattern: a gold-colored, ten-pointed starburst centered on a white background made of silk. The week before the reunion, I. W. McAdory, a former lieutenant in the 28th Alabama, had beseeched Owen, his uncle, to loan his comrades the flag for the special event. Though reluctant to do so, the director complied, thereby granting the aging graybacks one final roll call under the colors of their Lost Cause.

Photo courtesy of ADAH

William Drewey Bowen
copy print

It had been about four decades since Drewey Bowen had last hoisted the colors of the 16th Alabama Infantry. At his request, and based on his memory, a friend reproduced a striking facsimile of Bowen's old regimental flag. Then on a sunny day during the presidency of Theodore Roosevelt, the gray-bearded Rebel one more time raised the banner on high. A farmer from Franklin County, Bowen joined the Russell Valley War Hornets in the summer of 1861. That unit soon became Company H, 16th Alabama, and Private Bowen served as the regiment's color bearer. He was shot in the arm at Shiloh and wounded again at the Battle of Atlanta, but Bowen never relinquished his duty.

"Where the fight was hottest and heroism greatest, Drewey Bowen was always there," fellow veteran John Bankhead once commented, "defiant and unafraid, with the glorious light of battle in his eyes, and his flag to the breeze, an exemplar and inspiration to his comrades." High praise, indeed, yet it is unlikely that the passersby who later witnessed the septuagenarian fumbling with the flag knew anything of this wartime experience. It is also irrelevant, for Bowen knew what that war was about and what that flag meant—a conflict that only men such as him could ever truly understand.[28] *Photo courtesy of ADAH*

Appendix

Abercrombie, Robert Haden

Robert Abercrombie led his consolidated regiment at Nashville, where it ineffectually tried to hold a section of Hood's left flank in that disastrous battle. The colonel went on to North Carolina, where he and his depleted command surrendered with Gen. Joseph Johnston in April 1865. Abercrombie quietly resumed his law practice after the war. He and his wife, Fannie, raised six children. In 1891 Abercrombie was accidentally shot and killed by his son-in-law, who mistook him for a chicken thief.

Adams, Samuel

Samuel Adams was killed in action near Atlanta on 21 July 1864.

Angell, Joseph P.

Joseph Angell's term of service expired in the spring of 1862; it is unclear whether he reenlisted. In 1867 Joseph Angell married and moved to Arkansas, where he earned a living as a jeweler. Angell died in 1909.

Bagby, Simon Connell

Simon Bagby was killed at Fisher's Hill, 22 September 1864.

Bankhead, John Hollis

After recovering from his wound, John Bankhead resumed command of Company K, 16th Alabama. At the Battle of Atlanta on 22 July 1864, he was again wounded but again recovered and led the company until the end of the war. Bankhead became an active Democrat after the war, serving in the state legislature in the 1860s and 1870s. During Reconstruction, he was a member of the Ku Klux Klan. After a successful tenure as warden of the state penitentiary, Bankhead won election to the U.S. House in 1887, a seat he held until moving to the U.S. Senate in 1907. Bankhead died in 1920.

Barnum, David

At his request, David Barnum received a transfer to the Confederate navy, serving at Charleston until mid-1864, when he returned to the 5th Alabama to help offset the regiment's manpower shortage. Unhappy with his reassignment, Barnum appears to have deserted sometime during the final weeks of the war, at some point thereafter settling in St. Louis.

Battle, Cullen Andrews

Cullen Battle later participated in Jubal Early's ill-fated operations in the Shenandoah Valley. There Battle always seemed to have his men at the right place when danger threatened. At Cedar Creek he suffered a leg wound that left him unfit to take the field again. While he recuperated, Battle received promotion to major general, one of only a handful of Alabamians to attain such high rank during the war. In the autumn of 1865, he won election to the U.S. House, but the Republican-controlled Congress refused to seat any of the southern delegates, especially ex-Confederate officers, until new terms of Reconstruction had been established. At that point the former general returned to his law practice; he also briefly commanded a den of the Ku Klux Klan in Macon County. After Reconstruction he moved to North Carolina, where he became a newspaper editor. Battle died in Greensboro on 8 April 1905.

Beck, Franklin King

Franklin Beck ably commanded the 23rd Alabama throughout the siege of Vicksburg, but shortly after his parole following the capitulation, he suffered a serious leg fracture when his horse kicked him. Consequently, the colonel missed much of the Atlanta Campaign. He returned to duty in time to participate in Hood's forays into northern Georgia after Atlanta fell. On 12 October 1864, while conducting reconnaissance near Resaca, enemy cannon fire struck the mounted colonel, killing his horse and sheering off his recently healed leg at the thigh; he bled to death minutes later. Beck was survived by his wife, Martha, and their three children.

Bellamy, Richard Henry

After the surrender of Vicksburg and his parole, Richard Bellamy received a promotion to captain and a battery of his own, one he commanded with honor during the Atlanta Campaign. Shortly after the war Bellamy immigrated to Texas, where he engaged in merchandizing for nearly twenty years before returning to Russell County. In 1885 he married and took up farming. Bellamy died in 1907.

Bibb, Joseph Benajah

Joseph Bibb's 23rd Alabama did not participate in the fighting at Franklin but did push on with the rest of the army to Nashville, where it deployed as part of the right wing. During the Federal attack on 16 December, the 23rd helped repel a series of assaults against the Rebel right, but when the left wing disintegrated, the now-exposed Alabamians nearly bolted. Bibb and others managed to restore order, but as the 23rd was falling back, the colonel went down with a bullet through his lungs. Though he survived, he did not heed the advice of surgeons to retire: "The Confederacy has need of all hers sons," he brashly declared, "and death is preferable to defeat." The colonel returned to duty in time to lead the 23rd Alabama into battle one final time at Bentonville, North Carolina. Afterward, in addition to raising his two sons with his wife, Martha, Bibb actively resisted the process of Reconstruction in Alabama. In 1868, however, when friends urged him to run for a seat in the state legislature, he declined on the grounds of his "unwillingness to serve in a body containing negroes." Bibb never fully recovered from his severe wound and died of tuberculosis on 14 September 1869.[1]

Bickerstaff, James Henry

Though an amputee, Bickerstaff lived a long, prosperous life. In 1867 he married Emma Harrard, with whom he raised seven children. For a number of years, he served as tax collector for Russell County but primarily made his living as a farmer and brick manufacturer. Bickerstaff died on 18 May 1906.

Bickerstaff, William Jefferson

Mortally wounded during the first day's fighting at Murfreesboro, William Bickerstaff died on 14 February 1863.

Black, Thomas D.

Further details of Thomas Black's life are not known.

Bowen, William Drewey

William Bowen died in 1918.

Bozeman, Jefferson Elisha

The historical record for Jefferson Bozeman following the engagement at Montevallo is conflicting: he either withdrew with the main body to Selma, fighting there on 2 April, or he double backed to Tuscaloosa in time to help defend his school against another enemy cavalry column on 3 April. Regardless, the fighting was soon over for the young cadet. Bozeman completed his matriculation at the University of Alabama shortly after the war. He would go on to serve in the state legislature from 1874 to 1876. Bozeman died in 1897.

Brown, Samuel

Further details of Samuel Brown's life are not known.

Buchanan, Franklin

Recovering from his leg wound from the action in Mobile Bay, Franklin Buchanan received a special exchange in February 1865, but he did not participate further in the war. From 1868 to 1870, he served as president of the Agricultural College of Maryland, the forerunner of the University of Maryland. Buchanan died in 1874.

Buford, Jefferson

Frustrated by his trials in Kansas, Jefferson Buford resumed his law practice until the secession crisis. He predictably supported Alabama's secession but due to poor health could not participate in the armed struggle that followed. Buford died of heart of disease in August 1861.

Bullock, Edward Courtenay

In the summer of 1861, Edward Bullock helped organize the 18th Alabama Infantry, winning election as that regiment's colonel. Unfortunately, while stationed at Mobile, Bullock contracted typhoid fever and soon died; his many friends mourned his death. In 1866 the state legislature named a new county in his honor.

Bunn, Silas Mattison

Further details of Silas Bunn's life are not known.

Bunn, William Jasper

Following his wounding and capture at Spotsylvania, William Bunn spent the next seven months in prison at Elmira, New York, before receiving a medical parole. His role in the war was over. Bunn died in 1923.

Busteed, Richard

Richard Busteed died in 1898.

Byers, Joseph Pinson

After the war Joseph Byers moved to Oklahoma, where he died in 1913.

Campbell, John Archibald

During the secession crisis, John Campbell urged restraint but ultimately resigned his seat on the Supreme Court shortly after Alabama left the Union. He tried to act as an intermediary between the rival administrations over Fort Sumter, but his efforts to help preserve peace failed. Unfortunately, his lack of martial zeal tainted his reputation in the Confederacy. Nevertheless, Jefferson Davis appointed Campbell assistant secretary of war, but the position was mostly a sinecure. After the war Campbell moved to New Orleans and began a profitable law practice. In the early 1870s he moved to Baltimore, where he lived with his daughter. During those years, he also participated in two landmark Supreme Court cases, *Slautherhouse* and *Cruikshank*. Campbell died in 1889.

Canby, Edward Richard Sprigg

Edward Canby remained on active duty after the war, but while stationed in California in 1873, he was assassinated by Captain Jack, a chief of the Modoc Indians.

Cannon, William J.

William Cannon recovered from his injuries sustained at Frayser's Farm and returned to duty, receiving a promotion to captain. Cannon served in the 9th Alabama for the duration of the war.

Carter, Cecil

Though he survived and remained on Company A's roster until the war's end, Cecil Carter does not appear to have seen any further combat.

Chadick, Mary Jane

After the war Mary Jane Chadick moved to Tennessee with her husband, William.

Chadick, William Davidson

William Chadick resigned shortly after Shiloh for reasons of poor health. After the war he moved to Tennessee with his wife, Mary Jane. Chadick died in 1878.

Chilton, William Parish

By January 1865 William Chilton came to believe that Congress needed a more direct role in managing the war effort. To this end, the congressman proposed a resolution to create a committee on the conduct of the war, one modeled on its Northern counterpart, that could investigate military setbacks and recommend strategic courses of action. His resolution failed to pass. Nonetheless, the Alabamian remained a dedicated servant of the government right to the end, at which time he returned to his law practice in Montgomery. Chilton died in 1871.

Chitwood, John Campbell

Further details of John Chitwood's life are not known.

Clanton, James Holt

After Shiloh James Clanton's military record reflects a competent officer without any super-human dimensions. He gained promotion to brigadier general in November 1863, a year in which he organized three more cavalry regiments. For the most part, he defended his home state, most notably in trying to stop Rousseau's Raid in July 1864, and by monitoring Union forces around Pensacola. In March 1865 the general suffered a war-ending wound during a skirmish against Union forces advancing toward Mobile. Clanton was a vigorous political organizer during Reconstruction, helping resurrect Alabama's Democratic Party as a counterweight to the state's new Republican Party. In 1871, while fundraising in Tennessee, Clanton was gunned down on the streets of Knoxville by a former Union soldier.

Clanton, Nathaniel Holt

Further details of Nathaniel Clanton's life are not known.

Clare, William H.

While on medical furlough in Huntsville, Alabama, William Clare received a welcome visit from Mary Hadley; the two married in 1864. After recovering, Clare received promotion to major and served as assistant inspector general in the Army of Tennessee for the duration of the war.

Clay, Clement Claiborne

From 1861 to 1863, Clay served in the Confederate Senate. In 1864 the Davis administration sent him to Canada on a secret mission to orchestrate crises along that country's border with the United States. After the war Clay was briefly incarcerated at Fortress Monroe on false charges of complicity in the Lincoln assassination. While there, he occupied a cell adjacent to Jefferson Davis. The former senator was released eventually. Clay died in 1882.

Clayton, Henry DeLamar

Despite his lack of formal military training, Henry Clayton became one of the highest-ranking officers Alabama produced during the Civil War, consistently displaying sound and decisive leadership. In March 1861 he became colonel of the 1st Alabama Infantry, then stationed at Fort Barrancas, Florida. After commanding that unit for a year, he resigned and organized the 39th Alabama Infantry, leading that regiment at Murfreesboro, where he was seriously wounded. After promotion to brigadier general in April 1863, he ably commanded an all-Alabama brigade at Chickamauga and during the early phases of the Atlanta Campaign. Advanced to major general in July 1864, Clayton led a division in the Army of Tennessee, distinguishing himself at the Battles of Atlanta (where his command came closer than any other to breaching the Union lines), Ezra

Church, and Jonesboro. In December 1864 he participated in the Battle of Nashville, where his division bloodily repulsed several enemy attacks and then skillfully covered the general Confederate retreat, sparing Gen. John Bell Hood's army from total destruction. After the war the Alabamian showed little interest in the politics of Reconstruction and spent his postwar years farming and practicing law. Clayton died in 1889.

Clemens, Jeremiah

Jeremiah Clemens did not stay true to his vow. Appointed a major general in the Alabama State Militia, he was responsible for defending the northern part of the state. When Union forces overran the Tennessee Valley in early 1862, however, Clemens resigned his commission and proclaimed his loyalty to the Union. For the next couple of years, he resided in Federal-occupied Huntsville, where he rallied Alabama unionists in preparation for Reconstruction. But the strain of the whole ordeal affected Clemens's health, and he died in 1865, shortly after the war ended.

Cleveland, Morgan Smith

Morgan Cleveland was wounded again in late August 1864 while helping defend the Weldon Railroad. He served with the 8th Alabama through Appomattox. Details of Cleveland's life after the war, though, are not known.

Cobb, Williamson Robert Winfield

Williamson Cobb died of an accidental gunshot wound on 1 November 1864. Unmoved by this tragedy, the Confederate Congress unanimously voted on 17 November to expel its deceased member.

Coles, Robert Thompson

With the exception of writing *From Huntsville to Appomattox*, Robert Coles devoted most of his postwar life to his farm in Huntsville, where he and wife Lucy raised five children. Coles died in 1925.

Conaway, James Madison

James Conaway continued to fight with the 61st Alabama until his capture at Fort Mahone outside Petersburg in the closing days of the war. Paroled in June 1865, he returned to his family and resumed his quiet life of farming, though briefly serving as justice of the peace for Coosa County. Conaway died in 1899.

Conoley, John Francis

John Conoley fell ill during Hood's invasion of Tennessee, but he returned to duty in time to participate in the Battle of Selma, a literal defense of hearth and home for the colonel. After the war he served as probate judge from 1867 to 1874. Conoley died in 1883.

Conoley, Lewis Alexander

Lewis Conoley died of illness on 22 November 1864.

Crenshaw, Edward

It took almost a year for Edward Crenshaw's disfigured face to heal, but he did return to duty—as a marine lieutenant aboard the CSS *Tallahassee*. After the war he held a variety of local government posts in Butler County and in 1874 married Sarah Edith Brittain, raising two children with her. Crenshaw died in 1911.

Croxton, Milton E.

Milton Croxton was killed at Seven Pines, 31 May 1862.

Cumming, Kate

The war left Kate Cumming a bit jaded. "Every thing bespoke the malignity of the foe," she said of the war-torn Georgia countryside, "the modern Tartars had done their work well." But toward the end of her journal, she also indicted thousands of unnamed Southerners for not selflessly sacrificing everything for independence: "Had we been true to our God and country, with all the blessings of this glorious, sunny land, I believe we could have kept the North, with all her power, at bay for twenty years." With sentiments like this, it should come as no surprise that she became a vocal leader in the United Daughters of the Confederacy. In 1874 Cumming moved to Birmingham, where she was active in the Episcopal Church and in Lost Cause memorials. She never married. Cumming died in 1909.[2]

Curry, Jabez Lafayette Monroe

As a lame duck, Jabez Curry continued to promote the war effort until his departure from Richmond in February 1864. Thereafter, he served as a staff officer first in the Army of Tennessee and later in Roddey's Brigade. He was present at the Battle of Selma, where he barely escaped capture only to learn that his wife had died following a prolonged illness. In the spring of 1865, Curry returned home to care for his two young children, now motherless, and contemplate a future much different than the one he envisioned just four years earlier. After the war he became an ordained Baptist minister and dedicated the rest of his life to public education. In 1881 Curry became president of the Peabody Fund, a charity that sponsored biracial education throughout the South, and later helped create the Southern Education Board. He also served as a minister to Spain in the mid-1880s. Curry died in 1903.

Curtis, Alexander H.

Alexander Curtis died in 1878.

Davenport, Edward Henry Vance

Edward Davenport was killed near Groveton, Virginia, on 29 August 1862.

Dawson, Nathaniel Henry Rhodes

First Manassas was all the fighting Nathaniel Dawson ever wanted to see. When his twelve-month enlistment expired in the spring 1862, he resigned his commission and returned home to get married. In 1863 he won election to the Alabama legislature, where he supported the war effort. During the closing months of the war, he commanded a mounted home-guard battalion. Afterward, Dawson resumed his law practice, but he remained actively involved in politics, helping reorganize the Democratic Party in Alabama during Reconstruction and running unsuccessfully for governor in 1882. The brother of Reginald Dawson, Nathaniel died in 1895.

Dawson, Reginald Hebner

After the war Reginald Dawson moved his family to Dallas County. From 1883 to 1897, he served as president of the board of inspectors of state convicts, earning high praise for his humane treatment of Alabama's inmates. The brother of Nathaniel Dawson, Reginald died in 1906.

Deas, Zachariah Cantey

Zachariah Deas continued to command his Alabama brigade in the Army of Tennessee for the duration of the war. Shortly afterward he moved to New York City, where he continued to prosper as a businessman and stockbroker. Deas died in 1882.

DeLoffre, Andre

Out of a job with the burning of the University of Alabama, Andre DeLoffre moved to Mobile, where he taught French until 1875, when he returned to France.

Dollar, John Henry

John Dollar survived his wounds at Atlanta and returned to his unit, serving until the end of the war. Finding his community virtually destroyed by the war, Dollar stoically restarted his life. He resumed farming, built a log house, and fathered five more children with his wife, Mary. Eventually, he opened a blacksmith shop and earned extra income making pottery. All the while he remained active in the Primitive Baptist Church. Dollar died in 1920.

Duggar, Frederick Elijah

Frederick Duggar was killed during the Battle of Peach Tree Creek, 20 July 1864.

Ellison, Joseph Matthew

After the Valley Campaign, Joseph Ellison served in every major engagement in the East through Fredericksburg, after which he resigned his commission; the lieutenant believed that Col. James Cantey and Maj. Alexander Lowther were incompetent regimental officers who had unjustly denied him a captaincy. He later made a clean start as a company commander in a regiment of Georgia cavalry. Ellison survived the war and lived until 1908.

Falkner, Jefferson Manly

Jefferson Falkner died in 1907.

Fariss, Robert Clement

After Shiloh, Robert Fariss received promotion to full colonel, but poor health soon brought his military service to an end. While stationed at Mobile over the summer, he and many of the men of the 17th Alabama succumbed to various campground maladies. The colonel survived but resigned his commission and returned to his home in Montgomery where he remained for the duration of the war. He thereafter worked as a grocer in the city, where he raised seven children with his wife, Catharine. Fariss died on 19 November 1905.

Farragut, David

David Farragut received promotion to full admiral in 1866, the first naval officer in U.S. history to attain that rank. He died in 1870.

Farrand, Ebenezer

After the fall of Spanish Fort and Fort Blakely, Ebenezer Farrand scuttled several of his vessels, including the *Hunstville,* and then steamed the rest up the Tombigbee River to Nanna Hubba Bluff, Alabama. There on 10 May he formally surrendered the last ships of the Confederate navy, far from the open sea. For a few years after the war, Farrand lived in Montgomery, where he sold insurance. In 1871 he moved to Attalla, where he ran a hotel until his death in 1873.

Faust, Charles W.

Charles Faust was killed on 5 May 1864 during the Battle of the Wilderness.

Faust, David C.

Further details of David Faust's life are not known.

Feagin, Isaac Ball

For Isaac Feagin, the Battle of Sharpsburg did not end on that single, bloody day in September 1862. While covering part of the retreat across the Potomac River at Boteler's Mill on the night of 19 September, he suffered a grievous wound from Yankee artillery fire. His convalescence lasted several months, during which time he got married, but upon his return to the 15th Alabama, the captain was placed under arrest. Maj. Gen. D. H. Hill had not forgotten the "haystack episode" and wanted Feagin punished for alleged cowardice. Fortunately, a court-martial acquitted the captain. The testimony of his brigade commander, who insisted that Feagin "behaved with a gallantry consistent with his high reputation for courage," undoubtedly contributed to the verdict. The former merchant went on to become lieutenant colonel in the 15th Alabama, but at Gettysburg he lost his right leg, spent several months in a Union prison, and then received an invalid leave of absence for the duration of the war. Feagin enjoyed a happy postwar life, though. He and his wife, Sallie, raised eight children, while "the colonel" won election as Barbour County sheriff in 1866, Bullock County sheriff in 1876, and probate judge of Barbour County in 1880. Feagin died in 1900.

Figures, Henry Stokes

Henry Figures was killed during the Battle of the Wilderness on 6 May 1864. In 1867 Henry's father recovered his son's body from its makeshift grave in the Wilderness and interred the remains in the Maple Hill Cemetery in Huntsville.

Fitzpatrick, Benjamin

A manifestly weary Benjamin Fitzpatrick avoided direct participation in the Confederacy, preferring instead to reside quietly on his plantation throughout the conflict. He did offer charitable assistance to families and soldiers adversely affected by the war. In 1865 Fitzpatrick served as president of a mandatory constitutional convention, whose purpose was to formally abolish slavery and renounce secession. Soon thereafter, the Republican-controlled Congress repudiated the convention's work, and under the Reconstruction Acts disfranchised the former senator and many other Southern planters. Fitzpatrick died in 1869.

Forsyth, John

John Forsyth resumed editorial partisanship during Reconstruction, attacking the congressional plan and denouncing black freedom. He died in 1877.

Francis, John Clark

John Francis was mortally wounded at Rocky Face Ridge, Georgia, on 9 May 1864, dying two days later.

Fry, Birkett Davenport

In March 1864 Birkett Fry gained a special exchange, received promotion to brigadier general, and helped defend the Confederate left flank at Cold Harbor. He finished the war commanding garrison troops in South Carolina. Disgusted by the defeat of the Confederacy, Fry went into self-imposed exile in Cuba but in 1868 returned to his cotton business in Alabama. In 1881 he moved to Richmond, Virginia, where he continued his cotton trade until his death ten years later. Fry is buried in Oakwood Cemetery, Montgomery, Alabama.

Gaines, John F.

John Gaines was not saved by losing his right leg. Apparently, infection set in at the site of amputation. After months of suffering, Gaines finally died on 19 July 1865.

Galloway, Armistead L.

Armistead Galloway died of disease in Mississippi in the autumn of 1862.

Garland, Landon Cabell

Landon Garland retained his academic presidency throughout the war, even helping orchestrate a brief defense of the campus against Union raiders in 1865, but his dream of transforming the University of Alabama into the West Point of the South died with the Confederacy. In 1866 only one student enrolled for classes, prompting a despondent Garland to resign and accept a teaching position at the University of Mississippi. In 1875 he became chancellor of Vanderbilt University. Garland died in 1895.

Gilmer, James Nicholas

James Gilmer held various commands in the state militia during the 1870s. In 1889 he and his family moved to Seattle, Washington, where the former officer ran a collection agency. Gilmer died in 1920.

Goodgame, John Chapman

After Gettysburg, John Goodgame returned to the 12th Alabama and served until the surrender at Appomattox. A few years later he and his wife, Elverena, emigrated to Texas, where he served as a sheriff until getting killed in a shootout in 1876.

Goodloe, Albert Theodore

Albert Goodloe continued to serve in Company D, 35th Alabama, but the extent to which he participated in later battles is unclear. After the war Goodloe returned to his home near Nashville, where he became a physician.

Gorgas, Josiah

From 1866 to 1869, Gorgas managed the Brierfield Ironworks in Bibb County. He then accepted the vice chancellorship at the University of the South, later briefly serving in 1878–79 as president of the University of Alabama. Retiring to Tuscaloosa, Gorgas died of a stroke in 1883.

Gracie, Archibald

Archibald Gracie was killed in the Petersburg fortifications on 2 December 1864.

Granger, Gordon

Gordon Granger stayed in the regular army after the war, though at his prewar rank of colonel. He died in 1876 while stationed in New Mexico.

Griffin, Elihu Haulby

A couple of months after Gettysburg, Elihu Griffin received a parole and got married while on medical furlough; sadly, his brother Gabriel died in captivity. He later returned to duty but was wounded again near Petersburg in March 1865, then captured again when Grant's army occupied the Confederate capital in April. Griffin resumed his life as a farmer after the war and also joined the Masons. He and his wife, Elvira, raised a dozen children. Griffin died in 1914.

Grigg, Robert Pollard

Further details of Robert Grigg's life are not known.

Grubbs, H. W.

H. W. Grubbs was killed at Mechanicsville on 26 June 1862.

Hale, Stephen Fowler

Stephen Hale died of his wounds in July 1862, three weeks after receiving them during the Battle of Gaines' Mill (27 June).

Hall, Bolling, III

Bolling Hall recovered from his wound received at Chickamauga and became colonel of the 59th Alabama Infantry, a regiment formed from two of the battalions in Hilliard's Legion. The young colonel earned further combat laurels in 1864 at Drewry's Bluff, where he received a terrible thigh wound that incapacitated him for the rest of the war. In February 1866 Hall died from complications stemming from his battlefield wounds.

Haralson, Jeremiah

After leaving Alabama, Jeremiah Haralson held several government jobs in Washington, D.C., and Baltimore. Returning home in 1884, he ran as an independent for Congress but received a paltry 633 votes. Thereafter he lived itinerantly in the Southwest. In 1916, while hunting in Colorado, Haralson was killed by a wild animal.

Hastings, James S.

Further details of James Hastings's life are not known.

Hays, Charles

Charles Hays died in 1879.

Hearn, James Henry

For two months after being wounded at Jonesboro, James Hearn languished in a hospital at Macon, Georgia. It appears that he avoided having his arm amputated, but the sergeant suffered greatly from gangrene poisoning. After recovering from his wound and being furloughed, Hearn tried to make a go of farming in Elmore County. In 1868 he emigrated to Texas, where he finally found the agrarian stability and prosperity that had eluded him for so long in Alabama.

Hentz, Caroline Lee

Caroline Hentz died in 1856, so she never saw the military cataclysm that befell her cherished South. Her two sons, however, served in the Confederate army.

Herbert, Hilary Abner

Hilary Herbert eventually rose to full colonel in the 8th Alabama, ably leading the regiment at Gettysburg. At the Wilderness in May 1864, he received a disabling wound to his left arm that ended his military service. In 1867 Herbert married Ella Bettie Smith, with whom he raised three children. Herbert also emerged as one of Alabama's most important politicians in the post-war decades. Beginning in 1876, he won the first of eight consecutive terms to the U.S. House of Representatives, after which he served as secretary of the navy for the entirety of Grover Cleveland's second term (1893–97). A proponent of sea power, Herbert played a significant role in modernizing the U.S. Navy. Many of the warships commissioned during his years in Washington, D.C., went on to help win the Spanish-American War. Herbert died in 1919.

Herndon, Thomas Hoard

For his substantial role in the Battle of Atlanta, Thomas Herndon received praise up and down the chain of command. It would be many months before he could return to action, but the colonel did participate in one more fight: at Spanish Fort near Mobile. Herndon moved to Mobile after the war and soon returned to politics. A Democrat, he ran unsuccessfully for governor in 1872 but in 1878 won the first of three consecutive terms to the U.S. House. Herndon died in office in 1883.

Higley, John Hunt

John Higley increasingly served as acting brigade commander throughout the Atlanta Campaign, most notably during the big battle east of that city on 22 July. Toward the end of the summer, he received a leave of absence and does not appear to have returned. Perhaps Higley resented serving under the erratic General Baker without proper acknowledgement or consideration for promotion. In any event, history has at least recognized his solid contribution to the Confederate war effort. Once that war ended, though, he became a cotton factor and operated an insurance business in Mobile. Higley died in 1889.

Hobson, Edwin Lafayette

Edwin Hobson gained promotion to full colonel a month after his brilliant performance at Cedar Creek and retained command of Battle's former brigade until the end of the war. In November 1865 he married Fannie Archer, the woman to whom he described his exploits at Cedar Creek and the daughter of the owner of the Tredegar Iron Works. Together they raised ten children and eventually settled in Richmond, Virginia, where the former officer worked for his father-in-law. Hobson died in 1901.

Hodgson, Joseph

Joseph Hodgson later led the 7th Alabama Cavalry at the Battle of Selma, but the nighttime excursions around Nashville remained a highlight of the colonel's military experience. He stayed in Montgomery after the war, working as a newspaper propagandist for the Democratic Party during Reconstruction. In 1870 Hodgson won election to superintendent of public education in the state. He and his wife, Florence, raised three sons. Hodgson died in 1913.

Hopkins, Juliet Opie

Widowed in 1865 and bankrupted by the war, Juliet Hopkins moved to New York, where she lived with a relative. Later she moved to Washington, D.C., where she spent her last years. Hopkins died in 1890.

Houston, George Smith

In 1878 George Houston won election to the U.S. Senate, replacing the much-despised carpetbagger George Spencer. He only served one year before his death in 1879.

Huckabee, Caswell Campbell

C. C. Huckabee served briefly in the Alabama Senate (1865–66) but devoted most of his time trying to reclaim ownership of the Brierfield Ironworks. In 1872 the U.S. Supreme Court rejected his case on the grounds that the ironworks had become subject to the "right of conquest," meaning that the U.S. government could dispose of the facility as it saw fit. In 1882, however, Huckabee managed to become a joint owner once again almost twenty years after the Confederacy confiscated it from him.

Huguley, George Whitfield

George Huguley retained command of the 59th Alabama but was on a leave of absence when the regiment surrendered in April 1865. He later accompanied Jefferson Davis during part of the Confederate president's flight from Richmond. Huguley died in 1889.

Hurst, Marshall B.

Although Marshall Hurst served with the 14th Alabama until the final surrender in 1865, the two battles in June 1862, Frayser's Farm and particularly Gaines' Mill, remained his most vivid memories of the whole war. After the surrender Hurst resumed

his teaching career in Chambers County. In November 1865 he married Nannie F. Glasgow, with whom he raised two children. Over time Hurst became prominent in county affairs, serving as justice of the peace and as the county's unofficial historian. In 1905 he entertained his old comrades at a reunion of the 14th Alabama by playing the same fife that he had carried during the war. Four years later Hurst died after a prolonged illness.

Hutton, Aquila D.

Aquila Hutton recovered from his wound but did not return to the 36th Alabama; instead, he later joined a home-guard cavalry unit. After the war he worked for a commission house in New Orleans. While there in 1870, Hutton contracted pneumonia and died in August.

Hutton, William Bryan

William Hutton was mortally wounded on 3 May 1863 during the Battle of Chancellorsville.

Jackson, James Washington

After Cedar Mountain James Jackson fell ill but recovered in time to fight at Sharpsburg, where he was wounded in the arm. He again fell ill for an extended period, yet at Gettysburg was present to lead the 47th Alabama as a full colonel. He collapsed from heat exhaustion on the second day of that battle and never recovered his health, resigning from the Confederate service. Jackson died in July 1865.

Johnson, William Arthur

William Johnson eventually recovered from his wound, though only in time to surrender with his command in May 1865. Afterward he settled in Tuscumbia, where he earned a respectable living as a planter and cotton broker. Johnson died in 1891.

Johnston, Samuel Burr

Samuel Johnston was killed at Seven Pines on 1 June 1862.

Jones, Harvey Ellis

Ostensibly completing his education after the war, Harvey Jones married Marion Wilmer in 1869. For many years, he worked as a state railroad and tax commissioner before serving as a staff member for two Alabama governors, Thomas Jones and William Oates.

Jones, John William

In the 1890s John Jones worked as a revenue collector in Mobile. He died in 1909.

Jones, Richard Channing

Richard Jones recovered from his wound received at New Market Heights and eventually returned to duty, though not before getting married in October 1864. He was with his brigade at the final surrender the following year. Jones returned to his law practice after the war. He intermittently held various public offices, including brigadier general in the state militia in the late 1870s and state senator in the mid-1880s. From 1890 to 1897 Jones served as president of his alma mater, the University of Alabama. In 1901 he represented Wilcox County at the state constitutional convention. Jones died in 1903.

Jones, Robert Tingnal

Robert Jones was killed in action during the Battle of Seven Pines, 31 May 1862.

Jones, Thomas Goode

Thomas Jones simultaneously pursued planting and law after the war, but crop failures plunged him into debt. In the 1870s he entered politics as a Democrat, serving in turn as a city alderman, a state legislator, and finally as governor from 1890 to 1894. All the while Jones held the rank of colonel in the state militia. He also served as a judge and represented Montgomery County in the constitutional convention of 1901. Jones died in 1914.

Jowers, Joseph Demarcus

Joseph Jowers soon recovered from his wounds received at Frayser's Farm and served with the 8th Alabama through the Gettysburg Campaign, after which he was assigned to the provost guard of the Army of Northern Virginia.

Kelly, Samuel Camp

Samuel Kelly saw further action during the subsequent siege of Vicksburg. Paroled after that city's capitulation, he went on to fight at Chattanooga, Atlanta, Nashville, and Bentonville. Little is known of his postwar life other than that Kelly died in 1891.

Kidd, Reuben Vaughn

Reuben Kidd was killed at Chickamauga on 19 September 1863. A year after the war ended, Kidd's sisters sought to recover their brother's body, but his battlefield grave was never found.

Kimbrough, Julius A.

Julius Kimbrough was killed during the Battle of Sharpsburg, 17 September 1862.

Labuzan, Greene Marshall

Greene Labuzan would never again see his foe in battle, and in fact had not really "seen" him at all in Tuscaloosa, but he could take satisfaction in having played a very real, albeit very small, part in the larger saga of the Civil War. Labuzan became a lawyer after the war, but no further details of his life are known.

Lakin, Josephus Holtzclaw

J. H. Lakin died in 1909.

Lamkin, Thomas Peters

Thomas Lamkin was a proud participant in many veteran reunions after the war. He died around 1927, though the date is uncertain.

Lampley, Charles Harris D.

Harris Lampley was mortally wounded during the Battle of Atlanta; he died on 24 August 1864.

Law, Evander McIvor

After recovering from the wound received at Cold Harbor, Evander Law requested a new assignment with the cavalry. Thus, in the final months of the war, he commanded a brigade of horsemen as part of Joseph Johnston's operations in North Carolina. Resuming his teaching career after the war, Law eventually returned to South Carolina, where he dabbled in railroads, before finally settling in Florida, where he taught military science and edited a local newspaper. Law died in 1915.

Leadbetter, Danville

After the war Danville Leadbetter fled first to Mexico, then to Canada, where he died in 1866.

Leftwich, Lloyd

Lloyd Leftwich died in 1918, a victim of the Influenza Pandemic.

Leonard, John Owen

John Leonard recovered from his wound and a month after Chickamauga earned promotion to first lieutenant. The young officer fought with Company K until receiving a disabling leg wound at Ezra Church on 28 July 1864. But he did not long survive the war. Leonard moved to Florida, where he married Laura A. Blake in December 1865, but sadly died four years later on Christmas Day.

Lindsay, Robert Burns

A few months after leaving office, Robert Lindsay suffered a stroke and remained an invalid for the rest of his life. Lindsay died in 1902.

Little, George

George Little saw extensive action with Lumsden's Battery throughout the war, rising to the rank of captain. Thanks to his fluency in German, he also served on occasion as an interpreter for German American soldiers who deserted the Union army or were captured in battle. At Nashville in December 1864, the scholar turned soldier received a chest wound from a shell fragment. The war ended before he could return to duty. He resumed teaching afterward and also conducted numerous geological surveys of Mississippi and other parts of the Deep South. Little died in 1924.

Locke, Michael B.

Michael Locke died in 1871.

Logan, Andrew

In November 1863 Andrew Logan received promotion to sergeant, a rank he held until his discharge in July 1865. He presumably saw other action with his regiment, but his involvement in Streight's Raid was his most memorable experience. After returning home, Logan moved to Marion County, where he resumed farming. In 1876 he married Catherine Cothern, with whom he raised seven children. Logan died in 1911.

Lomax, Tennent

Tennent Lomax was killed at Seven Pines on 1 June 1862.

Lowery, William Fletcher

William Lowery died in 1920.

Loyd, William Pleasant

William Loyd married Margaret soon after the war and at some point moved to Mobile. Loyd died in 1901.

Lumsden, Charles L.

Charles Lumsden completed his Confederate service with the garrison around Mobile. He was killed in a sawmill accident in 1867.

MacIntyre, Edward Legare

Edward MacIntyre died of a morphine overdose in either 1865 or 1869.

Maffitt, John Newland

In February 1864, for reasons of health, John Maffitt relinquished command of the CSS *Florida*. He briefly skippered the ironclad *Albemarle* and finished the war as captain of the blockade-runner *Owl*. For a few years afterward, Maffitt served in the British merchant marine. He retired to Wilmington, N.C. Maffitt died in 1886.

Manasco, Jeremiah

Jeremiah Manasco died on 1 May 1862 from wounds received during the Battle of Shiloh.

Marrast, John Calhoun

Placed on indefinite sick furlough after Shiloh, John Marrast died in his Mobile home on 14 December 1863. He left behind Harriet, his wife of fourteen years, and their seven children.

Maury, Dabney Herndon

Dabney Maury returned to his native Virginia, where he founded a boy's school in Fredericksburg. In 1868 he helped organize the Southern Historical Society. Later in life he moved to Illinois to live with his son. Maury died in 1900.

Maury, Henry

Henry Maury survived his wound and, in the summer of 1863, led the 32nd Alabama in various attempts to relieve besieged Rebel forces at Vicksburg. In early 1864 he took command of the 15th Confederate Cavalry, serving with that unit along the Gulf Coast until the end of the war. Maury returned to his mercantile business in Mobile after the war and died in 1869.

Maxwell, James Robert

James Maxwell remained with Lumsden's Battery for the duration of the war. Afterward he wrote a lively account of his wartime experience in the unit. No further details of Maxwell's life are known.

McClelen, Bailey George

Bailey McClelen went on to fight in battles of greater significance—Second Manassas, Sharpsburg (where he was wounded), Chancellorsville, and Gettysburg (where he was again wounded and also captured)—but Dranesville always retained special meaning for the young man. Exchanged in September 1863, he received a discharge on account of his wounds and served in a home-guard unit for the duration of the war. Toward the end of the conflict, McClelen married Louisia Cordelia Walker, with whom he raised five children on a farm of some 200 acres. For more than forty years, he served as the surveyor of Calhoun County before his death in 1925.

McClellan, William Cowan

In early 1865 William McClellan returned to the ranks of the 9th Alabama and was captured shortly before Lee's final surrender at Appomattox. After returning to Limestone County, he married and took up farming. Unfortunately, after only a few years, he suffered apparent kidney failure, a health problem perhaps connected to his wartime ordeal. McClellan died in 1869.

McDaniel, James N.

Further details of James McDaniel's life are not known.

McInnis, Samuel N.

Samuel McInnis recovered from the wound he received during the Battle of Atlanta and served in Company A until the end of the war. Paroled in Georgia in May 1865, he returned home to a life of obscurity.

McKenzie, John C.

John McKenzie recovered from his wound received at Frayser's Farm. But in November 1862 he con-tracted a camp illness that forced him to resign his commission the following month. McKenzie later returned to the Confederate service in Stuart's Cavalry Battalion, a unit that operated in northern Alabama.

McKinstry, Alexander

Alexander McKinstry died in 1879.

McLemore, Owen Kenan

Owen McLemore was mortally wounded during the defense of Turner's Gap on 14 September 1862. He died sixteen days later.

McLeod, William A.

William McLeod was killed during the Battle of Ezra Church, 28 July 1864.

Middleton, William Armstrong

William Middleton spent the rest of the war as an invalid garrison soldier in Charleston, South Carolina. Afterward he fathered a prominent Alabama lawyer, but no further information on his life was discovered.

Milner, Willis Julian

Willis Milner died in 1921.

Mims, William J.

After a sixty-day furlough, William Mims returned to duty, received a promotion to major in November 1864, and was acting commander of the 43rd Alabama when it surrendered at Appomattox. Afterward, he and his family struggled to make ends meet during the early years of Reconstruction. That all changed, however, with the development of

Birmingham into a New South industrial city. The growing urban center raised the value of Mims's 800-acre cotton farm and increased the clientele for his law practice. Throughout these years, Mims was an active leader within the state's Democratic Party, and in the 1880s he served as tax collector for Jefferson County. He may not have been the country squire of his antebellum dreams, but the former major was among the minority of ex-Confederates who actually saw their net worth expand after the war. Mims died in 1891.

Mitchell, Julius Caesar Bonaparte

Shortly after Murfreesboro, Julius Mitchell defended the honor of Alabama when he and two other Alabama colonels submitted a petition of protest against Lt. Gen. Leonidas Polk, the corps commander, whose official report praised only the role South Carolinians played in the brigade attack on 31 December 1862. Colonel Manigault endorsed the petition, stressing the "heroic courage and fortitude displayed by [the Alabama regiments] on that bloody field." Subsequently, Mitchell served with the 34th Alabama through the Battle of Missionary Ridge, at which time he resigned his commission for health reasons and returned to Montgomery, where he served in the conscript bureau. After the war he resumed planting and also served as a railroad executive. Over the course of his life, Mitchell married twice, first to Jane Murdock, then after her death to her sister, Rebecca; with them he had three children. Mitchell died in Montgomery on 4 October 1869.

Moody, Young Marshall

After an extended medical furlough, Young Moody returned to command of the 43rd Alabama. In December 1864 he took over the brigade upon the death of Archibald Gracie and in March 1865 received promotion to brigadier general. He was captured one day before Lee's formal surrender at Appomattox. Moody and his wife, Floyd, took up residence in Mobile after the war. Before he could resume his business career, however, Moody died of yellow fever in the summer of 1866.

Moore, Richard N.

Richard Moore never recovered from the wound received in the attack on Snodgrass Hill; he died in October 1863, a month after the Battle of Chickamauga.

Moore, Sydenham

For a few weeks following Seven Pines, Sydenham Moore seemed to rally, but by midsummer his condition grew worse. On 20 August 1862 the colonel died of his wounds, leaving behind his wife of twenty years, Amanda Melvina, and their nine children. Their oldest son, Alfred, survived his father by only one year, falling at Chickamauga in September 1863.

Moren, Edward Hawthorne

Technically part of the home guard, Edward Moren hardly expected to do any real fighting and likely received word of Montgmery's surrender on 12 April 1865 with great relief. A war that held absolutely no glory for him had come to an end at last. The doctor continued his medical practice after the war but also pursued politics as a Democrat, serving as lieutenant governor (1871–73) and state senator (1884–85). Moren died in 1886.

Morgan, John Tyler

John Morgan denounced the North's Reconstruction policy after the war. In 1876 he won election to the U.S. Senate, where he served for the next thirty years. If fame eluded him as a general, it came as a senator, for he was the driving force in Congress behind U.S. efforts to secure rights to the Panama Canal. Morgan died in 1907.

Mundy, Frank Henry

Sent to the prison facility at Johnson's Island, Ohio, following his capture at Gettysburg, Frank Mundy remained there until the end of the war. Upon returning to Greene County after the war, he earned a living as a tax assessor; married his long-time sweetheart, Mary Jarvis Ustick, with whom he raised three children; and harassed local carpetbaggers during Reconstruction. Mundy died in 1896.

Murphey, Virgil S.

After being captured at Franklin, Virgil Murphey's personal ordeal only worsened. He was first interrogated by various Union staff officers, with whom he exchanged feeble words of bravado. Next, the colonel and over a hundred of his fellow countrymen were herded through the streets of Nashville, where freedwomen lining the way filled the air with curses. Finally, he arrived at the Union prison camp on Johnson Island, Ohio. Though demoralized by his fate, Murphey took pride in his belief that Franklin would forever stand as "a monument, as enduring as time to Southern valor." He survived the war and returned to his law practice. Murphey died of typhoid in 1890.[3]

Nall, Ducalion

Ducalion Nall never recovered from the wound he received at the Wilderness on 6 May 1864; he died later that autumn.

Norris, Thomas P.

Thomas Norris died in a Union prisoner-of-war camp during the war.

Nott, Josiah Clark

Disgusted by Reconstruction, Dr. Josiah Nott left Mobile in 1867. He soon settled in New York, where he resumed his medical practice and helped pioneer the new medical discipline of gynecology. Nott died of tuberculosis in 1873. When his body returned to Mobile for burial, the city conducted one of the largest funeral processions in its history.

Oates, William Calvin

William Oates continued to serve with distinction after Gettysburg, losing his right arm during an action around Petersburg in August 1864, but it was the dramatic failure and tragic losses at Little Round Top that would haunt the colonel for the rest of his life. Nevertheless, Oates enjoyed a distinguished political career following the war. Affiliating with the Democratic Party, he served in the state legislature throughout the 1870s, in the U.S. House throughout the 1880s, and was governor from 1894 to 1896. During the Spanish-American War, he held the honorary rank of brigadier general (and famously quipped, "I am now a Yankee general, formerly a Rebel colonel, right each time.") In 1901 he represented Henry County at the state constitutional convention. Oates died in 1910.

Oliver, Starke Hunter

Starke Oliver returned to command of his company for the duration of the Atlanta Campaign. By the end of the war, however, he had attained the rank of brevet lieutenant colonel in the consolidated 24th/28th/34th Alabama Infantry Regiment. After the war Oliver returned to Mobile, where he resided until his death in 1896. His postwar years were presumably happy ones as he and his wife, Kate, raised seven healthy children.

Owens, Robert Phillip

Robert Owens was mortally wounded and died at Franklin on 30 November 1864.

Parsons, Lewis Eliphalet

Although he denounced Radical Reconstruction, Lewis Parsons officially joined the Republican Party in 1869, in part because he embraced its economic vision but also in order to control its largely black constituency. Parsons died in 1895.

Pate, W. A.

Returning to duty after recovering from his wounds received at the Wilderness, W. A. Pate endured to the very end. After receiving his parole, he returned to his life of obscurity in Coosa County.

Patton, Robert Miller

When his term came to an end in July 1868, Robert Patton devoted the rest of his public life to promoting various railroad projects. Patton died in 1885.

Pelham, John

John Pelham was killed at Kelly's Ford, Virginia, on 17 March 1863.

Pettus, Edmund Winston

After the war Edmund Pettus resumed his law practice in Selma. In 1897 he won election to the U.S. Senate as a Democrat and died in office in 1907. In 1930 the state named a bridge across the Alabama River at Selma in his honor. On 7 March 1965 this bridge became the scene of a civil-rights-era atrocity—the infamous "Bloody Sunday" attack.

Phelan, Watkins

Watkins Phelan led Company F, 3rd Alabama Infantry for the duration of the war. Unfortunately, on 2 April 1865, Phelan was killed during the Army of Northern Virginia's general retreat from Petersburg. One week later his regiment stacked its arms in surrender.

Phillips, Philip

Philip Phillips declined serving a second term and returned to his law practice in 1855. He opposed secession and tried to leave the South in 1861, but his wife, Eugenia, was an ardent Confederate whom

Federal authorities briefly incarcerated in 1862 on charges of espionage. Thereafter, the two maintained a low profile until the end of the war. At that point Phillips moved to Washington, D.C., where he opened a law practice and argued over 400 cases before the U.S. Supreme Court. Phillips died in 1884.

Phillips, William Jackson

William Phillips languished at Rock Island Prison until the end of the war. On his return to Cherokee County, he discovered that his mother had passed away. A bit later he found happiness when he married Marry Frances Thornton, with whom he raised six children on a small farm in a log cabin he built with his own hands. Phillips died in 1923.

Pickett, Richard Orrick

During one of the 35th Alabama's engagements as rear guard for Van Dorn's army following the defeat at Corinth, Richard Pickett somehow fell into enemy hands. Fortunately, his captivity was brief, and he was soon exchanged. Shortly after returning to his unit, Pickett petitioned the Confederate government for a position as judge advocate general. When his request went unanswered, he resigned from the 35th Alabama to command the 10th Alabama Cavalry, a regiment that mostly patrolled the northern counties of the state. After the war he practiced law in Florence and served in the Alabama legislature (1886–87). Pickett died in 1898.

Posey, Sidney Cherry

During the war, Sidney Posey represented Lauderdale County in the state legislature, where his behavior evinced political neutrality. Under Reconstruction governor Lewis Parsons, he served as a circuit judge. Posey died in 1868.

Proskauer, Adolph

After Gettysburg, Adolph Proskauer periodically served as acting regimental commander until a neck wound at Spotsylvania in 1864 knocked him out of the war for good. Afterward he earned a living as a cotton merchant. A member of the state legislature in 1869, Proskauer joined the minority of seventeen who voted against ratifying the Fifteenth Amendment. In 1895 he moved to St. Louis. Proskauer died five years later.

Purifoy, John

John Purifoy stayed with the Jeff Davis Artillery until the unit was virtually destroyed at Spotsylvania in May 1864. After the war he actively engaged in state politics and government. Beginning in 1880, Purifoy served as (in order) a probate judge, a state legislator, a state auditor, a tax commissioner, the state treasurer, and the secretary of state. He married late in life, but he and his wife, Elizabeth, raised eight children. Purifoy died in 1927.

Ramsey, David Wardlaw

For three months after the *Mississippi's* destruction, David Ramsey increasingly shifted from commanding a shore battery to defending a line of entrenchments to the north of Port Hudson. A Union army under Maj. Gen. Nathaniel Banks invested the city in May 1863 and captured it in July. Ramsey spent the rest of the war as a prisoner on Johnson's Island, Ohio. After returning home, he married, completed his medical degree, and in 1883 was ordained a Baptist minister. Ramsey died in 1916.

Rapier, John Lawrence

John Rapier settled in Mobile after the war. In 1866 he became a newspaperman, eventually becoming the owner of the *Mobile Register*. From 1894 to 1897, he served as Postmaster of Mobile. Rapier died in 1905.

Richardson, Nicholas Davis

Nicholas Richardson died in Nashville in 1895.

Robbins, William McKendree

Within a matter of days after his wounding in the Wilderness, William Robbins returned to duty and served with the 4th Alabama until its surrender at Appomattox. He moved to North Carolina shortly after the war. There Robbins served as a Democrat in the U.S. House from 1873 to 1879. He also served on the Gettysburg Battlefield Commission that erected many of the markers identifying the location of Confederate brigades during that battle. Robbins died in 1905.

Roddey, Philip Dale

In August 1863 Philip Roddey gained promotion to brigadier general and continued to lead his brigade as the "Defender of North Alabama." In addition to harassing Union operations in the Tennessee Valley, he fought at Brice's Cross Roads and participated in Hood's invasion of Tennessee. Shortly after his involvement in the defeat at Selma in 1865, the general surrendered with Nathan Bedford Forrest. There is also some evidence to suggest that by the end of 1864, Roddey had met with Union military authorities for the purpose of negotiating Alabama's withdrawal from the Confederacy. After the war he lived for a time in Tuscaloosa before moving to New York, where he engaged in business. Roddey died in 1897 in London, where he had gone to negotiate the terms of a patent.

Rousseau, Lovell Harrison

After his successful 1864 raid on the Montgomery and West Point Railroad, Lovell Rousseau returned to Tennessee, where he helped repel Hood's invasion later that year. After leaving the service in November 1865, Rousseau won election to the U.S. House as a Republican. Returning to active duty in 1867, he went to Alaska to help finalize the nation's purchase of that territory. Afterward Rousseau assumed command of the Department of Louisiana until his death in 1869.

Royal, Benjamin F.

Further details of Benjamin Royal's life are not known.

Royston, Young Lea

Young Royston spent the rest of the war as the post commander at Selma. Afterward he lived as a cotton factor in Selma. He never married. Royston died in 1884.

Samford, William James

William Samford spent the next eighteen months after Champion Hill at the Union prison camp on Johnson's Island, Ohio. Happily, his incarceration was not unpleasant, for one of his college professors was also a prisoner and agreed to resume his instruction of the youth until the two were exchanged in early 1865. For the young man, the Civil War was not necessarily the defining period of his life. In 1865 Samford married Caroline Drake, with whom he raised eight children. Two years later he passed the bar and started a law practice in Opelika. Beginning in the early 1870s, he engaged in politics, which became his passion for the next three decades and culminated in his gubernatorial victory in 1900. His tenure as governor, however, was short lived; Samford died on 11 June 1901.

Sanders, John Caldwell Calhoun

John Sanders was killed at Globe Tavern, south of Petersburg, on 21 August 1864.

Sands, Robert Martin

Robert Sands remained with the 3rd Alabama Infantry for the duration of the war, rising to lieutenant colonel after the Battle of Gettysburg, where he was wounded in the leg. Sands died in 1903.

Sansom, Emma

In 1864 Sansom married Christopher B. Johnson, with whom she raised seven children. In either 1868 or 1879, she and her family moved to Texas, where Sansom died in 1900. In 1906 the United Daughters of the Confederacy erected a monument in her honor in Gadsden, Alabama.

Scott, Alfred Lewis

Alfred Scott remained with the 9th Alabama until his capture at Hatcher's Run in February 1865. After the war he farmed in Alabama for several years before immigrating to Texas with one of his brothers. He became a civil engineer in San Antonio. Scott died in 1915.

Scruggs, Lawrence Houston

On 3 July 1863, Lawrence Scruggs and his 4th Alabama Infantry helped beat back a Union cavalry attack at Gettysburg before limping off the field with the rest of the defeated Army of Northern Virginia. Although wounded again at Chickamauga, he served with the regiment until its surrender at Appomattox. Scruggs returned to the cotton business after the war and in 1872 married Mary Emma Cooley, with whom he raised five children.

Searcy, James Thomas

James Searcy saw action once again at Murfreesboro, but fell into Yankees hands when he stayed behind on the field to tend to his badly wounded brother, Reuben. When his younger brother died a few days later, James went to Camp Morton Prison in Indiana, where he stayed until exchanged in April 1863. "I return to Dixie glad enough to get back," he declared afterward, "and more fixed in my opinion of the Justice of our cause." He did not, however, return to Lumsden's Battery, serving instead as a sergeant major in the Army of Tennessee's reserve artillery battalion. Two years after the war, Searcy fulfilled his dream of becoming a doctor. Moreover, in 1868 he married Annie Ross, with whom he raised twelve children. From 1892 to 1919, Dr. Searcy held the office of superintendent of the Alabama Insane Hospital. Searcy died on 6 April 1920.[4]

Semmes, Raphael

Returning to the Confederacy shortly after his ship went down, Raphael Semmes commanded the James River Squadron at Richmond during the final days of the war, holding rank as both a rear admiral and a brigadier general. He practiced law after the war. Semmes died in 1877.

Sheats, Charles Christopher

Chris Sheats participated in the 1865 state convention that ratified the Thirteenth Amendment and repudiated the ordinance of secession. He joined the Republican Party but found the politics of Reconstruction frustrating. In honor of his wartime service, he gained appointment as consul to Denmark (1869–73) and later won election to one term in the U.S. House (1873–75). Sheats died in 1904.

Shelley, Charles Miller

After serving four consecutive terms in Congress, Charles Shelley accepted a position in the Treasury Department during the first Cleveland administration. In the 1890s he settled in Birmingham, where he practiced law. Shelly died in 1907.

Sherrod, Frederick Oscar Alexander

Frederick Sherrod fought with the 16th Alabama until he was captured during Hood's invasion of Tennessee in 1864. He settled in Birmingham after the war. In 1888 Sherrod succumbed to a spinal disease that impaired his brain before finally killing him.

Shorter, John Gill

John Shorter never regretted his conduct as governor and accepted his defeat with humility. He returned to his law practice in Eufaula, where he remained for the duration of the war. Afterward Shorter lived a private life until his death from tuberculosis in 1872.

Slaughter, John Nicholson

John Slaughter remained with of the 34th Alabama for the duration of the war. Though he frequently served as acting regimental commander and was wounded during the Battle of Atlanta and again at Nashville, he never rose above the rank of major. After the war Slaughter reunited with his wife, Celia; bought a farm; and fathered three children. Beginning in 1880, he became active in state politics as a Democrat. Slaughter died in 1909.

Smith, John Bass

John Smith lingered for weeks in a hospital before finally dying of his gunshot wounds later that summer. The lieutenant colonel's body servant, a slave named Tobe, returned to Jefferson County with his master's possessions, which included a gold Swiss watch, which became a treasured heirloom for generations of the Smith family.

Smith, Richard Huey

Evacuated to a hospital in Macon, Richard Smith's left arm was amputated at the elbow by surgeons. In September 1864 he returned home to face the challenge of having to farm with only one good arm. Though maimed, Smith did prosper during the postwar years. Evidently, one of his family's former slaves pitched in around the farm. Over time, Dick and Malinda raised a family that helped out as well. In all, the couple had six children, three of whom reached adulthood. A private man for most of life, Smith became something of a celebrity in the small town of Nectar, where he lived until his death on 15 December 1915.

Smith, William Russell

In the autumn of 1861, "Little Billy" Smith helped raise the 26th Alabama Infantry, serving as that regiment's first colonel. After winning a seat in the new Confederate Congress, however, he resigned his commission (and was reelected in 1863); Representative Smith worked to temper the war powers of Jefferson Davis. In 1865 he ran unsuccessfully for governor, but otherwise took no significant part in Reconstruction. After serving briefly as president of the University of Alabama, he returned to his law practice. In 1879 Smith moved to Washington, D.C., where he resided until his death in 1896.

Spencer, George Eliphaz

After losing his senate seat, George Spencer worked for a time as a lobbyist in Washington, D.C., before accepting a position as federal railroad commissioner. Sometime in the 1880s he moved to Nevada, where he made money investing in the region's silver mines. Spencer died in 1893.

Stabler, Malachi Lamar

Exchanged in February 1865, Malachi Stabler joined Company A, 38th Alabama Infantry in time to participate in the fighting around Spanish Fort. Stabler's fate thereafter is unknown, except that he died in 1925.

Stedham, James M.

Shipped to Camp Morton, Indiana, following his capture at Resaca on 15 May 1864, James Stedham developed acute dysentery, from which he died in March 1865.

Stewart, Jonathan Milton

Jonathan Stewart spent the remaining weeks of the war in various hospitals. The cavalryman recovered from his wounds sustained at Monroe's Crossroads but thereafter walked with a noticeable limp. He resumed farming after the war and remarried in 1873 following the death of his first wife. Stewart died in 1911.

Streight, Abel D.

Abel Streight spent the next nine months incarcerated at Libby Prison. In February 1864 he and several other officers executed a daring escape. Shortly thereafter, Streight returned to service, rising to the rank of brigadier general in March 1865. After the war he resumed his publishing career in Indiana, where also served as a state senator. Streight died in 1892.

Strickland, Jefferson

Jefferson Strickland died of disease in Virginia during the spring of 1862.

Strickland, Madison

Madison Strickland died of disease in Virginia during the spring of 1862.

Swayne, Wager T.

Wager Swayne got married in December 1868, retired from the army in 1870, and practiced law in Ohio until 1881, when he moved to New York. In 1893 he received the Medal of Honor for his combat performance at the Battle of Corinth (1862). Swayne died in 1902.

Talbot, Bailey Montgomery

Bailey Talbot was killed during the Battle of Peach Tree Creek, 20 July 1864. The closest his son, Bailey Jr., ever came to exacting revenge as per his father's request was to chase away every suitor who visited his widowed mother after the war.

Tarrant, Edward W.

Following his capture at Fort Blakely, Edward Tarrant spent the next few weeks in confinement on Ship Island, where the Union military evidently employed former slaves as prison guards. In May 1865 he and the rest of his men received their paroles. Tarrant immigrated to Texas sometime afterward. There he served the communities of San Antonio and Waco as a Methodist preacher. Tarrant died in 1921.

Tate, Isaac Henry

Isaac Tate never returned to the 15th Alabama and appears to have simply gone home. Described as "a good and brave soldier," he was undoubtedly missed by his comrades, particularly his brother. Toward the end of 1865, Tate married Sarah A. West, with whom he raised fourteen children. In the 1880s he moved from Chambers County to Henry County, where he made an unsuccessful go

as a merchant. He and his family immigrated to Texas in 1888, presumably living out the remainder of his years in peaceful quiet. Tate died in 1932.

Thompson, James Alford

James Thompson died of pneumonia on 22 January 1865 at the Alton Prison, Illinois.

Tomlin, James Ervin

Toward the end of August 1863, James Tomlin was again exchanged. He served with the 26th Alabama for the duration of the war, eventually rising to the rank of first sergeant of Company K, having been with that unit since October 1861. After the war Tomlin resumed his life as a farmer. He and his wife, Coredelia, raised two daughters. Tomlin died in 1923.

Turchin, John Basil

John Turchin went on to fight with valor at such battles as Chickamauga and Missionary Ridge before resigning his commission in 1864 due to illness. He held a government job in Chicago until 1873, when he bought some land in central Illinois and helped found the immigrant town of Radom. There he wrote books and articles that recounted his wartime exploits. Turchin died in 1901.

Turner, Benjamin Sterling

After losing his livery business in the Panic of 1873, Benjamin Turner shifted to farming, tilling 300 acres at one point. In the early 1890s he suffered a stroke and never fully recovered. Turner died in 1894.

Turpin, John Henry

Turpin was never exchanged, languishing at Johnson's Island in Ohio for the duration of the war. Receiving his parole, Turpin returned to Alabama, where he became a tax collector for the newly created Hale County, serving in that capacity for twenty-eight years. During Reconstruction, he was also a member of the Ku Klux Klan. In 1871 he married Donna Walthall, with whom he raised six children to adulthood.

Vance, Samuel W.

Samuel Vance did indeed do his duty bravely during the Battle of the Wilderness, and he continued to do so with the 11th Alabama until the end of the war. Further details of Vance's life, though, are not known.

Van Diver, Enoch M.

The debilitating nature of Enoch van Diver's wound sustained at Chancellorsville apparently prevented him from returning to his regiment. Instead, he served as a conscript officer in Alabama from December 1863 to April 1864. Thereafter until the end of the war, he spent some more time in the hospital for undisclosed reasons. Van Diver survived the war and died in 1922.

Waddell, James Fleming

In the weeks that followed, James Waddell's battery defended Vicksburg along a portion of the entrenchments southeast of the city, between the Railroad Redoubt and the Square Fort. After the surrender and his parole, Waddell received a promotion to major and command of the 20th Alabama Light Artillery Battalion, a unit he led throughout the Atlanta Campaign. After the war he practiced law in Russell County, where he served as probate judge in the late 1860s and state senator in the late 1880s. Waddell died in 1892.

Walker, Hickman Pierce

When the Confederate army in the Gulf District later surrendered, Hickman Walker headed west to keep fighting. By the summer of 1865, though, he realized that the war was truly over and returned home. Walker resumed his merchant livelihood, but he also pursued an active public life in Tuscaloosa, serving on several occasions as city alderman and trustee of public education.

Walker, Leroy Pope

After the war Leroy Walker earned a profitable living with his private law practice in Huntsville. Walker died in 1884.

Warner, Willard

In 1873 Willard Warner left politics and started the Tecumseh Iron Company in Cherokee County. In 1890, he closed the company and moved to Chattanooga, where he pursued a variety of business ventures and entered the political life of Tennessee. Warner died in 1906.

Watts, Thomas Hill

Bankrupted by the war, Thomas Watts started a successful law practice in Montgomery and eventually paid off his debts. Watts died of a heart attack 1892.

Weeks, John Leonard

John Weeks received his final parole in May 1865. In 1916 he received a pension for his wartime service. His one-time status as a deserter was evidently dismissed or ignored. Weeks died in 1926.

Westbrook, Marcus E.

Marcus Westbrook repeated the pattern of being a private in camp but a sergeant in battle throughout the war, during which he sustained two more combat wounds. His was the type of selfless character that enabled the Confederate army to fight for so long. After the war Westbrook returned to Cherokee County, where he discovered that Yankee raiders had gutted most of his hometown of Spring Garden. In 1866 he married his sweetheart, Mary Eliza, with whom he raised ten children. Westbrook died in 1911.

Whatley, George Croghan

George Whatley was killed during the Battle of Sharpsburg, 17 September 1862.

Wheeler, Joseph

A few months after Shiloh, Joseph Wheeler received promotion to brigadier general. By the summer of 1863, he was in command of a cavalry corps and gained notoriety for his many successful cavalry raids against Union lines of communication throughout the western theater. After the war Wheeler settled in Florence and briefly served in Congress (1882). He commanded U.S. volunteers during the Spanish-American War, fighting with distinction in the various actions around Santiago, Cuba. The old general died in 1906; Wheeler, Alabama, is named after him.

Whiting, Julian Wythe

Three days after Fort Morgan's surrender, Julian Whiting escaped and made his way back to Mobile, where he served on the staff of General Maury for the rest of the war. He stayed in Mobile after the war and went into banking. In 1871 Whiting helped organize the People's Bank, serving as president for twenty-nine years. He also served in the Alabama State Militia, rising to the rank of brigadier general. Whiting died in 1917.

Williams, James Madison

Believing he had faithfully done his duty, James Williams was nonplussed when Maj. Gen. Dabney Maury denounced his defense of Fort Powell as unsatisfactory and convened a court-martial. Acquitted of any wrongdoing, Williams later fought with the remnants of the 21st Alabama at Spanish Fort. After the war, with his wife, Lizzy, and their six children, Williams made his home in Mobile. After an unsuccessful go in the laundry business. he returned to his profession as a bookkeeper. For many years, he served as an officer in the Alabama State Militia and was always active with United Confederate Veterans. Williams died in 1903.

Wilmer, Richard Hooker

Richard Wilmer served as bishop of Alabama from 1861 until his death in 1900.

Wilson, James Harrison

Discharged from the regular army in 1870, James Wilson went into railroads. He came out of retirement to serve as a general of volunteers in both the Spanish-American War and the Boxer Rebellion. In his final years he authored several books and articles on American military history. Wilson died in 1925.

Wilson, Joseph Wyatt

Joseph Wilson went on to serve with honor in the 60th Alabama Infantry, a regiment formed in part by companies from the 1st Battalion, Hilliard's Legion.

Withers, Jones Mitchell

At the end of the summer of 1863, Jones Withers accepted command of the reserve forces in Alabama. His departure from the Army of Tennessee was unfortunate for General Bragg; the major general was one of the few officers who actually liked the irascible army commander. After the war Withers became editor of the *Mobile Tribune,* and in 1867 he was once again elected mayor of the city. Withers died on 13 March 1890.

Wood, Henry Black

Henry Wood's luck ran out later in 1863. At Gettysburg he was captured on the third day of fighting. After five months imprisonment at Fort Delaware, Wood died from either scurvy or typhus. When his son Willy grew up, the boy asked that people call him Henry, in honor of his fallen father.

Woodruff, Lewis Thompson

Lewis Woodruff resumed his business practice in Mobile, but his fortunes were short lived. On 25 May 1869, five years to the day of his terrible leg wound at New Hope Church, the former colonel died in a building fire.

Yancey, William Lowndes

William Yancey quickly faded into the background after Alabama's secession; he had, after all, fulfilled his purpose. Greatly disliking the hard work of political organizing and displaying little talent for governing, he operated mostly on the sidelines during the Civil War itself. Yancey conducted a fruitless diplomatic mission to England in 1861 and briefly served in the Confederate Congress before his premature death in 1863 at the age of forty-eight. As a secular prophet, few men possessed his ability to articulate the cogency of revolution—this was Yancey's ultimate legacy.

Zachry, Alfred Flourney

Alfred Zachry and his men arrived in time to participate in Lee's defensive operations against Grant's Overland Campaign. At the Battle of the Wilderness in May 1864, the 61st Alabama performed quite well, but at Spotsylvania it was badly shot up. In the latter battle Zachry suffered a horrific bullet wound to his left arm; the limb was subsequently amputated at the shoulder. While convalescing, the captain submitted his resignation. "I am no longer in condition to serve my country profitably," he wrote in his letter. For obvious reasons, the captain received an honorable discharge. Zachry died in 1868.[5]

Notes

Chapter 1

1. See Coles, *From Huntsville to Appomattox*.
2. Kenneth W. Noe, *Reluctant Rebels: The Confederates Who Joined the Army after 1861* (Chapel Hill: University of North Carolina Press, 2010).

Chapter 2

1. Fleming, *Civil War and Reconstruction in Alabama*, 5.
2. Thornton, *Politics and Power in a Slave Society*, 181.
3. Rogers et al., *Alabama*, 228–29; Fleming, *Civil War and Reconstruction in Alabama*, 5, 804–805.
4. McMillan, *Alabama Confederate Reader*, 4.
5. The slogan "Equality in the Union or Independence Out of It" was the long-running masthead of the *Spirit of the South*, a radical newspaper published in Eufaula, Alabama.
6. William R. Smith, *The History and Debates of the Convention of the People of Alabama* (Montgomery: White, Pfister, 1861), 26.
7. Dew, *Apostles of Disunion*, 57.
8. McMillan, *Alabama Confederate Reader*, 34.
9. Denman, *Secession Movement in Alabama*, 153.
10. McMillan, *Alabama Confederate Reader*, 57, 59.

11. Henry Barrett Learned, "The Relation of Philip Phillips to the Repeal of the Missouri Compromise in 1854," *Mississippi Valley Historical Review* 8 (1922): 310, 315–16.
12. Fleming, "Buford Expedition to Kansas," 39–40, 42–43.
13. Victoria V. Clayton, *White and Black under the Old Regime* (Milwaukee: The Young Churchman Co., 1899), 74.
14. *Dred Scott v. Sandford*, 60 U.S. 393 (1856), 516.
15. Walther, *William Lowndes Yancey*, 222.
16. Suzanne Rau Wolfe, *The University of Alabama: A Pictorial History* (Tuscaloosa: University of Alabama Press, 1983), 40, 51.
17. R. Bradley, "Tattered Banners," 12.
18. Smith, *History and Debates of the Convention*, 67–68.
19. Ibid., 29, 77–80, 117–18.
20. Ibid., 27, 95.
21. Ibid., 417.
22. Thomas G. Rodgers, "The Independent Blues of Selma, Alabama," *Military Images* 14 (1992): 16–17.
23. Ruth Ketring Nuermberger, *The Clays of Alabama: A Planter-Lawyer-Politician Family* (Tuscaloosa: University of Alabama Press, 2005), 168–69, 178, 182.
24. Thornton, *Politics and Power in a Slave Society*, 414–15.

25. Rogers, *Confederate Home Front,* 28.

26. George Little, *Memoirs of George Little* (Tuscaloosa: Weatherford Printing, 1924), 40.

Chapter 3

1. McMillan, *Alabama Confederate Reader,* 88.

2. Davis, *Battle at Bull Run,* 179.

3. McMillan, *Disintegration of a Confederate State,* 23; H. P. Watson to T. H. Watts, 31 Oct. 1864, Administrative Files (1863–65), SG24872, Alabama Department of Archives and History, Reel 18; Fleming, *Civil War and Reconstruction in Alabama,* 78–83.

4. Noel Crowson and John V. Brogden, eds., *Bloody Banners and Barefoot Boys: A History of the 27th Regiment Alabama Infantry, CSA* (Shippensburg, Pa.: Burd Street, 1997), 7.

5. Bailey, "An Alabamian at Shiloh," 152–53.

6. John G. Barrett, ed., *Yankee Rebel: Civil War Journal of Edmund DeWitt Patterson* (Chapel Hill: University of North Carolina Press, 1966), 27.

7. E. M. Law, "On the Confederate Right at Gaines's Mill," in Johnson and Buel, *Battles and Leaders,* 2:363.

8. U.S. War Department, *War of the Rebellion,* ser. 1, 11(2): 777–78 [hereafter cited as *Official Records;* all references are to series 1 unless otherwise noted].

9. Foote, *Civil War,* 1:513.

10. John C. Carter, ed., *Welcome the Hour of Conflict: William Cowan McClellan and the 9th Alabama* (Tuscaloosa: University of Alabama Press, 2007), 166.

11. William C. Harris, *Leroy Pope Walker: Confederate Secretary of War* (Tuscaloosa: Confederate Publishing, 1962), 26–27.

12. Edward Young McMorries, *History of the First Regiment, Alabama Volunteer Infantry, C.S.A.* (Montgomery, Ala: Brown Printing, 1904), 30–32.

13. Sword, *Southern Invincibility,* 53–56.

14. "Joe P. Angell," *Confederate Veteran* 18 (1910): 133.

15. *Official Records,* 5:491; Norman E. Rourke, ed., *I Saw the Elephant: The Civil War Experiences of Bailey George McClelen, Company D, 10th Alabama* (Shippensburg, Pa.: Burd Street, 1995), 21.

16. Edwin L. Drake, ed., *The Annals of the Army of Tennessee* (Jackson, Tenn.: Guild Bindery Press, 1878), 334.

17. "Wartime Sketch of W. D. Chadick," *Confederate Veteran* 6 (1898), 325.

18. John Wesley Brinsfield, *The Spirit Divided: Memoirs of Civil War Chaplains, The Confederacy* (Macon, Ga.: Mercer University Press, 2006), 104.

19. *Official Records,* 10(1): 558–59.

20. *Official Records,* 10(1):572–73; Emma Look Scott, "Major Clare and Mary Hadley," *Confederate Veteran* 16 (1908): 399–400.

21. Calvin J. Billman, "Joseph M. Ellison: War Letters (1862)," *Georgia Historical Quarterly* 48 (1964): 232.

22. Park, *Sketch of the Twelfth Alabama Infantry,* 29–30; Wheeler, *Confederate Military History,* 653.

23. *Official Records,* 11(1):970.

24. Griffin, *11th Alabama,* 97–100; *Official Records,* 11(1):986–98.

25. Battle, *Third Alabama,* 23.

26. M. T. Ledbetter, "With Archer's Brigade," *Southern Historical Society Papers* 29 (1901): 350–51.

27. Griffin, *11th Alabama,* 103.

28. William Stanley Hoole, ed., *History of the Fourteenth Regiment Alabama Volunteers* (University, Ala.: Confederate Publishing, 1982), 11–12.

29. Hilary A. Herbert, "History of the Eighth Alabama Volunteer Regiment, C.S.A.," *Alabama Historical Quarterly* 39 (1977): 68.

30. Barrett, *Yankee Rebel,* 46–47.

31. *Official Records,* 11(2):635–37.

Chapter 4

1. Krick, *Stonewall Jackson at Cedar Mountain,* 325.

2. John J. Hennessey, *Return to Bull Run: The Campaign and Battle of Second Manassas* (New York: Simon & Schuster, 1993), 355–56.

3. Daniel H. Hill, "The Battle of South Mountain, or Boonsboro," in Johnson and Buel, *Battles and Leaders,* 2:574.

4. Battle, *Third Alabama,* 59.

5. Joseph T. Glatthaar, *General Lee's Army, from Victory to Collapse* (New York: Free Press, 2008), 174.

6. Coles, *From Huntsville to Appomattox,* 52.

7. Hubbs, *Guarding Greensboro,* 153.

8. Battle, *Third Alabama,* 71–72.

9. William C. Oates, *The War between the Union and the Confederacy and Its Lost Opportunities* (New York: Neale, 1905), 211.

10. Pfanz, *Gettysburg,* 373.

11. *Official Records,* 12(2):208.

12. Hubbs, *Guarding Greensboro,* 137–39.

13. Annie M. Allen, "Lieut. Col. Owen Kenan

McLemore," *Confederate Veteran* 10 (1902): 368; *Official Records,* 19(1):922.

14. *Official Records,* 19(1):977; Laine and Penny, *Law's Alabama Brigade,* 24, 39.

15. Norman E. Rourke, ed., *I Saw the Elephant: The Civil War Experiences of Bailey George McClelen, Company D, 10th Alabama Infantry Regiment* (Shippensburg, Pa.: Burd Street, 1995), 30.

16. James R. Randall, "The Gallant Pelham," *Southern Historical Society Papers* 30 (1902): 344.

17. *Official Records,* 25(1):952, 956.

18. Battle, *Third Alabama,* 72–73.

19. Laboda, *From Selma to Appomattox,* 114–18.

20. Wayne Wood, *The Marble Valley Boys* (Birmingham, Ala.: Banner, 1986), 55–56.

21. Ernest B. Furgurson, *Chancellorsville 1863* (New York: Alfred A. Knopf, 1992), 266.

22. Hilary A. Herbert, "History of the Eighth Alabama Volunteer Regiment, C.S.A.," *Alabama Historical Quarterly* 39 (1977): 101–102.

23. *Official Records,* 27(2):646.

24. Ibid., 602.

25. Park, *Sketch of the Twelfth Alabama Infantry,* 10, 54.

26. *Official Records,* 27(2):391.

27. Ibid., 394.

28. LaFantasie, *Gettysburg Requiem,* 97–104.

29. Griffin, *11th Alabama,* 153.

30. *Official Records,* 27(2):593, 602.

31. B. D. Fry, "Pettigrew's Charge at Gettysburg," *Southern Historical Society Papers* 7 (1879): 92–93.

Chapter 5

1. Noe, *Perryville,* 280.

2. Cozzens, *Darkest Days of the War,* 173.

3. Cozzens, *No Better Place to Die,* 113.

4. Elaine Hendricks, ed., *"I Have Seen the Monkey Show": The Civil War Letters of Thomas Warrick of the 34th Alabama Volunteer Infantry* (Dadeville, Ala., 2004), 36–37.

5. Smith, *Champion Hill,* 307.

6. Sarah Woolfolk Wiggins, ed., *The Journals of Josiah Gorgas, 1857–1878* (Tuscaloosa: University of Alabama Press, 1995), 75.

7. W. Stanley Hoole, ed., "The Letters of Captain Joab Goodson, 1862–1864," *Alabama Review* 10 (1957): 150.

8. Cozzens, *This Terrible Sound,* 376–77.

9. Tucker, *Chickamauga,* 302.

10. Samuel H. Sprott, *Cush: A Civil War Memoir,* ed. Louis R. Smith and Andrew Quist (Livingston, Ala.: Livingston Press, 1999), 69.

11. Cozzens, *Shipwreck of Their Hopes,* 317.

12. Maxwell Elebash, "'When Shall Our Cup Be Filled?' The Correspondence of Confederate Soldiers James T. and Reuben M. Searcy," *Alabama Heritage* 31 (1994): 34.

13. Peter Cozzens, "Moving into Dead Men's Shoes: The Fight for Battery Robinett at the Battle of Corinth, Mississippi," *Civil War Times Illustrated* 36 (1997): 33.

14. *Official Records,* 20(1):670, 757–58.

15. Richard W. Smart, ed., *The Bore Every Burden: History of the 19th Alabama Infantry Regiment* (N.p., 1995), 29.

16. *Official Records,* 20(1):696–97.

17. Ibid., 770.

18. Ibid., 901–902.

19. Ibid., 794, 800.

20. Ronald S. Coddington, *Faces of the Confederacy: An Album of Southern Soldiers and Their Stories* (Baltimore: The Johns Hopkins University Press, 2008), 73.

21. William Milner Kelly, "A History of the Thirtieth Alabama Volunteers (Infantry), Confederate States Army," *Alabama Historical Quarterly* 9 (1947): 135, 137–38.

22. Albert Theodore Goodloe, *Confederate Echoes: A Voice from the South in the Days of Secession of the Southern Confederacy* (Nashville, Tenn.: Smith & Lamar, 1907), 77, 276.

23. *Official Records,* 24(2):96.

24. Ibid., 102.

25. Edward Young McMorries, *History of the First Regiment, Alabama Volunteer Infantry, C.S.A.* (Montgomery, Ala.: Brown Printing, 1904), 63–64.

26. *Official Records,* 30(2):407.

27. Ibid., 389–91; "Diary of Captain Edward Crenshaw," *Alabama Historical Quarterly* 1 (1930), 448.

28. Alice V. D. Pierrepont, *Reuben Vaughn Kidd: Soldier of the Confederacy* (Petersburg, Va.: McClures, 1947), 250, 335.

29. *Official Records,* 30(2):336.

30. Ibid., 352.

31. Lewellyn A. Shaver, *A History of the Sixtieth Alabama Regiment, Gracie's Alabama Brigade* (Montgomery, Ala.: Barrett & Brown, 1867), 16, 18.

32. *Official Records,* Supplement, 6:95–96.

33. "Poem: 'The Cherokees,'" Original 19th Alabama Infantry, 19thAlabama.org, http://www.19thalabama.org/cherokee.html.

Chapter 6

1. Wheeler, *Confederate Military History*, 60.
2. Trudeau, *Bloody Roads South*, 59.
3. William C. Oates, *The War between the Union and the Confederacy and Its Lost Opportunities* (New York: Neale, 1905), 344.
4. William F. Perry, "Reminiscences of the Campaign of 1864 in Virginia," *Southern Historical Society Papers* 7 (1879): 62.
5. Trudeau, *Bloody Roads South*, 132.
6. Griffin, *11th Alabama*, 182.
7. Foote, *Civil War*, 3:292.
8. Annette Tapert, ed., *The Brothers' War: Civil War Letters to Their Loved Ones from the Blue and Gray* (New York: Times Books, 1988), 198.
9. Park, *Sketch of the Twelfth Alabama Infantry*, 91.
10. Wiley, *Life of Johnny Reb*, 79.
11. McMillan, *Alabama Confederate Reader*, 429.
12. Glover Moore, *William Jemison Mims, Soldier and Squire* (Birmingham, Ala.: Birmingham Printing, 1966), 49.
13. John C. Carter, ed., *Welcome the Hour of Conflict: William Cowan McClellan and the 9th Alabama* (Tuscaloosa: University of Alabama Press, 2007), 201, 224, 245.
14. Battle, *Third Alabama*, 106.
15. Oates, *War between the Union and the Confederacy*, 346–47, 350.
16. Bowles, "Many a Gallant Soul," 66.
17. Hilary A. Herbert, "History of the Eighth Alabama Volunteer Regiment, C.S.A.," *Alabama Historical Quarterly* 39 (1977): 234.
18. S. W. Vance, "Heroes of the Eighth Alabama Infantry," *Confederate Veteran* 7 (1899): 492.
19. *Official Records*, 36(1):1083–84.
20. Griffin, *11th Alabama*, 182.
21. Rhea, *Battles for Spotsylvania Court House and the Road to Yellow Tavern*, 267–69.
22. "Letters of Major W. J. Mims, C.S.A.," *Alabama Historical Quarterly* 3 (1941): 221.
23. *Official Records*, 36(2):212.
24. E. M. Law, "From the Wilderness to Cold Harbor," in Johnson and Buel, *Battles and Leaders*, 4:138–41.
25. Charles S. Venable, "General Lee in the Wilderness Campaign," in ibid., 4:246.
26. Herbert, "History of the Eighth Alabama," 149–51.
27. Griffin, *11th Alabama*, 206.
28. Tapert, *Brothers' War*, 221–23.
29. Archibald Gracie IV, "Gen. Archibald Gracie," *Confederate Veteran* 5 (1897): 429–32.
30. Lewellyn A. Shaver, *A History of the Sixtieth Alabama Regiment, Gracie's Alabama Brigade* (Montgomery, Ala.: Barrett & Brown, 1867), 96.
31. Walter Jones, "The Flag of Truce at Appomattox," *Confederate Veteran* 39 (1931): 302–303.

Chapter 7

1. Boatner, *Civil War Dictionary*, 219.
2. Herman Hattaway and Archer Jones, *How the North Won: A Military History of the Civil War* (Chicago: University of Illinois Press, 1983), 584, 597.
3. Elbert D. Willett, *History of Company B, 40th Alabama Regiment, Confederate States Army, 1862 to 1865* (Northport, [Ala.]: Colonial, 1963), 74.
4. Davis, "Atlanta Campaign," 22.
5. Hiram Williams, *This War So Horrible: The Civil War Diary of Hiram Smith Williams*, ed. Lewis N. Wynne and Robert A. Taylor (Tuscaloosa: University of Alabama Press, 1993), 107.
6. Castel, *Decision in the West*, 504.
7. McDonough, *Nashville*, 44.
8. Daniel, *Soldiering in the Army of Tennessee*, 161.
9. *Official Records*, 45(1):705.
10. "Letter from General Clayton," *Southern Historical Society Papers* 5 (1877): 129.
11. *Official Records*, 31(2):771.
12. Ibid., 38(3):811; Larry D. Stephens, *Bound for Glory: A History of the 30th Alabama Infantry Regiment, C.S.A.* (Ann Arbor: Sheridan Books, 2005), 225–27.
13. J. H. Curry, "A History of Company B, 40th Alabama Infantry," *Alabama Historical Quarterly* 17 (1955): 195; Samuel H. Sprott, *Cush: A Civil War Memoir*, ed. Louis R. Smith and Andrew Quist (Livingston, Ala.: Livingston Press, 1999), 92.
14. *Official Records*, 38(3):834, 837.
15. George Little and James R. Maxwell, *A History of Lumsden's Battery, C.S.A.* (Tuscaloosa, Ala.: United Daughters of the Confederacy, 1905), 43–44.
16. Margaret Pace Farmer, *One Hundred Fifty Years in Pike County Alabama, 1821–1971* (Anniston, Ala.: Higginbotham, 1973), 50; *Official Records*, 38(3):897.
17. *Official Records*, 38(3):734.
18. Castel, *Decision in the West*, 403.
19. *Official Records*, 38(3):732.
20. Linda Ingram, *The Heritage of Tallapoosa*

County, Alabama, vol. 62 (Clanton, Ala.: Heritage Publishing Consultants, 2000), 160.

21. "Col. Thomas H. Herndon," *Confederate Veteran* 8 (1900): 542; *Official Records,* Supplement, 7:121–22.

22. *Official Records,* 38(3):785–86.

23. Ibid., 169.

24. "Col. Joseph B. Bibb and His Regiment," *Confederate Veteran* 11 (1903): 398.

25. Sword, *Confederacy's Last Hurrah,* 229.

26. Illene Thompson and Wilbur Thompson, *The Seventeenth Alabama Infantry: A Regimental History and Roster* (Bowie, Md.: Heritage Books, 2001), 109, 187.

27. Suzanne Rau Wolfe, *The University of Alabama: A Pictorial History* (Tuscaloosa: University of Alabama Press, 1983), 50; Little and Maxwell, *Lumsden's Battery,* 58.

28. *Official Records,* 45(1):695.

29. Robert G. McLendon, *History of the 53rd Regiment Alabama Volunteer Cavalry* (Norcross, Ga.: Olympic Printing, 2007), 272–73.

30. Illene Thompson and Wilbur Thompson, *Journey to Egypt Station: Pvt. James A. Thompson, a Confederate Soldier* (Huntsville, Ala., 1997), 58.

Chapter 8

1. McMillan, *Disintegration of a Confederate State,* 33.

2. Joseph H. Woodward II, "Alabama Iron Manufacturing, 1860–1865," *Alabama Review* 7 (1954): 207.

3. McMillan, *Alabama Confederate Reader,* 283, 289–91.

4. Marie Bankhead Owen, *The Story of Alabama: A History of the State,* 5 vols. (New York: Lewis Historical Publishing, 1949), 2:2.

5. Douglas Clare Purcell, "Military Conscription in Alabama during the Civil War," *Alabama Review* 34 (1981): 101.

6. Sterkx, *Partners in Rebellion,* 73; Parthenia Antoinette Hague, *A Blockaded Family: Life in Southern Alabama during the Civil War* (Boston: Houghton & Mifflin, 1888), 142.

7. William Stanley Hoole, *Alabama Tories: The First Alabama Cavalry, U.S.A., 1862–1865* (Tuscaloosa, Ala.: Confederate Publishing, 1960), 43.

8. Donald B. Dodd, "The Free State of Winston," *Alabama Heritage* 28 (1993): 13.

9. Michael E. Williams, "'God Will . . . Save Our Southland': I. T. Tichenor's Fast Day Sermon to the Alabama Legislature, August 21, 1863," *Alabama Baptist Historian* 38 (2002): 27; McMillan, *Disintegration of a Confederate State,* 82.

10. McMillan, *Disintegration of a Confederate State,* 103.

11. McMillan, *Alabama Confederate Reader,* 308.

12. Storey, *Loyalty and Loss,* 114.

13. Rogers, *Confederate Home Front,* 103, 144.

14. Rable, *Confederate Republic,* 186.

15. McMillan, *Alabama Confederate Reader,* 110; Anne Kendrick Walker, ed., "Governor John Gill Shorter: Miscellaneous Papers," *Alabama Review* 11 (1958): 282.

16. Lucille Griffith, "Mrs. Juliet Opie Hopkins and Alabama Military Hospitals," *Alabama Review* 6 (1953): 102, 104.

17. Richard Barksdale Harwell, ed., *Kate: The Journal of a Confederate Nurse* (Baton Rouge: Louisiana State University Press, 1959), 26, 39, 65, 84.

18. Bradley and Dahlen, *From Conciliation to Conquest,* 114.

19. Nancy Rohr, ed., *Incidents of the War: The Civil War Journal of Mary Jane Chadick* (Huntsville, Ala.: Madison County Historical Society, 2005), 93, 101, 124–25, 138, 225–26.

20. Dodd, "Free State of Winston," 15.

21. Frank E. Vandiver, *Ploughshares into Swords: Josiah Gorgas and Confederate Ordnance* (College Station: Texas A&M University Press, 1952), 170.

22. Willett, *Lightening Mule Brigade,* 59.

23. *Official Records,* 23(1):292.

24. Willett, *Lightening Mule Brigade,* 138–41.

25. Jessie Pearl Rice, *J. L. M. Curry: Southerner, Statesman, and Educator* (New York: King's Crown, 1949), 42–43, 192.

26. McMillan, *Alabama Confederate Reader,* 365.

27. Edwin C. Bearss, "Rousseau's Raid on the Montgomery and West Point Railroad," *Alabama Historical Quarterly* 25 (1963): 47.

28. *Official Records,* 39(1):544, 549.

29. Brewer, *Alabama,* 287; McMillan, *Alabama Confederate Reader,* 38.

30. Eric J. Wittenberg, *The Battle of Monroe's Crossroads and the Civil War's Final Campaign* (New York: Savas Beatie, 2006), 152.

31. Bruce Levine, *Confederate Emancipation: Southern Plans to Free and Arm Slaves during the Civil War* (New York: Oxford University Press, 2006), 123, 140.

32. Clark E. Center Jr., "The Burning of the

University of Alabama," *Alabama Heritage* 16 (1990): 35–37.

33. Jones, *Yankee Blitzkrieg*, 91–92, 185–86.

34. McMillan, *Disintegration of a Confederate State*, 118–19.

35. Charles A. Misulia, *Columbus, Georgia, 1865: The Last True Battle of the Civil War* (Tuscaloosa: University of Alabama Press, 2010), 156.

Chapter 9

1. Sidney Adair Smith and C. Carter Smith, eds., *Mobile: 1861–1865* (Chicago: Wyvern Press of SFE, 1964), 22.

2. Lash, "Yankee in Gray," 206, 209.

3. Walter Lord, ed., *The Freemantle Diary* (Boston: Little, Brown, 1954), 105.

4. Bergeron, *Confederate Mobile*, 125.

5. William Still, "Iron Afloat: Buchanan and the Mobile Squadron," *Journal of Confederate History* 1, no. 1 (1988): 98–99.

6. Bergeron, *Confederate Mobile*, 92.

7. Ibid., 102.

8. William Perry Fidler, "August Evans Wilson as Confederate Propagandist," *Alabama Review* 2 (1949): 41–43.

9. Bergeron, *Confederate Mobile*, 142; Craig L. Symonds, *Confederate Admiral: The Life and Wars of Franklin Buchanan* (Annapolis, Md.: Naval Institute Press, 1999), 202.

10. Sarah Woolfolk Wiggins, ed., *The Journals of Josiah Gorgas, 1857–1878* (Tuscaloosa: University of Alabama Press, 1995), 126.

11. R. L. Page, "The Defense of Fort Morgan," in Johnson and Buel, *Battles and Leaders*, 4:409.

12. O'Brien, *Mobile, 1865*, 63.

13. G. T. Cullins, "Siege of Spanish Fort, Near Mobile," *Confederate Veteran* 12 (1904): 354.

14. Hearn, *Mobile Bay and the Mobile Campaign*, 199.

15. Bergeron, *Confederate Mobile*, 192.

16. Lash, "Yankee in Gray," 212.

17. John M. Taylor, *While Cannons Roared: The Civil War behind the Lines* (Washington: Brassey's, 1997), 87.

18. Norman C. Delaney, "The End of the *Alabama*," in *The Civil War: The Best of American Heritage*, ed. Stephen Sears (New York: American Heritage, 1991), 149, 151.

19. Benjamin B. Cox, "Mobile in the War between the States," *Confederate Veteran* 24 (1916): 212.

20. Symonds, *Confederate Admiral*, 209, 214; J. D. Johnston, "The Battle of Mobile Bay," *Southern Historical Society Papers* 9 (1881): 474–75.

21. Still, *Iron Afloat*, 192.

22. John Kent Folmar, ed., *From That Terrible Field: Civil War Letters of James M. Williams, Twenty-First Alabama Infantry Volunteers* (Tuscaloosa: University of Alabama Press, 1981), 126, 128.

23. *Official Records*, 39(1):426.

24. Page, "Defense of Fort Morgan," 4:410; Hurieosco Austill, "Fort Morgan in the Confederacy," *Alabama Historical Quarterly* 7 (1945): 262, 264, 266.

25. Lonnie A. Burnett, *The Pen Makes a Good Sword: John Forsyth of the* Mobile Register (Tuscaloosa: University of Alabama Press, 2006), 142–44.

26. Reginald Horsman, *Josiah Nott of Mobile: Southerner, Physician, and Racial Theorist* (Baton Rouge: Louisiana State University Press, 1987), 254, 295.

27. Delany, *Confederate Mobile*, 344.

28. Waugh, *Last Stand at Mobile*, 72.

29. Edgar W. Jones, *History of the Eighteenth Alabama Infantry Regiment* (Birmingham, Ala.: C. David A. Pulcrano, 1994), 222, 240.

30. O'Brien, *Mobile, 1865*, 191.

31. E. W. Tarrant, "After the Fall of Fort Blakely," *Confederate Veteran* 25 (1917): 152.

32. *Official Records*, 49(1):283.

33. Dabney H. Maury, "The Defence of Mobile in 1865," *Southern Historical Society Papers* 3 (1877): 5, 9.

Chapter 10

1. *Southern Advocate*, 12 July 1865, quoted in Coles, *From Huntsville to Appomattox*, 303.

2. Robert H. McKenzie, "The Economic Impact of Federal Operations in Alabama during the Civil War," *Alabama Historical Quarterly* 38 (1976): 57.

3. Thomas Spencer, ed., "Dale County and Its People during the Civil War: Reminiscences of Mary Love Edwards Fleming," *Alabama Historical Quarterly* 19 (1957): 81–82.

4. John B. Myers, "The Alabama Freedmen and the Economic Adjustments during Presidential Reconstruction, 1865–1867," *Alabama Review* 26 (1973): 256–57.

5. Lonnie A. Burnett, *The Pen Makes a Good Sword: John Forsythe of the Mobile Register* (Tuscaloosa: University of Alabama Press, 2006), 156.

6. Loren Schweninger, "Alabama Blacks and the Congressional Reconstruction Acts of 1867," *Alabama Review* 31 (1978): 188.

7. Sarah Woolfolk Wiggins, "Alabama: Democratic Bulldozing and Republican Folly," in *Reconstruction and Redemption in the South*, ed. Otto H. Olsen (Baton Rouge: Louisiana State University Press, 1980), 53.

8. Mike Daniel, "The Arrest and Trial of Ryland Randolph, April–May 1868," *Alabama Historical Quarterly* 40 (1978): 132.

9. Allen W. Trelease, *White Terror: The Ku Klux Klan Conspiracy and Southern Reconstruction* (Baton Rouge: Louisiana State University Press, 1971), 123.

10. Rogers et al., *Alabama,* 250.

11. Melinda M. Hennessey, "Reconstruction Politics and the Military: The Eufaula Riot of 1874," *Alabama Historical Quarterly* 38 (1976): 116.

12. Owen, *History of Alabama and Dictionary of Alabama Biography,* 3:88.

13. Fleming, *Civil War and Reconstruction in Alabama,* 353.

14. Bond, "Social and Economic Forces in Alabama Reconstruction," 371.

15. Michael W. Fitzgerald, "Wager Swayne, the Freedmen's Bureau, and the Politics of Reconstruction in Alabama," *Alabama Review* 48 (1995): 190, 205, 210, 215.

16. Sarah Van Woolfolk, "Carpetbaggers in Alabama: Tradition versus Truth," in Woolfolk, *From Civil War to Civil Rights,* 69.

17. House Concurrent Resolution No. 43, *Black Americans in Congress, 1870–2007* (Washington, D.C.: U.S. Government Printing Office, 2008), 84.

18. Trelease, *White Terror,* 55.

19. Owen, *History of Alabama and Dictionary of Alabama Biography,* 4:1437.

20. Sarah Van Woolfolk, "The Political Cartoons of the *Tuskaloosa Independent Monitor* and *Tuskaloosa Blade, 1867–1873*," *Alabama Historical Quarterly* 27 (1965): 140, 148, 151.

21. Current, *Those Terrible Carpetbaggers,* 31.

22. Ibid., 154, 160, 164.

23. U.S. House, *The Condition of Affairs in the Late Insurrectionary States,* vol. 1, *Alabama,* 42nd Cong., 2nd sess., 1872, H. Rep. 22, 159, 170–71, 191, 208, 213.

24. Wiggins, *Scalawag in Alabama Politics,* 85.

25. William Warren Rogers Jr., *Black Belt Scalawag: Charles Hays and the Southern Republicans in the Era of Reconstruction* (Athens: University of Georgia Press, 1993), 70, 137.

26. U.S. Senate, *Elections in the State of Alabama,* 44th Cong., 2nd sess., S. Rep. 704, 170.

27. Lyn Johns, ed., "The Autobiography of Willis Julian Milner," *Journal of the Birmingham Society* 5 (1977): 13.

28. Robert Leslie James, *Distinguished Men, Women, and Families of Franklin County, Alabama* (N.p., 1930), 89.

Appendix

1. *Official Records,* 45(1):694; Owen, *History of Alabama and Dictionary of Alabama Biography,* 3:143.

2. Richard Barksdale Harwell, ed., *Kate: The Journal of a Confederate Nurse* (Baton Rouge: Louisiana State University Press, 1959), 281, 292.

3. Sword, *Confederacy's Last Hurrah,* 231.

4. Maxwell Elebash, "'When Shall Our Cup Be Filled?' The Correspondence of Confederate Soldiers James T. and Reuben M. Searcy," *Alabama Heritage* 31 (1994): 38–39.

5. William H. Davidson, *Word from Camp Pollard, C.S.A.* (West Point, Ga., Hester Printing, 1978), 293.

Bibliography

General and Reference Works

Allardice, Bruce S. *Confederate Colonels: A Biographical Register*. Columbia: University of Missouri Press, 2008.

Battle, Cullen A. *Third Alabama! The Civil War Memoir of Brigadier General Cullen Andrews Battle, CSA*. Edited by Brandon H. Beck. (Tuscaloosa: University of Alabama Press, 2000

Boatner, Mark M. *The Civil War Dictionary*. New York: Vintage Books, 1988.

Bradley, Robert. "Tattered Banners: Alabama's Civil War Flags." *Alabama Heritage* 96 (2010): 10–21.

Brewer, Willis. *Alabama: Her History, Resources, War Record, and Public Men, from 1540–1872*. Montgomery, Ala.: Barrett & Brown, Steam Printers and Book Binders, 1872.

Burton, John Michael. *Gracie's Alabama Volunteers: The History of the Fifty-ninth Alabama Volunteer Regiment*. Gretna, La.: Pelican, 2003.

Coles, R. T *From Huntsville to Appomattox: R. T. Coles History of the 4th Regiment, Alabama Volunteer Infantry, C.S.A., Army of Northern Virginia*. Edited by Jeffrey D. Stocker. Knoxville: University of Tennessee Press, 1996.

Fleming, Walter L. *Civil War and Reconstruction in Alabama*. New York: Columbia University Press, 1905.

Foote, Shelby. *The Civil War: A Narrative*. 3 vols. New York: Random House, 1958–74.

Freeman, Douglas Southall. *Lee's Lieutenants: A Study in Command*. 4 vols. New York: Charles Scribner's Sons, 1942.

Garrett, William. *Reminiscences of Public Men in Alabama, for Thirty Years*. Atlanta: Plantation, 1872.

Griffin, Ronald G. *The 11th Alabama Volunteer Regiment in the Civil War*. Jefferson, N.C.: McFarland, 2008.

Heritage Book Committee. *Heritage of Alabama Series of County Histories*. 67 vols. Clanton, Ala.: Heritage Publishing Consultants, 1998–2005.

Hubbs, G. Ward. *Guarding Greensboro: A Confederate Company in the Making of a Southern Community*. Athens: University of Georgia Press, 2003.

Johnson, Robert, and Clarence Buel, eds. *Battles and Leaders of the Civil War*. 4 vols. New York: Century, 1887.

Krick, Robert K. *Lee's Colonels: A Biographical Register of the Field Officers of the Army of Northern Virginia*. Dayton, Ohio: Morningside, 1992.

Laboda, Lawrence R. *From Selma to Appomattox: The History of the Jeff Davis Artillery*. Shippensburg, Pa.: White Mane, 1994.

Laine, J. Gary, and Morris M. Penny. *Law's Alabama Brigade in the War between the Union and the Confederacy*. Shippensburg, Pa.: White Mane, 1996.

Long, E. B. *The Civil War Day by Day: An Almanac, 1861–1865.* New York: Doubleday, 1971.

McMillan, Malcolm C., ed. *The Alabama Confederate Reader.* Tuscaloosa: University of Alabama Press, 1963.

———. *The Disintegration of a Confederate State: Three Governors and Alabama's Wartime Home Front, 1861–1865.* Macon, Ga.: Mercer University Press, 1986.

Owen, Thomas McAdory. *History of Alabama and Dictionary of Alabama Biography.* 4 vols. Chicago: S. J. Clarke, 1921.

Park, Robert Emory. *Sketch of the Twelfth Alabama Infantry.* Richmond, Va.: Wm. Ellis Jones, Book and Job Printer, 1906.

Rogers, William Warren, Jr. *Confederate Home Front: Montgomery during the Civil War.* Tuscaloosa: University of Alabama Press, 1999.

Rogers, William Warren, Jr.; Robert D. Ward; Leah R. Atkins; and Wayne Flint. *Alabama: The History of a Deep South State.* Tuscaloosa: University of Alabama Press, 1994.

Sifakis, Stewart. *Compendium of the Confederate Armies: Alabama.* New York: Facts on File, 1991.

Sword, Wiley. *Southern Invincibility: A History of the Confederate Heart.* New York: St. Martin's, 1999.

Tancig, W. J. *Confederate Military Land Units, 1861–1865.* South Brunswick, N.J.: T. Yoseloff, 1967.

U.S. War Department. *The War of the Rebellion, A Compilation of the Official Records of the Union and Confederate Armies.* 128 vols. in 4 series. Washington, D.C.: Government Printing Office, 1880–1901.

Warner, Ezra. *Generals in Blue.* Baton Rouge: Louisiana State University Press, 1981.

———. *Generals in Gray.* Baton Rouge: Louisiana State University Press, 1981.

Wheeler, Joseph. *Confederate Military History, Extended Edition.* Vol. 8, *Alabama.* Wilmington, N.C.: Broadfoot, 1987.

Wiggins, Sarah Woolfolk, ed. *From Civil War to Civil Rights—Alabama, 1860–1960: An Anthology from the Alabama Review.* Tuscaloosa: University of Alabama Press, 1987.

Wiley, Bell I. *The Life of Johnny Reb: The Common Soldier of the Confederacy.* Indianapolis: Bobbs-Merrill, 1943.

Yearns, Wilfred Buck. *The Confederate Congress.* Athens: University of Georgia Press, 1960.

Alabama Civil War Units

The following websites contain all of the significant published unit histories for Alabama during the war, listing also some important primary sources for various units:

Alabama Civil War Unit Bibliography, 19 March 2012, history-sites.com/~kjones/albiblio.html.

The Ohio State University, Alabama Regimental Bibliography, 2012, http://ehistory.osu.edu/USCW/features/regimental/alabama/confederate/albiblio.cfm.

Chapter 1

Zeller, Bob. *The Blue and the Gray in Black and White: A History of Civil War Photography.* Westport, Conn.: Praeger, 2005).

Chapter 2

Barney, William L. *The Secessionist Impulse: Alabama and Mississippi in 1860.* Tuscaloosa: University of Alabama Press, 1974.

Brantley, William H. "Alabama Secedes." *Alabama Review* 7 (1954): 165–85.

Denman, Clarence Phillips. *The Secession Movement in Alabama.* New York: Books for Libraries Press, 1971.

Dew, Charles B. *Apostles of Disunion: Southern Secession Commissioners and the Causes of the Civil War.* Charlottesville: University Press of Virginia, 2001.

Dorman, Lewy. *Party Politics in Alabama from 1850 through 1860.* Montgomery: Alabama Department of Archives and History, 1935.

Fleming, Walter L. "The Buford Expedition to Kansas." *American Historical Review* 6 (1900): 38–48.

Long, Durwood. "Political Parties and Propaganda in Alabama in the Presidential Election of 1860." *Alabama Historical Quarterly* 25 (1963): 120–35.

McWhiney, Grady. "The Revolution in Nineteenth-Century Alabama Agriculture." *Alabama Review* 31 (1978): 3–32.

Saunders, Robert. *John Archibald Campbell, Southern Moderate, 1811–1889.* Tuscaloosa: University of Alabama Press, 1997.

Thornton, J. Mills. *Politics and Power in a Slave Society: Alabama, 1800–1860.* Baton Rouge: Louisiana State University Press, 1978.

Walther, Eric H. *William Lowndes Yancey and the Coming of the Civil War.* Chapel Hill: University of North Carolina Press, 2006.

Wooster, Ralph A. *The Secession Conventions of the South.* Princeton, N.J.: Princeton University Press, 1962.

Chapter 3

Bailey, Hugh C., ed. "An Alabamian at Shiloh: The Diary of Liberty Independence Nixon." *Alabama Review* 11 (1958): 144–55.

Connelly, Thomas Lawrence. *Army of the Heartland: The Army of Tennessee, 1861–1862.* Baton Rouge: Louisiana State University Press, 1967.

Cooling, Benjamin Franklin. *Forts Henry and Donelson: The Key to the Confederate Heartland.* Knoxville: University of Tennessee Press, 1987.

Cooper, Norman V. "How They Went to War: An Alabama Brigade in 1861–62." *The Alabama Review* 24 (1971): 17–50.

Cunningham, O. Edward. *Shiloh and the Western Campaign of 1862.* New York: Savas Beatie, 2007.

Daniel, Larry J. *Shiloh: The Battle That Changed the Civil War.* New York: Simon & Schuster, 1997.

Davis, William C. *Battle at Bull Run: A History of the First Major Campaign of the Civil War.* Mechanicsburg, Pa.: Stackpole, 1995.

Frank, Joseph Allen, and George A. Reaves. *"Seeing the Elephant": Raw Recruits at the Battle of Shiloh.* Westport, Conn.: Greenwood, 1989.

Hamilton, James J. *The Battle of Fort Donelson.* New York: A. S. Barnes, 1968.

Jones, Kenneth W. "The Fourth Alabama Infantry: First Blood." *Alabama Historical Quarterly* 36 (1974): 35–53.

McDonough, James Lee. *Shiloh: In Hell before Night.* Knoxville: University of Tennessee Press, 1977.

Pearce, George F. *Pensacola during the Civil War: A Thorn in the Side of the Confederacy.* Gainesville: University Press of Florida, 2000.

Sears, Stephen W. *To the Gates of Richmond: The Peninsula Campaign.* New York: Ticknor & Fields, 1992.

Starbuck, Gregory J. "'Up, Alabamians!' The 4th Alabama Infantry at First Manassas." *Military Images* 8, no. 1 (1986): 25–29.

Sword, Wiley. *Shiloh: Bloody April.* New York: William Morrow, 1974.

Walker, Henry. "Young Men Go to War: The First Regiment Alabama Volunteer Infantry at Pensacola, 1861." *Gulf Coast Historical Review* 13 (1998): 6–34.

Chapter 4

Beidler, Philip D. "Alabama at Gettysburg." *Alabama Heritage* 10 (1988): 16–31.

Coddington, Edwin B. *The Gettysburg Campaign: A Study in Command.* New York: Charles Scribner's Sons, 1963.

Hennessy, John J. *Return to Bull Run: The Campaign and Battle of Second Manassas.* New York: Simon & Schuster, 1993.

Krick, Robert K. *Stonewall Jackson at Cedar Mountain.* Chapel Hill: University of North Carolina Press, 1990.

LaFantasie, Glenn W. *Gettysburg Requiem: The Life and Lost Causes of Confederate Colonel William C. Oates.* New York: Oxford University Press, 2006.

Pfanz, Harry W. *Gettysburg: The Second Day.* Chapel Hill: University of North Carolina Press, 1987.

Priest, John M. *Antietam: The Soldiers' Battle.* New York: Oxford University Press, 1989.

Rable, George C. *Fredericksburg, Fredericksburg!* Chapel Hill: University of North Carolina Press, 2001.

Sears, Stephen W. *Chancellorsville.* New York: Houghton Mifflin, 1996.

———. *Landscape Turned Red: The Battle of Antietam.* New York: Ticknor & Fields, 1983.

Trudeau, Noah Andre. *Gettysburg: A Testing of Courage.* New York: Harper Collins, 2002.

Tucker, Phillip Thomas. *Storming Little Round Top: The 15th Alabama and Their Fight for the High Ground, July 2, 1863.* Cambridge, Mass.: Da Capo, 2002.

Chapter 5

Ballard, Michael B. *Vicksburg: The Campaign That Opened the Mississippi.* Chapel Hill: University of North Carolina Press, 2004.

Connelly, Thomas Lawrence. *Autumn Glory: The Army of Tennessee, 1862–1865.* Baton Rouge: Louisiana State University Press, 1971.

Cozzens, Peter. *The Darkest Days of the War: The Battles of Iuka and Corinth*. Chapel Hill: University of North Carolina Press, 1997.

———. *No Better Place to Die: The Battle of Stones River*. Chicago: University of Illinois Press, 1990.

———. *The Shipwreck of Their Hopes: The Battles for Chattanooga*. Chicago: University of Illinois Press, 1994.

———. *This Terrible Sound: The Battle of Chickamauga*. Chicago: University of Illinois Press, 1992.

Daniel, Larry J. *Cannoneers in Gray: The Field Artillery of the Army of Tennessee, 1861–1865*. Tuscaloosa: University of Alabama Press, 1984.

———. *Soldiering in the Army of Tennessee*. Chapel Hill: University of North Carolina Press, 1991.

Grabau, Warren E. *Ninety-Eight Days: A Geographer's View of the Vicksburg Campaign*. Knoxville: University of Tennessee Press, 2000.

Hewitt, Lawrence Lee. *Port Hudson, Confederate Bastion on the Mississippi*. Baton Rouge: Louisiana State University Press, 1987.

Johnson, Curt, ed. "A Forgotten Account of Chickamauga by William F. Perry." *Civil War Times Illustrated* 32 (1993): 53–56.

Manigault, Arthur Middleton. *A Carolinian Goes to War: The Civil War Narrative of Arthur Middleton Manigault*. Edited by R. Lockwood Tower. Columbia: University of South Carolina Press, 1983.

McDonough, James Lee. *Chattanooga: A Death Grip on the Confederacy*. Knoxville: University of Tennessee Press, 1984.

Noe, Kenneth W. *Perryville: This Grand Havoc of Battle*. Lexington: University of Kentucky Press, 2001.

Smith, Timothy B. *Champion Hill: The Decisive Battle for Vicksburg*. New York: Savas Beatie, 2004.

Spruill, Matt, ed. *Guide to the Battle of Chickamauga*. Lawrence: University Press of Kansas, 1993.

Sword, Wiley. *Mountains Touched with Fire: Chattanooga Besieged, 1863*. New York: St. Martin's, 1995.

Tucker, Glenn. *Chickamauga: Bloody Battle in the West*. Indianapolis: Bobbs-Merrill, 1961.

Winschel, Terrence J. *Triumph and Defeat: The Vicksburg Campaign*. New York: Savas Beatie, 2004.

Chapter 6

Bowles, Pinckney Downie. "Many a Gallant Soul." *Civil War Times Illustrated* 38 (1999): 21–22, 62–68.

Glaathaar, Joseph T. *General Lee's Army: From Victory to Collapse*. New York: Free Press, 2009.

Lewis, Thomas A. *The Guns of Cedar Creek*. Laurel, 1988.

Matter, William D. *If It Takes All Summer: The Battle of Spotsylvania*. Chapel Hill: University of North Carolina Press, 1988.

Power, J. Tracy. *Lee's Miserables: Life in the Army of Northern Virginia from the Wilderness to Appomattox*. Chapel Hill: University of North Carolina Press, 1998.

Rhea, Gordon C. *The Battle of the Wilderness, May 5–6 1864*. Baton Rouge: Louisiana State University Press, 1994.

———. *The Battles for Spotsylvania Court House and the Road to Yellow Tavern, May 7–12, 1864*. Baton Rouge: Louisiana State University Press, 1997.

———. *Cold Harbor, Grant and Lee, May 26–June 3, 1864*. Baton Rouge, Louisiana State University Press, 2007.

Slotkin, Richard. *No Quarter: The Battle of the Crater, 1864*. New York: Random House, 2009.

Trudeau, Noah Andre. *Bloody Roads South: The Wilderness to Cold Harbor, May–June 1864*. Boston: Little, Brown, 1989.

———. *The Last Citadel: Petersburg, Virginia, June 1864–April 1865*. Boston: Little, Brown, 1991.

Chapter 7

Bradley, Mark L. *Last Stand in the Carolinas: The Battle of Bentonville*. Campbell, Calif.: Savas Woodbury, 1996.

Castel, Albert. *Decision in the West: The Atlanta Campaign of 1864*. Lawrence: University Press of Kansas, 1992.

Connelly, Thomas Lawrence. *Autumn Glory: The Army of Tennessee, 1862–1865*. Baton Rouge: Louisiana State University Press, 1971.

Davis, Stephen. "Atlanta Campaign: Actions from July 10 to September 2, 1864." *Blue & Gray Magazine* 6 (1989): 8–62.

Evans, David. "The Atlanta Campaign." *Civil War Times Illustrated* 28 (1989): 12–61.

Hughes, Nathaniel C., Jr. *Bentonville: The Final Battle of Sherman and Johnston*. Chapel Hill: University of North Carolina Press, 1996.

McDonough, James Lee. *Nashville: The Western Confederacy's Final Gamble*. Knoxville: University of Tennessee Press, 2004.

McDonough, James Lee, and Thomas L. Connelly. *Five Tragic Hours: The Battle of Franklin*. Knoxville: University of Tennessee Press, 1983.

Sword, Wiley. *The Confederacy's Last Hurrah: Spring Hill, Franklin, and Nashville*. Lawrence: University Press of Kansas, 1992.

Chapter 8

Bradley, George C., and Richard L. Dahlen. *From Conciliation to Conquest: The Sack of Athens and the Court-Martial of Colonel John B. Turchin*. Tuscaloosa: University of Alabama Press, 2006.

Bryant, William O. *Cahaba Prison and the Sultana Disaster*. Tuscaloosa: University of Alabama Press, 2001.

Jones, James Pickett. *Yankee Blitzkrieg: Wilson's Raid through Alabama and Georgia*. Athens: University of Georgia Press, 1976.

Martin, Bessie. *A Rich Man's War, a Poor Man's Fight: Desertion of Alabama Troops from the Confederate Army*. New York: Columbia University Press, 1932.

Napier, John H. III. "Montgomery during the Civil War." *Alabama Review* 41 (1988): 103–31.

Rable, George C. *The Confederate Republic: A Revolution against Politics*. Chapel Hill: University of North Carolina Press, 1994.

Sterkx, H. E. *Partners in Rebellion: Alabama Women in the Civil War*. Cranbury, N.J.: Associated University Press, 1970.

Storey, Margaret M. *Loyalty and Loss: Alabama's Unionists in the Civil War and Reconstruction*. Baton Rouge: Louisiana State University Press, 2004.

Todd, Glenda McWhirter. *First Alabama Cavalry, USA: Homage to Patriotism*. Bowie, Md.: Heritage Books, 1999.

Willett, Robert L. *The Lighting Mule Brigade: Abel Streight's 1863 Raid into Alabama*. Carmel, Ind.: Guild, 1999.

Chapter 9

Bergeron, Arthur W. *Confederate Mobile*. Baton Rouge: Louisiana State University Press, 1991.

Delany, Caldwell. *Confederate Mobile: A Pictorial History*. Mobile: Haunted Book Shop, 1971.

Friend, Jack. *West Wind, Flood Tide: The Battle of Mobile Bay*. Annapolis, Md.: Naval Institute Press, 2004.

Hearn, Chester G. *Mobile Bay and the Mobile Campaign: The Last Great Battles of the Civil War*. Jefferson, N.C.: McFarland, 1993).

Lash, Jeffrey N. "A Yankee in Gray: Danville Leadbetter and the Defense of Mobile Bay, 1861–1863." *Civil War History* 37, no. 3 (1991): 192–218.

Luraghi, Raimondo. *A History of the Confederate Navy*. Annapolis, Md.: Naval Institute Press, 1996.

Noles, Jim. "Confederate Twilight: The Fall of Fort Blakely." *Alabama Heritage* 91 (2009): 28–37.

O'Brien, Sean Michael. *Mobile, 1865: Last Stand of the Confederacy*. Westport, Conn.: Praeger, 2001.

Owsley, Frank L. "Incidents on the Blockade at Mobile." *Gulf Coast Historical Review* 4, no. 2 (1989): 38–48.

Schell, Sidney H. "Submarine Weapons Tested at Mobile during the Civil War." *Alabama Review* 45 (1992): 163–83.

Still, William N. "Iron Afloat: Buchanan and the Mobile Squadron." *Journal of Confederate History* 1, no. 1 (1988): 83–117.

———. *Iron Afloat: The Story of the Confederate Armorclads*. Nashville: Vanderbilt University Press, 1971.

Symonds, Craig L. "Damn the Torpedoes! The Battle of Mobile Bay." *Hallowed Ground* 9, no. 4 (2008): 16–24.

Tucker, Phillip Thomas. "The First Missouri Confederate Brigade's Last Stand at Fort Blakeley on Mobile Bay." *Alabama Review* 42 (1989): 270–91.

Waugh, John C. *Last Stand at Mobile*. Abilene, Tex.: McWhiney Foundation Press, 2001.

Wise, Stephen R. *Lifeline of the Confederacy: Blockade Running during the Civil War*. Columbia: University of South Carolina Press, 1988.

Zebrowski, Carl. "Frozen in Time." *Civil War Times Illustrated* 33 (1994): 24–28.

———. "Guardian of Mobile Bay." *Civil War Times Illustrated* 33 (1994): 20–22, 62–65.

Chapter 10

Bailey, Richard. *Neither Carpetbaggers Nor Scalawags: Black Officeholders during the Reconstruction of Alabama, 1867–1878*. Rev. 5th ed. Montgomery, Ala.: New South Books, 2010.

Bond, Horace Mann. "Social and Economic Forces in Alabama Reconstruction." In *Reconstruction: An Anthology of Revisionist Writings*, edited by Kenneth M. Stampp and Leon F. Litwack, 370–404. Baton Rouge: Louisiana State University Press, 1969.

Current, Richard Nelson. *Those Terrible Carpetbaggers: A Reinterpretation*. New York: Oxford University Press, 1988.

Fitzgerald, Michael W. "The Ku Klux Klan: Property Crime and the Plantation System in Reconstruction Alabama." *Agricultural History* 71 (1997): 186–207.

———. *The Union League Movement in the Deep South*. Baton Rouge: Louisiana State University Press, 1989.

Going, Allen J. *Bourbon Democracy in Alabama, 1874–1890*. Tuscaloosa: University of Alabama Press, 1951.

Herbert, Hilary A., et al. "Reconstruction in Alabama." In *Why the Solid South*, 29–69. Baltimore: R. H. Woodward, 1890.

Trelease, Allen W. *White Terror: The Ku Klux Klan Conspiracy and Southern Reconstruction*. Baton Rouge: Louisiana State University Press, 1971.

Wiener, Jonathan M. *Social Origins of the New South: Alabama, 1860–1885*. Baton Rouge: Louisiana State University Press, 1978.

Wiggins, Sarah Woolfolk. *The Scalawag in Alabama Politics, 1865–1881*. Tuscaloosa: University of Alabama Press, 1977.

Index

Hooker, Joseph, 85–86
Hopkins, Arthur, 243
Hopkins, Juliet O., *243*, 348
Houston, George S., 313, *330*, 348
Howard, Oliver O., 198
Hoyt, James, 84
Hubbard, George, 143
Huckabee, Caswell C., *249*, 348
Huguley, George W., *183*, 348
Huntsville, Ala., 233, 247, 311, 341–42, 344, 361
    photography in, 2, 112
Hurst, Marshall B., *75*, 348
Hurst, Nannie F. G., 348
Hutton, Aquila D., *149*, 348
Hutton, William B., *99*, 149, 348

Inzer, John, 126
Iron Brigade, 86, 108
Iron Production, 239, 271, 277, 307
    Brierfield Ironworks, 249, 346, 348
    Round Mountain Furnace, 237
    Shelby Ironworks, 234
    Tecumseh Iron Company, 361
Island No. 10. *See* New Madrid, Mo.
Iuka, Miss., battle of, 120, 316

Jackson, Andrew, 237
Jackson, James W., 83, *89*, 348
Jackson, John K., 49, 63
Jackson, Miss., 123
Jackson, Thomas J., "Stonewall," 47, 50, 66, 81–82, 85, 90, 97–98, 101, 104, 193
Jackson County, Ala., 262
Jefferson County, Ala., 9, 147, 180, 218, 263, 353, 358
Johnson, Andrew, 308, 314–16, 325
Johnson, Christopher B., 357
Johnson, William A., *261*, 348
Johnston, Albert S., 48–49, 64
Johnston, James D., 288–89
Johnston, Joseph E., 47, 49–50, 157, 195–96, 201, 337, 350
Johnston, Samuel B., *72*, 349
Johnston, Thomas M., 268
Jones, Bushrod, 150, 198, 216
Jones, Catesby R., 278
Jones, Edgar W., 300
Jones, Egbert J., 47, 57
Jones, Harvey E., *190–91*, 349
Jones, John W., *327*, 349
Jones, Nancy, 239
Jones, Richard C., *186*, 349
Jones, Robert T., *67*, 349

Jones, Thomas G., *193*, 349
Jonesboro, Ga., battle of, 198–99, 220, 341, 346
Joseph, Philip, 319
Jowers, Joseph D., *76*, 349

Kansas, 17–18, 25, 28, 339
Kansas–Nebraska Act (1854), 17–18, 22, 38
Keffer, John C., 309
Kelley, William D., 310
Kelly, Samuel C., *140*, 349
Kennesaw Mountain, Ga., battle of, 196, 208–10
Kidd, Reuben V., *151*, 349
Kimbrough, Julius A., *94*, 349
King, Porter, 55
King, William R., 16, 145
Kinston, N.C., battle of, 201
Knoxville, Tenn., 125, 159, 340
Ku Klux Klan, 311–13, 321–23, 326, 329, 337–38, 361

Labuzan, Greene M., *267*, 350
LaGrange Military Academy, 11
Lakin, Josephus H., *7–8*, 316, 350
Lamar County, 313
Lamkin, Thomas P., *6*, 350
Lampley, Charles Harris D., *213–14*, 350
Lauderdale County, Ala., 34, 54, 77, 90, 261, 309–10, 315, 355
Lavergne, Tenn., 138
Law, Evander M., 50–51, 85, 87–88, 92, 113–14, 125, 161, 164, 166, *182*, 186, 350
Lawrence County, Ala., 128, 137, 251, 264
Leadbetter, Danville, 276, *284*, 350
Lecompton Constitution (1857), 28, 38
Ledbetter, M. T., 73
Lee, Robert E., 50–51, 73, 81–88, 92, 97, 106, 117, 282, 300
    versus Grant, 161–67, 176, 189, 193, 195, 201, 296, 363
Lee, Stephen D., 123, 144–46, 198, 200, 219
Leftwich, Lloyd, *327*, 350
Leonard, John O., *153*, 350
Leonard, Laura B., 350
Lewis, David P., 312–13, 328, 331
Lewis, Dixon H., 16
Liddell, St. John R., 282
Lightfoot, James N., 94
Limestone County, Ala., 168, 322, 330, 352

Lincoln, Abraham, 18–19, 21, 32, 34–35, 38–39, 43, 45, 49, 58, 162, 166, 199, 225, 237, 246–47, 272, 296–97, 309, 341
Lincoln, Mary Todd, 56
Lindsay, Robert B., 312, 326, 350
Little, George, *43*, 350
Locke, Michael B., *148*, 350
Lockett, Samuel, 276
Logan, Andrew, *254*, 351
Logan, Catherine C., 351
Lomax, Tennent, 46–47, 71–72, 351
Longstreet, James, 51, 82, 87, 90, 123–25, 159, 161–62, 182
Loomis, John Q., 121, 131–32
Lovell, Mansfield, 121
Lowery, Mark P., 126, 196–97, 212–14, 224
Lowery, William F., *226*, 351
Lowndes County, Ala., 156, 327
Lowther, Alexander A., 343
Loyd, Margaret, *184*, 351
Loyd, William P., *184*, 351
Lumsden, Charles, 208, *225*, 351

Macaria, 278
MacIntyre, Edward L., *4*, 351
Macon County, Ala., 66, 72, 176, 182, 224, 273, 338
Madison County, Ala., 11, 33, 38, 52, 57, 60, 70, 112, 172, 239
Maffit, John N., 277, *285*, 351
Mahone, William, 71
Maine troops:
    4th Infantry, 113
    20th Infantry, 87
Manasco, Jeremiah, *62*, 351
Manassas, Va., first battle of, 11, 47–48, 55–57, 60, 70, 92, 97, 104, 112, 151, 182, 217, 265, 302, 343
    second battle of, 81–82, 90, 92, 151, 186, 352
Manigault, Arthur M., 121, 124, 126, 133–36, 154, 158, 197, 200, 215–19, 353
Marengo County, Ala., 181, 209, 308
Marion County, Ala., 152, 269, 351
Marion Light Infantry, 55
Marrast, Harriet, 351
Marrast, John C., *61–62*, 351
"Marseillaise," 41, 97
Martin, Jim, 311
Maury, Dabney H., 275–76, 280–82, 291, 299, 303, *305*, 351, 362

BEN H. SEVERANCE is an associate professor of history at Auburn University Montgomery and a former officer in the United States Army. He is the author of *Tennessee's Radical Army: The State Guard and Its Role in Reconstruction, 1867–1869.*